GARDNER WEBB COLLEGE

ESSAYS IN HONOR
E. H. CARR

D1281204

ESSAYS IN HONOUR OF E. H. CARR

edited by

C. ABRAMSKY

assisted by

BERYL J. WILLIAMS

ARCHON BOOKS
1974

Library of Congress Cataloging in Publication Data
Main entry under title:

Essays in honour of E. H. Carr

   Bibliography: p.
   1. Russia—History—20th century—Addresses, essays,
lectures. 2. Russia—History—19th century—Addresses,
essays, lectures. 3. Carr, Edward Hallett, 1892- —
Addresses, essays, lectures. I. Abramsky, Chimen,
1916-   ed. II. Williams, Beryl J. III. Carr, Edward
Hallett, 1892-
DK246.E85   1974   947'.008   74-3384
ISBN 0-208-01451-9

Editorial Matter, selection and tribute © C. Abramsky 1974
        Chapter 1 © Isaiah Berlin 1974 (abridged ed.
        originally published *T.L.S.* 31 December 1971)
        Chapter 2 © Monica Partridge 1974
        Chapter 3 © Arthur Lehning 1974
        Chapter 4 © G. A. Cohen 1974
        Chapter 5 © Beryl J. Williams 1974
        Chapter 6 © Eleonore Breuning 1974
        Chapter 7 © D. C. Watt 1974
        Chapter 8 © Roger Morgan 1974
        Chapter 9 © Alec Nove 1974
        Chapter 10 © John Erickson 1974
        Chapter 11 © Michael Kaser 1974
        Chapter 12 © R. W. Davies 1974
        Chapter 13 © Moshe Lewin 1974
        Chapter 14 © Maurice Dobb 1974
        Chapter 15 © Mary Holdsworth 1974
        Chapter 16 © Lionel Kochan 1974

All rights reserved. No part of this publication
may be reproduced or transmitted, in any form
or by any means, without permission.

First published 1974 by
THE MACMILLAN PRESS LTD
London and Basingstoke
and in the United States of America
under the imprint Archon Books by
THE SHOE STRING PRESS, INC.,
Hamden, Connecticut 06514

Printed in Great Britain

Contents

DK
246
E85
1974

PART FOUR: RELATED STUDIES

Tribute to E. H. Carr

C. ABRAMSKY

A group of scholars have joined in presenting this volume of scholarly papers in honour of E. H. Carr's eightieth birthday, which occurred on 28 June 1972.

ALONE in Western Europe, Carr has achieved a position of preeminence primarily in the field of Soviet studies. He saw with remarkable lucidity and an unrivalled mastery of sources the unique importance of the Russian Bolshevik Revolution, not only as completing the destruction of the old system – the burial of the ancient regime – but primarily as an enormous development in the idea of statecraft. In this process the Revolution consumed in internecine, bloody struggles some of its leading actors. Carr saw, and sees, Lenin and his colleagues more as builders of new, powerful, often tyrannical state institutions, rather than mere ideologues, or nihilists. He has given a masterly historical picture of how Russia was turned from a backward, reactionary country into one of the mighty 'super-powers' of the world.

For Carr the Soviet State, with the Bolshevik Party as almost the sole moving element, the driving force of the Revolution, was, and is, to paraphrase Marx on the capitalist system, 'the demiurgos', the all powerful creator of a complex machinery of state-bodies. He dismissed the classical socialist–Marxist theories on the 'withering or dying away of the State', as mere Shibboleth – obsolescences of history.

Carr has a grand vision of how a country the size of Russia was moulded, governed and shaped from above. The Party and the State, merged together, form in his Hegelian view the supreme embodiment and achievement of the Soviet Union. Everything else was, and is, subservient to the supreme architectural plan of the leaders, imposed on the country through the innumerable channels at the disposal of the State.

Such a vision of history was bound to raise many criticisms, and it is a great tribute to Carr's scholarship that some of his eminent critics have come to pay their respects to a man who has so enriched our knowledge of the most powerful convulsion in the world since the French Revolution.

E. H. Carr has written extensively on various aspects of European intellectual history of the nineteenth and twentieth centuries, as well as on diplomatic history and on philosophy of history. His biographic studies on Dostoyevsky, Herzen, Bakunin, Sorel and others are distinguished by a refined irony, an understanding for human weaknesses, and a compassion for man.

As a 'man of action' he wrote during the last war many editorials for *The Times*, in which he explained to the British public the need for a better understanding of Russia and its rightful place in the council of nations after the war. These editorials will be used extensively by future historians. They will remain the anonymous contribution of Carr to history.

E. H. Carr, however, will always be remembered for the monumental history of Soviet Russia. The eleven volumes, so far published, remind one architectonically of Mommsen's history of Rome.

Carr 'questioned and cross-examined' all the leaders and chief participants of the Russian Revolution, 'asked them for their motives' for various actions they had done. Like the illustrious Florentine, Carr could say that he 'entered the palaces of the Revolution: "and there I make bold to speak to them and ask the motives of their actions, and they, in their humanity, reply to me"'. The responses that Carr extracted from them form the backbone of the history of Russia from 1917 to 1929. May he soon finish his enormous task that he set himself over a quarter of a century ago.

PART ONE

Intellectual History in the Nineteenth Century

1 Georges Sorel

ISAIAH BERLIN

SOREL remains an anomalous figure. The other ideologists and prophets of the nineteenth century have been safely docketed and classified. The doctrines, influence, personalities of Mill, Carlyle, Comte, Darwin, Dostoevsky, Wagner, Nietzsche, even Marx, have been safely placed on their respective shelves in the museum of the history of ideas. Sorel remains, as he was in his lifetime, unclassified; claimed and repudiated both by the Right and by the Left. Was he a bold and brilliant innovator of devastating genius as his handful of disciples declare? Or a mere romantic journalist, as Mr Lichtheim calls him? A 'pessimist moaning for blood', in G. D. H. Cole's contemptuous phrase? Or, with Marx, the only original thinker (according to Croce) socialism has ever had? Or a notorious muddle-head, as Lenin unkindly described him? I do not volunteer an answer: I only wish to say something about his principal ideas, and also – to employ that much-abused word – the relevance of these ideas to our time.

I

Georges Sorel was born in 1847 in Cherbourg. His father was an unsuccessful businessman, and the family was forced to practise extreme austerity. According to his cousin, the historian Albert Sorel, Georges Sorel early showed exceptional mathematical gifts. In 1865 he became a student at the École Polytechnique in Paris, and five years later entered the Department of Public Works (Ponts et Chaussées) as an engineer. During the next twenty years he was posted to various provincial towns. During the débâcle of 1870 and 1871 he was in Corsica. In 1875 he fell ill in a hotel in Lyon, and was nursed by a servant called Marie David, a devoutly religious, semi-literate peasant from the borders of Savoy, with whom he set up a household. In his letters he refers to her as his wife, but in fact appears never to have married her, probably out of deference to the wishes of his family which was evidently shocked by this *mésalliance*. It appears to have been an entirely happy relationship. He taught her, and learnt from her, and, after her death in 1898, wore a sacred image that she had given him and worshipped her memory for the rest of his days.

Until the age of forty his life had been that of a typical minor French government official, peaceful, provincial and obscure. In 1889 his first book was published. In 1892, being then forty-five years old, having attained the rank of Chief Engineer and been rewarded with the rank of Chevalier of the Légion d'Honneur, he suddenly resigned. From this moment his public life began. His mother had left him a small legacy, and this enabled him to move to Paris. He settled in a quiet suburb, Boulogne-sur-Seine, where he lived until his death, thirty years later, in 1922. In 1895 he started to contribute to left-wing journals, and from then on became one of the most controversial political writers in France.

He appeared to have no fixed position. His critics often accused him of pursuing an erratic course: a Legitimist in his youth, and still a traditionalist in 1889, he was by 1894 a Marxist. In 1896 he wrote with admiration about Vico. By 1898, influenced by Croce, and also by Eduard Bernstein, he began to criticise Marxism and at about the same time fell deeply under the spell of Henri Bergson. He was a Dreyfusard in 1899, a revolutionary syndicalist during the following decade. By 1909 he was a sworn enemy of the Dreyfusards, and, in the following two or three years, an ally of the royalists who edited the *Action Française* and a supporter of the mystical nationalism of Barrès. He wrote with admiration about Mussolini's militant socialism in 1912, and in 1919 with still greater admiration about Lenin, ending with whole-hearted support for Bolshevism and, in the last years of his life, an unconcealed admiration for the Duce.

What credence could be placed in the thought of a man whose political views veered so violently and unpredictably? He did not claim to be consistent. 'I write from day to day,' he said in 1903 to his faithful correspondent, the Italian philosopher Benedetto Croce, 'following the need of the moment.' Sorel's writings have no shape or system, and he was not impressed by it in those of others. He was a compulsive and passionate talker, and, as is at times the case with famous talkers – Diderot, Coleridge, Herzen, Bakunin – his writings remained episodic, unorganised, unfinished, fragmentary, at best sharp, polemical essays or pamphlets provoked by some immediate occasion, not intended to be fitted into a body of coherent, developed doctrine, and not capable of it. Nevertheless, there is a central thread that connects everything that Sorel wrote and said, if not a doctrine, then an attitude, a position, the expression of a singular temperament, of an unaltering view of life. His ideas, which beat like hailstones against all accepted doctrines and institutions, fascinated both his friends and his opponents, and do so still not only because of their intrinsic quality and power, but because what in his day was confined to small coteries of intellectuals has now grown to world-wide proportions. In his lifetime Sorel was looked on as, at best, a polemical journalist, an autodidact with a powerful pen and occasional flashes of extraordinary insight, too wayward and perverse to claim for long the attention of serious and busy men. In the event, he has proved more formidable than many of the respected social thinkers of his day, most of whom he ignored or else regarded with unconcealed disdain.

II

The ideas of every philosopher concerned with human affairs in the end rest on his conception of what man is and can be. To understand such thinkers, it is more important to grasp this central notion or image (which may be implicit, but determines their picture of the world) than even the most forceful arguments with which they defend their views and refute actual and possible objections. Sorel was dominated by one *idée maîtresse*: that man is a creator, fulfilled only when he creates, and not when he passively receives or drifts unresisting with the current. His mind is not a mechanism or organism responsive to stimuli, analysable, describable and predictable by the sciences of man. He is, for Sorel, in the first place, a producer who expresses himself in and through his work, an innovator whose activity alters the material provided by nature, material that he seeks to mould in accordance with an inwardly conceived, spontaneously generated, image or pattern. The productive activity itself brings this pattern to birth and alters it – as it fulfils itself freely, obedient to no law, being conceived as a kind of natural spring of creative energy which can be grasped by inner feeling and not by scientific observation or logical analysis. All other views of what men are, or could be, are fallacious. History shows that men are essentially seekers not of happiness or peace or knowledge or power over others, or salvation in another life – at least these are not men's primary purposes; where they are so, it is because men have degenerated from their true humanity, because education or environment or circumstances have distorted their ideas or character or rendered them impotent or vicious.

Man, at his best, that is, at his most human, seeks in the first place to fulfil himself, individually and with those close to him, in spontaneous, unhindered creative activity, in work that consists of the imposition of his personality on a recalcitrant environment. Sorel quotes his political enemy Clemenceau as saying: 'Everything that lives, resists.' He believed in this proposition as strongly as he believed in anything in his life. To act and not be acted upon, to choose and not be chosen for, to impose form on the chaos that we find in the world of nature and the world of thought – that is the end of both art and science and belongs to the essence of man as such. He resists every force that seeks to reduce his energy, to rob him of his independence and his dignity, to kill the will, to crush everything in him that struggles for unique self-expression and reduce it to uniformity, impersonality, monotony, and, ultimately, extinction. Man lives fully only in and by his works, not by passive enjoyment or the peace and security that he might find by surrender to external pressures, or habit, or convention, by failure to use for his own freely conceived goals the mechanism of the laws of nature to which he is inevitably subject.

This is, of course, not a new idea. It lies at the heart of the great revolt against rationalism and the Enlightenment identified particularly with French civilisation, that animated the more extreme German Protestant sects after the Reformation, and which, towards the end of the eighteenth century, took the form of celebrating the primacy of the human will against material forces and calm, rational knowledge alike. This is not the place in which to discuss the origins of Romanticism. But one cannot understand Sorel, or the impact of his views, unless one realises that what caused the ferment in his mind was a passionate conviction which he shares with some of the early Romantic writers, that the pursuit of peace or happiness or profit, and concern with power or possessions or social status or a quiet life, is a contemptible betrayal of what any man, if he takes thought, knows to be the true end of human life: the attempt to make something worthy of the maker, the effort to be and do something, and to respect such effort in others. The notion of the dignity of labour, of the right to work, as opposed to the mere Pauline duty to engage in it, which is at the heart of much modern socialism, springs from this romantic conception, which German thinkers, notably Herder and Fichte, brought up in earnest Lutheran pietism, impressed upon the European consciousness.

Sorel's violent and lifelong disgust with the life of the Parisian bourgeoisie of his time, in its own way as ferocious as that of Flaubert with whom temperamentally he has something in common, is bound up with a Jansenist hatred of the twin evils of hedonism and materialism. The opportunism and corruption of French political life in the early years of the Third Republic, together with the sense of national humiliation after 1870, may have been a traumatic experience for him, as for many Frenchmen. But it seems unlikely that he would have felt differently in the greedy and competitive Paris of Louis-Philippe or the plutocratic and pleasure-seeking Paris of the Second Empire. An agonised sense of suffocation in the commercialised, jaunty, insolent, dishonourable, easy-going, cowardly, mindless, bourgeois society of the nineteenth century fills the writings of the age: the works of Proudhon, Carlyle, Ibsen, Marx, Baudelaire, Nietzsche, almost the whole of the best known Russian literature of the time, are one vast indictment of it. This is the tradition to which Sorel belongs from the beginning to the end of his life as a writer. The corruption of public life appears to him to have gone deeper than during the decadence of classical Greece, or the end of the Roman Empire. Parliamentary democracy, with its fraudulence and hypocrisy, appeared to him to be an odious insult to human dignity, a mockery of the proper ends of man. Democratic politics resembled a huge stock exchange in which votes were bought and sold without shame or fear, men were bamboozled or betrayed by scheming politicians, ruthless bankers, crooked businessmen, *avocasserie et écrivasserie* – lawyers, journalists, professors, all scrambling for money, recognition, power, in a world of contemptible fools and cunning knaves, deceivers and deceived, living off the exploited workers 'in a democratic bog' in a Europe 'stupefied by humanitarianism'.

III

The Western tradition of social thought has been sustained by two central doctrines. The first taught that the ultimate causes of human misery, folly and vice were ignorance and mental laziness. Reality, it was held by rationalists from Plato to Comte, is a single, intelligible structure: to understand it and explain it, and to understand one's own nature and place in this structure – this alone can reveal what, in a specific situation, can, and what cannot, be realised. Once the facts and the laws that govern them are known to him, no man, desiring as he does happiness or harmony or wisdom or virtue, can pursue any but the sole correct path to his goal that his knowledge reveals to him. To be a rational, even a normal, human being, is to seek one, or several, of the limited number of the natural ends of human life. Only ignorance of what they are, or of what are the correct means for their attainment, can lead to misery or vice or failure. The scientific or naturalistic version of this doctrine animated the Enlightenment and the forms which it took in the two centuries that followed – until, indeed, our own day.

Sorel rejected this entire approach. He saw no reason for believing that the world was a rational harmony, or that man's true perfection depended on understanding of the proper place assigned to him in it by his creator – a personal deity or an impersonal nature. Influenced by both Marx and the half-forgotten Italian thinker, Vico, of whom he was one of the few perceptive readers in the nineteenth century, Sorel believed that all that man possessed he owed to his own un-flagging labour. Certainly natural science was a triumph of human effort; but it was not a transcription or map of nature, as the positivists had claimed in the eighteenth century; they, and their modern disciples, were mistaken about this. There were two natures: artificial nature, the nature of science – a system of idealised entities – atoms, electric charges, mass, energy and the like – fictions compounded out of observed uniformities, particularly in regions relatively remote from man's daily concerns, like the contents of the world of astronomy, deliberately adapted to mathematical treatment that enabled men to identify some of the furniture of the universe, and to predict and, indeed, control parts of it. The concepts and categories in terms of which this nature had been constructed, were conditioned by human aims: they abstracted from the universe those aspects that were of interest to men and possessed sufficient regularity to make them capable of generalisation. This, of course, was a stupendous achievement, but an achievement of the creative imagination, not an accurate reproduc-tion of the structure of reality, not a map, still less a picture, of what there was. Outside this set of formulae, of imaginary entities and mathematical relationships in terms of which the system was con-structed, there was 'natural' nature – the real thing – chaotic, terrify-ing, compounded of ungovernable forces, against which man had to struggle, which, if he was to survive and create, he had at least in part to subdue; with the help, indeed of his sciences; but the symmetry, the coherence, were attributes of the first, or artificial nature, the construction of his intellect, something that was not found but made. The assumption that reality was a harmonious whole, a rational structure whose logical necessity is revealed to reason, a marvellously coherent system which a rational being cannot think or wish to be otherwise and still remain rational, and in which, therefore, it must feel happy and fulfilled – all this is an enormous fallacy. Nature is not a perfect machine, nor an exquisite organism, nor a rational system; it is a savage jungle: science is the art of dealing with it as best we can. When we extend such manipulation to men as well, we degrade and dehumanise them, for men are not objects but subjects of action. If Christianity has taught us anything, it has made us realise that the only thing of absolute value in the universe is the human soul, the only thing that acts, that imagines, that creates, that resists the impersonal forces which work against it and, unless they are resisted, enslave us and ultimately grind us into dust. This is the menace that perpetually hangs over us. Consequently life is a perpetual battle.

To deny this truth is shallow optimism, characteristic of the shallow eighteenth century for which Sorel, like Carlyle, felt a lifelong contempt. The laws of nature are not descriptions, they are, as he came to learn from William James (and perhaps also from Marx), strategic weapons. Croce had taught him that our categories are categories of action, that they alter what we call reality as the purposes of our active selves alter: they do not establish timeless truths as the positivists maintained. 'We consider as matter, or as the base, that which escapes, less or more completely, from our will. The form is rather what corresponds to our freedom.' Systems, theories, unrelated to action, attempting to transcend experience, that which professors and intellectuals are so good at, are only abstractions into which men escape to avoid facing the chaos of reality; scientific (and political) utopias are compounded out of them; the pseudo-scientific predictions about our future by which such utopias are bolstered, are nothing but modern forms of astrology. When such schemes are applied to human beings they can do dreadful damage. To confuse our own constructions and inventions with eternal laws or divine decrees is one of the most fatal delusions of men: this is what had happened in the French Revolution. The confusion of the two natures, the real and the artificial, is bad enough. But the *philosophes* were not, by and large, even genuine scientists: only social and political theorists who talked about science without practising it; the *Encyclopédie* had not improved one's real knowledge or skill. Ideological patter, optimistic journalism about the uses of science, were not science. They only lead to positivism and bureaucracy, *la petite science*; and when theory is ruthlessly applied to human affairs, its result is a fearful despotism. Sorel speaks almost the language of William Blake. The Tree of Knowledge has killed the Tree of Life. Robespierre and the Jacobins were fanatical pedants who tried to reduce human life to rules that seemed to them based on objective truths; the institutions they created crushed spontaneity and invention, enslaved and maimed the creative will of man.

Men, whose essence, for Sorel, is to be active beings, are perpetually menaced by two equally fatal dangers: a Scylla and a Charybdis. Scylla is weariness, the loss of nerve, decadence, when men relax from effort, return to the fleshpots, or else fall into quietism and become the victims of the trickery of the clever operators who destroy all honour, energy, integrity, independence, and substitute the rule of cunning and fraud, the dead hand of bureaucracy, laws that can be turned to their advantage by unscrupulous operators, aided and abetted by an army of experts – prostitutes and lackeys of those in power, or idle entertainers and sycophantic parasites, like Voltaire and Diderot 'the immoral buffoons of a degenerate aristocracy', bourgeois who aspire to ape the tastes of an idle and pleasure-loving nobility. Charybdis is the despotism of fanatical theorists – 'the savage frenzy of an optimist maddened by sudden resistance to his plans', who is ready to butcher the present 'to create the happiness of the future on its bones'. These alternations mark the unhappy eighteenth century.

How are men to be rescued from the horns of this dilemma? Only by moral strength: by the development of new men, fully-formed human beings not obsessed by fear and greed, men who have not had their imagination and emotion fettered by doctrinaires or rotted by intellectuals. Sorel's vision resembles that of Tolstoy and Nietzsche when they were young – of the fullness of life, as it was once lived by the Homeric Greeks, free from the corrosive effect of civilised scepticism and critical questioning. It is not the possession of common ideas, convictions bred by reasoning, that creates true human bonds, but common life and common effort. The true basis of all association is the family, the tribe, the *polis*, in which co-operation is instinctive and spontaneous and does not depend on rules or contracts or invented arrangements. Associations for the sake of profit or utility, resting on some artificial agreement, as the political and economic institutions of the capitalist system plainly do, stifle the sense of common humanity and destroy human dignity by generating a spirit of competitive opportunism. Athens created immortal masterpieces until Socrates came, and spun theories, and played a nefarious part in the disintegration of that closely knit, once heroic, community by sowing doubt and undermining established values which spring from the profoundest and most life-enhancing instincts of men.

Sorel began to write in this fashion when he was still a municipal engineer in Perpignan; his friend Daniel Halévy assures us that he had not then read a line of Nietzsche whom he later came to admire. But their charge against Socrates is identical: both Nietzsche and Sorel take the side of his accusers: it was Socrates, and his disciple Plato, arch-intellectuals, who planted the life-destroying seeds that led to the glorification of abstractions, academies, contemplative or critical philosophies, utopian schemes, and so the decline of Greek vitality and Greek genius.

Can decadence be averted? Where is permanent salvation to be sought? There is another ancient doctrine in which men have traditionally sought reassurance: teleology. History, it was thought, would be meaningless – merely a causal sequence, or a chaos of unrelated episodes, if it lacked some ultimate purpose. This was considered unthinkable: reason rejects the notion of a mere collocation of 'brute' facts; there must be advance or growth towards the fulfilment of some goal or pattern; the mind demands some guarantee that, despite all accidents and collapses, the story will have a happy ending; either Providence is leading us towards it in its own inscrutable fashion; or else history is conceived as the self-realisation from stage to stage of the great cosmic spirit of which all men and all their institutions, and perhaps all nature, is the changing and progressive expression. Or, perhaps, it is human reason itself that cannot and will not for ever be frustrated, and must, late or soon, triumph over all obstacles, both external and self-generated, and build a world in which men have become everything that, as rational creatures, they consciously or unconsciously seek to be. In its metaphysical or mystical or secular forms this amalgam of Hebraic faith and Aristotelian metaphysics dominated the ideas of the last three centuries and gave confidence to many who might otherwise have despaired.

These central intellectual traditions – the Greek doctrine of salvation by knowledge and the Judeo-Christian doctrine of history as theodicy – to which men have pinned their hopes, were all but rejected by Sorel. All his life he believed in two absolutes: that of science, and that of morality. Science, even though, or perhaps because, it is a human artifice, enables us to classify, predict, control certain events. The concepts and categories in terms of which science puts its questions may vary with cultural change: the objectivity and reliability of the answers do not. But it is a weapon, not an ontology, not an analysis of reality. The great machine of science does not yield answers to problems of metaphysics or morality: to reduce the central problems of human life to problems of means, that is, of technology, is not to understand what they are. To regard technical progress as being identical with, or even as a guarantee of, cultural progress, is moral blindness. Sorel devoted a series of essays to demonstrating the absurdity of the idea of general human progress which springs from confusion of technology with life, or of the preposterous claim, first advanced by men of letters in the late seventeenth century of their inevitable superiority to the ancients. As for theological or metaphysical beliefs in human perfectibility, they are only a pathetic clutching at straws, a refuge of the weak.

Neither science nor history offer comfort: Turgot and Condorcet and their nineteenth-century disciples are poor, deluded optimists who believe that history is on our side; so it will be, but only if we make it so, if we fight the good fight against the oppressors and exploiters, the dreary, life-destroying levellers, the masters and the slaves, and protect the sublime and the heroic against democrats and plutocrats, pedants and philistines.

Sorel has no doubt about what is health, and what is disease, whether in individuals or in societies. The Homeric Greeks lived in the light of values without which a society could not be creative or possess a sense of grandeur. They admired courage, strength, justice, loyalty, sacrifice, above all the struggle itself; freedom for them was not an ideal but a reality: the feeling of successful effort. Then (and this probably comes from Vico) came scepticism, sophistry, ease of life, democracy, individualism, decadence. Greek society disintegrated and was conquered. Rome, too, was once heroic, but it had given in to legalism and the bureaucratisation of life; the late Empire was a cage in which human beings felt stifled.

It was the early Church that had once held high the flag of man. What the early Christians believed is less important than the intensity of a faith that did not allow the corrosive intellect to penetrate. Above all, these men refused to compromise. The early Christians could have saved themselves from persecution by coming to terms with the Roman bureaucrats. They preferred faith, integrity and sacrifice. Concessions, Sorel repeats, always, in the end, lead to self-destruction. The only hope lies in ceaseless resistance to forces that seek to weaken what one instinctively knows that one lives by. When the Church triumphed and made its peace with the world, it became infected by it and therefore degenerated: the barbarians were converted to Christianity, but to a worldly Christianity, and so fell into decay.

The heroic Christianity of the martyrs is a defence against the decadent state, but it is itself intrinsically socially destructive. Christians (and Stoics too) are not producers: the Gospels, unlike the Old Testament or Greek literature, are addressed to paupers and anchorites. A society indifferent to riches, content with its daily bread, allows no room for vigorous, creative life. Christianity, like every ideology, like its secular imitation – the utopian socialism of a later day – 'cut the links between social life and the spirit, sowing everywhere germs of quietism, despair, death'. Too little was accorded to Caesar, too much to the Church – an organisation of consumers, not (in Sorel's sense) of producers. Sorel wishes to return to the firm values of the hardy Judean peasants or the Greek *polis*, where merely to question them was considered subversive. He is concerned neither with happiness nor salvation: only with the quality of life itself, with what used to be called virtue (which in his case much resembles Renaissance *virtù*). Like the Jansenists, like Kant and the Romantics, he values motive and character, not consequences and success.

The accumulation of public wealth in the hands of priests and monks played its part in the exhaustion and fall of the Roman West. But after decay there is always hope of a revival: does not Vico speak of a *ricorso*, when one cycle of history has ended in moral weakness and decadence, a new one, barbarian, fresh and simple and pious and strong, begins the story again? Sorel dwells on this with the enthusiasm of Nietzsche. He is fascinated by every example of resolute moral resistance to decay, and consequently by the story of the Church under persecution and of the Church militant; he takes little interest in the Church triumphant. It is in connection with movements of resistance and renewal that he develops (increasingly after falling under the influence of Bergson) the theories of which he became the most famous upholder: of the social myth, of permanent class war, of violence, of the general strike.

Even in the darkest moments of decadence, the social organism develops antibodies to resist the disease – men who will not give in, who will stand up and save the honour of the human race. The dedicated monastic orders, the saints and martyrs who preserved mankind from total contamination by late Roman society – what men today embody such qualities, possess the *virtù* of the great *condottieri* and artists of the Renaissance? There may be something of it in the American men of business, bold, enterprising, creative captains of industry who make their will prevail over nature and other men; but they are tainted by the general corruption of capitalism of which they are the leaders. There was, it seemed to Sorel, only one true body of this kind; those who are saved by work – the workers, the only genuinely creative class of our day. The proletarians, who are not morally caught in the toils of bourgeois life, appear to Sorel heroic, endowed with a natural sense of justice and humanity, morally impregnable, proof against the sophistries and casuistries of the intellectuals.

In the last years of the century, during the united front of the Left created by the Dreyfus Affair, and perhaps influenced by the reformist socialism of Bernstein in Germany which seemed to him to be at any rate based on economic realities, Sorel supported the idea of a political party of the working class. But soon he accepted the position of the syndicalist journalist, Lagardelle, in whose journal, *Le Mouvement Socialiste*, a good many of his articles appeared, that it is not opinions that truly unite men, for beliefs are a superficial possession, blown about by ideologists who play with words and ideas, and can be shared by men of different social formation who have basically nothing in common with each other. Men are truly made one only by real ties,

by the family – the unchanging unit of the moral life, as Proudhon and
Le Play had insisted – by martyrdom in a common cause, but above
all by working together, by common creation, united resistance to the
pressures both of inanimate nature which provides the workers with
their materials, and of their masters who seek to rob them of the
fruits of their toil. The workers are not a party held together by lust
for power or even for material goods. They are a social formation, a
class. It was the genius of Marx that discovered the true nature of
classes defined in terms of their relationship to the productive processes of a society torn, but also driven forward, by conflict between
capitalist and proletarian. Sorel never abandoned his belief in Marx,
but he used his doctrines selectively.

Sorel derives from Marx (reinforced by his own interpretation of
Vico) his conception of man as an active being, born to work and
create; from this follows his right to his tools, for they are an extension of his nature. The working tools of our day are machines.
Machinery is a social cement more effective, he believes, than even
language. All creation is in essence artistic, and the factory should
become the vehicle of the social poetry of modern producers. Human
history is more than the impersonal story of the evolution of technology. Inventions, discoveries, techniques, the productive process,
are activities of human beings endowed with minds but, above all,
wills. Men's values, their practice, their work, are one dynamic,
seamless whole. Sorel follows Vico in insisting that we are not mere
victims or spectators of events, but actors and originators. Marx, too,
is appealed to, but he is, at times, too determinist for Sorel, especially
in the versions of his more positivist interpreters – Engels, Kautsky,
Plekhanov, men inclined to *la petite science*, like bourgeois economists
and sociologists. Social and economic laws are not chains, not a con-
stricting framework, but guidelines to possible action, generated and
developed by, and in, action. The future is open. Sorel rejects such
determinist phraseology as 'tendencies working with iron necessity
towards inevitable results' and the like, of which *Das Kapital* is full.
Marxism 'is a doctrine of life good for strong peoples; it reduces
ideology to the role of a mere instrument'. History for Sorel is what
it was for Hegel, a drama in which men are authors and actors; above
all it is a struggle between the forces of vitality and those of decay,
activity and passivity, dynamic energy versus cowardice and surrender.

Marx's deepest single insight for Sorel is his notion of the class
war as the matrix of all social change. Creation is always a struggle:
Greek civilisation for Sorel is symbolised by the sculptor who cuts
the marble – the resistance of the stone, resistance as such, is essential
to the process of creation. In modern factories the struggle is not

merely between men – workers – and nature which provides raw material, but between workers and employers who seek to extract surplus value by exploiting other men's labour power. In this struggle, men, like steel, are refined. Their courage, their self-respect, their solidarity with each other, grow. Their sense of justice develops too, for justice, according to Proudhon (to whom Sorel's debt is greater than even to Marx), is something that springs from the feeling of indignation aroused by the humiliation inflicted on others. What is insulted is what is common to all men – their humanity which is ours; the insult to human dignity is felt 'by the offender, by the injured man, and by the third party'; this common protest which they all feel within them, is the sense of justice and injustice. It is this that united some among the socialists with the liberal bourgeoisie against the chicanery of the Army and the Church during the Dreyfus case, and created Sorel's bond with Charles Péguy who was never a Marxist but was prepared to work with anyone who did not wish to see France dishonoured by a cynical miscarriage of justice. In 1899 he speaks of the 'admirable ardour' with which the Allemanist workers are marching for 'truth, justice, morality' by the side of Jaurès whom he was soon to attack so violently for lacking these very qualities.

Justice in particular is for Sorel an absolute value, proof against historical change. His conception of it may, as in the case of Kant and Proudhon, be rooted in a severe upbringing. Sorel dreaded sentimental humanitarianism: when people cease to feel horror at human crimes this will, he thinks, mean a collapse of their sense of justice. Better wild retribution than indifference or a sentimental tendency to forgiveness characteristic of humanitarian democracy. It is his indignation with what he saw as the dilution in the public life of France in his day of the sense of justice – to him a kind of intuitive sense of absolute moral pitch – that drove him from one extreme remedy to another had caused him to reject anything that he suspected of inclining towards compromise with stupidity or wickedness. It is the absence of the sense of absolute moral values, and of the decisive part played in human life by the moral will, that, for Sorel, is Marx's greatest single weakness: he is too historicist, too determinist, too relativist. Sorel's uncompromising voluntarism is at the heart of his entire outlook; there is in Marx too much emphasis on economics, not enough ethical doctrine.

The carrier of true moral values today is the proletariat. Only workers have true respect for work, for family, for sacrifice, for love. They are 'frugal, dignified, honest'. For him, as for Fernand Pelloutier, the true founder of French Syndicalism, they are beings touched by grace. For Sorel they were what peasants were for Herzen, what 'the Folk' was for Herder and the populists, what 'the Nation' was for

Barrès. It is this traditionalism, which he shared with a certain type of conservative, and the quality of his domestic life with the simple and religious Marie David, that may have deepened his sense of the gulf between the moral dignity of the workers and the character and values of the pliable and the clever who rose to success in democracies. He found, or thought he found, this farouche integrity in Proudhon, in Péguy, in Pelloutier and other uncompromising fighters for justice or independence at whatever cost; he looked for it in the royalist *littérateurs*, in ultra-nationalists, in all resistance to time-serving supporters of the Republic and its demagogues. Hence his lack of sympathy for the populist nationalism of Déroulède, as for the entire Boulangist front. He might have approved of the *Croix de Feu*, but never of Poujadism.

Sorel's relationship to Marx is harder to define: classes and the class war as the central factor in social change; universal, timeless ideals as disguises for temporary class interests; man as a self-transforming, creative, tool-inventing being; the proletariat – the producers – as the bearer of the highest human values; these ideas he never abandoned. But he rejected the entire Hegelian–Marxist teleology which fuses facts and values. Sorel believed in absolute moral values: the historicism of the Hegelian–Marxist tradition was never acceptable to him, still less the view that issues of basic moral or political principle can be solved by social scientists, psychologists, sociologists, anthropologists; or that techniques based on imitation of the methods of natural science can explain and explain away ideas or values, to the permanence and power of which all history and art, all religion and morality, testify; or can, indeed, explain human conduct in mechanistic or biological terms, as the positivists, the blinkered adherents of *la petite science*, believe.

Sorel regards values, both moral and aesthetic, though their forms and applications may alter, as being independent of the march of events. Hence he regards sociological analysis of works of art, whether by Diderot or Marxist critics, as evidence of their profound lack of aesthetic sense, blindness to the mystery of the act of creation, and to the part that art plays in the life of mankind. Yet he shows little consistency when engaged on exposing the motives of the enemy; then he is more than ready to use all the tools of psychological or sociological analysis, provided by those who probe for true springs of action by 'unmasking' interests disguised as unalterable laws or disinterested ideals. Thus he fully accepts the Marxist view that economic laws are not laws of nature, but human arrangements, created, whether consciously or not, in the interests of a given class. To look upon them as objective necessities, as bourgeois economists do, is to reify them, an illusion that plays into the hands of that class to whose advantage it is to represent them as being eternal and unchangeable. But then he draws the un-Marxist, voluntarist corollary that freely chosen effort and struggle can change a great deal; and parts company with the orthodox who insist on a rigorous and predictable causal correlation between productive forces and the superstructure of institutions and ideas. The moral absolutes must not be touched: they do not alter with changes in the forces or relations of production.

History for Sorel is more of a wild flux than Marx supposed: society is a creation, a work of art, not (as, perhaps, the state is) a mere product of economic forces. Marx's economism he regards as overstated; this may have been necessary (as Engels, in effect, admitted) in order to counter idealistic or liberal-individualist theories of history. But in the end such theories may, he thinks, lead to a belief in the possibility of predicting the social arrangements of the future. This is dangerous and delusive utopianism. Such fantasies may stimulate the workers, but they can arm despotisms too. Even if the workers win their fight against the bourgeoisie, yet, unless they are educated to be creative, they too may generate an oppressive élite of doctrinaire intellectuals from within their own class. He accuses Marx of relying altogether too much on that Hegelian maid-of-all-work, the world spirit, although Marx is credited with understanding that science (and especially economic science) is not 'a mill into which you can drop any problem facing you, and which yields solutions'. Methods of application are everything. Did not Marx himself once declare, 'Whoever composes a programme for the future is a reactionary'?[1] Nor, according to Sorel, did Marx believe in a political party of the working class; for a party, once in the saddle, may well become tyrannical and self-perpetuating, no matter what its manifestoes state. Marx, after all, Sorel tells us, believed in the reality of classes alone.

This is a greatly Sorelified Marx: Sorel rejects everything in Marx that seems to him political – his notion of the workers' party, his theory of, and practical measures for, the organisation of the revolution, his determinism, above all the doctrine of the dictatorship of the proletariat which Sorel regards as a sinister recrudescence of the worst elements of repressive Jacobinism. Even the anarchist classless society with which true human history is to begin is virtually ignored by Sorel: evidently it is too much of a conceptual, ideological construction. 'Socialism is not a doctrine', he declared, 'not a sect, not a political system; it is the emancipation of the working classes who organise themselves, instruct themselves and create new institutions.' The proletariat is for him a body of producers at once disciplined and inspired by the nature of the labour they perform. It is this that makes them a class and not a party. The proletarians are not simply the discontented masses; the proletarian revolution is not merely a revolt of poor against rich, of the *popolo minuto* of the Italian communes, organised and led by a self-appointed general staff, the kind of rising advocated by Babeuf or Blanqui; for this can happen anywhere and at any time. The true social revolution of our day must be the revolt of a heroic class of producers and makers against exploiters and their agents and parasites – something that cannot happen unless – this was Marx's crucial discovery – a society has reached a certain stage of technological development, and the truly creative class has developed a moral personality of its own. (It is this emphasis on the intrinsic value and revolutionary character of the culture of the producers – the proletariat – that appealed to Gramsci and caused him to defend Sorel against his detractors.) Sorel does not seem to have contemplated a society so mechanised as to generate a technocratic bureaucracy involving both managers and workers, in which social dynamism is stifled by the organisation required by the sheer size of the industrial system. According to Daniel Halévy, France at the turn of the century, and in particular Paris and its environs, were relatively unindustrialised compared with England or Germany. Sorel is closer to Proudhon's world than to that of General Motors or I.C.I.

Only conflict purifies and strengthens. It creates durable unity and solidarity; whereas political parties, which anyone, of whatever social formation, can enter, are ramshackle structures, liable to opportunist coalitions and alliances. This is the vice of democracy. Not only is it the sham denounced by Marxists – a mere front for capitalist control – but the very ideal of democracy – national unity, reconciliation of differences, social harmony, devotion to the common good, Rousseau's General Will raised above the battle of the factions – all this destroys the conditions in which alone men can grow to their full stature – the struggle, the social conflict. The most fatal of all democratic institutions are parliaments, since they depend on compromise, concessions, conciliation; even if we forget about the 'ruses, equivocation, hypocrisy' of which the syndicalists speak, political combinations are the death of all heroism, indeed of morality itself. The member of parliament, no matter how militant his past, is inevitably driven into peaceful association, even co-operation, with the class enemy, in committees, in lobbies, in the chamber itself. The representative of the working classes, Sorel observed, becomes 'an excellent bourgeois very early'. The hideous examples are before our eyes – Millerand, Briand, Viviani, the spellbinding demagogue Jean Jaurès with his easily acquired popularity. Sorel had once hoped for much from these men, but was disillusioned. They all turned out to be squalid earthworms, rhetoricians, grafters and intriguers like the rest.

Sorel goes even farther. Creative vitality cannot exist where everything gives, where it is too soft to resist. Unless the enemy – not the parasitic intellectuals and theorists, but the leaders of the capitalist forces – are themselves energetic and fight back like men, the workers will not find enemies worthy of their steel, and will themselves tend to degenerate. Only against a strong and vigorous opponent can truly heroic qualities be developed. Hence Sorel's characteristic wish that the bourgeoisie might develop stronger sinews. No serious Marxist could begin to accept this thesis, not even the mildest reformist, not even those who, like Bernstein, denied the validity of the Marxist historical libretto and declared in language worthy of Sorel himself: 'The goal is nothing: the movement is everything.' Sorel averts his gaze from the aftermath of the ultimate victory of the working class. He is concerned only with rises and falls, creative societies and classes and decadent ones. No perfection, no final victory, is possible in social existence; only in art, in pure creation, can this be achieved. Rembrandt, Ruysdael, Vermeer, Mozart, Beethoven, Schumann, Berlioz, Liszt, Wagner, Debussy, Delacroix, the Impressionist painters of his own day – these were capable of reaching an unsurpassable summit in their art. Hence his attack on those who sell their genius for fame or money. Meyerbeer can be despised but not blamed: he was a true child of his age and milieu: his gift was as vulgar as the audience which he knew how to please; not so Massenet, who prostituted his more genuine talent to please the bourgeois public. Something of this kind, he seems to think, is true of Anatole France, too.

The total fulfilment that is possible in art, in science, in the case of individual men of genius, cannot occur in the life of society. Hence Sorel's distrust of the entire Marxist scenario: the expropriation of the expropriators, the dictatorship of the proletariat, the reign of plenty, the withering away of the state. He ignores practical problems; he is not interested in the way in which production, distribution, exchange, will be regulated in the new order, nor whether there is any possibility of abolishing scarcity without performing at least some tasks that can hardly be described as creative. Marxists can scarcely be blamed if they did not regard as their own a man who wished to preserve the enemy in being lest the swords of his own side rusted in their scabbards, who had nothing to say about the ideal of a free society of associated producers combining to fight inanimate nature, but, on the contrary, declared, 'Everything may be saved if the proletariat, by its use of violence ... restores to the middle classes something of its former energy', a man who did not seem to care about the problems of poverty and misery as such, and protested against sabotage of factories, because this was wilful destruction of the fruits of someone's creative labour. No man could claim to be a Marxist if he condemned revolutionary terror as a political act and damned Jacobins as tyrants and fanatics – men on whom Marx, to some degree, and even more Lenin, looked as their legitimate ancestors. Sorel denounces activity that springs from morally impure feelings, from motives infected by bourgeois poisons: 'The fierce envy of the impoverished intellectual,' he declares, 'who would like to see the rich merchant guillotined, is a vicious feeling that is not in the least socialist.' He cares only for the preservation of heroic vitality and courage and strength which may decline if total victory leaves the victor no enemy.

Sorel was aware of the oddity of his position, and took perverse and somewhat malicious pleasure in exposing the weakness or confusions of his allies. He pronounced socialism to be dead in the early years of our century. He made no effort to influence any active social or political group. He remained true to his professions: isolated, independent, a man on his own. If he has any parallel within the socialist movement, it is with the equally independent and unpredictable Viennese critic and journalist Karl Kraus – also concerned with morality, and the preservation of style in life and literature.[2] Even Bernard Shaw, who admired vitality, style, Napoleonic qualities, the 'life force', had a greater affinity with him than learned theorists like Kautsky, Plekhanov, Guesde, Max Adler, Sidney Webb, and the other pillars of European socialism. To him they were everything that he despised most deeply – arid, cerebral, latter-day sophists, clerks and glossators who turned every vital impulse into abstract formulae, utopian blueprints, learned dust. He poured the vials of his scorn upon them. They repaid him by ignoring him completely.

Jaurès called Sorel the metaphysician of Syndicalism. And, indeed, Sorel believed that in every human soul there lay hidden a metaphysical ember glowing beneath the cinders. If one could blow this into a flame, it would kindle a conflagration that would destroy mediocrity, routine, cowardice, opportunism, corrupt bargains with the class enemy. Society can be saved only by the liberation of the producers, that is, the workers, particularly those who work with their hands. The founders of Syndicalism were right: the workers must be protected against domination by experts and ideologists and professors – the intellectual elite of Plato's hideous dream – what Bakunin (with Marx in mind) had called 'pedantocracy'. 'Can you conceive,' asked Sorel, 'of anything more horrible than government by professors?' In these days such men, he observes, tend to be, as often as not, *déraciné* intellectuals, or Jews without a country – men who have no home, no hearth of their own, 'no ancestral tombs and relics to defend against the barbarians'.

This is, of course, the violent rhetoric of the extreme Right – of De Maistre, of Carlyle, of German nationalists, of French anti-Dreyfusards, of anti-Semitic chauvinists – of Maurras and Barrès, Drumont and Déroulède. But it is also, at times, the language of Fourier and Cobbett, Proudhon and Bakunin, and would later be spoken by Fascists and National Socialists and their literary allies in many countries, as well as those who thunder against critical intellectuals and rootless cosmopolitans in the Soviet Union and other countries of Eastern Europe. No one was closer to this style of thought and expression than the so called left-wing Nazis – Gregor Strasser and his followers in the early days of Hitler, and in France men like Déat and Drieu la Rochelle.

There is an anti-intellectual and anti-Enlightenment stream in the European radical tradition, at times allied with populism, or nationalism, or neo-medievalism, that goes back to Rousseau and Herder and Fichte, and enters agrarian, anarchist, anti-Semitic and other anti-liberal movements, creating anomalous combinations, sometimes in open opposition to, sometimes in an uneasy alliance with, the various currents of socialist and revolutionary thought. Sorel, whose hatred of democracy, the bourgeois republic and above all, the rational outlook and liberal values of the intelligentsia was obsessive, fed this stream, indirectly at first, but towards the end of the first decade of our century more violently and openly until, by 1910, this caused a breach between him and his left-wing allies.

Doubtless his devout upbringing, his deep roots in traditional, old-fashioned, French provincial life, his unspoken but profoundly felt patriotism, played their part: what seemed to him the demoralisation and disintegration of traditional French society plainly preoccupied him throughout his life and intensified his basic xenophobia and hostility to those who seemed to him to wander beyond the confines of the traditional culture of the West. His anti-intellectualism and anti-Semitism sprang from the same roots as those of Proudhon and Barrès. But there was also the decisive influence of the philosophy of Henri Bergson. With his friend Péguy, Sorel attended Bergson's lectures, and, like Péguy, was deeply and permanently affected.

It was from Bergson that he derived the notion, which he could equally well have found in the francophobe German Romantics a century earlier, that reason was a feeble instrument compared with the power of the irrational and the unconscious in the life both of individuals and societies. He was profoundly impressed by Bergson's doctrine of the unanalysable *élan vital*, the inner force that cannot be rationally grasped or articulated, which thrusts its way into the empty and unknowable future, and moulds both biological growth and human activity. Not theoretical knowledge but action and only action, gives understanding of reality. Action is not a means to pre-conceived ends, it is its own policy-maker and pathfinder. Prediction, even if it were possible, would kill it. We have an inner sense of what we are at, very different from, and incompatible with, the outside view, that is, calm contemplation that classifies, dissects, establishes clear structures. The intellect freezes and distorts. One cannot render movement by rest, nor time by space, nor the creative process by mechanical models, nor something living by something still and dead – this is an old Romantic doctrine that Bergson revivified and developed. Reality must be grasped intuitively, by means of images, as artists conceive it, not with concepts or arguments or Cartesian reasoning. This is the soil which gave birth to Sorel's celebrated doctrine of the social myth which alone gives life to social movements.

There is another source, too, whence the theory of myth may have sprung – the teachings of the founder of modern sociology, Emile Durkheim, who stood at the opposite extreme from Bergson. Rational and sternly positivist, he believed, like Comte, that science alone could answer our questions; what science could not do, no other method could achieve; he was implacably opposed to Bergson's deep irrationalism. Durkheim, who became the leading ideologist of the Third Republic, taught that no society could remain stable without a high degree of social solidarity between its members; this in its turn depended on the prevalence in it of dominant social myths bound up with appropriate ritual and ceremonial; religion had in the past been by far the most powerful of the forms in which this sense of solidarity found natural expression. Myths are not for Durkheim false beliefs about reality. They are not beliefs about anything, but beliefs *in* some-thing – in descent from a common ancestor, in transforming events in a common past, in common traditions, in shared symbols enshrined in a common language, above all, in symbols sanctified by religion and history. The function of myths is to bind a society, create a structure governed by rules and habits, without which the individual may suffer from a sense of isolation and solitude, may experience anxiety, feel lost, which in its turn leads to lawlessness and social chaos. For Durkheim myths are ultimately a utilitarian, if uncontrived, spontaneous and natural, response to a quasi-biological need; his account of their function is treated by him as an empirical discovery of a Burkean kind, of a necessary condition for social stability. Sorel abhorred utilitarianism, and in particular the quest for social peace and cohesion by cautious republican academics, as an attempt to muffle the class war in the interests of the bourgeois republic.

For Sorel, the function of myths is not to stabilise, but to direct energies and inspire action. They do this by embodying a dynamic vision of the movement of life, the more potent because not rational, and therefore not subject to criticism and refutation by university wiseacres. A myth is compounded of images that are 'warmly coloured', and affect men not as reason does, nor education of the will, nor the command of a superior, but as ferment of the soul which creates enthusiasm and incites to action, and, if need be, turbulence. Myths need have no historical reality; they direct our emotions, mobilise our will, give purpose to all that we are and do and make; they are, above all, not utopias, which from Plato onward, are descriptions of impossible states of affairs, fantasies in the heads of intellectuals remote from reality, evasion of concrete problems, escape into theory and abstraction. Sorel's myths are ways of transforming relationships between real facts by providing men with a new vision of the world and themselves: as when those who are converted to a new faith see the world and its furniture with new eyes. A utopia is 'the product of the intellectual labour of theorists who, after observing and discussing the facts, seek to build a model against which to measure existing societies ... they are constructions which can be taken to pieces ...', their parts can be detached and fitted into other structures – bourgeois political economy is just such an artificial entity. But myths are wholes perceived instantaneously by the imagination. They are, in effect, political aspirations presented in the form of images 'made warm' by strong feeling. They reveal, as mere words cannot, hitherto invisible potentialities in the past and present, and so drive men to concerted efforts to bring about their realisation. The effort itself breeds new vitality, new effort and militancy in an endless dynamic process, spiralling upwards, which he called 'giving an aspect of reality to hopes of immediate action'.

The Christian vision of the Second Coming that is at hand is, for Sorel a myth of this kind – in its light men accepted martyrdom. The Calvinist belief in the renovation of Christianity was a vision of a new order that was not of this world, but fired by it the believers successfully resisted the advance of secular humanism. The idea of the French Revolution, referred to with fervour at civic gatherings in French provincial towns, lives on as a vague but ardent image that commands loyalty and stimulates action of a particular kind, but a myth that cannot, any more than a hymn, or a flag, be translated into a specific programme, a set of clear objectives. 'When masses of men become aroused, then an image is formed which constitutes a social myth.' This is how the Italian Risorgimento presented itself to the followers of Mazzini. It is by means of myths that socialism can be converted into a kind of social poetry, can be expressed in action but not in prose, not in treatises intended merely to be understood. The French revolutionary armies in 1792 were inspired by an ardent myth, and won; the royalist forces lacked it, and were defeated. The Greeks lived and flourished in a world filled with myths until they were subverted by the Sophists, and after them by rootless Oriental cosmopolitans who flooded into Greece and ruined her. The analogy with the present is all too patent.

Sorel's myth is not a Marxist idea. It has a greater affinity with the modernist psychologism of Loisy or Tyrrell, William James's doctrine of the will, Vaihinger's 'philosophy of "as if"', than with Marx's rationalist conception of the unity of theory and practice. The notion of 'the people', the 'folk' – good, simple and true, but unawakened, as it is conceived by populists, both radical and reactionary, of the eternal 'real nation' in the thought of nationalists, as opposed to its corrupt or craven representatives – Barrès's 'la terre et les morts' – these are Sorel's, not Durkheim's myths. Unsympathetic critics might say the same of most Marxists' use of the concept of the true, dialectically grasped interests of the proletariat, as opposed to its actual 'empirical' wishes, perhaps even of the notion of classless society itself, provided that its outlines remain blurred. The function of a myth is to create 'an epic state of mind'. Sorel's insistence on its irrationality is, perhaps, what caused Lenin to dismiss him so curtly and contemptuously.

What is to be the myth of the workers? What is to raise them to the state of heroic grandeur, above the grey routine of their humdrum lives? Something which, Sorel believes, already inspires those activists in the French *syndicats* who had found their leader in the admirable Fernand Pelloutier who has rightly kept them from contamination by democratic politics – the myth of the general strike. The syndicalist general strike must not be confused with the ordinary industrial or 'political' strike which is a mere effort to extort better conditions or higher wages from the masters, and presupposes acquiescence in a social and economic structure common to owner and wage slave. This is mere haggling and is the very opposite of the true class war. The myth of the syndicalist general strike is a call for the total overthrow of the entire abominable world of calculation, profit and loss, the treatment of human beings and their powers as commodities, as material for bureaucratic manipulation, the world of illusory consensus and social harmony, of economic or sociological experts no matter what master they serve, who treat men as subjects of statistical calculations, malleable 'human material', forgetting that behind such statistics there are living human beings, not so much with normal human needs – to Sorel that does not appear to matter much – but free moral agents able collectively to resist and create and mould the world to their will.

The enemy for Sorel is not always the same: during the Dreyfus Affair it was the nationalist demagogues with their paranoiac, Jacobin cries of treason, their fanatical search for scapegoats and wicked incitement of the mob against the Jews,[3] who play this role. After their defeat, it is the victors – the 'counter-church' of the intellectuals, the intolerant, dehumanising, republican 'politico-scholastic' party, led by academic despots, bred in the Ecole Normale – who increasingly become the principal targets of his fury. The general strike is the climax of mounting militancy and 'violence', when, in an act of concentrated collective will, the workers, in one concerted move, leave their factories and workshops, secede to the Aventine, and then arise as one man and inflict a total, crushing, permanent, 'Napoleonic' defeat upon the accursed system that shuffles them into Durkheim's or Comte's compartments and hierarchies, and thereby all but robs them of their human essence. This is the great human uprising of the children of light against the children of darkness, of fighters for freedom against 'merchants, intellectuals, politicians' – the miserable crew of the masters of the capitalist world with their mercenaries, men promoted from the ranks, bought off and absorbed into the hierarchy, careerists and social planners, right-wing and left-wing power- or status-seekers, promoters of societies based on greed and competition, or else on the stifling oppression of remorselessly tidy rational organisation.

Did Sorel believe, did he expect the workers to believe, that this final act of liberation would, or could, in fact, occur as a historical event? It is difficult to tell. He had nothing favourable to say of the general strikes, designed to secure specific concessions, that broke out (during his most syndicalist phase) in Belgium in 1904, above all in the abortive Russian Revolution of 1905. This, for him, was Péguy's *mystique* reduced to mere *politique*. Moreover, if he believed, as he appeared to, that if the enemy weakened so would the class of producers, would not total victory lead to the elimination of the tension without which there is no effort, no creation? Yet without a myth it is impossible to create an energetic proletarian movement. Empirical arguments against the possibility or desirability of the general strike are not relevant. It is, one suspects, not intended as a theory of action, still less as a plan to be realised in the real world.

The weapon of the workers is violence. Although it gives its name to Sorel's best-known work ('my standard work', as he ironically referred to it) its nature is never made clear. Class conflict is the normal condition of society, and force is continuously exerted against the producers, that is, the workers, by the exploiters. Force does not necessarily consist in open coercion, but in control and repression by means of institutions which, whether by design or not, have the effect, as Marx and his disciples have made clear, of promoting the power of the possessing class. This pressure must be resisted. To resist force by force is likely to result, as in the case of the Jacobin revolution, in the replacing of one yoke by another, the substitution of new masters for old. A Blanquist *putsch* could lead to mere coercion by the state – the dictatorship of the proletariat, perhaps even by its own representatives, as the successor to the dictatorship of capitalists. Dogmatic revolutionaries easily become oppressive tyrants: this theme is common to Sorel and the anarchists. Camus revived it in his polemic with Sartre. Force, by definition, represses; violence, directed against it, liberates. Only by instilling fear in the capitalists can the workers break their power, the force exerted against them.

This, indeed, is the function of proletarian violence: not aggression, but resistance. Violence is the striking off of chains, the prelude to regeneration. It may be possible to secure a more rational existence, better material conditions, a higher standard of living, security, even justice for the workers, the poor, the oppressed, without violence. But the renewal of life, rejuvenation, the liberation of creative powers, return to Homeric simplicity, to the sublimity of the Old Testament, to the spirit of the early Christian martyrs, of Corneille's heroes, of Cromwell's Ironsides, of the French revolutionary armies – this cannot be attained by persuasion, without violence as the weapon of liberty.

How the use of violence can in practice be distinguished from the use of force is never made clear. It is merely postulated as the only alternative to peaceful negotiation which, by presupposing a common good, common to workers and employers alike, denies the reality of class war. Marx, too, talked about the need for revolution to purify the proletariat from the filth of the old world and render it fit for the new. Herzen spoke of the cleansing storm of the revolution. Proudhon and Bakunin spoke in similarly apocalyptic terms. Even Kautsky declared that revolution raises men from degradation to a more exalted view of life. Sorel is obsessed by the idea of revolution. For him, faith in revolutionary violence and hatred of force entails, in the first place, the stern self-insulation of the workers. Sorel fervently agrees with the syndicalist organisers of the *bourses de travail* (a peculiar combination of labour exchanges, trades councils, and social and educational centres of militant workers) that proletarians who allow themselves any degree of co-operation with the class enemy are lost to their own side. All talk of responsible and humane employers, reasonable and peace-loving workers, nauseates him. Profit-sharing, factory councils that include both masters and men, democracy which recognises all men as equal, are fatal to the cause. In total war there can be no fraternisation.

Does violence mean more than this? Does it mean occupation of factories, the seizing of power, physical clashes with police or other agents of the possessing class, the shedding of blood? Sorel remains unclear. The conduct of the Allemanist workers who marched with Jaurès (then still well thought of) at a certain moment of the Dreyfus Affair is one of his very few allusions to the correct use of proletarian violence. Anything that increases militancy, but does not lead to the formation of power structures among the workers themselves, is approved. The distinction between force and violence appears to depend entirely on the character of its function and motive. Force imposes chains, violence breaks them. Force, open or concealed, enslaves; violence, always open, makes free. These are moral and metaphysical, not empirical, concepts. Sorel is a moralist and his values are rooted in one of the oldest of human traditions. That is why Péguy listened to him, and why his theses do not belong only to their own times but retain their freshness. Rousseau, Fichte, Proudhon, Flaubert, are Sorel's truest modern ancestors; as well as Marx the destroyer of rationalisations, the preacher of class war and of the proletarian revolution; not Marx the social scientist, the historical determinist, the author of programmes for a political movement, the practical conspirator.

I V

The doctrine of myths and its corollary, the emphasis on the power of the irrational in human thought and action, is a consequence of the modern scientific movement, and the application of scientific categories and methods to the behaviour of men. The relatively simple models of human nature which underlay the central ideas of social and political philosophers until quite far into the nineteenth century were gradually being superseded by an increasingly complicated and unstable picture as new and disturbing hypotheses about the springs of action were advanced by psychologists and anthropologists. The rise of doctrines, according to which men were determined by non-rational factors, some of them refracted in highly misleadng ways in men's consciousness, directed attention to actual social and political practice and its true causes and conditions, which only scientific investigation could uncover, and which severely limited the area of free will or even made it vanish altogether. This naturalistic approach had the effect of playing down the role of conscious reasons by which the actors mistakenly supposed themselves, and appeared to others, to be motivated. These may well have been among the most decisive causes of the decline of classical political theory which assumes that men who are, to some degree, free to choose between possibilities, do so for motives intelligible to themselves and others, and are, *pro tanto*, open to conviction by rational argument in reaching their decisions. The penetration of the 'disguises', of concealed factors – psychological, economic, anthropological – in individual and social life by examination of their actual role, transformed the simpler model of human nature, with which political theorists from Hobbes to J. S. Mill had operated, and shifted emphasis from political argument to the less or more deterministic descriptive disciplines that began with Tocqueville and Taine and Marx, and were carried on by Weber and Durkheim, Le Bon and Tarde, Pareto and Freud, and their disciples in our time.

Sorel rejected determinism, but his theory of myths belongs to this development. His social psychology is an odd amalgam of Marxism, Bergsonian intuitionism, and Jamesian psychology, in which men, once they realise that they are, whether they know it or not, shaped by the class conflict (which he treats as a historical datum), can, by an effort of the will reinforced by the inspiration of the appropriate myth, freely develop the creative sides of their nature, provided they do not attempt to do so as mere individuals but collectively, as a class. Even this is not entirely true of individual men of genius – especially of artists, who are capable of creation in adverse social conditions by the strength of their own indomitable spirit. Of this dark process James and Croce and Renan seemed to him to show a deeper understanding than the blinkered sociological environmentalists. But Sorel is not a consistent thinker. His desperate lifelong search for a class, or group, which can redeem humanity, or at least France, from mediocrity and decay, is itself rooted in a quasi-Marxist sociology of history as a drama in which the protagonists are classes generated by the growth of productive forces, a doctrine for which he claims objective validity.

v

The effect of Sorel's doctrine upon the revolutionary syndicalist movement was minimal. He wrote articles in journals, collaborated with Lagardelle, Delesalle and Péguy, offered homage to Fernand Pelloutier, and talked and lectured to groups of admirers in Paris. But when Griffuelhes, the strongest personality since Pelloutier among the syndicalists, was asked whether he read Sorel, he replied, 'I read Alexandre Dumas'. Sorel was himself what he most despised in others

– too intellectual, too sophisticated, too remote from the reality of the workers' lives. He looked for biblical or Homeric heroes capable of the epic spirit and was constantly disappointed. During the Dreyfus case, he denounced the anti-Dreyfusards who seemed to him to stand for lies, injustice, and unscrupulous demagoguery. But after the Dreyfusards had won, he was in turn disgusted by the ignoble political manœuvring, cynicism and dissimulation of the friends of the people. Jaurès's humanity and eloquence seemed to him mere self-interested demagoguery, democratic claptrap, dust in the workers' eyes, no better than Zola's rodomontades, or the silver periods of Anatole France, or betrayals by false friends of the workers, the worst of whom was Aristide Briand, once the fervent champion of the general strike.

He continued to live quietly in Boulogne-sur-Seine. For ten years, until 1912, he took the tram to attend Bergson's lectures, and on Thursdays came to the gatherings in the offices of Péguy's *Cahiers de la Quinzaine* which he dominated. There he delivered those vast monologues about politics and economics, classical and Christian culture, art and literature, which dazzled his disciples. He drew on a large store of unsystematic reading; but what lingered in his listeners' memories were his mordant paradoxes. Péguy listened reverently to *le père Sorel*, but in the end, when Sorel, disillusioned with the syndicalists who had gone the way of all workers into the morass of social democracy, began to look for new paladins against political impurity, and denounced the radical intellectuals, especially the Jews among them, too violently, even he became uncomfortable. When Sorel's anti-Semitism became more open and more virulent, and he did an unfriendly turn to Julien Benda (a ferocious critic of Bergson and of every form of nationalism, whom Péguy nevertheless greatly admired), and finally entered into an alliance with the militant royalists and chauvinists led by Maurras and the mystical Catholic nationalists grouped round Barrès, men who alone seemed to him independent, militant, and not tainted by the republican blight, this proved too much for Péguy, and he requested Sorel not to return. Sorel was deeply wounded. He preferred talk to writing. The audience of gifted writers and intellectuals was necessary to him. He began to frequent the bookshop of a humbler follower, and went on talking as before.

The flirtation with the reactionaries in the so-called Cercle Proudhon did not last long. In 1912 Sorel acclaimed Mussolini, then a flamboyant socialist militant, as a *condottiere* who, one day, 'will salute the Italian flag with his sword'. By 1914 he was once again on his own. When war broke out he felt abandoned: Bergson, Péguy, Maurras, even Hervé, all rallied to the defence of the Republic. During the war he was depressed and silent. He corresponded with Croce, who seemed to him critical and detached, and told his friend Daniel Halévy that the war was nothing but a fight between Anglo-American finance and the German General Staff. He did not seem to care greatly which gang emerged victorious.

After the war, in his letters to Croce, he criticised the beginnings of Fascism but, perhaps under the influence of Pareto, and Croce's initial pro-Fascist moment, pronounced Mussolini a 'political genius'. Lenin excited him far more. He saw him as a bold and realistic re-juvenator of socialism, the greatest socialist thinker since Marx, who had roused the Russian masses to an epic plane of revolutionary feel-ing. Lenin was Peter the Great or Robespierre, Trotsky was Saint-Just; their concept of the Soviets seemed to him pure syndicalism: he took it at its face value, as he did, perhaps, Mussolini's denunciation in 1920 of 'all states, past, present and future'. He applauded the Bolsheviks' contempt for democracy, and, still more, their ferocious attitude to intellectuals. He declared that the mounting terror of the Bolshevik Party was less harmful than the force which is was designed to repress; in any case it was probably the fault of its Jewish members. He averted his eyes from the strengthening of the party apparatus, and would not speak of Russia as a socialist state, since this concept seemed to him, as it had seemed to Marx, a blatant contradiction in terms.

To use the state as a weapon against the bourgeoisie was, he declared, like 'Gribouille who threw himself into the water to avoid getting wet in the rain'. He still thought well of Mussolini, but he thought better of Lenin to whom he wrote a passionate paean. By this time few listened to him; he was living in solitude and poverty – he had invested too much of his property in Tsarist and Austrian bonds. His death, a few weeks before Mussolini's march on Rome, passed unnoticed. His last uttered word is said to have been 'Napoleon...'.

Of the two heroes of his declining years, Lenin ignored him; Musso-lini, in search of distinguished intellectual ancestry, claimed him as a spiritual father. Fascist propaganda found useful ammunition in Sorel's writings: the mockery of liberal democracy, the violent anti-intellectualism, the appeal to the power of irrational forces, the calls to activism, violence, conflict as such, all this fed Fascist streams.[4] Sorel was no more a Fascist than Proudhon, but his glorification of action, honour, defiance, his deep hatred of democracy and equality, his contempt for liberals and Jews, are, like Proudhon's brand of socialism, not unrelated to the language and thought of Fascism and National Socialism; nor did his closest followers fail to note (and some among them to be duly influenced by) this fact. The ideological link of his views with what is common to romantic Bolshevism and left-wing strains in Fascism is painfully plain. 'The cry "death to the intellectuals",' he wrote hopefully in his last published collection of articles, 'so often attributed to the Bolsheviks, may yet become the battle-cry of the entire world proletariat.'

At this point, one might be tempted to bid Sorel goodbye as an eccentric visionary, a penetrating and cruel critic of the vices of parliamentary democracy and bourgeois humanitarianism – of what Trotsky once called 'Kantian–Quaker–liberal–vegetarian nonsense', a writer chiefly read in Italy, both in leftist and nationalist circles, duly superseded by Pareto, Mosca and Michels, a friend of Croce, a minor influence on Mussolini, the inspirer of a handful of radicals both of the Right and the Left, a half-forgotten extremist safely buried in the pages of the more capacious histories of socialist doctrines. Yet his ghost, half a century later, is by no means laid.

VI

Sorel, like Nietzsche, preached the need for a new civilisation of makers and doers, what is now called a counter-culture or an alternative society. The progressive Left in the nineteenth century believed in science and rational control of nature and of social and individual life, and on this based their attacks upon tradition, prejudice, aestheticism, clericalism, conservative or nationalist mystiques, whatever could not be defended by rational argument – these men have, to some extent, won. The technocratic, post-industrial society in which we are said to be living is governed by men who make use of skilled, scientific experts, rational planners, technocrats. The theory of convergence used to inform us, in its heyday, now evidently past, that societies on both sides of the Iron Curtain are conditioned by similar forces in all essential respects, whatever the differences in kind or degree of individual liberty enjoyed by their members.

This is the kind of order – democracy both real and sham – based on respect for blueprints and specialists, that Sorel most deeply feared and detested. A society of consumers without authentic moral values of their own, sunk in vulgarity and boredom in the midst of mounting affluence, blind to sublimity and moral grandeur, bureaucratic organisation of human lives in the light of what he called *la petite science*, positivist application of quasi-scientific rules to society – all this he despised and hated. Who would revolt against it? The workers had not fulfilled his expectations. They failed to respond to his trumpet calls; they continued to be preoccupied with their material needs; their mode of life remained hopelessly similar to that of the petite-bourgeoisie, one day to be the main recruiting-ground of Fascism, a class which Sorel regarded as the greatest source of moral contamination. He died a disappointed man.

Yet, if he were alive today, the wave of radical unrest could scarcely have failed to excite him. Like Fanon and the Black Panthers, and some dissenting Marxist groups, he believed that the insulted and the oppressed can find themselves and acquire self-identity and human dignity in acts of revolutionary violence. To intimidate the cowardly bourgeoisie (or, in Fanon's case, imperialist masters) by audacious acts of defiance, though Sorel did not favour terrorism or sabotage, is in tune with his feeling and his rhetoric. Che Guevara's or Fanon's concern about poverty, suffering and inequality was not at the centre of Sorel's moral vision; but they would have fulfilled his ideal of revolutionary pride, of a will moved by absolute moral values.

The idea of repressive tolerance, the belief that toleration of an order that inhibits 'epic' states of mind is itself a form of repression, is an echo of his own view. The neo-Marxist dialectic according to which all institutions and even doctrines are frozen forms of, and therefore obstacles to, the ever-flowing, ever-creative, human *praxis*, a kind of permanent revolution, might have seemed to him, even if he had understood the dark words of Hegelian neo-Marxism, mere incitement to anarchy. The metaphysics of the School of Frankfurt, and of Lukács (who was in his youth affected by Sorel's views), would surely have been roundly condemned by him as the latest utopian and teleological nostrums of academic pedants, visionaries or charlatans.

In England anti-liberal critics – Wyndham Lewis and T. E. Hulme – took an interest in his ideas. Hulme translated the *Reflexions*. They found his emphasis on self-restraint and self-discipline sympathetic. Like them he hated disorder, bohemianism, the lack of self-imposed barriers, as symptoms of self-indulgence and decadence. But the revolt of those whom a German writer has recently described as the Anabaptists of affluence, the preachers of an alternative society uncontaminated by the vices of the past, might well have made an appeal to him. He would have been disturbed by their sexual permissiveness; chastity was for him the highest of virtues; their slovenly habits, their exhibitionism, their addiction to drugs, their formless lives would have enraged him; and he would have denounced their neo-primitivism, the Rousseauian belief that poverty and roughness are closer to nature than austerity and civilised habits, and therefore more authentic and morally pure. He regarded this as false and stupid and attacked it all his life. But the present state of Western society would have seemed to him a confirmation of Vico's prophecy of social disintegration as a prelude to a second barbarism, followed by a new, more virile civilisation, a new beginning in which men would again be simple, pious and severe. Barbarism did not frighten him.

He might have found reasons for acclaiming the Cultural Revolution in China. 'If Socialism comes to grief,' he once observed, 'it will evidently be in the same way as Protestantism, because it will be alarmed at its own barbarity,' with the implication that it must not stop but plunge on – barbarism is, after all, an antidote to decay. This is instinctively believed by all those today who have opted out of a wicked society, as Sorel, who admired the early Christians and Puritans for their renunciation, so ardently wished the workers to do. Sparta rather than Athens. This alone created an unbridgeable gulf between Sorel and the easy-going, generous, humane Jaurès. It is this very quality that appeals to the grimmer dynamiters of the present.

But the strongest single link with the revolutionary movements of our day is his unyielding emphasis on the will. He believed in absolute moral ends that are independent of any dialectical or other historical pattern, and in the possibility, in conditions which men can themselves create, of realising these ends by the concerted power of the free and deliberate collective will. This, rather than a sense of the unalterable timetable of historical determinism, is the mood of the majority of the rebels, political and cultural, of the past two decades. Those who join revolutionary organisations, and those who abandon them, are more often moved by moral indignation with the hypocrisy or inhumanity of the regime under which they live (or alternatively with similar vices in the revolutionary party which, disillusioned, they leave), than by a metaphysical theory of the stages of history – of social change by which they do not wish to be left behind. The reaction is moral more than intellectual, of will rather than reason; such men are against the prevailing system because it is unjust or bestial rather than irrational or obsolescent. More than seventy years ago Eduard Bernstein became convinced that Marxism failed to provide an acceptable view of the ends of life, and preached the universal values of the neo-Kantians. So did Karl Liebknecht, who could not be accused of lack of revolutionary passion. This is far closer to Sorel's position, and connects him with modern revolutionary protest.

Yet, of course, this anti-rationalism was, to some degree, self-refuting. He knew that if faith in reason is delusive, it is only by the use of rational methods, by knowledge and self-knowledge and rational interpretation of the facts of history or psychology or social behaviour, that this could be discovered and established. He did not wish to stop invention and technology; he was no Luddite, he knew that to break machines is to perpetuate ignorance, scarcity and poverty. He might have admitted that the remedies offered by the modern insurgents are delusions; but this would not have troubled him. He proposed no specific economic or social policies. Like Hegel's opponents in post-Napoleonic Germany he appealed to love, solidarity, community; this, in due course, offered sustenance to 'extra-parliamentary' oppositions both of the Right and of the Left. If Fanon, or the militants of the Third World, or the revolutionary students were not healers, he might have recognised them as the disease itself. This is what Herzen said about himself and the Nihilists of his own generation. His lifelong effort to identify and distinguish the pure from the impure, the physicians from the patients, the heroic few who should be the saviours of society – workers, or radical nationalists, or Fascists, or Bolsheviks – ended in failure. Would he have tried to find them in colonial peoples, or Black Americans or students who have mysteriously escaped contamination by the false values of their society? We cannot tell. At any rate, the dangers of which he spoke were, and are, real. Recent events have shown that his diagnosis of the malaise is anything but obsolete.

He was almost everything that he so vehemently denounced, an alienated intellectual, a solitary thinker isolated from men of action who achieved no relationship with the workers and never became a member of any vigorous, co-operative group of producers. He, whose symbol of creation was the cut stone, the chiselled marble, was productive only of words. He believed implicitly in family life and for twenty-five years had none. The apostle of action felt at home only in bookshops, among purveyors of words, talkers cut off, as he had always been, from the life of workers and artists. He remained eccentric, egocentric, an outsider of outsiders. This is an irony that, one may be sure, could scarcely have escaped him.

No monument to him exists. Ten years after his death, so Daniel Halévy tells us, Rolland Marcel, the director of the Bibliothèque Nationale in Paris, came to Halévy with an odd story. He had recently met the Ambassador of Fascist Italy who informed him that his Government had learnt that Sorel's grave was in a state of disrepair: the Fascist Government offered to put up a monument to the eminent thinker. Soon after this, the Ambassador of the U.S.S.R. approached him with an identical proposal on behalf of the Soviet Government. Halévy promised to get in touch with Sorel's family. After a long delay he received a communication which said that the family regarded the grave as its own private affair and that of no one else. Halévy was delighted. The message was dry, brusque and final. It might have come from Sorel himself.

The prophet of concerted collective action, of pragmatic approaches, prized only absolute values, total independence. He was to be the modern Diogenes bent on exploding the most sacred dogmas and respected beliefs of all the establishments of his enlightened age. Sorel is still worth reading. The world about and against which he was writing might be our own. Whether he is, as he wished to be, 'serious, formidable, sublime', or, as often as not, perverse, dogmatic and obsessed, with all the moral fury of perpetual youth (and this fiery, not wholly adult, outraged feeling, may in part account for his affinity with the young revolutionaries of our time, his ideas come at us from every quarter. They mark a revolt against the rationalist ideal of frictionless contentment in a harmonious social system in which all ultimate questions are reduced to technical problems, soluble by appropriate techniques. It is the vision of this closed world that morally repels the young today. The first to formulate this in clear language was Sorel. His words still have power to upset.

NOTES

1. *Réflexions sur la violence* (Paris, 1930) p. 199. This letter, by Marx, which Professor L. J. Brentano reported as having been sent to Marx's English friend, Professor Beesly, in 1869, has never, so far as I know, been found. Nor does the sentiment sound very Marxian, although Eduard Bernstein is reported to have said that it seemed to him to be so.

2. Marxism is in danger of becoming 'a mythology founded on the maladies of language', he wrote in a letter to Croce. This could well have been said by Kraus.

3. Destined, Sorel declared in 1900, to become a formidable weapon.

4. A romantic, bitterly anti-democratic nineteenth-century Russian reactionary once declared that when he thought of the bourgeois in their hideous clothes scurrying along the streets of Paris, he asked himself whether it was for this that Alexander the Great, in his plumed helmet, had ridden down the Persian hosts at Arbela. Sorel would not have repudiated this sentiment.

2 Alexander Herzen: His Last Phase

MONICA PARTRIDGE

ALEXANDER HERZEN'S sense of history, his understanding of contemporary events and the people who made them, his political judgements and political programme during the last year of his life, deserve reappraisal. New material which has become available with the publication of the Soviet Academy edition of his works[1] makes possible a more complete understanding of his ideas and his endeavours at that time. He was more in sympathy with the international working-class movement than is generally supposed, and his thought was more an amalgam of ideas held by the most radical European socialists than it was the political liberalism first attributed to him by the younger generation of Russian revolutionaries.

A young Russian admirer of Herzen and a budding positivist philosopher, G. N. Vyrubov, noticed when he met Herzen in Geneva in August 1866 that 'usually so lively and gay, he was sad and dejected. He was depressed about the sudden fall in circulation of *The Bell* and complained about ingratitude.'[2] Perhaps Vyrubov, who lived to enjoy a ripe old age, surviving until 1913, is to some extent responsible for the apocryphal image of Herzen in these last years as a spent force, a weary, defeated and ageing man who had outlived his time. It should be remembered, however, that Karakozov's terrorist attempt on the life of Alexander II had occurred in April 1866, only a few months before the visit Vyrubov refers to. This event sharpened the focus of Herzen's thoughts, initiating a new phase whose final shape became clear only in 1869. A rather different impression of Herzen was formed by another Russian of the younger generation, Boborykin. The first Russian journalist ever to appear at a Congress of the First International (in September 1868), Boborykin wondered:

Was there in him the chagrin of a man who had not found for himself a permanent home and who recognised that he would not mean as much to his fellow-countrymen as he had a few years earlier thought? There were sad notes in him which broke through. But it could not possibly be said that the pessimism which overtook him after the June Days of 1848 had deepened or that it had suppressed him spiritually. It seemed to me, on the contrary, that with his move to the Continent he began to look less gloomily at European reaction, at the then Bonapartism, and placed higher hopes on French youth ... and, while not turning formally into a social democrat, a follower of Marx's theory, nevertheless, in spite of his long-standing dislike of the author of *Capital* ... in a letter to Ogaryov written in his last year, acknowledged Marx as a great innovator in the struggle of the proletariat.[3]

In 1863 Herzen had been committed by Ogaryov and Bakunin to identify *The Bell*'s editorial policy with enthusiastic partisan support of the Polish insurrection, in spite of his own more sober and correct judgement that the uprising was insufficiently organised, likely to fail, at best could result in political, not social, change and therefore should not be encouraged. Of the most eminent European revolutionaries, Herzen stood alone with Proudhon and Blanqui in this attitude. Blanqui too felt that even a successful outcome could achieve only political independence under a hierarchical state. He saw that 'ces imbéciles [i.e. "nos révolutionnaires"] ont l'idée fixe que toute insurrection triomphante profite nécéssairement à la Révolution'.[4] *The Bell*'s circulation declined sharply as the result of its partisanship. Endeavouring to re-establish his news-sheet as the open forum of free uncensored speech, Herzen thereafter but too late remained soberly adamant. 'After '63 and '64 I decided to stand on guard and, as far as I could, to avoid our making any general mistakes, prevent any common blunders,' he told Ogaryov. 'We lost *The Bell* and the press abroad because of our enthusiasms.'[5]

This does not mean that he was unwilling to hand over the press to others. By 1864 he was already weary of carrying the enormous burden of work which the practical running of his press involved. A Russian merchant who visited him in London in 1864, in answer to a question from Herzen, reported 'that "Russia has hardly been looking at *The Bell* recently. Instead of you we have our own publicist, Chernyshevsky. We find your *Bell* poor and you are no longer in fashion." "Yes, I see that," replied Herzen. "I have had no visitors recently and the publication does not sell. We should give it up.... I work only with Ogaryov and he is ill. What can I do? ... I would have given it to Utin *but he refused*.... Let Chernyshevsky come. I would give my press to him with both hands." '[6]

The facts regarding *The Bell*'s decline and Herzen's relations with the 'younger generation' need not be repeated her. It is sufficient to recall that when Utin, a leader of the student movement inside Russia in 1861 and then a member of the 'Land and Liberty' secret organisation, escaped arrest and arrived in London in 1863, Herzen welcomed him warmly there. He invited him to join *The Bell*'s editorial board. But Utin, refusing, moved to Switzerland where other young Russians joined him. In the last days of 1864 and the New Year of 1865 Herzen travelled to Geneva in a further attempt to collaborate with the younger generation of the Russian emigration in Switzerland. It was decided then to transfer Herzen's press to Geneva and *The Bell* appeared there from 25 May 1865 onwards. But the fundamental disagreement over editorial policy, which had been the cause of Utin's original refusal to join the editorial board, had not been satisfactorily resolved. The two different possible policies at the root of the disagreement had been plainly stated and *The Bell*'s position equally plainly announced in the editorial dated 1 January 1865:

> *The Bell* will remain what it has been – *the organ of social development in Russia*. It will be, as before, against everything which hinders such development and for everything which assists it.... Propaganda may be clearly divided into two kinds. On the one hand there may be the word, advice, analysis, accusation, theory; on the other, the formation of [revolutionary] circles, the formation of internal and external contacts. We shall devote our whole authority, our whole ability, to the former. The latter cannot be done from abroad.[7]

Utin and his friends thought it could. They also took exception to Herzen's authoritarian tone. They maintained that *The Bell* should be devoted wholly to the organisation of revolutionary circles and especially to 'Land and Liberty'. In this attitude they carried with them Ogaryov, torn from now onwards between loyalty to Herzen and attraction to the revolutionary enthusiasms of the 'younger emigration'. Herzen remained adamant; and when Karakozov attempted to assassinate Alexander II on 4 April 1866, the gulf widened beyond the point where it could be bridged. The *attentat* strengthened his view that the members of the 'young emigration' were not only romantic but irresponsible. Herzen, who by his publications abroad had virtually single-handed created the Russian revolutionary movement, was now in 1866 made sharply to understand what he had gradually been realising since 1863: that it is easier to start revolutionary agitation than to stop it or even keep it under control. His own words, misunderstood or, at any rate, misapplied, had started a line of thought leading directly to the attempt at tyrannicide which appalled him both on practical and humane grounds. The essays written after the June Days in Paris of 1848 and his pamphlets written for the Free Russian Press had provided the 'new' men with ready-made conclusions and slogans, but, as was now becoming painfully apparent to Herzen, these were being used by the 'new' men out of context, without reference to the facts and arguments which led to them. They took his slogans at their face value in rather the same way as his own generation had accepted Hegel's maxims unrelated to the philosophy as a whole, until he himself had undertaken the task of the thorough study of Hegel, and had published in Russia his essays on philosophy upon which this younger generation of revolutionaries had been reared.[8]

Herzen had concluded one of his essays written immediately after the June Days with the peroration:

> The world will not know liberty until everything religious and political is transformed into something simple and human.... Blood flowed in rivers but they [the French Provisional Government, M.A.P.] could find no word of love or reconciliation.... What will become of this bloodshed? Who knows? But whatever comes it is enough that out of this orgy of madness, revenge, strife, retribution there will perish a world which stifles the new man, prevents him from living, from making himself at home in the new [conditions]. That is excellent and therefore long live chaos and destruction! *Vive la mort!*...[9]

From this and similar passages the younger generation had taken their main text; and they had evolved a concept of nihilism much more materialist than Herzen's, a form of nihilism which provided the ideology for Karakozov's shot at the Tsar. In the first editorial of *The Bell* to be published after the shooting, Herzen announced:

> The shot on 4 April gave us no cause for rejoicing. We expect disaster to follow and were indignant that some fanatic should have taken responsibility into his own hands.... History forces her way forward by means of murder only among barbaric and decadent people. Murder is of most use to individuals who seek to change dynasties.... We do not need bullets ... we are progressing along the main highway in full strength.... It is impossible to stop us. We can be diverted only from one path into another, from the course of gradual development into the path of general uprising.... No, our voice is not needed in the cathedral choir of exultation, hate, protest, demonstration.... Let servile Pharisees who corrupt young

men to the point of false idolatry join the choir. The sound of our voice is not in harmony with them.[10]

In adopting this attitude to the *attentat* Herzen was not changing his intellectual tune. He had never been a political anarchist, although some of his most influential writing had been taken to mean such by the next generation. He was in 1866 as in 1848 an iconoclast, that is, a philosophical anarchist. His cry, then as now, was not for cannons to destroy but for the destruction of canonised truths, the questioning of intellectual prejudices found to be outworn or invalid. The policy of terrorism emerged because his new destructive slogans had been clapped on to the surface of the old political concept of history instead of his newer social interpretation of it. Herzen had, in any case, welcomed the bloodshed and destruction only as a *fait accompli* which could be of use only if pushed further, because it could produce nothing useful if left at the *juste milieu*. The peroration had been written, moreover, before the savagery of the political reaction had started.

Of all the lessons learnt from 1848, the most far-reaching in Herzen's subsequent thought resulted from the Government reaction which revealed itself in its full fury only in 1849; it was a lesson strengthened by the abortive Polish insurrection of 1863. Thereafter the basis of his thought on revolutionary methods was that unsuccessful revolution begets counter-revolution which invariably leaves a worse situation than before; and he therefore shared Blanqui's conviction of the paramount importance of a practical approach and the need for patient and meticulous preparation and organisation. The concept of history as a mass movement, the need at all costs to avoid counter-revolutionary action and the necessity of thorough preparation all underlay Herzen's own contribution to socialist theory with special regard to Russia, that is, his 'Russian Socialism', whose originality lay in the idea that the educated classes of student and 'repentant nobleman' should go 'to the people' to prepare soil deep enough to ensure that real social change might not only be implanted, but take root.

By 1866 Herzen's ideas were, largely through Chernyshevsky and the work of secret presses and of people within Russia, beginning to give rise to a wide-scale mass movement such as he had hoped for. Through his technique of exerting relentless pressure on the Government, he had by propaganda from his press, already played an influential part during the 1850s in bringing about the first Act of Emancipation of the serfs in 1861. This had yet to be completed. The year 1870 would be a crucial time when these seeds sown in 1861 would either bear full fruit or decay.[11] His open letter to the Tsar published in *The Bell* of 25 May 1865, and, indeed, the continued preoccupation of *The Bell* at this time with this question of serfdom, a preoccupation which was seen, incorrectly, by many readers to spring from lack of other ideas or from 'liberalism', resulted from his conviction of the need for continuous pressure on the Tsar; and it was entirely consistent with his earlier approach and technique. Thus Herzen's reaction to the Karakozov shot was not simply a matter of internal disagreement with and temperamental difference from the younger generation of the emigration over this incident itself. He feared its practical consequences on a broad scale. He feared it would precipitate violent Government measures (as, indeed, it did), affect the climate of public opinion in Russia, and so destroy something partially achieved without making any practical contribution at all to the building of socialism. His editorial of 1 May, and a series of essays 'Order Prevails' ('Poryadok torzhestvuet') which followed, were more than a piece of fine journalism written out of personal pique, more than repetition of old ideas by an ageing revolutionary who had no new ideas to offer. They were the result of Herzen's sudden full realisation of how completely the younger generation had misunderstood him; and a vigorous effort to explain the abstract and more positive basis of his slogans of destruction. 'We will speak later of nihilism,' he wrote, 'but here we wish to call attention to those dutiful people who keep repeating a word, parrot-like, without understanding what it means. They are capable of understanding that nihilism is – a woman who sits with her feet stuck up on the table drinking champagne ... but we want to explain to them that *nihilism* in a serious sense means – *knowledge and scepticism, study instead of faith, understanding instead of obedience.*' The Government had been forced to bring in the Act of Emancipation because it was afraid; afraid of the sure, inexorable growth of the whole, broad-based progressive movement. Karakozov's 'act of vengeance' had not only been unsuccessful; it had provided an excuse to the Government to act

with savage pleasure. Reaction has been justified. The Tsar's terrorists have been justified.... We are not concerned whether they understand or what they understand. The problem is to make them realise what they are up against, what they have to be afraid of.... The redoubtable enemy ... which they fear and are fighting is ... socialism. Is not this a step forward? ... it is impossible to stop this movement which frightens them and which is carrying the Continent towards other destinies.... Over the last five years we have ... disintegrated, forgetting that we have been granted not our *rights* but an indulgence. It is time to concentrate our energies again.[12]

And he again appealed to his readers, but especially those who sympathised with Karakozov, to recognise that history is mass movement, and that socialism, which could not *ipso facto* be achieved except by social change, must proceed in Russia from the peasants themselves, not from something imposed on them from outside:

> We can foresee many people laughing at the expression 'Russian Socialism'. Will not people laugh at anything which they do not understand? ... By 'Russian Socialism' I mean that kind of socialism which proceeds from the land and from peasant life, from the actual division and actual redistribution of fields, from communal ownership and communal management – and this together with the proletarian workshops represents progress towards economic *justice* such as socialism in general strives after.[13]

Having failed to persuade Utin and his friends to collaborate in restrengthening *The Bell* as an open forum, Herzen in March 1865 initiated proceedings whereby it became a limited company. He, Ogaryov, their printer Cziernecki, Peter Dolgorukov, F. V. Luginin (alias Bakst) and V. I. Kasatkin all became shareholders. The last, who had contributed a substantial sum towards costs, became Herzen's chief assistant with responsibility for the practical management. A man of some literary ability, he had had experience in publishing before leaving Russia, and was a member of 'Land and Liberty'. Luginin, a member of the secret society *Velikorus*, had participated in the formation of the Russian reading-room in Heidelberg; and Prince Dolgorukov, a contributor to *The Bell*, had published a number of works in continental journals and a book *La Vérité sur la Russie*. The limited company thus represented an attempt to reflect in its composition all shades of progressive opinion. Kasatkin proved incompetent. The arrangement failed to work. Herzen was obliged to resume private ownership. He eventually suspended publication (until 1 July 1867). Although *The Bell*'s circulation had dropped so dramatically since 1863, Herzen's own personal reputation in Russia as leader of the Russian emigration abroad was still considerable. Pressed by both Ogaryov and the younger men to reopen it as the organ of 'Land and Liberty', he remained firm in preferring to stop publication than again to permit that reputation to be exploited by those whose methods he deemed harmful to the cause of socialism. Observation of the foreign and especially Russian *émigré* colonies in Geneva strengthened his resolve. They were displaying all the tendencies for petty intrigue and quarrels which he had deplored among the foreign refugees in London. His conviction of the impossibility of the creation of socialism by such people increased: 'One phalange after another appears on the platform with alarming rapidity – and one phalange after another drops into oblivion ... or into the mud, unable to hang on. They are all a Monte Rosa, with nothing to peg a rope to. There is no soil. There is soil only in the social basement.'[14]

Failing to gain the support of the younger men, for whom the vigorous material and political anarchism of Bakunin was much more attractive, Herzen adopted an attitude to the activities of the Russian emigration in Geneva of apprehensive dissociation. In June 1869 he wrote to his son that Bakunin was

> going from one meeting to another. He is rushed around like a social midwife – first to Lausanne, then to Lök. Everywhere he preaches general destruction – conservatives turn pale, pastors utter oaths ... and then he leaves them to begin his sermon again. In an abstract sense he is right, but in practice he goes beyond all possible limits. Furthermore, the young generation of Russians accept his programme *à la lettre*. Students meet in order to form themselves into robber bands. Bakunin advises them to burn all documents, to destroy things but to save people. This is where the stupidity of the Government and obstinate miserliness of the bourgeoisie has led. In this destructive framework which the old student Bakunin and our young Bakuninists dream about, nothing will take shape in the near future, but the débâcle has begun.... In Lausanne the *Grand Conseil* has threatened the workers with soldiers.[15]

While Bakunin was rushing about Switzerland inciting workers to revolution and the young nihilists struggled to surpass their European brethren in conspiracy, Herzen anxiously watched the course of events in Russia. On 1 January 1869 he wrote to Edgar Quinet that 'the Russian boat is going to hurl itself fatally in a year's time (in 1870) against a formidable rock. There is no pilot to turn it. It is the end of the period for the re-purchase of land. It will be the consummation of the emancipation of the serfs. We are waiting for the Government and the nobility. This is much more important for us than war-cries and the crusades of Henri Martin.'[16] According to the 1861 Act of Emancipation the peasants had been given nine years in which to fulfil certain obligations with regard to the payment for their land.

Of the Russian revolutionaries, Herzen alone attached great importance to the fact that Russia had not yet completed the destruction of her feudal system, and interpreted it to mean not that she was necessarily at a backward stage but at a different stage of historic growth as compared with the rest of Europe.

He reviewed his situation after 1866 with characteristic realism, stoicism and imaginative invention. He recognised that the days of

The Bell's effectiveness were over. He recognised that propaganda of the kind he himself had started could now most effectively come from one of the numerous illegal presses now existing in Russia and for whose creation he himself was responsible. He recognised that he stood in isolation. And he recognised that he still was nevertheless not without influence in Russia or in Europe. He wrote to Ivan Turgenev: '*Tempora mutantur*. Different times require different weapons.'[17] He closed *The Bell*. Its last editorial of 1 December 1868 took the form of a letter to Ogaryov:

> Our journal was never an end but a means, a tool.... We have repeated a hundred times the important part of our dearer convictions. Round them an indestructible crust has formed. We have a youth so irrevocably socialist, so filled with audacious logic, so strong in intellectual realism and in negation in all the realms of clerical and governmental fetishism that we have no need to fear – *the idea* will not perish!

The younger generation must be allowed to go its own way. Unfortunately the 'seed' had deviated from normal growth after germination because of the unnaturally long incubation period. It was growing too fast and 'it is doubtful whether it will be able to withstand being forced without an unfortunate crisis or mishap. One must just wait for the crisis to pass ... and, above all, know how to wait.... And in our language "wait" has never meant *to cross one's arms*. It is a thousand times better to look for a new route.'[18]

The new route which Herzen started to explore led back into the enemy camp. The fact that his writings from Europe had been superseded in Russia by publications both written and published there, represented a significant step forward. He proposed taking the next. He decided to attempt publication of his own works, but within Russia instead of from abroad, and openly, not at secret presses. It was a bold idea. For when in 1852 the Buturlin Committee had banned Iskander's writings from abroad, they had also banned the re-publication of works of his which had been published earlier within Russia; they had even ordered that all back numbers of *Notes of the Fatherland*, the journal in which they had originally appeared, be withdrawn from all stores and libraries; they had banned even the appearance of the name Herzen or Iskander.

By the end of 1868 Herzen was already in touch with the editors of a St Petersburg journal *The Week* (*Nedelya*), who agreed to publish a series of articles by him. The first of the series, to which he gave the title 'Out of Boredom' ('Skuki radi'), appeared in one of the last numbers of that year under the new pseudonym of 'Nionsky'. On receiving his copy, Herzen wrote immediately to tell Ogaryov: 'My article has been printed without alteration. After one or two articles I must try them under my own name.'[19] Evidently there was disagreement on the editorial board as to the wisdom of publication. Nevertheless, three weeks later Herzen received a letter of thanks from the editor and he told Ogaryov of

> a request to send more. *Ergo*, victory on that side.... They [the editorial board] not only are not afraid. They are actually boasting.... I am sending the third instalment very soon.... And so *la porte est ouverte* and, if you wish, you can send as well. If *The Week* has accepted so enthusastically, then others also will accept. I am afraid the *The Week* is not read much. But I think that all this is not without considerable significance.[20]

Herzen was not so much out of touch with the atmosphere in Russia as was supposed. He continued with the cycle. The second article of the cycle (it was a series of physiological sketches of the French bourgeoisie of the Second Empire) appeared in February 1869 and a third in April. He was paid a 'laughable' sum for them, he told Ogaryov, 'but all Petersburg is reading them. Why should we go on churning things out here – just to provide ourselves with something to read?'[21] Evidently many readers soon guessed the identity of 'Nionsky' from the writer's highly characteristic style. After the appearance of the third article the Ministry of Home Affairs, having warned the editors following the publication of each earlier one, suspended *The Week* for six months. The fourth essay, therefore, did not appear in Herzen's lifetime, since he died at the beginning of 1870.

The interest roused by the published essays was probably the reason for a request from two publishers for permission to re-publish in Russia a collection of all Herzen's works previously published there. A certain P. I. Blaramberg sought out in Geneva and proposed to Ogaryov (Herzen being absent) that he and Baron N. Wrangel should publish in Petersburg all Herzen's former works other than his novel, and including the two cycles of his philosophical essays.[22] Almost immediately after this, Herzen received a second request from Arkady Skalon, a publisher and owner of a bookshop and reading-room in Kharkov. Since he had not yet entered into any contract with Wrangel, of whom neither he nor Ogaryov knew anything, and since Skalon was known to them as being the pupil of Chernyshevsky's friend, Irina Vedensky, around whom a secret political circle had formed, Skalon's proposal was more attractive. Herzen eventually gave his permission to Skalon, who wished to undertake the work not, like Wrangel, as a commercial venture but out of a desire to participate in circulating Herzen's writings within Russia. On 11 June 1869 Skalon applied to the Kiev authorities for permission to publish a manuscript *Hesitations (Variations on Old Themes): An Anthology of Articles by I.* On being requested to supply the name of the author, he replied that it was 'the political emigrant' Herzen. Permission for publication was refused. A year later, six months after Herzen's death, a Moscow publisher by the name of E. A. Troyan published an anthology of Herzen's articles containing all his early literary works under the same title of *Hesitations* but without any initial. Soon after this appeared a second volume which contained the important cycle of philosophical essays, *Letters on the Study of Nature.* This was immediately censored and as many copies as could be found were confiscated. Only then did it transpire that 'E. A. Troyan' was Skalon.[23]

Herzen had not been unduly discouraged by the temporary suspension of *The Week*, nor by the refusal of permission made to Skalon by the Kiev authorities. Guerrilla warfare depended on continuous audacious attacks followed by tactical rapid retreat. Accepting his position of isolation, he intended to fight now only as a guerrilla and was optimistic that other opportunities for attack would present themselves. When Ogaryov, a few months before Herzen's death, again suggested reviving *The Bell*, the latter wrote:

> I cannot understand what you think *The Bell* can consist of. *Polar Star* can still be kept going with 'homework', i.e. articles written in advance. But *The Bell*? And where are your correspondents? My own relationship with regard to the Paris journals means that I can have in them permanent space for a Russian section – in *Le Siècle* or *Liberté* ... or even *Le Temps*. And besides, for whom shall we publish *The Bell*? Where is its public? Pyatkovsky has proposed to me that I should contribute to the new journal which they are about to publish – and you know what the frontiers for that are from the affair of Shchapov and Louis Blanc's letters. Whatever you may say, Shchapov was acquitted (did you read Spasovich's speech?). On that precedent I could publish three-quarters of *The Bell* in Moscow.... I am not just raising objections, Ogaryov, and would be only too glad to be convinced otherwise.... And remember, too, that our physical energy for work is declining, as well as Cziernecki's for printing.[24]

The 'Shchapov affair' to which Herzen refers had occurred the previous month. Shchapov had been prosecuted for the publication in St Petersburg in November 1866 of Louis Blanc's *Letters on England* which the Petersburg censors had declared to contain passages 'extremely harmful in their orientation and in contravention of the existing laws regarding publication and the general criminal code'. The defence of Shchapov had been undertaken by a brilliant barrister, V. D. Spasovich. He had succeeded in procuring the verdict that 'in spite of radicalism the book contained no statements likely to prove harmful to existing beliefs or dangerous to the existing law of the Russian Empire'.[25] As a consequence Shchapov was acquitted and the ban on the book removed.

Particularly since 1848 and his resultant preoccupation as to how to avoid political reaction, Herzen, like Lassalle, had come to conceive the state (which to Herzen for practical purposes meant the Russian state) as playing a positive role in the attainment of socialism. The state should not be quickly and completely destroyed, as Bakunin and his young Russian followers advocated; it should be subjected to constant pressure which would force it into becoming, ultimately, the servant of the people; and by 'people' he understood both the peasant and the proletarian worker. 'The state,' he wrote, 'has no specially defined form – it may serve reaction and revolution alike, whichever has force on its side.... The state is a transitional form. But from this it does not follow that it is obsolete.' Nor does it follow that Herzen, though he 'preferred revolution without bloodshed', was opposed to the use of force. On the contrary, he advocated it. Pressure by the revolutionary forces, both from inside and outside Russia, could speed the pace of the advance to socialism. Hence the value, however small, of his own guerrilla sorties.

If he shared with Lassalle a belief in the necessity and positive role of the state and also in the value of propaganda, Herzen shared with Karl Marx an appreciation of the international proletarian movement which was rapidly developing and in 1869 was reaching the peak of its nineteenth-century success. Stemming from the English Chartist movement, and in contrast to the old conspiratorial methods of European revolutionaries, it had concentrated on finding new forms of organisational structure and on new social and political activities. One historian states that its attention had been shifted 'to the open propaganda of socialism and communist ideas and to the building of mass organisations of labourers in the city and on the land ... the general trend was away from relatively small groups of active revolutionary conspirators who were isolated from their environment and towards mass political parties'.[26] Similarities with this and Herzen's own ideas for advancing Russia's progressive movement are striking.

If, as Herzen fervently hoped, Russia achieved full emancipation in 1870, thereby passing out of her period of feudalism; and if she were to pass, as he also hoped, directly to her social revolution without the development of a capitalist bourgeois class, then the Russian peasant and worker, unimpeded by the barrier of the bourgeoisie's existence, might in 1869 be nearer than was supposed (at any rate by European socialists) to the attainment of socialism. The new methods being used by the European proletariat for acquiring their social and democratic rights promised to be more helpful than old methods which led simply to political *coups d'état*.

It is not generally appreciated that, while in London, Herzen had been more closely connected with *émigrés* of the socialist and working-class wing of the revolutionary movement than with such men as Ledru-Rollin and Mazzini, whose objectives were not socialist and whose contacts with Herzen are better known. Jean-Baptiste Bocquet, a foundation member of the First International and member of its General Council in 1864-5, who, as a member of the committee of *The Working Man*, had taken some initiative in the International's formation, had been closely associated with Herzen in Paris as early as 1848. He was present in Herzen's apartment a few hours before his arrest for participation in the June Days, and he returned directly there for refuge on being released from imprisonment in the Bastille some time later. Subsequently, and indeed during the time when he was organising the demonstration of 1849 at the Château d'Eaux, Bocquet was engaged by Herzen as tutor to his children. Herzen's relations with Bocquet continued in London. Another foundation member of the First International and French representative on the International Committee which preceded it, Joseph Domengé, was also invited by Herzen to act as tutor to his son. (Invitations to give lessons to his children seem to have been a better method for helping *émigré* friends financially than for helping his own children educationally.) Domengé and Herzen had appeared on the same public platform in London in 1853 as speakers at the meeting to celebrate the Polish insurrection of 1830. Herzen subsequently saw him 'quite often ... and always with the greatest and most sincere pleasure'.[27] He included him among 'the small number I love among the small number of my friends',[28] words written in the autumn of 1854 at the time of the formation of the International Committee, when Domengé would 'always' visit the Herzen household 'three times a week'.[29] In 1857 Domengé returned to the Continent for a time and thereafter Herzen saw less of him, until 1865 when he himself went abroad and closer relations were resumed. Domengé once more was invited to act as tutor in the Herzen household.

Of all the French political *émigrés* in London, Herzen was closest to Alfred Talandier; and Talandier was the most deeply involved in the international working-class movement. He was a prime mover behind the idea of an international alliance of the English Chartist organisation with French, German and Polish refugee organisations, and he became corresponding Treasurer of the International Association at its formation in August 1856. He was a member of the French secret masonic society of the *Philadelphes*, probably also of the *Commune Révolutionnaire*, and when the First International was founded in September 1864 Talandier became a member of its General Council. Friendship between Herzen and Talandier was cemented by Talandier's contribution of an article for the all-important first number of Herzen's *Polar Star*. Subsequently Talandier assisted Herzen with the French translation of several works and articles. The Talandier and Herzen families also became close, and it was Herzen who, gaining Michelet's support, secured for Talandier a post as tutor at the military college of Sandhurst (a post which might be considered somewhat inappropriate for one so deeply involved in revolution). Two other radically-minded French political *émigrés* whom Herzen knew in London, Élie and Élisée Reclus, returned to live in Paris in 1855. The extent of Herzen's trust in them is demonstrated by the fact that they from time to time acted as agents in bringing parcels to Herzen from Russia via Maria Reichel.[30] On returning to the Continent Herzen re-established contact with Élisée, a member also of the First International and future participant in the Paris Commune; and in February 1869 Élisée joined the company of those invited to act as tutor to Herzen's children.[31]

In the light of such contacts, and others which cannot be mentioned for reasons of space, Herzen's interest in the international working-class movement is no matter for surprise. He was directly involved in the foundation of the International Association. When, in the autumn of 1854, Armand Barbès, imprisoned since 1848, proposed visiting London on being amnestied, Ernest Jones suggested that the workers' demonstration planned at that time to protest against the proposed visit to England of Napoleon III should also be a demonstration of welcome to Barbès. The 'Welcome and Protest Committee' was set up. Neither the welcome nor the unwelcome guest arrived; but the Committee decided to justify its existence by concerning itself with international questions in general. A subcommittee of four, including Talandier, was set up. The subcommittee sent out deputations to other national organisations with a view to appointing members to sit on a new committee. Herzen was approached and offered to collaborate; he had been publicly recognised in international circles in London since his speech delivered at the meeting of 29 November 1853, held to commemorate the Polish revolt of 1830. On 25 January 1855 the subcommittee resolved to call itself the International Com-

GARDNER WEBB COLLEGE LIBRARY

mittee. From this Committee a subcommittee composed of Ernest Jones, the German committee members and Herzen was then asked to 'prepare the announcements' for a demonstration to take place at St Martin's Hall on 27 February. The announcement informed the public that 'Mr Herzen is the head of Russian democratic literature and the most distinguished exile of his country; as such, the representative of its proletarian millions. He will be at the demonstration in St Martin's Hall and will, we trust, receive a welcome that will show the world that the English can sympathise with the Russian people while they desire to strike at the Russian tyrant.'[32] After the meeting at St Martin's Hall a permanent International Committee was set up. Herzen, surprisingly, was not a member. The death of Nicholas I a few weeks after the meeting intensified his activity on his Russian publications. This, together with the anti-Russian feeling at the outbreak of the Crimean War, were major reasons for his public withdrawal from the affairs of the international movement. But he never lost personal interest in it. The interest was sharpened by the setting-up of the First International in 1864 and may have had something to do with his decision to return to the Continent to live.

The First Congress of the First International took place in September 1866 in Geneva. It was held, therefore, at a time when Herzen's attitude against anarchistic, terroristic, secret organisational methods had been hardened by Karakozov's attempted tyrannicide. At the beginning of September 1866 he travelled to Geneva where he stayed throughout the time of the Congress. Though he did not intend personally to participate, he wished to follow events at first hand. A significant occurrence was the presence there of Blanquist students, some of whom Herzen had already met during earlier visits to Paris. They had responded to the appeal, signed by working-class members of the International's General Council, that students of all nations should support them in forming 'the great federation of peoples' and participate in the forthcoming Congress. Blanqui himself travelled to Switzerland secretly to support them. The Blanquist students clashed with the mandated Parisian representatives and, monopolising the floor against Blanqui's advice, were eventually physically ejected. After the Congress, at the beginning of October, Herzen went to Fribourg to meet 'one of the *most noble* people in Europe'.[33] It was Blanqui. The early part of that year had been the time when Blanqui had encouraged the Paris students to unite with the Paris workers. They had together organised effective civil demonstrations in Paris. And one may suppose that one subject of conversation between the two men turned upon the question of the role of students in the progressive movement. At this juncture Blanqui was faced with the problem of

restraining students from precipitate militant action, as Herzen faced
the problem of how to curb the violent revolutionary methods of the
'young emigration'.

Herzen did not travel to Lausanne at the time of the Second Congress
of the International held in September 1867. Nor, though warmly
invited to do so, did he participate in the First Congress of the League
of Peace and Freedom which immediately followed it in Geneva. He
was already moving towards a realisation of the need to dissociate
himself from the activities of the 'young emigration', encouraged in
their conspiratorial activity by Bakunin and Ogaryov. The endless
congresses and meetings seemed to achieve nothing practical and led
instead to internal squabbles and splits in the ranks. Herzen also considered that Russians were 'not wanted' at such meetings because of the
anti-Russian attitude caused by 'official' Russia's militancy in Europe.
Since Russians could not enter the European movement on equal
terms, they should not enter at all but should concentrate on their own
special problem. He explained the reason for his non-participation in
an open letter to the organiser of the Congress, expecting it to be read
in public:

> If I have been invited to participate it is not because of my qualities
> as a Russian but in the profound belief that I am as little Russian
> as possible. And this is what I cannot, I will not and I must not
> accept. I belong with all the fibres of my heart to the Russian
> people ... and this is not ... a blind instinct ... but the consequence
> of what I see in the Russian people.... There was a time when
> Russians, too crushed and too unhappy, appeared defeated and
> confused before the proud future republicans of France and the
> proud free-thinkers of Germany. Since then the stars have greatly
> changed. Though we have not had the strength and time to trans-
> plant into our hard and bitter climate the frail liberties of Western
> institutions, yet military despotism, government *du bon plaisir*,
> omnipotent and unbridled police methods, absence of personal
> security have struck such deep roots in continental soil that com-
> plete equality exists between us – except that there is a difference
> between those trying to escape from prison and those who have only
> just been put in.[34]

The letter was not read. Probably its notion outraged the Europeans.
Ogaryov and Bakunin both participated. Indeed, Ogaryov was elected
vice-president and secretary of the Russian contingent (composed of
the 'young emigration'). Herzen asked Ogaryov for a full account of
the proceedings, a request with which Ogaryov complied; and he was
not wrong in believing that the Congress would achieve nothing

useful. Garibaldi, elected chairman, exhorted all present to have faith
in God; several atheists present thereupon immediately packed their
bags and left; Bakunin wondered how he might 'withdraw' and then
delivered a bellicose speech declaring war on almost everything;
according to Ogaryov the affair ended 'miserably'.

The claim has been made that Bakunin at this time stood for the
international movement whereas Herzen did not.[35] This is an over-
simplification. It is crucial for an understanding of Herzen's whole
Weltanschauung to remember that he fully supported the International,
which eventually he came to believe was capable of representing
the way for the European working-class movement to progress towards
socialism. But he opposed Bakunin's Pan-Slavism because he saw
Russia as being historically set apart from the whole of the rest of
Europe, including Poland and other Slavonic peoples. Unlike Russia
these other Slav peoples were linked by their historic fate, civilisation
and development with Europe. Thus Herzen stood both for the international progressive movement which might save Europe through her
proletariat, and also for a separate Russian progressive movement,
whose very separateness might enable her to found a new form of
socialist society built on non-capitalist foundations and shaped from
ethical standards which were instinctive rather than legal standards
inherited from Roman law.[36]

At the Second Congress of the League of Peace and Freedom held
in Berne the following year (1868), Herzen maintained the same
attitude of interested non-participation.[37] Nevertheless, he manifested
a particularly lively interest in the Third Congress of the First International held in Brussels a few weeks earlier. Perhaps he would have
travelled to Brussels but for the fact that he was suffering severely
from diabetes. However, he read with particular interest the reports
of Boborykin. Subsequently the two men met quite frequently in
Paris. The following year (1869) he again followed the International's
Congress, though again from a non-committed distance. He asked
Ogaryov to 'send all that comes out about the Basle Congress', assur-
ing him that 'I shall follow [it] ... but I am afraid that Bakunin will
go too far again'.[38] His especial interest in the International is seen
by the fact that, with Serno-Solovyovich, he helped to found the library
at its Geneva Section.[39]

By 1869 Herzen found the intellectual atmosphere in Switzerland
impossible. The 'desire to work' attracted him to Brussels. He felt he
needed '*Anregung* in my environment. It does not exist in Switzerland
and Italy – but it is in Brussels and Paris.'[40] This was the time when
he embarked on his plan for guerrilla warfare in Russia and planned
publication about Russia in left-wing European journals. He also had

plans for re-publishing in Europe his own earlier works, particularly his memoirs. In Brussels and Paris he would be in closer touch 'with the booksellers'. Paris was the 'centre of activity'. Arriving in Brussels by July 1869, he divided his time between the Belgian capital and Paris until November, when he rushed to Florence for family reasons which engulfed him until his own death in Paris three months later.

Having escaped from the antipathetic atmosphere of the Russian *émigré* colony in Switzerland, he resumed old friendships with such people as Élisée Reclus, very soon to participate in the Commune, whom he now invited to give lessons to his youngest daughter; with Tessier du Motay; with Edgar Quinet; with Massol; with Le Lubez; and, not least, with the Belgian foundation member of the International, César de Paepe. The latter had been a champion of Herzen's viewpoint when, at the London Conference of the International in September 1865, he had repeated Herzen's theme of the two Russias, the oppressor Government and the oppressed people, first publicly expressed by Herzen at the Polish anniversary meeting in 1853. 'You want to check Russian influence,' de Paepe asked the meeting. 'Which influence? That of the Government? Then I ask that the influence of *all* governments in Europe be checked.... If you mean to check the influence of the Russian people, then I say that they are the same as any other people.'[41] By September 1869 Herzen, now in Brussels, was in close personal touch with de Paepe with whom he discussed political tactics and the working-class movement.[42]

Herzen sensed the impending Paris Commune. From Paris he wrote to his son, then in Florence: 'When I look closely at the strength of the social movement, into its depths and its passions, I can see clearly that the present struggle between the world of capital and the world of labour is not far off,' and he warned his son that, 'it is time for you to consider this with respect to yourself personally'.[43] His son must learn how to support himself by his own labour. In October he reported that, 'there is chaos here and we are sitting on top of a volcano'.[44] He preferred a seat on that volcano to the peace of Switzerland.

The cycle of essays *To an Old Comrade* (they were published posthumously) proved to be Herzen's final *profession de foi*. Addressed to Bakunin and Ogaryov, they were designed to start a polemic. The essays reiterate and reaffirm conclusions so profoundly held by Herzen after Karakozov's *attentat* and clarify views which developed from them. 'The slowness and confusion of the movement of history angers and chokes us,' he explained. 'It seems intolerable and many of us, betraying what our intellect tells us, try to go too fast and try to make others go too fast.' The new revolutionary methods essential for success 'must include everything, containing all the elements of contemporary activity and of all human aspirations. You can create neither a Sparta nor a Benedictine monastery in our world.' Unable to 'believe in the revolutionary way followed up to the present', he was 'trying to understand *human progress* in the past and in the present, in order to know how to keep in step with it, neither falling behind nor going so far ahead that other people cannot follow me, cannot keep up'. The newest element in socialist thought was that it had changed from being a faith to being a science. Therefore the new method must insist on greater knowledge and understanding. The use of knowledge and understanding must replace the use of bloodshed. Thus 'for the social revolution nothing is necessary except *understanding and force*, knowledge and – opportunity'. The new socialist order must be 'not only a sword which destroys but a force which preserves. In delivering its blow to the old world, it must not only save everything worth saving, but must leave untouched whatever is varied and individual. Woe to the revolution which is poor in spirit, which is able out of all the past and present to build nothing but a dull workshop.' The new order would be created by 'the workers' who, 'uniting of their own accord, forming their own "state within the state", achieving their rights with regard to capitalists and property owners, political and religious frontiers, will be the first link and the first element of the future economic set-up'. Fearing the danger of political reaction, he warned that this international union of workers must organise itself internally before resorting to action in the outside world. It was essential 'to gather the troops together quietly. Threats without strength do harm.' He added that to recommend 'gradualism' in the circle in which he moved 'requires if not more then certainly as much courage and independence as it requires to take the most extreme of extreme attitudes in all questions'. However, he found gradualism necessary because, confronted with such a diversity of possible paths, to take the wrong one was only too easy. To understand which route 'is shorter, better, more possible is a matter of tactics, a matter of revolutionary strategy'. Reviewing the present international situation, he saw that the moment had come for the workers to assume power; not the power of political dictation but the power of self-management. 'The international association of workers, all their possible associations ... must with all their might strive after a position of non-interference of the Government in their *work* ... they must constitute themselves a free parliament of the fourth estate and work out, continue working out, their own internal organisation which will be the basis for the future.' This call for the workers to organise their own affairs is particularly interesting. It applied not only to the international movement but in Russia also. Herzen had realised, even before history had realised it, that the notion he had introduced into his 'Russian Socialism', of the intellectual acting as 'leaven' for the peasant's uprising by instructing him in his messianic destiny, had somehow gone awry. In July 1869, before the Populist movement had reached its height, Herzen detected where the fallacy of his own idea lay:

The masses themselves, on whom lies the entire weight of [reshaping] existence ... with their phalanx of workers, seek words and understanding – but they look with unbelief at people who preach the aristocracy of science and who summon them to arms. And observe, these preachers are not from among the people, but ... old students, living in abstractions. They are further away from the people than are [the people's] enemies whom they curse.... And therefore they suggest that it is possible to introduce an economic revolution from a *tabula rasa* erasing the whole field of history as it has been so far, without even thinking that this field, for all its stubble and its weeds, is the only soil which the people in reality have, it is their whole morality, the only thing with which they are familiar, their only consolation. It is more difficult to fight the conservatism of the people than the conservatism of the throne and the pulpit.[45]

In Bakunin Russia produced a revolutionary who unsuccessfully challenged Karl Marx for the control of the international progressive movement. In Herzen she produced a revolutionary who challenged Bakunin unsuccessfully for the control of the Russian revolutionary movement and whose intellectual position was much closer to that of Marx.

NOTES

1. A. I. Gertsen, *Sobranie sochinenii v 30 tomakh* (Moscow: Akademia Nauk, 1954-66). Future quotations from Herzen in this article will be from this edition.

2. G. N. Vyrubov, 'Revolyutsionnye vospominaniya', *Gertsen v vospominaniyakh sovremennikov* (1956) p. 290.

3. P. D. Boborykin, 'A. I. Gertsen', ibid., p. 314.

4. Quoted from M. Dommanget, *Blanqui et l'opposition révolutionnaire à la fin du Second Empire* (Paris, 1960) p. 44.

5. xxx (i) 91.

6. B. P. Koz'min, *Iz istorii revolyutsionnoi misli v Rossii* (Moscow, 1961) p. 516. This book contains an excellent and detailed account of Herzen's relations with the 'younger emigration'. See also 'Gertsen, Ogaryov i "Molodaya Emigratsiya"', *Literaturnoe Nasledstvo*, XLI-XLII (1941) pp. 1-178.

7. *Kolokol*, no. 193, 1 January 1865, p. 1581.

8. Published under the collective titles *Dilettantism in Science* (*Diletantizm v nauke* (1843) and *Letters on the Study of Nature* (*Pis'ma ob izuchenii prirody*) (1845).

9. VI 46-8.

10. *Kolokol*, no. 219, 1 May 1866, p. 1789.

11. By the 1861 Act the "temporarily bound" peasants were permitted to receive their portions of land and fulfil the required obligations to landlords and Government only after nine years, i.e. 1870.

12. *Kolokol*, nos. 233 and 234, 1 February 1867, p. 1904.

13. Ibid., pp. 1902-3.

14. XXX 577.

15. XXX 134.

16. XXX 10.

17. XXX 53.

18. XX (i) 399-400.

19. XXX 21.

20. XXX 41-2.

21. XXX 62.

22. See *Literaturnoe Nasledstvo*, LXIV (1958) 706.

23. See ibid., LXII (1955) 571-4.

24. XXX 97.

25. XXX (i) 419.

26. B. I. Nicolaevsky, 'Secret Societies and the First International', in M. M. Drachkovitch (ed.), *The Revolutionary Internationals, 1864-1943* (Stanford University Press, 1966) p. 40.

27. XXV 173.

28. XXV 206.

29. XXV 227.

30. XXVI 90.

31. XXX 207.

32. *The People's Paper*, no. 145, 10 February 1855. See also no. 144, 3 February 1855.

33. XXVIII 226, 228. Herzen describes his meeting with Blanqui in the article 'Order Triumphs'.

34. 'Un fait personnel', XX (i), 16-17.

35. As does, for instance, R. Hostetter in *The Italian Socialist Movement*, I (Stanford University Press, 1958).

36. In this he reveals an affinity with Slavophils such as Ivan Kireyevsky, and does not differ from views he himself held in the 1840s.

37. See the article 'Les Russes au Congrès de Berne', XX 380.

38. XXX 189.

39. B. P. Koz'min, 'K voprosu ob otnoshenii A. I. Gertsena k 1 Internatsionalu', *Istoricheskie Zapiski*, LIV (1955) 435.

40. XXX 73.

41. *The General Council of the First International: The London Conference, 1865*, p. 246.

42. XXX 197.

43. May 1869, XXX 119; see also p. 199.

44. XXX 222.

45. XX (ii) 575-93.

3 Bakunin's Conceptions of Revolutionary Organisations and Their Role: A Study of His 'Secret Societies'

ARTHUR LEHNING

AFTER the failure of the Polish insurrection in 1863, Bakunin no longer believed in national liberation movements as a social and revolutionary force. From now on he advocated a social revolution on an international scale. He was of the opinion that the fall of the Second Empire would inaugurate a new 1848 and that one should be prepared for these events. His main task he saw from now on as finding revolutionaries who would work together intimately to influence the coming events and avoid the mistakes of 1848. To this end he created in 1864 in Florence a secret society, to which he soon gave international ramifications. In one way or another, such a society existed for ten years. It consisted only of those men and women who temporarily worked together with Bakunin on the basis of his programme, though remnants were left long after his death.[1] These societies express rather the evolution of his ideas than the functioning of an organisation. Most of the drafts, programmes and projects Bakunin wrote for those rather ephemeral, or even non-existent, bodies are a fundamental source of his political and social ideas. They were not meant to be ideological or theoretical discourses; they reflect and are connected with his revolutionary activities for a decade.

Why Bakunin chose this way to propagate his ideas, we do not know. He might have thought that the doctrine conceived by 1864 would have found little response if openly proclaimed. Already in 1835 Bakunin had suggested an intimate small circle with his brothers and sisters and their friends: the first idea of a private union of the most intimate comrades, so to speak, the first of his secret societies.

The family circle was in fact the most ideal group to which he ever belonged, the model for all his organisations and his conception of a free and happy life for humanity in general.[2] Later, in connection with his activities for a national liberation movement of the Slavs and the establishment of a democratic Slav federation, he had already tried to create, in 1848 and 1849, political secret societies.[3] However, the organisation he wanted to create in 1864 was of an altogether different character. Just as the Jesuits founded the best secret society, which had existed for two hundred years with the relentless aim of destroying all liberty in the world, so his society 'de longue haleine', which would survive after his death, was founded for the triumph of liberty.[4] It may be recalled that when Adam Weishaupt founded his Order of the Illuminati on 1 May 1776, it was for exactly the same purpose.

Only a fragment of what Bakunin wrote in the decade after 1864 was published during his lifetime. His influence on his contemporaries depended mainly on the spoken word and on that elusive gift called personality; it is impossible to 'convey to posterity that sense of overwhelming power which was always present to those who knew him in his life'.[5] Another factor should be added to explain his influence: his enormous epistolary activity.[6] He had the rare capacity to convince people to devote their lives to his cause and the dexterity to form intimate bonds with people quickly, if they seemed useful to him for the revolutionary cause.[7]

The sceptical and critical Alexander Herzen recognised in Bakunin's character an exceptional superior quality and even greatness, in that, having grasped two or three characteristics of his environment, he detached from it the revolutionary current and immediately set about propelling it further, intensifying it, making it a passionate, vital question.[8]

The story of Bakunin's secret societies, then, must be viewed in the light of his personal approach and activity. There is, it seems, no other example in the nineteenth-century social history of this unique phenomenon but that of Buonarroti. He too built up on an international scale, though over a much longer period, an elaborate underground network, on a freemason pattern, sometimes using masonic institutions, to work for his egalitarian creed of 1796, for a social revolution and for the republicanisation of Europe. For forty years the principles remained the same: the leadership was secret; the existence of the higher grades was unknown to the lower; protean in character, this network took advantage of and used other societies. According to Buonarroti, such a secret society could not be a democratic institution in its purpose or its forms, nor could it consist of a single grade and equal participation. There should be more grades, 'formant entre eux une suite croissante de doctrines et d'autorité de manière que des idées morales et politiques les plus simples, on remonte, par échelons, aux plus complexes et plus hardies et, qu'au grade le plus élevé en doctrine appartienne le droit de diriger tous les autres' – in other words, a secret society as defined by Adam Weishaupt.[9]

One of the tasks of Buonarroti's secret societies was to prepare public opinion through 'secondary', i.e. more open, societies, so that at the time of revolution *les hommes sages* of the inner circle of the society might be called on to exercise supreme power. Thus the revolutionary authority would fall into the hands of wise and vigorous revolutionaries, devoted to equality:

> Il faut ... que la même volonté dirige l'affranchissement et prépare la liberté ... au commencement d'une révolution l'autorité suprême ne doit pas être déléguée par le choix libre du Peuple.... Qui donc pourra exercer utilement le droit de désigner les hommes auxquels l'autorité révolutionnaire suprême doit être confiée? Ceux qui sont embrasés de l'amour de l'égalité et ont le courage de se dévouer pour en assurer l'établissement....

The experience of the revolutionary Government of Robespierre had taught that such a political dictatorship could be used to establish the *égalité de fait*. The *douce communauté* could only be established with the help of this authority, because only the use of force could 'entraîner les irrésolus et contenir les récalcitrants'. Only in a society where private property was abolished could democracy and sovereignty of the people function.

All this was a precise and elaborate theorisation of Buonarroti's own experience, when, in April–May 1796, Babeuf's 'Secret Directory' tried to overthrow the post-Thermidorian Directory and to establish a kind of state communism: a Babouvist Committee of Public Safety to prepare an egalitarian regime. Thus Buonarroti established through his political societies the Jacobin trend in European socialism.[10] The aim of Bakunin's work was to reverse this trend.

There was in Buonarroti's multifarious activities and gradualism an essential factor which was completely absent from the structure Bakunin outlined for a secret society. Buonarroti worked at the same time in many directions on different ideological levels for more immediate republican or democratic aims, and this was also reflected in his secret underground network with its different ideological strata. Bakunin had only one aim in mind, and there was no 'gradual' ideology or theory.

Secret societies were of course a permanent and widespread

phenomenon in Europe since the end of the Napoleonic Empire, and
one with which Bakunin was familiar. In Dresden in 1842 he had
studied the classic book of Lorenz von Stein, the first extensive survey
of French socialist theories and social movements. There he read the
story of Babeuf, and in the vast underground revolutionary movements
in Europe during the Restoration and the July Monarchy, the name of
Buonarroti is omnipresent. Bakunin knew Buonarroti's famous book
of 1828, the *Conspiration pour l'égalité*, with its detailed description
of its communist aims and its revolutionary tactics.

Bakunin stressed the historical importance of Babeuf's attempt but
added that, at that moment, the strength of the French Revolution
was already exhausted.[11] He also spoke with admiration of Buonarroti,
the 'greatest conspirator of his age', an 'homme de fer', 'un caractère
antique', but he rejected his theory of establishing equality through
the force of the state. Babeuf and his friend, Bakunin wrote, had the
cult of equality 'au détriment de la liberté': they were Jacobin
socialists. The state would confiscate all private property, administer
it in the general interest, provide upbringing, education, livelihood
and pleasures equally for all, and require physical or mental labour
from every citizen. All communal autonomy, all individual initiative
in the world, all liberty would disappear. The whole society would
present a picture of monotonous and forced uniformity. The Government would exercise absolute power over all members of society.
Bakunin was also well aware of the specific character and role of
Buonarroti's underground organisations, i.e. in transmitting 'Babeuf's
communist testament' as a 'sacred trust' to future generations: thanks
to the secret societies, the communist ideas took root in the popular
imagination.[12]

In May 1843, in Zürich, Bakunin met Wilhelm Weitling, who in
1838 had written the communist programme for a secret organisation
of German *proscrits*, the 'League of the Just', which entertained close
relationships with the secret revolutionary republican societies of a
Babouvist character led by Blanqui and Barbès. After Marx and
Engels had joined the secret 'League of the Just' in 1847, it took the
name 'Communist League', propagating its ideas mainly through the
German Workers' Education Society, which published in February
1848 the *Manifesto of the Communist Party*, by order of the secret
League.

During his stay in Paris in 1845-7 and in Brussels in 1847-8,
Bakunin got first-hand information on the leading members and movements of the secret societies and about the mysterious leadership behind them, and he was intimately acquainted then, and again in 1848
in Breslau, with the conspiring Poles.

After his return to London from eleven years in prison and exile, he met in 1862-3 Giuseppe Mazzini. Garibaldi, whom he had visited in Caprera, recommended Bakunin to Giuseppe Dolfi, grand master of the Tuscan freemasonry in Florence, where Bakunin arrived on 26 January 1864. Mazzini wrote to Dolfi of the arrival of Bakunin 'whose name is honoured by democrats all over the world', and the Garibaldian Agostino Bertani, whom Bakunin had visited in Genoa upon his arrival in Italy, recommended him to Dolfi with the words: 'Un noto e fervente apostolo di riforme sociale e politico.'[13]

In Florence Bakunin came in contact with other freemasons like Giuseppe Mazzoni, a former member of the triumvirate of the provincial Government of Tuscany in 1849. In the following years Mazzoni was to belong to his intimate circle. In Florence Bakunin became a member of the lodge 'Il Progresso Sociale', founded in 1863.[14] In Paris, in the 1840s, he had been admitted to a lodge;[15] whether this fact had facilitated his Italian connection is not known and is open to doubt. In the Italian milieu of freemasonry and traditional conspiracy, he expected to find a fruitful environment for his plans. When, a few years later, a prospective candidate whom Bakunin wanted to recruit for his 'Fraternité' protested against the paraphernalia of mystery and secrecy, Bakunin said: 'They aren't necessary. We invented that for the Italians.'[16] For some time Bakunin also thought of using freemasonry for his purpose. He regarded freemasonry as the international of the revolutionary bourgeoisie. In Florence he may have tried to revolutionise the lodge or to form a lodge independent of the Grand Orient. Documents are lacking to provide us with details of any such attempts. He wrote a long manuscript on freemasonry (which is lost), but some fragments 'Catéchisme de la Franc-maçonnerie', written in 1865, have been preserved. Within a year, however, he declared that he never really thought to find anything seriously worth while in freemasonry, though it was conceivably useful as a mask.[17]

In July of the same year, he informed his friends in London that during the last three years he had been engaged in the foundation of a secret international social revolutionary society, of which he was sending them a complete programme. He could report positive results. Friends were to be found in Sweden, Norway, Denmark, England, Belgium, France, Spain and Italy. There were also Poles and a few Russians.[18] The 'complete programme', which is in fact the first extensive and comprehensive exposition of his ideas, has been preserved.[19]

In an anonymous article, published in 1873, Bakunin has given the following account of the foundation of the 'Fraternité':

In 1864, during his stay in Italy, Bakunin with some of his Italian friends formed an intimate Alliance [to provide a counterbalance to the Republican Alliance, which was founded just before this by Mazzini and which had a religious direction and exclusively political aims]. This first socialist society in Italy adopted the name of the 'Alliance of Social Democracy', which, as a result of the German state communists giving the term 'social democracy' a compromising doctrinaire and state meaning, was changed into the 'Alliance of Socialist Revolutionaries'. Arising as an affirmation of socialism against the religious-political dogmatism of Mazzini, the Alliance asserted in its programme atheism, a total negation of all authority and state, liquidation of juridical law and the denial of civil law, in exchange for the free rule of humanity and collective ownership; it declared labour to be the basis of social organisation, which in his programme was shown as a voluntary federation from the bottom upwards. Into the Alliance, at first a purely Italian organisation, Frenchman and Poles soon entered, and much later people from other countries.[20]

If this short résumé of the vicissitudes of the different societies is a correct version, then the Italian organisation preceded the international 'Fraternité'. Bakunin certainly started his enterprise during his stay in Florence, and recruited some adherents. Among the first Italians were Mazzoni, Gambuzzi, Fanelli, Tucci and Saverio Friscia – those who formed in Naples in 1866 the Italian section or 'family', according to Bakunin's vocabulary.[21] They published secretly a *Programma della Rivoluzione democratico sociale italiana* and subsequently linked up with and influenced the federalist democratic movement in southern Italy. In this, Bakunin successfully counteracted the national-revolutionary ideology and the enormous prestige of Mazzini and Garibaldi, which led in 1869 to the foundation of the Italian section of the first International.

During his stay in Stockholm (8 September to 12 October 1864) he enrolled three Swedes, among them August Sohlman, the editor of a democrat paper. On his way back he may have recruited in Norway, a few Poles in London, among them a certain Colonel Bogdanov, as well as Alfred Talandier and Fernando Garrido,[22] and in Paris Élisée and Élie Reclus.[23] The last of these, as probably the others, understood this intimate circle to be a useful means for progressive men in different countries to be in contact, but not in the sense of Bakunin's real purpose, a secret organisation to co-ordinate ideology and action. On behalf of August Sohlman, Bakunin wrote an exposé to explain the purpose of his projected society. The document, partly in the form of a letter to Sohlman, was entitled 'Société internationale secrète de l'émancipation de l'humanité. But de la société'. The aim was stated as:

Cette Société a pour but de rallier les éléments révolutionnaires de tous les pays pour en former une alliance vraiment sainte de la liberté contre la sainte Alliance de toutes les tyrannies en Europe: religieuse, politique, bureaucratique et financière.

The manuscript is not complete, but it is likely that the missing pages consisted of a concise document, a 'Catéchisme' and a 'Programme d'organisation provisoirement arrêté par les frères fondateurs'.[24] The last page indeed contained the sentence: 'Si vous dites "oui" à toutes ces questions, alors lisez les pages qui suivent, car vous êtes des nôtres. Sinon, ne lisez pas.' These texts are still unknown.

In the *Catéchisme révolutionnaire* of 1866 the aim of the society is stated as 'the triumph of the principle of Revolution in the world and consequently the radical overthrow of all presently existing religious, political, economic and social organisations and institutions and the reconstitution first of European and subsequently of world society on the basis of *liberty, reason, justice* and *work*'.

In the 'Swedish manuscript' Bakunin explains why such an alliance should be secret:

Une telle organisation ne pourra jamais être formée qu'en secret. Faite publiquement, au grand jour, elle produirait des paroles, pas d'actions, – et contre la Sainte Alliance, il faut des actions. Aucun homme ne consentirait à conspirer en public avec des étrangers pardessus le marché, contre l'État dont il est le sujet. Il se compromettait inutilement et ne servirait aucune cause, parce que tous ces projets trahis par la publicité, seraient étouffés à leur naissance même par les gouvernements dont les moyens matériels d'action sont toujours supérieurs aux nôtres. Le secret est donc indispensable. Mais pas seulement le secret: *il faut, pour qu'une telle alliance devienne possible, que les hommes qui la forment ayent à peu près, et si faire se peut, tout à fait les mêmes convictions philosophiques, religieuses, politiques et sociales.* Autrement ils ne s'accorderaient jamais, et si même, malgré les différences qui les séparent, ils parvenaient même, à force de sacrifices mutuels, à former une entente temporaire, leur union se dissoudrait infailliblement avant même que son but fut atteint. L'histoire est là qui nous prouve par mille exemples l'inutilité, je dirai plus, la nuisibilité d'unions formées par des éléments héterérogènes. L'égoisme, la vanité et la sottise des hommes rendent déjà si difficile toute entente sérieuse et durable entre des hommes d'opinions identiques. Ajoutez-y la différence des intérêts et des idées, et votre alliance ne durera pas six mois. Ajoutez-y surtout le scepticisme maladif et blasé qui recontre avec un sourire ironique et amer toute généreuse entreprise, l'indifférence qui succède si souvent dans les hommes à une exaltation et à un entraînement momentanés, le dégout qui est le résultat ordinaire d'un contact trop intime avec les hommes, dont chacun a des grandes ou des petites faiblesses, maladies journalières mais terribles, et qui rongent dans la racine toute grand action, maladies qui ne purent être vaincues que par une conviction sérieuse, prodonde et pour ainsi dire religieuse, que par une persévérance calme à l'extérieur, mais à l'intérieur passionnée. Et vous direz avec moi, que *pour produire une alliance des peuples efficace et réelle*, il faut d'abord le faire en secret et qu'ensuite et surtout, *il peut lui donner pour base un grand principe identique, assez large et assez élevé pour devenir, pour les hommes qui le reconnaissent une sorte de religion, pour leur donner une foi assez forte pour lutter contre les difficultés, les obstacles et les dégoûts journaliers, et pour leur inspirer le sacrifice de leur vanité et de leurs intérêts.*

In the *Revolutionary Catechism* (1866) the revolutionary purpose is clearly defined in the following paragraph:

That the elements of social revolution are already widespread in practically all the countries in Europe, and their fusion into an effective force is merely a matter of mediation and concentration. That this must be the task of the dedicated revolutionaries of every land, gathered at once into both public and private association with the twofold object of broadening the revolutionary front and at the same time paving the way for simultaneous concealed action in all countries in which action proves initially possible, through secret agreement among the most intelligent revolutionaries of those countries.[25]

'Aucun peuple en Europe ne se levera plus que pour réaliser les idées de l'émancipation politique et sociale et il faut adopter *notre programme* qui en est la juste expression,' Bakunin wrote in the 'Swedish manuscript' of 1864. To prepare a simultaneous international uprising, 'il faut une organisation secrète préalable'.

Il n'y a de vivant et d'énergique en Europe que le peuple, surtout les ouvriers des fabriques et des villes. Si cette armée se lève simultanément, dans toute l'Europe, nous sommes sauvés. Si elle ne se lève pas ensemble, mais par corps séparés, isolés l'un après l'autre, il y a grande chance à ce que nous soyons battus. Si elle ne se lève pas du tout, nous et la liberté avec nous sommes perdus.

This does not mean that Bakunin ever thought that these small groups could or should start a revolution. Revolutions, he wrote, cannot be brought about either by individuals or by secret societies. They derive from circumstances, from the inevitable course of events, and they can only be successful if they have the support of the masses. There are moments in history when revolutions are impossible, and others when they are inevitable. They ferment for a long time in the depths of the instinctive consciousness of the masses, then they explode, often triggered by apparently trivial causes. But propaganda and action could prepare the revolution. All that a well-organised secret society can do is first to assist the birth of the revolution by sowing ideas corresponding to the instincts of the masses, then to organise, not the army of the revolution – the army must always be the people – but a kind of revolutionary general staff made up of devoted, hard-working, sincere friends of the people, 'without ambition or vanity' and 'capable of acting as intermediaries between the revolutionary idea and the popular instinct'.[26]

Apart from his mania of writing fantastically elaborate statutes, which were never put into practice, one cannot deny that if one, like Bakunin, rejected the democratic state as well as Jacobin political dictatorship, this idea is not devoid of a realistic political point of view.

Bakunin did not mean that there could be a revolution without violence, but that this should not be directed against persons, rather against institutions. The revolution should, however, not develop a new authority, i.e. the right to coerce. Those who carry out the repression will do so with the approval of the revolutionaries; this is the only legitimation for violence in a revolution, since law does not exist. The unavoidable violence should be short, and not lead to an organisation invested with authority to repress. Not only in these programmes, but in all his public writings, he rejected the idea of a 'revolutionary Government', of 'Committees of Public Safety', including the so-called 'dictatorship of the proletariat'. For such a new authority, such a 'proletarian state', would in theory 'represent' the workers, but would lead in practice to a new ruling class.

To influence revolutionary events would be the task of 'invisible pilots in the thick of the popular tempest' – a kind of 'invisible dictatorship' without insignia, titles or official rights, having none of the paraphernalia of power – to prevent in particular the establishment of a new state with a new bureaucracy. The triumph of the Jacobins or the Blanquists would be the death of the revolution. Political butchery has never killed off any party and has proved powerless against the privileged classes, since power stems far less from men than from positions made available to privileged men by the organisation of things, in the first place the institutions of the state. Therefore, positions and things should be attacked, property and the state destroyed. Then there would be no need to destroy men and 'to condemn ourselves to the inevitable reaction which is unfailingly produced in every society by the slaughter of men'. The inevitable result of a bloody revolution based on a centralised revolutionary state would be a military dictatorship under a new master. This new authority would be revolutionary in name only. In practice, it would be a new reaction whose effect would be once again to condemn the popular masses to enslavement and exploitation at 'the hands of a new quasi-revolutionary aristocracy'.

For the triumph of revolution, *the unity of revolutionary thought and action must find an agent* in the thick of the popular anarchy[27] which would constitute the very life and all the energy of the revolution. Bakunin denied that such an agent, i.e. the revolutionary secret society, would be contrary to the free development of the people, because it was free of vested interest, of ambition; it was anonymous and did not reward any of its members with profit or honour or official power; its organisation would be from the bottom upwards and in accordance with the people's customs and instincts. After the triumph of the revolution there should be no establishment of any sort of state control over the people, 'even one that appears to be revolutionary itself,[28] because all domination would inflict the old slavery on the people in a new form'. The chief aim and purpose of the organisation should therefore be to help the people towards self-determination on the lines of the most complete equality and the fullest human freedom in every direction without the least hindrance from any sort of domination, even if it be temporary or transitional; that is, without any sort of government control.[29] In all his public writings, moreover, Bakunin was to stress this point again and again.

In one of his few writings published at the time, written in August 1870 after the first news of the French defeats, he advocated a social revolutionary uprising to start in the provinces, to fight the enemy of the interior as well as the invader, and summarised the essence of his theory on revolution:

La révolution n'est plus la révolution lorsqu'elle agit en despote, et lorsque, au lieu de provoquer la liberté dans les masses, elle provoque la réaction dans leur sein. Le moyen et la condition, sinon le but principal de la révolution, c'est l'anéantissement du principe de l'autorité dans toutes ses manifestations possibles, c'est l'abolition complète de l'État politique et juridique, parce que l'État, frère cadet de l'Église, comme l'a fort bien démontré Proudhon, est la consécration historique de tous les despotismes, de tous les privilèges: la raison politique de tous les asservissements économiques et sociaux, l'essence même et le centre de toute réaction. Lorsque au nom de la révolution, on veut faire de l'État, ne fut-ce que de l'État provisoire, on fait donc de la réaction et on travaille pour le despotisme, non pour la liberté: pour l'institution du privilège contre l'égalité.[30]

This was the essence of the ideas on revolution he had propagated since 1864. Ever since he was a member of the International, since June or July 1868, he had rejected the theory that the working class should organise in a political party with the purpose of conquering political power, and by 1872 large parts of the International had accepted his view, which found its historical expression in the resolution drafted by Bakunin at the Congress of St Imier in September 1872, that if the proletariat seized political power, it would become itself a dominating and exploiting class and that therefore the destruction of all political power was the first duty of the proletariat; every organisation of political power, nominally provisional and revolutionary, to bring about this destruction could only be another deceit, and would be just as dangerous for the proletariat as all existing governments.[31]

By the power of its determined propaganda that would really penetrate to the people, and by organisation among the people themselves, it would be possible to demolish governments and to make it for ever and everywhere impossible for them to exist, leaving the revolutionary mass movement free to mature fully and to organise itself, from the base to the top, through the process of spontaneous federation, the most complete freedom, and taking good care that this movement should never be able to reconstitute authorities, governments, states. Such ambitions would have to be countered by the natural influence – which must never be an official influence – of the members of the society dispersed in all countries and powerful only on account of their active solidarity and the unity of their programme and aims.[32]

In the same vein he wrote a long letter in March that year to Celso Ceretti, one of the young Italian militants who had rallied to his cause and who founded the International in Italy. Speaking of the possibility that Government persecution might oblige the public and legal organisations of the sections based on the Romagna to transform themselves into secret organisations, Bakunin suggests that well before that it would be advisable to form

des *nuclei* composés des membres les plus sûrs, les plus dévoués, les plus énergiques, en un mot des plus intimes. Ces *nuclei*, intimement reliés entre eux et avec les *nuclei* pareils qui s'organisent dans les autres régions de l'Italie et de l'étranger, auront une double mission : d'abord ils formeront l'âme inspiratrice et vivifiante de cet immense corps qu'on appelle l'Association internationale des Travailleurs et ensuite ils s'occuperont des questions *qu'il est impossible de traiter publiquement*. Ils formeront le pont nécessaire entre la propagande des théories socialistes et la pratique révolutionnaire.[33]

Elsewhere Bakunin remarks that even three men united in this sense 'forment déjà, selon moi, un sérieux commencement de puissance'.[34] In his programme of 1866 he wrote: 'One hundred revolutionaries, strongly and earnestly allied, would suffice for the international organisation in the whole of Europe. Two, three hundred revolutionaries will suffice for the organisation of the greatest country.'

Indeed, when Bakunin, after the French defeat at Sedan, advocated immediate social revolution, to start in the provinces, he openly proclaimed these principles in his *Lettre à un Français*, which amounts to a programme of action, written in August 1870:

Que doivent donc faire les autorités révolutionnaires – et tâchons qu'il y en ait aussi peu que possible – que doivent-elles faire pour étendre et pour organiser la révolution? Elles doivent non la faire elles-mêmes par des décrets, non l'imposer aux masses, mais la provoquer dans les masses. Elles doivent non leur imposer une organisation quelconque, mais en suscitant leur organisation autonome de bas en haut, travailler sous main, à l'aide de l'influence individuelle sur les individus les plus intelligents et les plus influents de chaque localité, pour que cette organisation soit autant que possible conforme à nos principes. Tout le secret de notre triomphe est là.[35]

Bakunin wrote to Nechaev that in Russia there is an enormous number of people, seminarists, children of peasants and the lower middle class of important civil servants, who could help the people in its fight for freedom. 'But this world must be organised and *filled with moral purpose*.' And Bakunin adds, 'your system will only corrupt them'. For the moral improvement, one should arouse directly and consciously in minds and hearts the desire to free all the peoples of the world. This should be the whole content of the propaganda. The secret organisations to be created should be a force to help the people and become a training-ground for the moral education of its members.[36] The 'Fraternité', in Bakunin's view, as he often explained, should not only work out the principles but also develop the character, the solidarity, the mutual confidence of its members.

To expose the 'grand principe identique', Bakunin subsequently wrote countless programmes and statutes containing his philosophical, political and social ideas as well as, in broad lines, the concrete plan for a revolution. All this was intended for those he had recruited for his 'Fraternité'. He wanted to educate those who had embraced his cause and to work out practical measures to be taken in the course of a revolution. This has nothing to do with the technical rules for a *coup d'état*, but only with practical measures, the first steps to be taken towards reconstruction after the destruction of the old power. It seems a much more realistic approach than the belief in a hypothetical 'dialectic historical process', or the belief that all problems would be solved once a revolutionary Government were established. There is no room in the world, wrote Bakunin, for predetermined plans, or established or predicted laws.

Many elements of his doctrine are to be found in his 'Swedish manuscript' – his ideas on religion, on federalism, on liberty. From Hegel he got the idea that the purpose of world history was liberty, but after five years' intensive study of his writings he repudiated the Hegelian abstractions and the identification of the real with the rational he had once admired. The way to liberty was to achieve self-awareness and to act. In his famous article of 1842, where class conflict is advanced as a motive force in the historical process, Bakunin no longer follows the Hegelian trichotomy: no mediation, no reconciliation between thesis and antithesis. The quintessence of the philosophy of history and the conception of the revolution, which determined Bakunin's thought and activity for the next three decades, was that the historically new emerges through the complete destruction of the old. That is the implication of the usually misquoted and misunderstood famous phrase: 'The passion for destruction is also a creative passion.' At the same time, Feuerbach's substitution of anthropology for theology formed the basis of his atheist humanism:

Le monde est plus que jamais partagé aujourd'hui entre deux systèmes éternellement opposés: le principe théologique et le principe humanitaire, celui de l'autorité et celui de la liberté. Le vieux système part de cette idée fondamentale que l'humanité est mauvaise par elle-même et que, pour reconnaître la vérité, elle a besoin de *révélation divine*, pour reconnaître la justice, *les lois divines et pour les observer d'autorité et d'instructions divines, à la fois religieuses et politiques, de l'Église et de l'État.*[37]

The revolution, then, should be the transformation of all institutions and social organisations, the only way to 'moraliser les hommes', and not establish a new 'droit juridique'. We shall find this formulated in the fragments of his freemason manuscripts and again in *Fédéralisme, socialisme et antithéologisme* (1867): 'Dieu est, donc l'homme est esclave. L'homme est intelligent, juste, libre, donc Dieu n'existe pas.' The *Revolutionary Catechism* of 1866 starts: 'Denial of the existence of a real extra-terrestrial individual God, and consequently of any revelation and any divine intervention in the affairs of the human world.' All this would find a definite form in the fragments taken from his great manuscript of 1871, published as *God and the State*.

The only moral law is this: 'Soyez libre et respectez, secondez la liberté de votre prochain, car elle est la condition sine qua non de la vôtre. La liberté de l'un est nécessairement solidaire de la liberté de tous.' Bakunin repudiated Rousseau – the inventor of 'l'Être-Suprême, le Dieu abstrait et stérile des déistes' – whom he called 'l'écrivain le plus malfaisant du siècle passé':[38]

C'est bien à tort que Jean-Jacques Rousseau et beaucoup de monde après lui ont prétendu que la liberté de tout homme est limitée par celle de tous les autres. De cette manière, l'ordre qui s'établit parmi les hommes apparait comme une sorte de *contrat social* par lequel chacun renonce à une partie de la liberté au profit de tous, c'est-à-dire au profit de *la communauté*, pour mieux assurer la partie restante et l'État, représentant de l'intérêt général, en surgit non comme sa confirmation, mais comme la négation, ou si l'on veut la limitation de la liberté individuelle de chacun, au profit de la communauté toute entière. Dans ce système philosophique, comme dans le système théologique, dont d'ailleurs il procède directement, l'État apparait donc toujours comme quelque chose de supérieur et de transcendant à la communauté.

L'ordre dans la société loin de devoir être une limitation de la liberté des individus qui la composent, doit au contraire résulter de son plus grand développement possible et son extension pour ainsi dire infinie. La liberté n'est donc plus la limitation, mais bien la confirmation de la liberté de tous, et elle n'est juste et complète que dans l'entière solidarité de chacun et de tous. Pour que je sois libre, il faut que mon droit et mon humanité soient reconnus, que leur image me soit renvoyée comme par la réflection d'un miroir par la conscience libre de tous les autres.[39]

In a manuscript 'Programme de la Société de la Révolution. Première partie. Principes théoriques, which is difficult to date but probably written in 1867, we find a very concise formulation in nine-points, some of them annotated:[40]

La liberté individuelle de chacun ne devient réelle et possible que par la liberté collective de la société, dont par une loi naturelle et fatale il fait parti....

L'homme naturel ne devient un homme libre, il ne s'humanise et ne se moralise, ne reconnaît en un mot et ne réalise en lui-même et pour lui-même son propre caractère humain et son droit qu'à mesure seulement qu'il reconnait ce même caractère et ce droit dans tous ses semblables. Dans l'intérêt de sa propre humanité, de sa propre moralité et de sa liberté personelle, l'homme doit donc vouloir la liberté, la moralité et l'humanité de tous.

Respecter la liberté d'autrui est donc le devoir suprême de tout homme. L'aimer et la servir – voilà la seule vertu. C'est la base de toute morale; il n'en existe point d'autre.

La liberté étant le produit et la plus haute expression de la solidarité, c'est-à-dire de la mutualité, elle n'est complètement réalisable que dans l'égalité. L'égalité politique ne peut être fondée que sur l'égalité économique et sociale. La réalisation de la liberté par cette égalité – voilà la justice.[41]

L'organisation politique doit être basée sur la commune, l'unité politique de la nation sera l'union fédérale des provinces. L'ordre doit couronner la liberté[42] et 'toute organisation politique doit partir de bas en haut, de la circonférence au centre'.

The same words are to be found, two years later, in the *Revolutionary Catechism*: the nation should be nothing else than 'the federation of autonomous provinces', and Bakunin summarises the political aim of the revolution as follows:

C'est l'abolition du droit historique, du droit de conquête et du droit diplomatique. C'est l'émancipation complète des individus et des associations du joug de l'autorité divine et humaine; c'est la destruction absolue de toutes les unions et agglomérations forcées des communes dans les provinces, des provinces et des conquis dans l'État. Enfin, c'est la dissolution radicale de l'État centraliste, tutélaire, autoritaire, avec toutes les institutions militaires, bureaucratiques, gouvernementales, administratives, judiciaires et civiles. C'est, en un mot, la liberté rendue à tout le monde, aux collectifs, associations, communes, provinces, régions et nations et la garantie mutuelle de cette liberté par la fédération.[43]

For the future Bakunin envisaged a completely new political structure. The development of the European working men's associations would give rise to new political and economic conditions and eventually, bursting the bounds of the present-day communes, provinces and even states, will provide the whole of human society with a new constitution 'no longer divided into nations but into different industrial groupings and organised according to the requirements not of politics but of production'.

In the *Revolutionary Catechism*, Bakunin speaks of free productive associations having become their own masters, which would expand one day beyond national frontiers and form one vast economic federation, with a parliament informed by detailed statistics on a world scale, which would decide and distribute the output of world industry among the various countries so that there would no longer or hardly ever be industrial crisis, stagnation, disasters and waste of capital: 'Human labour, emancipation, each and every man will regenerate the world.' It goes without saying that this is the foreshadowing of what under the determined influence of Bakunin was to become the ideology of federations of the International like the federations of Italy and Spain, under the name of revolutionary collectivism: a federation of free economic federations. Such an occasional glimpse of a socialist, or in this case a 'syndicalist', utopia is rare in these documents.

Bakunin's entire activity was focused on the revolution to be expected after the fall of Napoleon III. A revolution in France would, he hoped, influence revolutionary movements in Spain and Italy and could spread to the Slav peoples of Austria, Poland and the Ukraine and reach the peasant masses in Russia.

In the documents of the 'Fraternité internationale' of 1868, he deals with the immediate measures to be taken during a revolution, which must set out from the first radically and totally to destroy all state institutions. And in another manuscript, 'Fraternité internationale. Programme et objet', of the end of 1868, the 'positive side' of 'Revolutionary Politics' reads:

> Organisation spontanée des groups insurectionnels en communes provisoires, envoi immédiat de délégués avec mandats impératifs au foyer révolutionnaire, fédération d'urgence de toutes les communes, permanence des barricades et de tout centre de résistance, division du corps des délégués en comités parfaitement distincts et indépendants les uns des autres, qui pourront se répartir ainsi: comités locaux et fédérés du travail, comités locaux et fédérés de l'instruction publique, comités locaux et fédérés pour la détention provisoire des capitaux, comités locaux et fédérés pour la remise temporaire de capitaux entre les mains des associations agricoles et industrielles, comités locaux et fédérés d'organisation communale, comités locaux et fédérés des relations internationales etc., etc., le tout formant la grande Alliance

fédérative de la solidarité révolutionnaire, fonctionnant sous l'inspiration directe des masses populaires et sous leur sanction immédiate.[44]

Here we find for the first time the expression 'federation of the barricades',[45] and it may be recalled that two years later the Paris Commune acted, or tried to act, according to these principles. As for Blanqui, so for Bakunin the revolution was an art, but these precise 'positive' and 'negative' instructions seem much more relevant to a social revolution than the pure insurrectional *Instructions pour une prise d'armes* of Blanqui.

In June or July 1868 Bakunin joined the International. In September, with the minority which had left the League of Peace and Freedom, he founded the 'International Alliance of Social Democracy'. Bakunin has given the following account of this event, which subsequently had many repercussions in the International:

[Bakunin] proposed to the minority members of socialist revolutionaries, who had left the League, to enter the International as a mass, preserving at the same time an intimate connection with, and expanding, their Union of Social Revolutionaries in the form of a secret society. The proposal to enter the International was accepted unanimously; but with regard to the Union, the French and Italians wished to preserve its inner intimate character of a secret society. It should appear at the same time as an open organisation under the name the 'International Alliance of Social Democracy'. They even wished that the Alliance be organised completely independently of the International Association, being satisfied that its members be composed separately as members of that Association. Bakunin argued against this on the basis that such a new international organisation would appear in a most undesirable collaboration in a workers' organisation. These debates ended with the following resolution to found an open International Alliance of Social Democracy and to declare it an integral member of the International, the programme of which was recognised as obligatory for each member of the Alliance.[46]

The General Council agreed, on 9 March 1869, to accept the Geneva Section of the International Alliance, after the Alliance had been dissolved as an international body. In the meantime, another secret organisation linked up with the 'Fraternité': the secret Alliance. Bakunin wrote several drafts to link up this Alliance with the 'Fraternité', which was, however, dissolved in January 1869, but may have been reconstructed in one form or another. The secret Alliance never really existed. It was only in September 1872, in Zürich, that a new 'Alliance' or 'Fraternité' was founded: the *Alliance Socialiste Révolutionnaire*. The programme was written by Bakunin, between 2 and 5 September, and adopted on 13 September, after a discussion with his Italian and Spanish friends.

Bakunin's original French text exists only as a draft. There is however a complete Italian translation. These unpublished manuscripts prove that the programme was in broad lines identical with previous projects of the 'Fraternité'. According to the statutes there were international, national and provincial 'frères'. Cafiero, Costa, Nabruzzi, Fanelli and Malatesta were, at the moment, the only Italian international 'frères'; besides these there were Farga Pellicer, James Guillaume, Marselau and possibly Ralli.

A few months earlier Bakunin had formed a 'Russian Brotherhood' with Ross, Ralli, Golstein and El'snich. The text of its programme, too, is lost. However, the Zürich group[47] published in September 1873 a Russian pamphlet *To the Russian Revolutionaries*, summarising this programme.[48] Bakunin regarded this publication as a breach of confidence. The group printed it because they considered the text to be an excellent exposé of anarchist principles; they left out everything which alluded in one way or another to the secret organisation. But Bakunin was not convinced and severed his relations with Ralli and his group.

As in 1866, the Italian section of the new 'Fraternité' was the only one which had an objective existence.

After Bakunin became a member of the International, his activities for the next six years were mainly directed towards Switzerland, France, Italy, Spain and Russia. A man like Bakunin, with a revolutionary past of many years and a great prestige among democrats and revolutionaries in all countries, obviously became a member of the International to propagate and to work for his ideas. For the same reason, in September 1864, Marx accepted the invitation to become a member of the 'Provisional General Council'.

After the Basle Congress of the International, in September 1869, Marx became alarmed at the influence of Bakunin. 'If he is not careful, he will be excommunicated,' he wrote to Engels in 1869.[49] That happened indeed three years later, after a long underground campaign and personal attacks. The fact that the Bakuninist collectivist and anti-state ideas took more and more root in the federations was explained by intrigues and 'complots' on the part of the 'fripouille allianciste'.

It was especially in the development of the Spanish Federation that Bakunin's 'Alliance' became an important factor in the 'lutte des tendances'. The question became an important point on the agenda of The Hague Congress of the International. Engels had prepared a long report[50] for the Congress to prove that in Spain such a secret Alliance existed. This, the *Alianza*, was this time indeed a real existing organisation. Engels, however, was not well informed – although Paul Lafargue, who had provided most of the incriminating material, had told him that the *Alianza* was a Spanish affair and that Bakunin had nothing to do with it, as far as an organisation was concerned. He added that it was an excellent idea to form a secret society with the most forceful and intelligent militants, with a view to a possible dissolution and eventual rebuilding of the Spanish International.[51]

A committee of the Congress dealing with the question of the 'Alliance' produced an 'amazing document', 'a blend of naïvity and irrelevance'.[52] The actual existence of the Alliance could not be proved, but Bakunin had 'tried and perhaps succeeded' in forming a 'society called Alliance'. According to Engels, this society, of which the existence could not be proved, was one and the same as the Spanish *Alianza*.

The conclusion of the report was that the programme of the Alliance – which Alliance was meant was not clear, they were all mixed up: those which had existed, or those Bakunin 'had intended and perhaps succeeded in creating', or the public Geneva Alliance, or the Spanish *Alianza* – was opposed to that of the International. This was, of course, not the case.[53] The International had no official programme. The Provisional Rules of 1864 and the Statutes of 1866 were vague enough to admit all kinds of organisations of different schools of thought. The policy of the International was worked out at its congresses or especially by its federations.

It is true that the Bakuninist programme was not in accordance with the Marxian resolution of the conquest of political power, adopted at The Hague. But these resolutions had to be confirmed by the federations, and in this case the quasi-totality of the International did not. The accusation that Bakunin wanted to replace the programme of the International by that of the 'Alliance' was likewise unjustified. Again and again Bakunin stressed the point that it was very important that the programme of the International should be general enough to unite the workers of all countries.[54]

Engels stated in his report that Bakunin was trying to destroy the International. That, of course, was polemical humbug. All this can only be explained by the fact that Marx and Engels identified the General Council with their point of view, and the International with the General Council.

If, finally, one asks what really did exist in terms of organisation, the answer must be: very little indeed. The Alliance 'had no list of members, no agreed rules or programme (since Bakunin's numerous drafts were all made on his own responsibility), no officers, no subscriptions, and no regular meetings. A political association having none of these attributes was a myth.'[55] Nevertheless, Bakunin believed and made others believe in this myth. He thought that 'certaines existences imaginaires' were very useful and that one shouldn't disdain them altogether. In the whole of society, he wrote, there is a quarter of reality, and at least three-quarters of imagination, 'et ce n'est point sa partie imaginaire qui a agi de tout temps le moins puissamment sur les hommes'.[56] James Guillaume, who belonged from 1868 to 1874 to Bakunin's most intimate circle, stated that the secret Alliance was nothing more than an intimate group among the most devoted accepting its programme.[57]

From the description of Mikhail Sazhin, intimately allied to Bakunin from 1870 to 1874, and with his French and Russian circles, one can draw the same conclusion: there was, he wrote, 'no secret pact among us. All the time during our friendship and my collaboration with Bakunin, as well as with our mutual friends like Guillaume and Schwitzguébel, there has been no secret society or conspiracy. When I saw Bakunin, in the summer of 1871, my "novitiate" had by then lasted for a year.'

> When I appeared there I met some people who arrived before me, Italians, Spaniards and Swiss, whom I already knew. He suggested that I should speak openly about Russian affairs.... So from this meeting it is necessary to count my association with the 'mythical' Alliance, or as Michel said, with the 'holy of holies'. There were no 'dagger-fights', no statutes, initiation ceremonies or any other rites connected with secret societies, and no plots either. It continued like this up to the end. Occasionally we came together to consider matters, and sometimes we came individually. This was done most frequently by me and the Italians, as we lived nearer to him than any of the others.[58]

The 'Fraternité', then, was a Bakuninist 'party' or rather a 'party' of Bakunin: the ideal union of all those who had embraced his creed.[59] It was his most personal achievement by which he succeeded in influencing decisively the orientation of large parts of the European labour movement towards the ideology of revolutionary collectivism and libertarian socialism. It was in this way he chose to convey his message of liberty and by which he made a lasting impact on history.

NOTES

1. José Garcia Viñas died in 1931. Errico Malatesta in 1932. With them the last original members of Bakunin's intimate circle had gone.

2. A. A. Kornilov, *Molodye gody Mikhaila Bakunina. Iz istorii russkogo romantizma* (Moscow, 1915) pp. 195-7.

3. The 'Slav Friends', made up of a few people who shared his ideas, chiefly spokesmen of the Slovak, Croat and Slav movements. Cf. Franco Venturi, *Roots of Revolution: A History of the Populist and Socialist Movements in Nineteenth Century Russia* (New York, 1966) p. 55.

4. MS. entitled 'Société internationale secrète de l'émancipation de l'humanité. But de la société', Sohlman Archives, Kungl. Biblioteket, Stockholm, 80 pp., quoted subsequently as Swedish MS. Apart from the Swedish MS. all manuscripts here mentioned are in the possession of the International Institute of Social History (I.I.S.G.), Amsterdam. References to pages of unpublished manuscripts are omitted. All italics in Bakunin's quotations are from the original.

5. E. H. Carr, *Michael Bakunin* (New York, 1961) pp. 439, 456 (1st ed., London, 1938).

6. His diary, e.g., mentions on one day twenty-four letters. Many of them were of the length of a pamphlet. Unfortunately, most of his correspondence from 1864 to his death in 1876 is lost: nearly all his letters to Spain, Italy, the Jura, and an important part of his Russian correspondence. Bakunin and his friends destroyed letters and documents on several occasions.

7. Mikhail Sazhin, 'Vospominaiya o Bakunine', *Katorga i Ssylka* (Moscow), XXVI (5) (1926) 18; reprinted in *Mikhailu Bakuninu 1876-1926. Ocherki istorii anarkhicheskogo dvizheniya v Rossii* (Moscow, 1926) p. 180. Sazhin (who after 1870 called himself Arman Ross) characterised Bakunin's method as follows: 'For Bakunin the acquaintance with people who were willing to work for the sake of the revolution was particularly characteristic. Usually he did not enter into any relations, and repelled such people from whom it was impossible to draw any benefit for the revolution. By words, stories, theoretical considerations and programmes he gave each new person a secondary importance, and tried realistically and practically to define one's abilities, one's suitability for particular aspects of activity. He would therefore give someone a certain task, which corresponded with his abilities; if the person wished to be useful as a writer, Bakunin proposed to him, or asked him, to write something, etc. In this way he gradually learnt to know the person, and it happened sometimes that he terminated all practical relations with him because of his inability.' *Katorga i Ssylka*, p. 13.

8. A. I. Herzen, 'Bakunin i pol'skoe delo', in 'Byloe i dumy', *Sobranie sochineniya*, XI (Moscow, 1957) 359.

9. 'Eine geheime Verbindung im strengsten Verstande nenne ich diejenige, deren Ursprung, Zweck, Mittel, Einrichtung und Daseyn, nur ihren Eingeweihten, und so viel einige dieser Stücke in ihrem ganzen Umfang betrifft, nur den Geprüftesten ihrer Mitglieder bekannt sind.' Adam Weishaupt, *Über die geheime Welt und Regierungskunst* (Frankfurt, 1795) p. 45.

10. See Arthur Lehning, *From Buonarroti to Bakunin: Studies in International Socialism* (Leiden, 1970) pp. 30-90.

11. In fact, by 1796 there no longer existed a popular movement to support

Babeuf. Daniel Guérin called him an 'enragé à retardement'.

12. Michel Bakounine, *Œuvres*, v (Paris, 1911) 336-8; i (Paris, 1895) 36-7, 215.

13. *Archives Bakounine*, i 1, 'Michel Bakounine et l'Italie, 1871-1872, La polémique avec Mazzini' (Leiden, 1961) pp. xv-xvi.

14. Elio Conti, *Le Origini del socialismo a Firenze (1860-1880)* (Rome, 1950) pp. 69-97.

15. M. A. Bakunin, *Sobranie sochineniya i pisem 1818-1876* (Moscow, 1934) iii 538-9; Carr, *Michael Bakunin*, p. 233.

16. Carr, *Michael Bakunin*, p. 233.

17. *Pis'ma M. A. Bakunina k A. I. Gertsenu i N. P. Ogarevu* (Geneva, 1896) p. 164.

18. Ibid., p. 171.

19. MS. I.I.S.G., a copy made by Walerian Mroczkowski and the Princess Obolenskaya. The greater part is published in Max Nettlau, *The Life of Michael Bakounine: Michael Bakunin. Eine Biographie* (London, 1896-1900) pp. 209-34.

20. *Istoricheskoe razvitie Internatsionala. Chast' I* (Zürich, 1873) pp. 301-2. The article of Bakunin, 'The International Alliance of Social Revolutionaries', was signed 'the editor'. The text will be reprinted in *Archives Bakounine*, v.

21. See in general Max Nettlau, *Bakunin e l'Internazionale in Italia dal 1864 al 1872*, preface by Errico Malatesta (Geneva, 1928) chaps. v-viii. Giuseppe Mazzoni (1808-80) founded in 1863, with Giuseppe Dolfi, a 'democratic society' in Florence, with a strongly anticlerical character.

22. Alfred Talandier (1822-90), revolutionary democrat, a *proscrit* of 1852, who in 1864 entered the Provisional General Council of the International; Fernando Garrido y Tortosa, the Spanish democrat and Fourierist. They are mentioned as members of the 'Fraternité' by Albert Richard, 'Bakounine et l'Internationale à Lyon, 1868-1870', *Revue de Paris*, iii 17 (1 Sep 1896) 121.

23. Élisée Reclus (1830-1905) was then already an anarchist. Writing to Bakunin in 1875, he spoke of himself as a 'frère indépendant'. Élie Reclus (1827-1904) always had a more sceptical attitude towards anarchism. Bakunin wrote of them: 'Ce sont deux savants et en même temps les hommes les plus modestes, les plus nobles, les plus désintéressés, les plus purs, les plus religieusement dévoués à leurs principes que j'aie recontrés dans ma vie.' *Archives Bakounine*, i 1, p. 245. Summarising the theoretical principles of the 'Fraternité', Max Nettlau wrote: 'Europe was to be reconstructed on the basis of local autonomy and federation, irrespective of present state boundaries; work was to be done by the widest application of the principle of association; privilege was to be abolished by the abolition of the right of inheritance, all property of any importance devolving upon the death of the present owner to a fund for the education, instruction and apprenticeage of all children, in order to give within a generation an equal start to all. These ideas and corresponding revolutionary action, wherever possible, were to be realised by groups and societies of all kinds which would be secretly formed and their action co-ordinated, controlled and inspired in a thoroughly revolutionary sense by the national and international brethren. Élie and Élisée Reclus accepted this idea, which at that time, when Mazzini and Blanqui had gathered the nationalists of several countries and the authoritarian socialists of France in similar societies, was a very practical thought, conceived before the International Working Men's Association was ever founded. Élisée Reclus was long since an anarchist at heart and willing to support all efforts towards this aim;

there was no anarchist movement at that time and Bakunin's attempt was the nearest approach to it.' Max Nettlau, 'Élisée Reclus and Michael Bakunin', in *Élisée and Élie Reclus in Memoriam* (Berkeley Heights, Calif: Oriole Press, 1927) pp. 197-8.

24. Cf. a document dated Stockholm, 12 Oct 1864, by which Sohlman was admitted, with several reservations made by him, as a 'frère' of the society. The 'catechism' and the 'programme' are also mentioned in a letter to Sohlman from London, dated 27 Oct, asking him to have these documents read to Colonel Pavel Bogdanov, a Russian who took part in the Polish insurrection. Obviously, Bakunin had recruited him during his stay in London.

25. Nettlau, *Biographie*, p. 212.

26. 'Programme et objet de l'Organisation révolutionnaire des frères internationaux' (1868), in *L'Alliance de la Démocratie socialiste et l'Association internationale des Travailleurs. Rapport et documents publiés par ordre du Congrès de La Haye* (London, 1873) p. 132.

27. Here, as often elsewhere, Bakunin uses the term 'anarchy' in the sense of a revolutionary disorder, 'un désordre salutaire'. On 1 Apr 1870 he wrote to Albert Richard: 'Il faut que l'anarchie, le réveil de la vie spontanée, de toutes les passions locales sur tous les points, soient aussi grands que possible, pour que la révolution soit et reste vivante, réelle, puissante.' Bibliothèque de la Ville de Lyon, MS. 5401/12.

28. Bakunin added here 'even yours'; the quotation is from a letter of 2 June 1870 to Sergei Nechaev, *Archives Bakounine*, IV, 'Michel Bakounine et ses relations avec Sergej Nečaev, 1870-1872' (Leiden, 1971) p. 237.

29. Ibid.

30. Michel Bakounine, *Œuvres*, II (Paris, 1907) 107-8.

31. *Archives Bakounine*, II, 'Michel Bakounine et les conflits dans l'Internationale, 1872' (Leiden, 1965) p. 141.

32. From a letter to T. Garcia Morago, 21 May 1872, MS. I.I.S.G.

33. Letter to Celso Ceretti, 13-27 Mar 1872, *Archives Bakounine*, I 2, 'Michel Bakounine et l'Italie, 1871-1872. La Première Internationale en Italie et le conflit avec Marx' (Leiden, 1963) pp. 251-2.

34. Michel Bakounine, 'Circulaire à mes amis d'Italie', ibid., p. 308.

35. *Œuvres*, II 228.

36. *Archives Bakounine*, IV 235.

37. Swedish MS.

38. Michel Bakounine, *Œuvres*, III (Paris, 1908) 121; v 318-19.

39. Swedish MS. The same formulations are to be found in the *Revolutionary Catechism* of 1866.

40. MS. after a copy made by Max Nettlau. The manuscript was in the hands of Kropotkin, but seems to be lost in the Kropotkin Museum in Russia.

41. Cf. Buonarroti's: 'La Liberté est une partie de la justice; la justice toute entière est dans l'égalité; la liberté sociale ne peut se concevoir sans l'égalité.' Lehning, *From Buonarroti to Bakunin*, p. 90.

42. Cf. Proudhon's well-known phrase: 'Liberty is not the daughter but the mother of order.' 'Solution du problème social', in *Œuvres complètes*, VI (Paris, 1868) 87.

43. Nettlau, *Biographie*, p. 233.

44. MS. I.I.S.G.

45. In the documents of the 'Fraternité internationale' of 1868, dealing with

the immediate measures to be taken during a revolution, Bakunin also writes: 'The Commune will be organised by the standing Federation of the Barricades and by the creation of a Revolutionary Communal Council composed of one or two delegates from each barricade, one to each street or district, vested with plenary but accountable and rescindable mandates.' *L'Alliance de la Démocratie socialiste* ... , p. 130.

46. *Istoricheskoe razvitie Internatsionala*, pp. 311-12.

47. In August 1873 a split took place between Ross and the other members, after fifteen months of close collaboration with Bakunin, who had formed with them, in August 1872, the Slav Section of Zürich, affiliated to the Jura Federation of the International.

48. *K russkim revolyutsioneram. Revolyutsionnaya obshchina russkikh anarkhistov* [n.p.], no. 1 (Sep 1873) 14 pp. The text of this pamphlet (based on Bakunin's programme of the 'Russian Brotherhood') will be reprinted in *Archives Bakounine*, v, which will contain also the unpublished French and Italian versions of the programme of the 'Fraternité' of 1872, the *Alliance Socialiste/Revolutionnaire*.

49. Karl Marx, Friedrich Engels, *Historisch-kritische Gesamtausgabe*, 3. Abteilung: *Der Briefwechsel zwischen Marx und Engels 1868-1883*, iv (Berlin, 1931) 213.

50. Originally published in Karl Marx and Friedrich Engels, *Sochineniya*, XIII 2 (Moscow, 1940); now reprinted in *Gaagskii Kongress Pervogo Internatsionala, 2-7 sentyabrya 1872g. Protokoly i dokumenty* (Moscow, 1970) pp. 305-15.

51. Letter of Lafargue to Engels, 29 May 1872. Friedrich Engels, Paul et Laura Lafargue, *Correspondance*, iii (Paris, 1959) 468.

52. Carr, *Michael Bakunin*, p. 449. For all relevant documents, see *Archives Bakounine*, ii.

53. In fact the Geneva Alliance had been admitted by the General Council on 27 July 1869, and its programme declared not contrary to the International.

54. A similar view was held by Engels, who explained that the International had the task of welding in one great army the totality of the workers of Europe and America able to start the fight. It could therefore not take the principles of the *Communist Manifesto* as a starting-point. In September 1871, however, Marx and Engels tried to give the International this special programme, 'le coup longtemps préparé'. The answer was a revolt of most of the federations against the General Council, after the Jura Federation had sounded the alarm.

55. Carr, *Michael Bakunin*, p. 439.

56. Letter to Johann Philipp Becker, 4 Dec 1869, quoted in *Archives Bakounine*, i 2, p. xxxvii.

57. James Guillaume has given the following account of Bakunin's conception: 'Pendant son séjour au Locle, [Bakounine] me fit en effet des confidences: il me parla d'une organisation secrète qui unissait depuis plusieurs années, par les liens d'une fraternité révolutionnaire, un certain nombre d'hommes dans différents pays, plus particulièrement en Italie et en France; il me lut un programme contenant des choses qui répondaient entièrement à mes propres aspirations, et me demanda si je ne voudrais pas me joindre à ceux qui avaient créé cette organisation. Ce qui me frappa surtout dans les explications qu'il me donna, c'est qu'il ne s'agissait point d'une organisation du type classique des anciennes sociétés secrètes, dans laquelle on dût obéir à des ordres venus d'en haut: l'organisation n'était autre chose que le libre

rapprochement d'hommes qui s'unissaient pour l'action collective, sans formalités, sans solennité, sans rites mystérieux, simplement parce qu'ils avaient confiance les uns dans les autres et que l'entente leur paraissait préférable à l'action isolée.' James Guillaume, *L'Internationale. Documents et souvenirs (1864-1878)*, I (Paris, 1905) 130. Ross confirms this statement: 'Guillaume is right when, in his four-volume book about the International, he says that all stories, and even accusations, about the existence of the "Alliance" are the purest fantasy. I repeat once more that during the whole of the six or seven years of my intimate friendship with Bakunin, Guillaume and others, there was nothing that could indicate that there was ever a plot, or a secret alliance, between us.' Mikhail Sazhin, *Katorga i Ssylka*, p. 14.

58. Ibid., p. 19.

59. When Bakunin occasionally speaks of 'our party' he uses this term in the same way as Blanqui: a *groupement* of those who had accepted his special trend of revolutionary socialism and who belonged to the movement of which Blanqui was the leader; what name Blanqui gave to his secret organisation is unknown. See Maurice Dommanget, *Les Idées politiques et sociales d'Auguste Blanqui* (Paris, 1957) p. 346.

4 Being, Consciousness and Roles: On the Foundations of Historical Materialism

G. A. COHEN

It is not the consciousness of men that determines their being, but, on the contrary, their social being that determines their consciousness.
KARL MARX, Preface to *A Contribution to the Critique of Political Economy**

THE thesis exhibited above is obscure. It is not clear what sort of evidence should weaken confidence in it, nor what sort may be adduced in its support. But that it is not clear does not show that it cannot be clarified. A satisfactory clarification must fulfil three requirements:

1. It must state what evidence has to be like to confirm it, and to disconfirm it.
2. The thesis so elucidated must be recognisable. It must be reasonable to claim it as a more express version of the thesis Marx maintained and which historians have affirmed and denied in controversy over particular issues.[1]
3. The thesis must remain interesting. It must become neither trivially true nor trivially false. (A clarification which passes the second test thereby passes the third, unless historians have been more confused than I am willing to suppose.)

It is easy to list the requirements and difficult to produce formulations which meet them. The present paper does not aspire to their production. Its object is to suppress misconceptions which surround the problem, and to take some preliminary steps towards its solution.

I begin by examining a familiar argument which purports to prove the thesis, or something like it. I then consider arguments which would show not merely that it is not but that it cannot be true. Next, I locate the thesis within the theory of historical materialism, which is briefly expounded. The exposition exploits the concept of a role, which is analysed in the final section of the paper.

I

At Marx's graveside Engels presented what has been considered at once a sufficient explication of and a compelling argument for the basic outlook of historical materialism. Arguments akin to Engels's have been propounded, crudely and otherwise, by many Marxists, including, as we shall see, Marx himself. According to Engels:

> Marx discovered the law of development of human history: the simple fact ... that mankind must first of all eat, drink, have shelter and clothing, before it can pursue politics, science, art, religion, etc.; that therefore the production of the immediate material means of subsistence and consequently the degree of economic development attained by a given people or during a given epoch form the foundation upon which the state institutions, the legal conceptions, art and even the ideas on religion of the people concerned have been evolved, and in the light of which they must, therefore, be explained....

Let us not ask whether what Engels argues for deserves to be called a 'law of development', even if his reasoning is successful. Let us assess the argument without insisting that its conclusion state what is properly a law of any kind.

The passage contains four inferences. The first inference is implicit. The rest are signalled by the words 'therefore', 'consequently' and 'therefore', in that order. The structure of the argument is as follows:

1. Men must eat (etc.) if they are to engage in politics (etc.).
∴ 2. Men must produce food (etc.) if they are to engage in those activities.
∴ 3. The activity of material production is the foundation on which those activities rest. (*See first 'therefore'.*)
and ∴ 4. The degree of economic development is also part of that foundation. (*See 'consequently'.*)
∴ 5. The activity of material production (together with the degree of economic development) explains those activities. (*See second 'therefore'.*)

Let us call (2) the 'indispensability claim'. It asserts that material production is indispensable to all other human activity. I shall first comment on the inferences I have exposed, and then offer additional remarks on the indispensability claim.

Consider then the inference from (1) to (2). I think we can assume that Engels would not regard (2) as relevantly true unless material production absorbs more than a negligible amount of human energy. He would have abandoned his argument had he thought the average historical working day was, say, one hour long. He meant to affirm not only that men must produce, but that they must devote a great deal of themselves to the task, and also, though this imputation is more conjectural, that the task is not intrinsically attractive. Now does (2), thus glossed, follow from (1)? I think it does in all relevant circumstances. A look at the irrelevant ones will explain my meaning.

They are those in which the writ of the Curse of Adam does not run, and the earth supplies the requisites of survival with little human help. Marx said nature is then 'too lavish', for she

'keeps man in hand, like a child in leading-strings'. She does not impose upon him any necessity to develop himself.... It is the necessity of bringing a natural force under the control of society, of economising, of appropriating it or subduing it by the work of man's hand, that first plays the decisive part in the history of industry

and hence, we may add by way of interpretation, in history *sans phrase*. In Arcadia the fruit falls from the tree into man's lap and men make no history because they do not have to: history is a substitute for nature.[2] But Engels calls what he is trying to demonstrate 'the law of development of human history', and whatever that is, it cannot be expected to hold where history is in abeyance. If, then, we set aside such cases, and consider nature as it usually is, niggardly, and resistant to human desire and design, we can confidently endorse the derivation of the indispensability claim, as glossed above, from proposition (1).

It will simplify the issue, without distorting it, if we do not inspect one of the three remaining inferences, that carried by the word 'consequently', and which leads us from (3) to (4). Let us elide proposition (4) and therefore also the parenthesis in proposition (5). Two steps are left, from (2) to (3), and from (3) to (5).

Let us designate 'mental production'[3] those activities which Engels proposes to explain by reference to material production, the production of the means of subsistence. Then our two inferences are: since material production is indispensable, it is the foundation of mental production; since it is the foundation of mental production, it explains the character of mental production.

Now there is really only one inference worth examination here, because to call material production the *foundation* of mental production is either already to assert that it explains it, or it is merely to repeat the indispensability claim in the form of an arresting architectural image. The image tends to arrest thought. For it has encouraged many, and doubtless Engels here, to suppose both that (3) is obviously true and that it obviously entails (5); whereas in the sense in which it is obviously true, (3) just repeats (2), and in that sense, as opposed to another in which it means something like (5), (3) does not obviously entail (5). We have really one inference, which is either from (2) to (3) or from (3) to (5), depending on how we read 'foundation'. That inference is from the indispensability of material production to the conclusion that the character of mental production is largely explained by it. As it stands, unsupplemented by further considerations, the inference is deplorable. The indispensability of material production does not guarantee for it the asserted explanatory role. Moreover, the reverse explanatory relation is compatible with material production's indispensability. Men must work and must organise themselves to do so, yet it might be true that the way they work and the forms of organisation they adopt are determined by political and cultural complexes which develop autonomously and which maintain a strong grip on men.

So much for Engels's inferences. Now some further remarks on the claim that material production is indispensable. The claim is impregnable, but it cannot make material production prior to mental as far as explanation is concerned. For mental production is also indispensable to life. It is indispensable because it is indispensable to material production, and indispensability is a transitive relation. We can mark two ways in which material production requires mental production. The second might be contested, but a Marxist is committed to both.

1. Mental activities enter into material production, and the capacity to perform those activities depends on mental production and general culture.
2. On a Marxian view religion and/or law and/or ideology are essential to secure order *in* the labour process (to discipline the labouring agents) and an ordering *of* the labour process (to organise production). Men will not submit to the deprivations inherent in labour in the absence of legal or religio-moral sanctions, and work will not proceed smoothly unless production relations enjoy a sharpness of definition which only law or something like it can provide.

There is, finally, yet another difficulty in arguing for the secondary role of mental production on the basis of the indispensability claim. For even if mental production were dispensable, it would remain unavoidable for beings with human attributes. Even if we absurdly suppose that it is unnecessary to survival, we can still predict that a society will express itself culturally as confidently as we can predict that it will devote energy to work. If, therefore, the indispensability of material production is thought significant *because* it renders material production unavoidable, then its indispensability would be no argument for the dominance of material over mental production, even if mental production were dispensable.

Let me now substantiate my earlier comment that Engels is not alone in his espousal of arguments of the sort we have reviewed. In Volume I of *Capital*, Marx replies to a critic who conceded that economic life was central in modernity, but denied it was so in the Middle Ages or in antiquity. Marx thinks it significant and appropriate to point out 'that the Middle Ages could not live on Catholicism, nor the ancient world on politics'.[4] This shows he fell into the same mistake as Engels did.

Consider also Brecht's pungent reminder, 'Erst kommt das Fressen, dann kommt die Moral' ('Grub comes before morality'), which is obviously true in one sense, and which, in my opinion, is also true, *but not obviously*, in a more important sense. My criticism of Engels is intended to remove the spurious self-evidence such claims have when they are used to enunciate momentous theses.

I think it possible to fill the gaps in Engels's argument, to argue persuasively from roughly his premises to roughly his conclusions. I shall not, however, present a refurbished argument here. Instead, I shall next examine arguments purporting to show that the Marxian attempt to distinguish what is fundamental and what is derivative in society is not only a failure, but in principle misconceived.

II

Perhaps the most formidable and certainly the most indefatigable purveyor of such arguments is Professor John Plamenatz, who has developed them in a number of publications.[5] What Engels thought must be true, more or less *a priori*, Plamenatz thinks cannot be true, can be known not to be true without consulting the evidence of history. He thinks the basic distinctions of historical materialism, between being and consciousness, between foundation and superstructure, cannot be properly drawn, because the elements the historical materialist would distinguish are, as a matter of logic, too intimately bound to one another. I have elsewhere[6] shown why this appears true but is in fact false as far as the relation between the economic structure and the legal superstructure is concerned. Here I deal with the problem more generally, though I take the liberty of drawing on the results just mentioned in so far as they are generalisable.

In *Man and Society* Plamenatz discusses what he calls 'sides of social life' (economy, religion, science, politics, art, etc.) and he lodges two claims. The first is that *it is not plausible to regard any 'large' side of social life as derivative from any other.* Unlike many of his anti-Marxist contentions, this one is not argued for on conceptual grounds. It relies on an appeal to our intuitive appreciation of history and society. The second claim, which is conceptual, is that *moral and other ideas cannot be determined by any side, or combination of sides, of social life, since they enter into every one of them.*

We shall later[7] distinguish the thesis that being determines consciousness from the theory to which it is connected – that the economic foundation determines the character of a non-economic superstructure. We may see the two claims just reported as respectively directed against the theory and the thesis. The first challenges the theory, since if it is correct, the economy cannot be designated as a 'foundation':

> If we take something like fashion in dress, we can show that it greatly depends on certain other things which it hardly influences. But if we take larger sides of social life, like religion or science or government, it is no longer plausible to treat any of them as fundamental or derivative in relation to the others.[8]

Plamenatz is willing to assert that fashion is 'much more affected by the rest of social life, or even by some other part of it, than it affects it'. This is what he means when he allows it is derivative.[9] Indeed, Plamenatz is prepared to say that this can be *shown*. Most people would find his judgement about fashion intuitively acceptable. But Plamenatz thinks it can be demonstrated, and, if this is so – in fact, even if it is not so – the intuition must be grounded in a principle of interpretation which, if it were made explicit, might well enable some rational judgement about the relative strength of the larger factors Plamenatz mentions. I am not saying it is easy to unearth the principle. I am saying that the claim about fashion implies that there is one, and that if we had it, we might be able to say that government is more fundamental than science, or vice versa, in Plamenatz's sense of 'fundamental', even though we can say little using intuitive resources alone. The principle, in conjunction with the available empirical evidence, might license the judgement that one large side of social life influences another more than it is influenced by it.

The force of my objection is that it is not easy to be sure in advance of conceptual and empirical work what judgements are plausible in this area. We require a clarification of the idea of a side of social life, so that we can establish the identity of each; a clarification of the idea of A affecting B more than B affects A; and a careful study of the historical record, in the light of such clarifications. I realise that this is an enormous programme. But it is inappropriate to make confident judgements without embarking upon it.

I turn to the second contention:

> Since claims and duties and mental attitudes are involved in all social relations, in every side of social life, no matter how primitive, since they are part of what we mean when we call a human activity social, we cannot take any side of social life and say that it determines ... men's moral and customary relations and their attitudes towards one another.[10]

For Plamenatz, A determines B if, given a particular form of A, there arises a particular form of B,[11] or, as we might also put it, if variations in A explain variations in B. On this use of 'determine' it is conceptually in order to assert that the character of men's ideas and customs is determined by the stock of instruments of production available to them, and/or by their level of economic development. Each of the latter can be described without referring to customs and ideas. Plamenatz might respond by saying that in that case what is described is not a 'side of social life'. Be that as it may, Marxists – and it is Marxism Plamenatz is discussing – are not obliged to assert that what they isolate as fundamental may be styled a 'side of social life' in Plamenatz's sense. As I understand historical materialism, economic activity is central only because the economic structure, which is not an activity or set of activities, is central; and while moral and other ideas may enter the activity, the structure may be so conceived that it is free of all such superstructural encumbrances.[12]

But Plamenatz is wrong even on his own ground. For it is not clear that a side of social life, as he conceives it, is incapable of determining the ideas associated with it, as he understands determination. The ideas associated with a side of social life may vary as and *because* the side as a whole varies, and this will meet his sense of 'determine'. But to make good these objections, I should like to focus on a more extended formulation of the second claim, which derives from Plamenatz's book on *Ideology*.

III

The second of the claims introduced in the last section disputes the thesis which is our epigraph: Plamenatz maintains that social existence *cannot* determine consciousness because consciousness is integral to, gives shape to, social existence. This is argued at length in chaps. ii and iii of *Ideology*. The following presentation achieves as close an approximation as any to the structure of his argument, which is never offered in step-wise form. The key terms and phrases are Plamenatz's own:

      1. Social being consists of institutions.
      2. Institutions are conventional modes of behaviour.[13]
∴ 3. Social being consists of conventional modes of behaviour.
but   4. Conventional modes of behaviour involve the use of ideas
and   5. If A involves B, A cannot determine B.
∴ 6. Conventional modes of behaviour do not determine the ideas they involve.
∴ 7. Social being does not determine the ideas it involves.

The trouble begins with the first premise, which cannot pass unless it conforms to what Marx meant by 'social being'. I shall question premise (1) in the next section. Here I examine the derivation of sub-conclusions (3) and (6).

The derivation of (3) exploits an ambiguity in the term 'institution'. Setting aside the exegetical issue raised in the last paragraph, premise (1) can appear ($\neq$ is) acceptable only if we contemplate institutions composed of relations between persons[14] (and things), such as a latifundium, or a feudal manor, or a corporation, or stock exchange. But none of these is – as premise (2) requires – a conventional mode of behaviour. Premise (2) can appear acceptable only if we think of institutions which are practices, such as the institutions or practices of slavery, serfdom, marriage, punishment, etc. A set of relations is not an institution in this sense. It is the locus of practices but it is not itself a practice. It follows that sub-conclusion (3) rests on an equivocation.

We turn to the passage from (4) and (5) to (6).

Until we are told what concept of involvement figures in premise (5), it cannot be assessed, and therefore cannot be accepted. Plamenatz tells us little. Hence it is entirely open that, in any sense of 'involve' in which (4) is true, (5) is false, so that the transition to (6) embodies further equivocation.

Plamenatz thinks the thesis that all ideas are determined by forms of social activity 'suggests that there are forms of social activity which do not involve the use of ideas'.[15] Pending receipt of more information about involvement, one must wonder why he imputes the suggestion, since it does not appear present in causal claims generally. I do not suggest that the production of sound is not involved in blowing a trumpet when I say that blowing a trumpet causes sound. In one plain sense of 'involve' causal assertions always suggest the contrary of what Plamenatz says they do, for whenever an effect occurs, one may say that what caused it involved its occurrence.

Plamenatz also espouses this variant of (5), which I shall call (5)(i): if A involves B, B cannot determine A. For he says[16] that 'the thought that forms part of an action' can no more 'affect' the action than 'the shape of something' can 'affect' that thing. The analogy is unhappy, since the shape of a bridge can make it weak, and the shape of a chemical compound, the arrangement of its atoms, can decide what its further properties are. But whatever the merits of the analogy are, one may be satisfied of the dubious character of the principle (5)(i) it is intended to illustrate by reflecting that the respiratory organs both cause and are involved in respiration.

If we drop the notion of involvement and express (5) and its variant in the alternative language of wholes and parts, which Plamenatz also employs, we still get negative results. (5) becomes: if B is part of A, A cannot affect B; and (5)(i) becomes: if B is part of A, B cannot affect A. But the surface of a sphere may melt as a consequence of the sphere's rapid rotation, even though, one may add, every sphere necessarily has a surface. That defeats the alternative version of (5). As for its revised variant, it founders on the fact that the furnace which is part of a locomotive causes the locomotive (furnace included) to move.

Of what relevance, it may be asked, are trumpets, bridges, chemical compounds, respiratory organs, rotating spheres and locomotives to a discussion of the way *social* phenomena are connected? The answer is as follows. Natural objects and processes may be intimately connected, thoroughly involved with one another, and yet in unquestionably causal relation. Professor Plamenatz writes as though social phenomena are either quite unrelated or related too closely to admit of causal connection. A review of simple facts of nature indicates that he has not catered for the possibility that social facts too may be very closely linked and yet bound together by causation.

IV

We must now inquire whether premise (1) ('Social being consists of institutions') harmonises with the sense Marx attached to 'social being' when he said it determined consciousness. Harmony is required since the conclusion of Plamenatz's argument is intended as a denial of Marx's thesis.

Marx wrote: 'It is not the consciousness of men which determines their existence, but their social existence determines their consciousness.' In other words, *the consciousness of a person is determined by the social existence of that person.* That the thesis may be expressed in this individualised form is less clear from its familiar abbreviation, '(social) being determines consciousness', but the full formulation merits preferential attention.

Let us now look at premise (1), in the light of our italicised interpretation of the thesis. Can an institution, in any sense of the word, *be* the social existence of a person? Certainly not if by an institution we understand a practice. And if by an institution we understand a set of social relations, then a man's social existence is surely not an institution, but his emplacement, his particular situation, within the set. A person's social existence is, I am proposing, his *place* in society, the role(s) he occupies in the institution(s) to which he belongs. But of course we must add that what Marx meant by 'social being' was a particular one or set of a man's social roles, namely, his economic role(s).[17] Taken by itself, the structure of the sentence leads us to identify social being with a social role. Its occurrence inside Marx's thought ensures that the role is an economic one.

For Marx, then, a person's social existence is the economic role he occupies. And though role-defined behaviour, the *performance* of a role, may ($\neq$ does) involve the use of ideas in a causation-excluding sense, the same cannot be said for a man's *occupancy* of a role.[18] 'If a man occupies the role of a shopkeeper he will have the ideas of a shopkeeper as a result' suffers from no conceptual difficulties, not even apparent ones.[19] The desired causal relation is perfectly assertable. The extent to which such assertions are true is another matter. I think they are to an important extent, and that when they are false this is due to empirical facts about man and society, not to conceptual difficulties.

The construal I have put on the being/consciousness thesis has more than linguistic propriety in its favour. Its further merit is that it fits the thesis into the rest of the doctrine of the Preface to *The Critique of Political Economy*. It enables us to establish the relation[20] between being and consciousness on the one hand and foundation and superstructure on the other. They are connected but distinct pairs. The foundation is an economic structure, a set of production relations,[21] whereas the social being of a person is his position in it; and the superstructure is a set of non-economic institutions (of law, politics, religion, education, etc.) in which persons participate with a consciousness grounded in their being.[22]

The heart of the theory of the Preface is that as society increases the volume of productive power at its disposal, changes in its division of labour (work roles) and in its division of property (ownership roles)[23] are functionally required. An array of roles well suited to the achieved level of the productive forces tends to be established because it is so suited and tends to perdure as long as it remains so. The arrays of roles in the period of history to which the theory is addressed divide role-occupants into classes bearing antagonistic interests. Accordingly, there is a permanent disposition towards class struggle, victory tending to go to the class capable of and interested in maintaining or introducing the array of roles indicated by the current technology. The function of superstructural institutions is to stabilise, by many means, the existing role-array, but they also become (what they always are in some measure) the theatre of social conflict when convulsive changes are in the offing. None of this occurs except through the agency of human beings, whose actions are inspired by their ideas, but whose ideas are more or less determined by their economic roles.

Plamenatz experiences difficulty when he confronts Marxian theoretical constructions because he is disposed to see in society only a collection of activities, not positions; or, what comes to the same thing, he concentrates on what he calls 'social life' and fails to distinguish it from the social structure in which it occurs. Hence he takes it for granted[24] that anyone who speaks of 'social existence' must or should have something like 'forms of social activity' or 'conventional modes of behaviour' in mind, when the phrase invites or at the very least permits a quite different interpretation. In his emphasis on men engaged in sundry social behaviours, Plamenatz misses what Marx aptly called the *anatomy* of society.[25]

Plamenatz writes:

> Social conditions consist, presumably, in social relations, and these relations are defined in terms of conventional modes of behaviour. John is the husband of Mary (1) if he behaves towards her in the ways required or expected of a husband, or (2) if it is recognised that he has the right and duty to do so.[26]

What is first said about John is strictly speaking false. His behaving in that or in any other way is not sufficient for his being Mary's husband. Nor is it necessary, since if it were, husbands could not be criticised for failing their wives. The second characterisation of husbandhood is closer to the truth, though it would be closer still if it were put the other way around ('If John is the husband of Mary, then it is recognised ...'), since John could acquire the relevant rights and duties other than by marrying Mary.

Speaking less strictly, one may allow that each definition captures a sense of 'husband', regardless of the rules laid down by Church and State. But my principal criticism is that Plamenatz conceals the large difference between the alternatives when he casually juxtaposes them. The difference between definitions featuring behaviour and definitions featuring rights and duties is that the first specify the kinds of actions performed in society and the second specify its roles. Only the second may be used to reveal the network of ties connecting society's members. The social network and social activity are of course intimately related, just as the anatomy and physiology of an organism are. But the network and the activity are nevertheless different, not least with respect to their relevance and propriety in explanations of social phenomena.

In this section I have leaned heavily on the concept of a role, which must now be explained.

V

We need a specially tailored concept of role for our purposes. I shall distinguish three familiar concepts ordinarily expressed by the term 'role': the concepts of a social role, a dramatic role, and a function. The technical concept we need is a development of the first of these commonplace concepts.

'Judge', 'industrialist', 'farmer', 'soldier', 'teacher', 'physician', 'electrician' – such descriptions may be used to denote persons in virtue of the social roles they occupy. Each such role imposes duties upon and affords rights to its occupant. Right and duty are frequently identical in content. Thus a physician has the right and the duty to dispense medicine, a soldier the right and the duty to bear arms. I have elsewhere[27] defined 'social role' as follows: 'A description under which a person falls allocates him to a social role or position in the measure that the attribution to him of some rights and/or duties is inseparable from the application of the description.'

The phrase 'or position' is added to highlight the fact that one can occupy a role without playing it, for[28] one naturally speaks of occupying rather than playing a position. People occupy roles without playing them when they lack the will or ability to play, or when obstacles prevent their doing so. They retain their rights and duties, but they do not exercise and fulfil them. The distinction between occupancy and performance helps us to see how the first may causally explain the second. What is more, a role which is not even occupied may be part of the social structure. Examples will be found in the 'Situations Vacant' columns of newspapers. Not every post there advertised is well enough established to qualify as an unoccupied role in the social structure, but some are. Certainly, the role of president has not disappeared from those American universities which have lost their president and have not yet hired a new one.

Now if one specifies and relates all the social roles in a society, one has characterised it as a social structure. The relevant relations between roles show up in the rights and duties occupants of roles have by virtue of their occupancy vis-à-vis occupants of other roles by virtue of their occupancy.

But society is not only a structure. It is also to some extent, or in certain ways, a drama; and to some extent, or in certain ways, a system. And there is a concept of role corresponding to each of these two further ways of conceiving society. (The sociologist Erving Goffman is the acknowledged master of the dramaturgical conception of society. Talcott Parsons is the most famous exponent of the systemic view. Each makes crucial but quite different use of the term 'role'.)

The role of Hamlet is not a social role. Typically, the social role of the person who plays the role of Hamlet is that of an actor. And even if an actor plays Hamlet and no other role every night for decades, his social role is that of an actor, more specifically, of an actor of the role of Hamlet, not the role of Hamlet. It is his right and duty to play Hamlet, which is not a social but a dramatic role. It may seem odd to attribute this right and duty to him, but not when one reflects that he may legitimately complain if he is prevented from appearing on stage as Hamlet, and others may legitimately complain if he decides not to appear.

The term 'role', then, may denote a position in society, a part in a play, and – this is our third concept – a function in a system or scheme. When we say of a piston that it plays a role within a mechanical system, we mean that it fulfils a function within that system. Functions may also attach to persons, as in 'Corporal Smith's function in the strategic scheme is to detect the enemy's movements'. Bagehot thought the function or role of the monarch in the British political system is to dignify the constitution, or, as we might unkindly put it, to deflect attention from the sordid doings of government. But this is not the monarch's social role in the defined sense.

Having distinguished three types of role, we may now note that there usually are dramatic and functional aspects to social roles proper. Consider a judge. His social role is defined by his duty to render sound verdicts and sentences, his right to question counsel, and so on. But judges often perform that role with a great show of solemnity and sobriety. One may then say that they play a role, drawing attention not to their performance of a social role in the defined sense, but to the dramatic quality of the performance. (The histrionic aspect can become mandatory, in which case one may say it is part of the judge's (social) role to play a (dramatic) role.) Finally, one may say that it is the role of a judge to help maintain social stability, thereby specifying the judge's function. The social role is so articulated that its effective performance should contribute to the fulfilment of the associated function. But the means does not always secure the end, and the space between them is the difference between social roles and roles in the sense of functions.

Other examples. One may hypothesise that the role of mothers is to preserve and transmit tradition, meaning that is their function, but they may fail to do so while impeccably carrying out the duties of their social role. One may say, with Schumpeter, that the function of the entrepreneur is to introduce innovations, but his social role, the position which enables him to do that, will be defined, differently, in terms of his rights and duties vis-à-vis shareholders, managers, workers, other entrepreneurs, etc.

Persons standing in the production relations which compose an economic structure occupy economic roles, which are a species of social role. Typical economic roles are the ownership roles of landowner, serf, wage-labourer, shopkeeper and merchant; and the work roles of building labourer, electrical engineer, personnel manager and blacksmith. A person's 'being', in the sense of Marx's thesis, is the economic role he occupies. Enough has been said to show that his occupancy of it does not involve his having a particular consciousness in a sense which excludes its being a result of that occupancy. 'Derivative' elements are not integral to social being in that way. But if we left the analysis here they would be integral in another way, for a different reason.

For social roles are defined with reference to rights and duties which, being normative properties, are inadmissible by historical materialism as constitutive features of economic positions: they belong in the superstructure. The remedy is to construct a concept of social role parallel to the one defined, but which is not normative. This is achieved by replacing reference to rights and duties with reference to powers and constraints. Economic roles in the required technical sense will be determined not by what persons are *de jure* entitled and obliged to do, but by what they are *de facto* able and constrained (= not able not) to do. The procedure for constructing power-analogues of rights has been given in detail elsewhere,[29] and the construction of constraints corresponding to duties may be accomplished in a similar fashion. The same article shows how a historical materialist may acknowledge, without damage to his theory, that it is usually rights and duties which guarantee powers and constraints. The 'concession' is unembarrassing, since it is compatible with the thesis that rights and duties have the content they do because their having it helps maintain powers and constraints appropriate to the given state of the productive forces. The relationship between the positive and the normative is an aspect of the fact, which every clear-minded Marxist should insist on, that *the base needs a superstructure*. To elaborate further would be to reproduce the material of the earlier article.

NOTES

* Marx–Engels, *Selected Works* (Moscow, 1958) I 363. The phrase 'social being' is a translation of 'gesellschaftliches Sein', which may also be rendered 'social existence'. The two translations are used indifferently throughout the present paper.

1. Such as the relation between the emergence of Protestantism and the rise of capitalism in Europe, the reason for the arrested development of capitalism in Asia, the persistence of the Jews as a distinct ethno-religious group, the essence of the conflict in the American Civil War, the impetus behind late nineteenth-century American imperialism, the sources of fascist strength, and many other questions.

2. *Capital* (Moscow, 1961) I 513-14. This is why history (sometimes called 'pre-history') stops once nature has been transformed into man's home. Marxian optimism about the future complements Marxian pessimism about the past.

3. For justification, see *The German Ideology* (London, 1965) p. 37.

4. *Capital*, I 82 n. Marx goes on to make subtler claims which escape the present criticism.

5. *German Marxism and Russian Communism* (London, 1954); *Man and Society* (London, 1963) vol. II; *Ideology* (London, 1970).

6. 'On Some Criticisms of Historical Materialism', *Proceedings of the Aristotelian Society*, supp. vol. (1970). (Hereafter referred to as 'O.S.C.'.)

7. See below, p. 89.

8. *Man and Society*, II 283.

9. Ibid.

10. Ibid., pp. 284-5. Note that the nature of Plamenatz's argument is such that, according to him, no number of sides of social life, including all of them, can have the determining role in question.

11. Ibid., p. 278.

12. By extension of the method used to extrude law from the economic structure in O.S.C.

13. Or, as he also says, 'forms of social activity'. Nothing depends on which alternative we select.

By 'conventional modes of behaviour' Plamenatz means all modes of behaviour governed by rules or norms, not just behaviour (like shaking hands to signify welcome) which is, as we say, merely a convention.

14. That Plamenatz sometimes means institutions in this sense is shown by the fact that he also says (p. 48) that social conditions consist of social relations. Indeed, an alternative version of his argument, which would not improve it, begins as follows:

1. Social being consists of social relations.
2. Social relations are defined by conventional modes of behaviour.
∴ 3. Social being is defined by conventional modes of behaviour.

The rest would be as before, and the equivocation besetting the original derivation of (3) would give way to difficulties concerning his use of 'define'.

15. p. 42: '... the contrast [Marx] makes between social existence and consciousness is odd and misleading. Taken literally, it suggests that there are forms of social activity that do not involve the use of ideas.' From this it appears that Plamenatz takes Marx's 'social being' to be a set of forms of social activity. This unwarranted supposition is refuted in the next section.

16. p. 66.

17. To avoid further typographical barbarism, I shall henceforth use 'economic role' to mean 'economic role or roles'. The set of economic roles a single man occupies may be thought of as a single composite economic role.

18. The distinction here introduced is elaborated and defended in the next section.

19. Apparent ones arise for the different claim: 'If a man does what a shopkeeper does, performs that role, he will have the ideas of a shopkeeper as a result.'

20. See *Ideology*, p. 47, for uncertainty about this matter, which is generally neglected in Marx studies.

21. This identification is explained and defended in O.S.C.

22. Note that 'forms of social consciousness' are mentioned in the Preface alongside reference to the superstructure, and not as part of it.

23. For the characterisation of these two types of roles see O.S.C.

24. See above, note 15.

25. In the Preface. In the Introduction (unpublished by Marx) to the same work he used a similar image, referring to society's 'skeleton structure'. See *The Critique of Political Economy* (Chicago, 1904) p. 310. See also the *Grundrisse* (Berlin, 1953) p. 554, where the same analogy is used in the context of economic theory.

26. *Ideology*, p. 48 (I have inserted the numbers).

27. See 'Beliefs and Roles', *Proceedings of the Aristotelian Society* (1966-7) pp. 20-2, for further discussion of the definition.

28. Outside the special context of sports or games, which are not discussed here. I am not giving an exhaustive account of 'role' and its cognates.

29. See O.S.C.

PART TWO

Diplomatic History and International Relations

5 The Revolution of 1905 and Russian Foreign Policy

BERYL J. WILLIAMS

RUSSIAN foreign policy at the turn of the twentieth century can perhaps best be understood in the context of what has been termed 'conservative nationalism'.[1] Under Witte the Ministry of Finance had presided over an economic policy designed to give Russia the where-withal to take her full place as a European great power – a developed industry, a modern army and an efficient communication system. The theories behind the internal policies of the end of the nineteenth century, associated with the influential figure of Konstantin Pobedo-nostsev, were simultaneously concerned with the development of Russia as a powerful and united state. The autocracy was to be strong and centralised, ruling a nation unified in faith, government and, as far as possible, language. To Pobedonostsev and many of the bureau-cracy in the 1890s Witte's economic Westernisation did not promise political reform. On the contrary, it served as a method not of changing but of strengthening the autocracy and the state. Given unity and centralisation at home and a position as a great power in Europe, Russia would be in a position to fulfil her unique mission as a partially Asiatic power.

By the early years of the twentieth century Russia's expansion into the maritime regions of the Far East and into Central Asia, which had been a feature of Russian policy since the mid-nineteenth century, was being extended into dominance over neighbouring and weaker Asiatic states. Without political annexation, which would run the risk of clashes with other interested European powers, Russia was establish-ing a form of economic imperialism destined to lead, in the fullness of time and with the collapse of the power concerned, to peaceful absorption achieved through diplomatic agreement with the other great powers. A policy of diplomatic control, economic dependence and political influence, already a long-established, if not always successful, policy with regard to the Balkans, was well advanced by

1904 in several areas of Asia.[2] The motives behind this policy were a complex mixture of natural extension from existing areas of control; a search for markets and resources; a desire to protect what were seen as Russian interests from foreign, normally English, competition; and a search for great-power standing. The concept of a 'civilising mission in Asia' was heard frequently in military and bureaucratic circles by the 1890s, and was not only confined to local agents engaged in the 'great game'.[3]

In the Far East, where the policy was most fully developed, Witte achieved considerable success in his aim of dominating northern China by controlling the trade and economic resources of Manchuria. Russian control of the Chinese Eastern Railway and the Russo-Chinese Bank, as well as administrative control of the major railway and urban centres such as Harbin and Port Arthur, gave her a dominant influence in the area. Benckendorff, the Russian Ambassador in London, described Manchuria in 1903 as 'a question where Russian interests predominate'.[4]

In Persia a similar and equally successful policy had been developed, with the exception of a railway network.[5] The establishment of a troop of Persian Cossacks under Russian officers, the acquisition of concessions, the establishment of a bank, and above all loans amounting to over £3 million to the Shah, secured for Russia a dominant influence in the north and aroused the lively apprehension of the British.[6] Witte later declared in his memoirs that 'the entire northern part of Persia was intended, as if by nature, to become in the future, if not a part of the Russian Empire, then in any case a country under our complete protection'.[7]

Military and local officials talked, in terms which went beyond northern Persia, of a trans-Persian railway, a port on the Persian Gulf and ultimate control of all Persia, including Seistan, as well as Afghanistan and possibly Tibet.[8] In both the Middle East and the Far East local officials and right-wing extremists talked, and occasionally acted, in extreme terms. To those in charge of Government policy, economic expansion was intended to be kept strictly within the bounds of what could be achieved peacefully and absorbed. Nevertheless, the official policy of the Foreign Office was not necessarily far behind its unofficial advance guard. As late as October 1904, despite the Russo-Japanese War, the Foreign Minister wrote, with regard to Persia, that Russian policy was 'to preserve the integrity and the inviolability of the possessions of the Shah, without seeking territorial accretions for ourselves, without allowing the hegemony of a Third Power, gradually to subject Persia to our dominant influence ... in other words our task is to make Persia politically an obedient and useful, i.e. sufficiently powerful, instrument in our hands, and economically, to preserve for ourselves the large Persian market for a free application of Russian labour and capital'.[9] These words could equally have applied to either China or Turkey.

The success of the policy depended on Russia achieving a powerful and independent voice in European diplomacy. Count Lamsdorff, the Foreign Minister at the beginning of the twentieth century, was a close friend and admirer of Witte,[10] and the policy of the Ministry of Finance was backed by the Foreign Office, always provided it did not clash with the demands of European alignments. The basis of Russian foreign policy since the early 1890s had been the Franco-Russian alliance, but Lamsdorff did not see this as necessarily tying him in any way. His policy, and that of Witte, was to keep Russia in an independent, mediating position in European affairs – what a career diplomat described with approval as retaining 'les mains libres'.[11]

The outbreak of the Russo-Japanese War was the result of the breakdown of the above policy, not necessarily inherent in the policy itself.[12] If a danger of war was felt to be inherent in the process, it was more likely to be in Central Asia against England than in the Pacific. The war was a symptom of the dangers of the arbitrariness of the Russian Government structure rather than the faulty nature of the policy as such.

At first the war had relatively little effect on Foreign Office thinking. Lamsdorff saw no reason to abandon his European strategy. Even after the Dogger Bank incident brought Russia to the brink of war with England, he described Russia's position as that of 'une rich épousée', still benefiting from being a desirable ally for other powers and as yet uncommitted.[13] More remarkably, the forward policy in Persia was not radically slowed down. The financial cost of the operation had been causing disquiet since before the war, and once war was engaged in the Far East it was officially reviewed. In February 1904, just after the outbreak of war, Count Kokovtsov, the Finance Minister, informed the Tsar of a Persian request for a new loan. This was approved but with reservations. In June a special conference under Lamsdorff reconsidered the economic implications of Russia's Persian policy and agreed with Kokovtsov that financial aid should be given 'only if the expenditure brought real advantages to our interests'.[14] But no sizeable withdrawal in Russian policy was considered and in October, the same month as the Dogger Bank incident, Lamsdorff issued instructions to the new Russian Ambassador in Teheran which laid down a forward policy not only in the north but also in the Gulf and rejected any compromise with England. Consulates were established in the south (for example at Bandar Abbas) and attempts were made to control the Persian Army financially. The ministerial conference on Persia late in August 1905 preserved the Russian veto on railways which, it was feared, would lead to economic competition in the north from cheaper British imports.[15]

By the summer of 1905, however, the situation was beginning to change. Defeat of the army in the Far East, revolutionary disturbances in European Russia and the naval catastrophe at Tsushima in May 1905 altered the situation. It was obvious by May that the war could not be won without large reinforcements and reorganisation – which the revolutionary situation in Russia and the unpopularity of the war made virtually impossible. A Council of War declared that the preservation of internal order must take precedence over the war effort and, as attention focused on home affairs, negotiation with the Japanese began to be considered.[16] The question was how far this would affect the general orientation of foreign policy.

The next two years were to see considerable debate as to the future of Russian foreign policy.[17] The conclusion of the Anglo-Russian agreement in August 1907 and the Near Eastern crisis of 1908-9 have often been interpreted as the result of a radical reorientation of policy, a shift of interest from Asia to Europe associated with the name of Alexander Isvolsky.[18] To some extent this is what happened, but it is probably a mistake to see it as the result of a specific policy. The formulation of foreign policy during these vital years was subjected to considerable pressures, as much internal as international, and everyone's, including the new Foreign Minister's, prime attention was focused on internal events during 1905-6.[19]

The contradictions inherent in the policy of conservative nationalism became violently apparent in the early months of 1905. The results of the hoped-for industrial growth and national cohesion were seen to be workers' and peasants' uprisings, national minority movements, revolutionary agitation and a strong liberal movement demanding political reform. The confusion of internal policies and the uncertainty of the Government in dealing with them are reflected in foreign policy. As always at times of crisis, the relatively automatic running of the bureaucracy broke down and the personal and arbitrary nature of Tsarist control, a personal control Nicholas II had been deliberately enforcing since before the Russo-Japanese War,[20] became more apparent. Foreign policy was, and remained after the creation of the Duma, the prerogative of the Tsar. Particularly, as at this period, when there was no strong or experienced minister in control of foreign policy, his personal control made any coherent policy, or one directly related to long-term national interests, almost impossible.[21] Lamsdorff was described by the French Ambassador as 'a Minister of Foreign

Affairs "à la russe", which is to say that he did not have charge of the foreign policy but only the diplomacy of Russia, with the mission of adapting the latter to the former'.[22] Isvolsky possibly had more direct influence over Nicholas II, but he also told Kokovtsov that he had been instructed by the Tsar not to keep the Council of Ministers informed as to the affairs of the diplomatic service.[23] Specific issues, such as the possibility of negotiation with England in 1906-7 over Central Asia, were debated in the Council of Ministers. At such discussions the military were represented and, in so far as they concerned Asia, the Minister of Finance.[24] Nevertheless, the decision remained with the Tsar. Nicholas II's arbitrary and vacillating control over foreign affairs during this period made the situation confusing, but it cannot be said that the advice he received was either clear or consistent.

Basically, the problem concerned a choice of allies. The defeats in the Far East and the revolutionary situation meant that Lamsdorff's balancing policy would be difficult to retain, at least in the short term. During the Russo-Japanese War Wilhelm II made two overtures to Russia regarding the possibility of a Russo-German alliance – in October 1904 after the Dogger Bank incident and at Björkö in July 1905.[25] On both these occasions the Tsar appeared to be personally in favour, and Witte also hoped for a Russo-German agreement with which France would be associated.[26] The possibility of a Russo-German alliance divorced from France, and presumably involving the end of the Franco-Russian alliance, as a revival of the Dreikaiserbund with Austrian and possibly Italian adherence, was raised by Lamsdorff after the renewal of the Anglo-Japanese alliance in August 1905 and its extension to India. Russo-Austrian relations had been good since 1903 and it is possible that this idea was taken seriously by Russia, but it failed to meet with German approval.[27]

There were many arguments in favour of a closer rapprochement with Germany at that time and they were particularly attractive in court and among right-wing circles.[28] The dynastic ties between St Petersburg and Berlin were strong, and at a time of revolution much was heard of a monarchical solidarity pact as a bulwark against revolution.[29] The right wing were particularly vocal in their pro-German sympathies during crisis-points in the revolutionary period – the summer and autumn of 1905 and again in the summer of 1906 when, after the dissolution of the first Duma, a new wave of violence was feared. Right-wing associations sprang up over the spring and summer of 1905 calling for strong monarchical control, if necessary by dictatorial means, and these tended to be pro-German in foreign policy. In 1906 there was some talk in these circles of German aid to put down the revolution. Similarly, after the change in the fundamental laws in June 1907 there was considerable right-wing and pro-German activity in the press and court circles.[30]

Witte, who finally persuaded the Tsar to accept a constitution in October 1905, saw the right wing as one of the greatest dangers. He complained to the English Chargé d'Affaires early in November that 'the real danger . . . was not liberalism but the worst form of reaction'.[31]

There were also considerations of more weight than monarchical sentiment. Germany was by far Russia's most important trade partner,[32] and a new commercial treaty was signed in July 1904.[33] The war and the revolutionary situation disrupted the flow of wheat exports from Odessa,[34] and commercial circles were apprehensive. A closer political link would preserve Russia's only large grain market in Western Europe and hopefully enable Russia to control the effects of German competition in Russia itself and in the Near and Middle East.[35]

Probably of more influence on Government thinking were the arguments of the military. Defence of Russia's long western frontier was the War Office's first military priority, with the preservation of order at home second and Central Asian security third.[36] By the summer of 1905 the military situation on the Western front was acknowledged to be deplorable. Military strength was reduced as reinforcements were sent to the Far East, morale was low and combat-readiness non-existent.[37] A year later General Palitsyn was to declare that the military situation was worse on the Western front than in the Far East and that security in Europe could only be ensured by an agreement with Germany. He therefore argued that any agreement with England in Asia should be strictly limited.[38] The naval situation, after the sending of the Baltic fleet to the Pacific, was if anything worse, and the navy acknowledged its incapacity to defend either Kronstadt or the capital if a war were to break out in the Baltic.[39] Germany, it was argued, was the natural, 'strong', ally of Russia, particularly at a time of military weakness.[40]

Alternatively, there was the policy, already considered at the end of the 1890s and raised again by Benckendorff in London in 1903,[41] of an agreement with England over Central Asia. The French Ambassador in St Petersburg regarded this as likely early in April 1904 and saw the encouragement of it as a major part of his instructions.[42] The English also believed the Russian Government to be in favour of this in the spring and summer of 1904,[43] although the Dogger Bank episode obviously put an end to any immediate possibility of negotiations.

Between Björkö and the dissolution of the first Duma (July 1905–July 1906) the Government wavered between a rapprochement with

England or Germany and concessions or repression at home. The lack of a consistent policy was commented on by all observers.[44] The Tsar, insistent upon his own autocratic power, was also indecisive in implementing it. Personnel changes were frequent and arbitrary. The Council of Ministers remained individually responsible to the Tsar and did not form a united Government body. The nearest the Government came to a unified force was when, on 26 October 1905, the Tsar empowered Witte to 'unify all government activities'.[45] The result, as Dr Dillon had commented in July 1904, was that Russian policy was 'the resultant of conditions of which some elude analysis, most are bound up with her internal structure, and all are proof against diplomatic reagents'.[46] The Tsar was more influenced by court cliques than by the official Government of the day,[47] and his most important adviser was probably D. F. Trepov, the Governor-General of St Petersburg who was made Assistant Minister of the Interior in control of police and military affairs in May 1905. Under Witte's administration he became Palace Commandant. His concern was for the personal safety of the Tsar and his family rather than the implementation of any consistent policy.[48]

Witte's personal success in persuading the Tsar to opt for conciliation on the home front in October took the Council of Ministers, who had not been informed, by surprise,[49] but the October Manifesto, to his dismay,[50] did not lead to a restoration of peace. November and December were the most dangerous months the Government had yet faced. A renewed strike movement in November, the Moscow uprising, peasant and national minority movements, army mutinies and a financial crisis brought the Government to the edge of disaster. There was felt to be a 'danger that the existing regime, and even the state itself, would collapse'.[51]

The strike movement and the St Petersburg Soviet were suppressed by Durnovo by the end of December. Early in January Witte, who had already made one overture to England through Dillon in October, proposed to London a quick settlement through a monarchical pact on the lines of Björkö, by-passing the slow channels of regular diplomacy.[52] The decision to seek an agreement with England seems to have been made by Witte and Lamsdorff during the crisis months of October–December 1905. Although he was later specifically associated with this policy, Isvolsky did not initiate it. Together with the Russian Ambassadors in London and Paris he had been an advocate of agreement since at least 1904,[53] but he seems to have been appointed because he was an advocate of the alliance and would be acceptable to the liberals, more than because of a change of policy in May 1906. Lamsdorff and Witte were both removed from office in a Cabinet reshuffle – but for internal reasons: the former because of his refusal to work with the Duma and the latter because the Tsar wished to be rid of him.[54] Indeed, the English were apprehensive that Isvolsky's appointment would lessen the chances of an alliance rather than strengthen them. Isvolsky was widely regarded as pro-German and had hoped for a transfer to Berlin. The English Under-Secretary minuted on the report merely 'I feel certain that he will follow the current of the moment which does not appear to be unfriendly at present'.[55]

The Cadets, who dominated the first Duma, tended to equate a constitutional regime at home with an English alliance – as did Isvolsky and some of his supporters in the diplomatic service.[56] Isvolsky told Milyukov in 1906 that 'basic political reform will bring us closer to Europe'.[57] It is possible that Witte, even if reluctantly, also assumed this connection. At the same time as the overture to England in October 1905 he started negotiations to include 'men of public confidence', including Shipov and Guchkov, in the Cabinet.[58] In the summer of 1906 Isvolsky and Stolypin, with the Tsar's approval, also started secret talks with Cadet leaders. One proposal even considered Milyukov as Minister of Foreign Affairs,[59] but was rejected by Milyukov.

The Cadets before 1908 normally supported Isvolsky as the best Foreign Minister they were likely to get. Isvolsky was in fact by far the most constitutionally-minded of the Council of Ministers and was barely tolerated by them. His influence generally seems to have been small.[60] Before Stolypin's increasing use of extraordinary legislation after November 1906, which seems to have estranged them,[61] he was associated with the Premier and they co-operated well in the field of foreign affairs. Both were associated with the Octobrists – Isvolsky was actually a member of the party and Stolypin was closely connected to it through his brother.[62]

It is difficult, however, to discern any clear policy formation either in the internal or external fields. Witte's negotiations with Shipov failed over his insistence on the appointment of a well-known proponent of repression, P. N. Durnovo, as Minister of the Interior,[63] while Trepov's and the Tsar's support for the negotiations with the Cadets in May 1906 was motivated by fear of violence if Goremykin's threat to dissolve the Duma was carried out.[64]

The crisis of July 1906 was a typical piece of arbitrary compromise by Nicholas himself. The Duma was dissolved – with little in the way of violent reaction. Negotiations with the Cadets were broken off, but Goremykin was replaced by Stolypin and the extreme right-wing members[65] dismissed – all without any consultation with the Council of Ministers as such. The negotiations with England continued, but increasingly, as the Government recovered its position, a right turn was felt in home affairs which culminated in the new electoral law of 3 June 1907.[66]

Formal negotiations between England and Russia were launched on 7 June 1906.[67] The decision with regard to this was crucially influenced by French diplomatic pressure and financial extremity.[68] Whether or not Russian finances were sound at the beginning of the Russo-Japanese War,[69] it was obvious from the beginning of hostilities that further loans would be necessary if the gold standard was to be retained.

Negotiations for loans were started in both Paris and Berlin as a result of a decision of the Finance Committee a month after the Japanese attack.[70] A loan from the German firm of Mendelssohn was agreed in January 1905,[71] but Berlin could not raise the amounts of money that would be needed. It was obvious by 1905 that an appeal would have to be made to France, and after the Peace of Portsmouth Rouvier offered a loan which included English participation.[72] Witte hoped throughout the summer of 1905 to obtain an international loan which would include Germany and thus retain Russia's freedom of action. An international consortium which included the house of Mendelssohn negotiated in October in a strike-bound St Petersburg, but discussions were broken off by the October Manifesto.[73] Again in 1906 Witte warned Berlin that German non-participation in the projected international loan would mean Russia's increasing political dependence on England and France.[74] The French Government, to the fury of the Russian liberals, went to considerable trouble to pressure its own financial houses, who were not surprisingly uncertain as to how far Russia was a sound investment, and Rouvier forced a small loan in October 1905.[75]

The Russian Government's need for money was undeniable by the end of 1905. The failure of the October Manifesto to restore public confidence resulted in a run on the banks. Gold flowed out of the country and by December notes were being issued over the reserve. Early in December the new Finance Minister considered stopping the issue of notes. The Finance Committee still hoped to avoid this, but the threat of a commercial and industrial crisis during the December uprising in Moscow meant that the withdrawal of gold had to be artificially controlled. The Government was faced with coming off the gold standard or admitting bankruptcy. Loan repayments to Berlin due in December were delayed.[76]

Two days after the Moscow uprising was suppressed, Kokovtsov left for Paris to negotiate a small loan, but the cost of pacifying operations in Moscow and the provinces meant that the 100 million roubles advanced at $5\frac{1}{2}$ per cent and a small loan from Berlin did not wipe out the deficit.[77] Under the advice of Raffalovich, the agent of the Finance Ministry in Paris, and Noetzlin, the director of the Bank of France and the Low Countries, Kokovtsov started negotiations which led in April to the large international loan, with English participation, to cover the entire Russian debt.[78]

It was realised by all involved that French co-operation would have to be paid for. Although in November 1905 the Tsar had opposed a rapprochmement with England as unnecessary,[79] he himself suggested co-operation against Germany at the Algeciras Conference to Kokovtsov before the latter left for Paris.[80] Witte's approach to London at the same time clearly shows the connection between the political and financial policies.[81] The Russian delegates at Algeciras were instructed to give full support to the French and English,[82] and Germany withdrew from the international loan. As the British Chargé d'Affaires wrote from St Petersburg in February, 'the main preoccupation of everyone is ... not the Duma or the government but finance'.[83] The French Government, who had throughout pressurised St Petersburg towards a closer collaboration with England, was not concerned with the Duma either and readily accepted the Russians' legal arguments that the loan did not need Duma ratification.[84]

The degree of influence that the Russian dependence on the French money market had on the decision to negotiate with England is difficult to assess in detail. Most Soviet writers give it prime importance,[85] whilst J. P. Sontag has recently argued that it played 'a decidedly ancillary role', and that the negotiations were used 'to achieve diplomatic goals it [the St Petersburg Government] had already decided on'.[86] It is certainly true that high finance was not a subject which normally preoccupied European chancelleries, and that Algeciras was as much a good opportunity to show support for a policy already considered, as a necessary price for French credit. However, as M. Griault has stressed, the loan compromised Russia and the French certainly saw it in this light.[87] This loan, more than most, was regarded by all observers as having a political character. Nevertheless, the fact that the agreement with England was actually concluded as late as August 1907 when the Government was both solvent and stable shows perhaps the force of the other considerations behind the policy.

These factors were largely military and they related to the situation in Central Asia. Russian expansion in Central Asia, her influence in the Middle East and her expanding railway network along the borders of Afghanistan were making the defence of India an increasingly expensive and politically explosive issue for the British Government.[88] On their side, as the boundaries became virtually conterminous and as increasing communications made troop deployment faster and more efficient, the Russians both talked of expanding their influence in Asia and worried that the English would threaten what were seen as existing Russian spheres of influence or strategic interests. The ever-present possibility of a renewed war in Asia would, after the renewal of the Anglo-Japanese treaty in August 1905, probably involve fighting both powers, not just one, and made the idea of a settlement of outstanding conflicts in Asia more attractive – if not essential.[89] Kuropatkin's argument that the western frontier was of the greatest importance to Russian security was not questioned. Nevertheless, the western frontier was not threatened from outside in 1905-6, however troubled it might be internally. After the Reval meeting in 1908, military and naval chiefs or staff met to consider possible German actions in the Baltic if war broke out, and the Franco-Russian military conversations of 1906 assumed that future military planning would be anti-German.[90] But in 1906 there was no immediate danger from Germany, whereas Kitchener's proposals for increased Indian defence were regarded by the Russians as a threat to Central Asia and the independence of Afghanistan. A British establishment of control over Seistan was also feared.[91]

In February 1906 there was also a panic in St Petersburg regarding a possible revival of the war with Japan with increased Japanese strength in South Manchuria and Korea, and General Unterberger (Governor-General of the Amur Region) pressed strongly for reinforcements in November.[92] Naturally, there were voices who talked in revanchist terms.[93] Isvolsky complained to Benckendorff of military members of the Council called to discuss the negotiations with England who had learnt nothing and forgotten nothing from before the Russo-Japanese War.[94] There were groups in favour of war with Japan who argued in terms reminiscent of Plehve's 'small victorious war' that a campaign against the Japanese would be a way of fighting sedition at home. It cannot be said, indeed, that the military showed any marked enthusiasm for an agreement with Great Britain, which ran counter to so many traditions of the 1890s.

Nevertheless, it is noticeable that responsible army leaders on the whole supported Isvolsky and Kokovtsov's reiterated statements of the need to ensure peace[95] and prevent any drift towards the war of revenge that the English had feared in 1905.[96] The need for peace is a *leitmotif* of all the discussions. Witte declared in 1905 'we need 20 to 25 years to be occupied only with ourselves and to have quiet in foreign relations'.[97] The obvious reasons were the internal situation which did not allow Russia to pursue an aggressive foreign policy,[98] and the state of the armed forces. The military situation made any threat of another war in the immediate future a great danger to the country. Lamsdorff recognised as early as March 1905 that 'we positively do not have the foundation for entering on a struggle with England'.[99] It was later stated that as late as 1908 the army 'was not capable of fighting'.[100]

During these years the army was engaged on the vital task of ensuring order at home, and the constant threat of disorder among the armed forces overhung the entire period. Isvolsky referred to the Government's 'grave doubts' as to whether army discipline could be maintained after the Potemkin mutiny and disorders at Sevastopol in the summer of 1905.[101] Reports of mutinies reached St Petersburg from several regiments in the non-Russian borderlands and from Samara, Rostov and Kursk in the autumn.[102] In October there was a serious mutiny at Kronstadt, and Soviets of Soldiers' Deputies were organised in Moscow and Chita in November.[103] The Government blamed these on revolutionary agitators, and social democratic influence increased in the army throughout the year and was important in the uprisings at Kronstadt and Sveaborg in July 1906.[104]

Moreover, the areas which would be fields of operation in a war against England or Japan were heavily affected. Trouble along the Trans-Siberian Railway, at Irkutsk and at Harbin was affecting the war effort before the Peace of Portsmouth.[105] In October Vladivostok was virtually in the hands of mutineering reservists, and the Manchurian army disintegrated as it was withdrawn.[106] Trouble was reported in December at Krasnoyarsk and Harbin, and the entire state of Far Eastern defence gave considerable cause for alarm throughout 1906. In November of that year the Council of State Defence admitted that the Japanese were in a position to seize Manchuria, lay siege to Vladivostok and capture the mouth of the Amur.[107]

The Caucasus was in a state of civil war and under the flimsiest of control from Central Russia during the last months of 1905 and early 1906. December 1905 saw the height of the revolutionary movement at Tbilisi,[108] and in November 1905 the suppression of a mutiny at Tashkent led to a renewed strike wave.[109] In June 1906 the British Consul in Batum reported that army strength in Central Asia had declined by 15 per cent over the previous twelve months and that many battalions were under strength. Except for the Cossacks, all branches of the army in the area were reported to be unreliable.[110] In the border areas the revolutionary movement was linked to national minority demands; both the social democrats and the liberals had gained considerable support in these areas as a result of the Government's russification policy.[111] Ironically, the effects of the revolution spread from Russia into neighbouring areas and had an effect – against Russian interests – on constitutional movements in Persia and Turkey.[112] The two were linked in a Turkish invasion of certain border areas of Persia near the Caucasian border which began in 1905 and caused a minor diplomatic crisis early in 1908.[113] The British Ambassador explained Isvolsky's warlike posture over this by the effect the troops were having on an area (Azerbaijan) already badly troublesome.[114] The French Chargé d'Affaires reported that the troops in the area were not numerous and scarcely able to cope normally.[115] Although Isvolsky and Palitsyn proposed a limited war to remove the Turks, Stolypin firmly reiterated the argument used by both the above throughout 1905-6. 'A new mobilisation in Russia,' he said, 'would give strength to the revolution, from which we are only just beginning to recover. It is possible that in a few years, when we are fully pacified, Russia will again speak in her former language. But at the present time any policy except the most severely defensive would be the delirium of an abnormal government and it would bring in its wake danger for the dynasty.'[116]

The Persian revolution which forced a constitution on the Shah in December 1905 complicated the situation and was regarded as advantageous to Great Britain. The movement could be expected to lessen Russian influence in Teheran and make Russian aims in the area more difficult to attain.[117] St Petersburg was also worried by German influence in the Near and Middle East – a fear which became increasingly apparent as the negotiations progressed. The danger the Baghdad Railway and especially possible branch lines into Persia represented to Russian interests in Persia and Russian security in Central Asia was stressed in the discussion in the Council of Ministers,[118] and German influence on Persia was one factor in Isvolsky's aggressive stand over the frontier dispute with Turkey.[119]

The conclusion of the various conferences was not an abandonment of Russian aims in Asia. As Isvolsky put it, 'a choice must be made between an agreement capable of firmly securing at least a part of our interests, and rivalry under circumstances in which we lack the assurance that questions which concern us would not be decided without us and to the detriment of all our advantages'.[120] In other words, the Russian aim was to concentrate on securing those areas regarded as essential to Russian interests until such time as Russia would again be strong enough to talk in her 'former language'.

In Central Asia this meant northern Persia with a demarcation line which secured Teheran, although it abandoned Seistan and the Gulf, at least temporarily, to British influence.[121] Afghanistan was recog-

nised as within the British sphere of influence in exchange for
significant rights of border relations and commercial concessions,
which gave Russia the substance of her immediate interests. As
Isvolsky argued, Russia had not, in fact, been prepared to push her
demand in 1900 for direct relations and 'could hardly have chosen to
go to war with England over Afghanistan'.[122] Tibet, which was
accepted as being an English concern, was described by Benckendorff
as 'un bon débarras et rien de plus'.[123]

The agreement was intimately bound up with a settlement in the
Far East with England's ally, Japan. The two were negotiated parallel
to each other and their interconnection was realised by all concerned.
Isvolsky referred to them as jointly giving Russia the 'necessary
stability in foreign affairs'.[124] The policy of negotiation with Tokyo
led to considerable debate in St Petersburg. Apart from revanchist
groups, the opposition came from commercial concerns with an
interest in keeping Russia's protectionist position in Manchurian trade,
and it was as a concession to these that Isvolsky in 1908 abandoned
the free port policy with regard to Vladivostock. The Japanese
demands for free access for their ships along the Amur and Sungari
rivers and extensive shipping rights were hotly opposed during the
negotiations as leading to a 'Japanese economic conquest of Manchuria and the whole of the Far East'. The liberal paper, *Rech*, also
opposed Isvolsky's policy of settlement with Japan and proposed a
project close to Milyukov's heart, an Anglo-American-Russian agreement which would be anti-Japanese and which would secure the 'open-
door policy' in China.[125] Isvolsky rejected this both in 1906 and again
when the Americans proposed it three years later.

In November 1906 a committee agreed with Isvolsky that, in view
of a possible outbreak of conflict, the Japanese demands had to be
met to ensure peace.[126] The agreement, like those in Central Asia,
redefined Russia's essential interests. In practice it returned to a policy
similar to that advocated by Kuropatkin in 1903.[127] It ensured to
Russia recognition of northern Manchuria as her sphere of influence
and, leaving the south and Korea to the Japanese, enabled her to
consolidate and strengthen her position by a continuation of the pre-
1904 policy in more rigidly defined areas and under tighter control.
In fact considerable improvement in Russia's position had been made
by the time the Chinese Revolution occurred, in 1911. An English
War Office report of 1907 described Harbin as 'practically a Russian
town' which had been 'converted into an entrenched camp'.[128]
The plans for municipal government, interrupted by the war, were
continued under the active Director of the Chinese Eastern Railway,
General Horvath. In March 1908 a municipal council was elected

under Russian control, and by the time the situation started to attract Anglo-American attention the railway administration was holding powers equivalent to a colonial government and was described as such by Russian visitors.[129] Direct annexation was considered in 1910 but rejected, although in the opinion of the Minister of Finance 'the annexation of northern Manchuria was for the Russian Government an imperative necessity' and Russia was merely awaiting a favourable time.[130]

As Kuropatkin had realised earlier, economic control of northern Manchuria with Japanese support proved more rewarding than competing with her further south. This was to be Isvolsky's policy in 1909 when faced with competing railway development by international and especially American railway syndicates. The American scheme for internationalising railways in China was regarded in St Petersburg as threatening Russian interests.[131] Although the Finance Minister and Witte had earlier been in favour of selling the Chinese Eastern Railway to an American company (the Amur railway was started in 1908), Isvolsky firmly opposed any sale in 1909.[132] Faced with a choice between an agreement with either America or Japan, Isvolsky, to the annoyance of the Cadets, again chose Japan. The new Russo-Japanese treaty in July 1910 was in fact more aggressive than the earlier one and bordered 'close on a defensive alliance'.[133] As Isvolsky argued, 'if we reject the American proposal we will call forth the temporary cooling off of American friendship, but America will not declare war on us for this and its fleet will not arrive in Harbin, while in this connection Japan is considerably more dangerous'.[134] As always, the policy of Isvolsky, as had been the case before 1903, was the consolidation of economic and political control in areas where Russian dominance would not be challenged and through methods which would not lead to war. By 1912 Russian control of northern Manchuria had been extended to Mongolia – an area recognised as a Russian sphere of influence by Japan, although not by England, in 1907[135] and which replaced Tibet and southern Manchuria as a growth point for Russian interests.

Similarly, in the Middle East Isvolsky's policy of 'backs to the Asians' was more apparent than real. Afghanistan, despite the Amir's refusal to ratify the Anglo-Russian agreement,[136] caused little friction apart from a prolonged border incident in the form of some Jamshedi tribesmen who crossed into Russian territory.[137] In Persia, however, the Russians pursued an active policy of reconsolidating their hold on the north, threatened both by Germany and by the constitutional movement. At a series of conferences on Persia between 1908 and 1910 all the old aims and ambitions of re-establishing Russian influence over the whole of the country, including the Gulf, were reiterated. Vorontsov-Dashkov (Governor-General of the Caucasus) was typical in his statement that 'our influence in the east, close to the Caucasus – on Persia and Asia Minor – has been shaken but we will repair it and with great interest when Russia gets stronger'.[138]

Isvolsky was not against strengthening Russia's position in northern Persia and perhaps eventually extending it, but he insisted on the need to work for the moment within the framework of the Anglo-Russian alliance and complained unceasingly of Russian local agents who ignored instructions.[139] Nevertheless, he and Stolypin were hard put to it to restrain the Tsar and his military advisers from full-scale intervention on the side of the Shah.[140] In October 1908 Russian forces occupied Tabriz and the following year invaded Azerbaijan. By 1910 Russia's position in Persia was, if anything, stronger than it had been in 1904.

Isvolsky's desire to restrain his subordinates in this area was not due to a genuine reversal in Foreign Office policy with regard to Teheran, but more to the urgent need during the Balkan crisis of 1908-9 to co-operate with the British. As he had pointed out in the Council of Ministers which approved the Anglo-Russian agreement in August 1907, trouble could break out on the European front – especially the Balkans – at any time. If Russia's position in Asia was not stable, she could not 'raise her voice in solution of European problems and we will be a second-class power. We must put our interests in Asia in appropriate order or else we shall ourselves become an Asiatic state.'[141]

The underlying interest in the negotiations with England was a settlement of the Straits question in Russia's favour. The motives might be internal and Asiatic, the gains were to be European. A future control of Constantinople would be the crowning achievement of the whole policy of 'peaceful penetration', and was the goal of Isvolsky's whole programme. It had been referred to as a justification for agreement by Zinoviev in 1906.[142] Isvolsky, like many Octobrists, had neo-Panslavic ideas, but a settlement of the Straits question would increase Russia's standing, both at home and abroad, as a European great power far more effectively than a small victorious war in Asia.

The British declared sympathy, although not in any binding sense, during the negotiations,[143] but in this area German goodwill was also vital. Isvolsky had never seen the Anglo-Russian agreement as anti-German. Regarded as a Germanophile, and in close contact with the German Ambassador at St Petersburg, he was anxious not merely to keep Germany informed but positively to improve Russo-German relations in areas of conflict.[144] He attempted to initiate negotiations with regard to the Baghdad Railway in 1906 but failed.[145] However, the Baltic was an area where Russo-German interests were closely intertwined and where, like the Straits, Isvolsky could hope to complete the work of Gorchakov in overthrowing the remnants of the Treaty of Paris in 1856. Benckendorff also saw the Anglo-Russian agreements as leading to English support for Russian aims in the Baltic.[146]

In fact Isvolsky's aims in the Baltic went a good deal further than London realised and were distinctly anti-British in character. A Russian squadron landed on the Åland Islands in June 1906, ostensibly to prevent arms smuggling by revolutionaries. Isvolsky's aims became apparent at Swinemünde in August 1907 when he proposed to Germany plans for a Russo-German alliance to exclude all non-littoral states from Baltic affairs and to close its entrance in time of war. The plan, which was also to enable Russia to refortify the Åland Islands, was still being drawn up in October when the scheme foundered on Swedish objections.[147]

Another feature of the Swinemünde discussions, which also came to nothing, was Isvolsky's hope of renegotiating the Mürzsteg agreement of 1903 with Austria on terms more favourable to St Petersburg and thus developing Russia's aims in the Balkans by preserving the Russo-Austrian agreement and if possible associating England with it.[148] Indeed, Isvolsky's aims over 1906-7 seem to have been basically the establishment of a general European détente. As a French diplomatist said: 'Isvolsky wants to be friends with the whole world.'[149] In this his policy was much nearer to that of his predecessors than either he or Witte in their respective memoirs later allowed. The internal situation made the preservation of peace essential. Nevertheless, by keeping in good relations with both England and Germany Russia could be the third 'laughing party' as mediator in any future Anglo-German war[150] – a policy reminiscent of Lamsdorff's 'mains libres'. Neither French loans nor the Anglo-Russian entente was regarded as involving a basically anti-German standpoint. They were both short-term necessities whilst Russian internal stability and her Asiatic position were re-established after the Russo-Japanese War. Once Russia was strong again she could, in Stolypin's words, 'speak with her old voice'. This needed clever diplomacy to ensure peace whilst preserving essential Russian bases on which a forward policy in Asia could be re-established in the future. It also meant the development of Russia as a strong military power – reforms of the army and especially of the fleet. Isvolsky was one of the few members of the Council of Ministers and the Council of State Defence who supported the Tsar's decision to give priority to the development of a modern fleet.[151] To Isvolsky his policy depended on Russia reacquiring her status as a European great power and this, in the first decade of the twentieth century, meant the construction of dreadnoughts and participation in the arms race at sea. Stolypin referred to the fleet as a 'lever' for great-power status, and lamented the Duma's obstructionist tactics over this issue.[152] Although in fact it was the navy's minimum programme which was implemented and the fleet was confined to the Baltic – perhaps one reason for Isvolsky's interest in the area – Russia spent as much as England on its fleet between 1906 and 1914.[153]

Isvolsky said in this connection in 1907: 'At present we are talking about a war with Germany, but this is not the only combination; perhaps in the future political situation this will change and our present relations with Germany will be still more strengthened and develop into an alliance with her.' Once a modern fleet was built, he added, Russia 'will acquire great value as an ally'.[154] The British Ambassador at St Petersburg summed up the policy as to place 'Russia in an exceedingly favourable position. He [Isvolsky] would be on the best of terms with the two great Central Powers, he would have an ally in France; he would have removed all uneasiness to Russia from the part of Great Britain.'[155] The policy succeeded in Persia only because the British Foreign Minister chose to allow it to. In November 1908 Benckendorff warned his chief with regard to Persia that 'we are fond of assuming the standpoint that we may choose between a rapprochement with England and one with Germany. In reality we have to choose between isolation, which would be the outcome of a German–English understanding, or a rapprochement with England.'[156]

But if the policy on the whole succeeded in Asia, it failed in the two areas where its first successes were to have been achieved: in the Baltic and the Balkans. Its failure meant that the aim of balancing between the two developing power blocs collapsed. By the time Isvolsky left the Foreign Office, the catastrophe of his Balkan policy of 1908-9 had finally linked Russia to the Triple Entente, with which she was to enter the war in 1914, a mere nine years after 1905. The much-needed period of peace and reconstruction essential for Russia's aims both internally and externally was not achieved. With Isvolsky's removal and Stolypin's assassination the possibility, already much modified, of balance between autocracy and constitutionalism at home also came to an end.

NOTES

1. E. C. Thaden, *Conservative Nationalism in Nineteenth Century Russia* (Seattle, 1964); I. J. Lederer (ed.), *Russian Foreign Policy* (New Haven, 1962) pt I.
2. B. H. Sumner, *Tsardom and Imperialism in the Far East and the Middle East, 1880-1914* (London, 1942); D. J. Dallin, *The Rise of Russia in Asia* (New Haven, 1949). With regard to the Bosphorus, see *Krasny Arkhiv*, XVIII (1926) 18-25.
3. Sumner, *Tsardom and Imperialism*, p. 16.
4. J. A. White, *The Diplomacy of the Russo-Japanese War* (Princeton, 1964) pp. 26-8; E. H. Zabriskie, *American–Russian Rivalry in the Far East, 1895-1914* (Philadelphia, 1946) pp. 87-8; *British Documents on the Origin of the War, 1898-1914*, IV, no. 181b (hereafter cited as *B.D.*).
5. See F. Kazemzadeh, *Russia and Britain in Persia, 1864-1914* (New Haven, 1968) for a detailed study of Russian policy in Persia.
6. Grant Duff to Grey, 27 Feb 1906, no. 53, F.O. 371/106.
7. S. Witte, *Vospominaniya* (Berlin, 1922) II 407-8.
8. Kazemzadeh, *Russia and Britain in Persia*, pp. 401-2; P. C. Terenzio, *La Rivalité anglo-russe en Perse et en Afghanistan* (Paris, 1947) p. 81; B. G. Martin, *German–Persian Diplomatic Relations, 1873-1912* (The Hague, 1959) pp. 89-90.
9. Kazemzadeh, *Russia and Britain in Persia*, pp. 460-2; *Krasny Arkhiv*, LIII (4) (1932) 13-14.
10. G. Katkov and M. Futrell, 'Russian Foreign Policy, 1880-1914', in G. Katkov *et al* (eds.), *Russia Enters the Twentieth Century* (London, 1971) p. 27; E. de Schelking, *Recollections of a Russian Diplomat* (New York, 1918) p. 168; C. L. Seeger (ed.), *Memoirs of Alexander Iswolsky* (London, n.d.) p. 178.
11. M. de Taube, *La Politique russe d'avant-guerre et la fin de l'Empire des Tsars, 1904-17* (Paris, 1928) pp. 100-1.
12. R. E. Pipes, 'Domestic Policy and Foreign Affairs', in Lederer (ed.), *Russian Foreign Policy*, p. 154; for details, see A. Malozemoff, *Russian Far Eastern Policy, 1881-1914* (Berkeley, 1958).
13. Taube, *La Politique russe d'avant-guerre*, p. 19.
14. B. V. Anan'ich, 'Krizis ekonomicheskoi politika tsarizma v Persii v 1904-6 gg', *Istoricheskie Zapiski*, LXXIV (1963) 247.
15. Kazemzadeh, *Russia and Britain in Persia*, pp. 457-72; *Krasny Arkhiv*, LVI (1) (1953) 49-57; LIII (4) (1932) 13-30.
16. White, *The Diplomacy of the Russo-Japanese War*, p. 206; B. Romanov, 'Konets Russkoi-Yaponskoi voiny', in *Krasny Arkhiv*, XXVIII (3) (1928) 201; R. Griault, 'La Révolution russe de 1905 d'après quelques témoignages français', *Revue Historique*, CCXXX (1963) 101.
17. The Soviet scholar I. V. Bestuzhev has attempted to relate these debates to a struggle between social classes for influence in Government circles in *Bor'ba v Rossii po voprosam vneshnei politiki, 1906-10* (Moscow, 1961). The book is an expansion of two articles, in *Istoricheskie Zapiski*, LXIV (1959) and *Voprosy Istorii*, VI (1960).
18. F. Stieve, *Isvolsky and the World War* (London, 1926) p. 12; Bestuzhev, *Bor'ba v Rossii*, p. 25; E. M. Rosental, *Diplomaticheskaya istoriya russko-*

frantsuskogo soyuza v nachale XXv. (Moscow, 1960) p. 176; Taube, *La Politique russe d'avant-guerre*, pp. 100-1.

19. Rosental, *Diplomaticheskaya istoriya*, p. 4; H. Isvolsky, 'The Fateful Years, 1906-11', *Russian Review* (1969) pp. 194-6.

20. Malozemoff, *Russian Far Eastern Policy*, p. 223; Pipes, in Lederer (ed.), *Russian Foreign Policy*, p. 154.

21. See B. Nolde, *L'Alliance franco-russe* (Paris, 1936) pp. 166-8; Pipes, in Lederer (ed.), *Russian Foreign Policy*, p. 150; Bestuzhev, *Bor'ba v Rossii*, p. 52.

22. Quoted in G. H. Bolsover, 'Aspects of Russian Foreign Policy, 1815-1914', in B. Pares and A. J. P. Taylor (eds.), *Essays Presented to Sir Lewis Namier* (London, 1956) p. 325.

23. H. H. Fisher (ed.), *Memoirs of Count Kokovtsov: Out of My Past* (Stanford, 1935) p. 215; Bestuzhev, *Bor'ba v Rossii*, p. 75.

24. *Krasny Arkhiv*, LXIX-LXX (1935) 'K istorii anglo-russkogo soglasheniya 1907 g.'

25. *Krasny Arkhiv*, V (1924) 6-24, 46-8; *Die Grosse Politik*, XIX 454-502.

26. Witte, *Vospominaniya*, II 405-6.

27. White, *The Diplomacy of the Russo-Japanese War*, pp. 92-3. The idea was also talked of in November 1906 regarding the Balkans; see Bestuzhev, in *Istoricheskie Zapiski*, p. 176.

28. Bestuzhev, *Bor'ba v Rossii*, pp. 45-6.

29. Ibid., p. 157; H. Isvolsky (ed.), *Alexandre Iswolsky. Au Service de la Russie. Correspondance diplomatique, 1906-11* (Paris, 1937) I 39-40.

30. H. Rogger, 'The Formation of the Russian Right, 1900-6', *California Slavic Studies*, III (1964) 78; Bestuzhev, *Bor'ba v Rossii*, p. 142; Isvolsky, *Correspondance diplomatique*, I 92-3.

31. Spring-Rice to Lansdowne, 9 Nov 1905, F.O. 1703/650.

32. Bestuzhev, *Bor'ba v Rossii*, pp. 38, 44; A. V. Ignat'ev, *Russko-angliiskie otnosheniya nakunune pervoi mirovoi voiny 1908-14* (Moscow, 1962) p. 16; M. S. Miller, *The Economic Development of Russia, 1905-14* (London, 1926).

33. O. Crisp, 'Financial Aspect of the Franco-Russian Alliance, 1894-1914', unpublished Ph.D. thesis (London, 1954) p. 384.

34. Griault, in *Revue Historique*, p. 105.

35. Bestuzhev, *Bor'ba v Rossii*, pp. 38-41; *Krasny Arkhiv*, LXIX-LXX (1935) 21-2.

36. Dnevnik A. N. Kuropatkina, *Krasny Arkhiv*, II (1922) 83; White, *The Diplomacy of the Russo-Japanese War*, p. 47.

37. Note of French Minister of War, 28 July 1908, M. des A. E., N. S. (Eur.) 16; K. F. Shatsillo, 'O disproportsii v razvitii voorushennykh sil Rossii nakanune pervoi mirovoi voiny 1906-14 gg.', *Istoricheskie Zapiski*, LXXXIII (1969) 128.

38. Ignat'ev, *Russko-angliiskie otnosheniya*, p. 63; Bestuzhev, *Bor'ba v Rossii*, p. 137; A. M. Zaionchkovsky, *Podgotovka Rossi k mirovoi voine v mezhdunarodnom otnoshenii* (Leningrad, 1926) pp. 134-6.

39. K. F. Shatsillo, *Ruskii imperializm i razvitie flota* (Moscow, 1968) p. 48.

40. Bestuzhev, *Bor'ba v Rossii*, p. 137.

41. See R. P. Churchill, *The Anglo-Russian Convention of 1907* (Cedar Rapids, Iowa, 1939), and *B.D.*, IV.

42. Spring-Rice to Lansdowne, 27 Apr 1904, no. 206, F.O. 1627; M. Bompard, *Mon ambassade en Russie 1903-8* (Paris, 1937) p. 236.

43. Hardinge to Lansdowne, 2 July 1904 and 13 July 1904, no. 330, 351, F.O. 1680.

44. Kokovtsov, *Memoirs*, p. 32; V. I. Gurko, *Features and Figures of the Past* (Stanford, 1939) pp. 376, 394; Spring-Rice to Lansdowne, 9 Nov 1905, no. 650, F.O. 1703: 'Count Witte told me with some heat that the system of government was in absolute chaos, that at the first outbreak the government was powerless.'

45. Gurko, *Features and Figures of the Past*, p. 397.

46. *Contemporary Review* (July 1904) p. 41. See also E. J. Dillon, *The Eclipse of Russia* (London, 1918).

47. Bestuzhev, *Bor'ba v Rossii*, p. 53; G. Alexinsky, *Modern Russia* (London, 1913) p. 175; Spring-Rice to Grey, 9 May 1906, no. 304, F.O. 371/122, stated that the real Government was 'a small court camarilla' round Trepov.

48. Gurko, *Features and Figures of the Past*, p. 483.

49. Kokovtsov, *Memoirs*, p. 68.

50. Gurko, *Features and Figures of the Past*, pp. 416-17. See also T. H. von Laue, 'Sergei Witte and the Russian Revolution of 1905', *American Slavic and East European Review* (1958).

51. Gurko, *Features and Figures of the Past*, p. 449.

52. Rosental, *Diplomaticheskaya istoriya*, pp. 229-30; Bompard, *Mon ambassade en Russie*, p. 240; Churchill, *The Anglo-Russian Convention of 1907*, pp. 110-11.

53. Seeger (ed.), *Memoirs of Alexander Iswolsky*, pp. 24, 39.

54. Gurko, *Features and Figures of the Past*, pp. 455-7; G. P. Gooch, *Studies in Diplomacy* (London, 1942) p. 291. Witte, in fact, resigned.

55. Johnstone to Grey, 9 May 1906, no. 56, F.O. 371/125, and 7 May 1906, no. 6, Tel. 371/121; N. F. Grant (ed.), *The Kaiser's Letters to the Tsar* (London, n.d.) pp. 228-33.

56. Isvolsky, *Correspondance diplomatique*, II 60-3.

57. Quoted in T. Riha, *A Russian European* (Notre Dame, Ind., 1969) pp. 123-4.

58. Gurko, *Features and Figures of the Past*, pp. 404-5.

59. Ibid., pp. 486-93; Seeger (ed.), *Memoirs of Alexander Iswolsky*, pp. 190-1; Riha, *A Russian European*, p. 128; Kokovtsov, *Memoirs*, pp. 150-1.

60. Gurko, *Features and Figures of the Past*, p. 471; Kokovtsov, *Memoirs* pp. 142, 165, 203.

61. Baron Rosen, *Forty Years of Diplomacy* (New York, 1922) II 48.

62. H. Isvolsky, in *Russian Review*, p. 194. See also E. Chmielewski, 'Stolypin and the Ministerial Crisis of 1909', *California Slavic Studies*, IV (1967) 4, for Stolypin's contacts with the Octobrists.

63. Gurko, *Features and Figures of the Past*, pp. 404-5.

64. Ibid., p. 483; Seeger (ed.), *Memoirs of Alexander Iswolsky*, p. 198.

65. Stishinsky and Shirinsky-Shikhmatov.

66. Gurko, *Features and Figures of the Past*, p. 493.

67. *B.D.*, IV, no. 224.

68. For a detailed study of the pressure which French diplomats exerted in this direction, see Rosental, *Diplomaticheskaya istoriya*, Bompard to Delcassé, 12 May 1904, *Documents diplomatiques français*, 2nd ser., v 50.

69. Crisp maintains that they were (op. cit., p. 384), but see Griault, 'Sur quelques aspects financiers de l'alliance franco-russe', *Revue d'Histoire Moderne et Contemporaine*, VIII (1961) 68-9.

70. Crisp, op. cit., p. 384.

71. Kokovtsov, *Memoirs*, p. 42.

72. O. Crisp, 'The Russian Liberals and the 1906 Anglo-French Loan', *Slavonic Review* (1961) pp. 499-500; *Krasny Arkhiv*, XVI (12) (1925) 427, zaem 1906 g.

73. Crisp, in *Slavonic Review*, p. 501; Kokovtsov, *Memoirs*, pp. 70-3; Griault, in *Revue d'Histoire* ... , p. 73.

74. Rosental, *Diplomaticheskaya istoriya*, p. 206.

75. Crisp, in *Slavonic Review*, p. 501.

76. Griault, in *Revue d'Histoire* ..., p. 73; Rosental, *Diplomaticheskaya istoriya*, pp. 172-4; Crisp, in *Slavonic Review*, p. 498; Kokovtsov, *Memoirs*, pp. 83-5.

77. Griault, in *Revue d'Histoire* ..., pp. 73-4; Rosental, *Diplomaticheskaya istoriya*, pp. 175-81.

78. Kokovtsov, *Memoirs*, pp. 107-15; Crisp, in *Slavonic Review*.

79. Rosental, *Diplomaticheskaya istoriya*, p. 233; Kokovtsov, *Memoirs*, pp. 90-7.

80. Kokovtsov, *Memoirs*, pp. 90-1.

81. Griault, in *Revue d'Histoire* ..., p. 73. A telegram from Bompard relating to the sending of an envoy to London concerning financial questions referred to 'en échange, la Russie est prête à entrer en collaboration sur les questions irritantes qui séparent les deux pays' (2 Jan 1906).

82. *Krasny Arkhiv*, IV (1930-1) 10, 'Rossiya i Alzhezirasskaya Konferentsiya'.

83. Spring-Rice to Grey, 28 Feb 1906, no. 156, F.O. 371/122.

84. Griault, in *Revue d'Histoire* ..., p. 75.

85. See particularly Rosental, *Diplomaticheskaya istoriya*, p. 171, and Ignat'ev, *Russko-angliiskie otnosheniya*, p. 14.

86. J. P. Sontag, 'Tsarist Debts and Tsarist Foreign Policy', *American Slavic and East European Review*, IV (1968) 538-40. See also the article by Pipes in Lederer (ed.), *Russian Foreign Policy*.

87. Griault, in *Revue d'Histoire* ..., p. 73; Rosental, *Diplomaticheskaya istoriya*, p. 176.

88. See B. J. Williams, 'The Strategic Background to the Anglo-Russian Entente of 1907', *Historical Journal*, IX 3 (1966).

89. Isvolsky actually said, in explaining the Anglo-Russian negotiations in Berlin in October 1906, that the extension of the Anglo-Japanese treaty to cover India made an agreement with Britain essential. *Die Grosse Politik*, XXII, no. 7364.

90. Ignat'ev, *Russko-angliiskie otnosheniya*, p. 67; M. N. Pokrovsky, *Vneshnyaya politika Rossii v XX veke* (Moscow, 1926) pp. 37-8; P. Renouvin, 'Les Relations franco-russes à la fin du XIXᵉ s.', in *Cahiers du monde russe et sovietique* (1959-61) I 133.

91. Council of Ministers meeting, 1/13 Feb 1907, *Krasny Arkhiv*, LXIX-LXX (1935) 19-25.

92. Bestuzhev, in *Istoricheskie Zapiski*, p. 158.

93. See Bestuzhev, ibid., p. 164, for details.

94. Isvolsky, *Correspondance diplomatique*, I 378.

95 Kazemzadeh, *Russia and Britain in Persia*, p. 487; *Krasny Arkhiv*, LXIX-LXX (1935).

96. *B.D.*, IV, nos. 26, 117.

97. Perepiska S. yu Witte, A. N. Kuropatkina v 1904-5 g., *Krasny Arkhiv*, XIX (1926) 80.

98. See comments of Sazonov and Isvolsky in conference of 11/24 Aug 1907, *Krasny Arkhiv*, LXIX-LXX (2-3) (1935) 36. Isvolsky argued at the council in April that war and internal events 'prevent us from designs incompatible with the real strength of the country' (ibid., p. 27).

99. Lamsdorff to Benckendorff, 31 Mar 1905, quoted in O. F. Solov'ev, 'K voprosu ob otnoshenii Tsarskoi Rossii k Indii v XIX–nachale XX veke', *Voprosy Istorii*, VI (1958) 105.

100. A. L. Sidorov, 'Iz istorii podgotovki tsarizma k pervoi mirovoi voine', *Istoricheskii Arkhiv*, II (1962) 120.

101. Seeger (ed.), *Memoirs of Alexander Iswolsky*, p. 204; Rosental, *Diplomaticheskaya istoriya*, p. 169.

102. Gurko, *Features and Figures of the Past*, p. 417; V. A. Petrov, *Ocherki po istorii revolyutsionnogo dvizheniya v russkoi armii v 1905 g.* (Moscow, 1964) pp. 383-4.

103. Gurko, *Features and Figures of the Past*, pp. 417-18; J. Keep, *The Rise of Social Democracy in Russia* (Oxford, 1963) p. 238.

104. E. Yaroslavsky, *Istoriya VKP* (Moscow, 1926-30) II 697. Keep, *The Rise of Social Democracy in Russia*, pp. 271-3, argues that the S.D.s had little real control over army mutinies in 1905.

105. White, *The Diplomacy of the Russo-Japanese War*, pp. 221-2.

106. Gurko, *Features and Figures of the Past*, pp. 417-18; *Krasny Arkhiv*, XII (1925) 289; Keep, *The Rise of Social Democracy in Russia*, pp. 261-4.

107. Bestuzhev, in *Istoricheskie Zapiski*, p. 163.

108. D. Lang, *A Modern History of Georgia* (London, 1962) p. 164.

109. R. Pierce, *Russian Central Asia, 1867-1917* (Berkeley, 1960).

110. Stevens to Nicolson, 30 June 1906, no. 19, F.O. 371/860; Nicolson to Grey, 19 June 1906, no. 378, F.O. 371/122. The military position in Central Asia was acknowledged by the Russians to be very unsatisfactory. See Council of Ministers, 14/27 Apr 1907, *Krasny Arkhiv*, LXIX-LXX (1935) 27.

111. Pierce, *Russian Central Asia*, pp. 257-8.

112. See I. Spector, *The First Russian Revolution: Its Impact on Asia* (Englewood Cliffs, N.J., 1962).

113. See Bestuzhev, in *Istoricheskie Zapiski*, p. 156; Martin, *German–Persian Diplomatic Relations*, pp. 93-5.

114. Nicolson to Grey, 8 Feb 1909, no. 92, F.O. 371/727.

115. Panafieu to Pichon, 21 Feb 1908, no. 50, M. des A. E., N. S. (Eur.) 16.

116. Quoted in P. N. Efremov, *Vneshnaya politika Rossii 1907-14* (Moscow, 1961) pp. 78-9; Kazemzadeh, *Russia and Britain in Persia*, p. 528.

117. Kazemzadeh, *Russia and Britain in Persia*, p. 480.

118. Council meeting, 1/13 Feb 1907, *Krasny Arkhiv*, LXIX-LXX (1935) 19-22.

119. Martin, *German–Persian Diplomatic Relations*, p. 136.

120. *Krasny Arkhiv*, LVI (1) (1933) 60.

121. For details, see Churchill, *The Anglo-Russian Convention of 1907*, and *B.D.*, IV.

122. *Krasny Arkhiv*, LXIX-LXX (1935) 33-5.

123. Isvolsky, *Correspondance diplomatique*, I 374-6.

124. Meeting of 14/27 Apr 1907, *Krasny Arkhiv*, LXIX-LXX (1935) 26. See E. W. Edwards, 'The Far East Agreements of 1907', *Journal of Modern History* (1954).

125. Bestuzhev, in *Istoricheskie Zapiski*, pp. 158-62.

126. Ibid., p. 162.

127. White, *The Diplomacy of the Russo-Japanese War*, pp. 47-8.

128. 'Military Resources of the Russian Empire', General Staff, 1907, W.O. 33/419, p. 262.

129. Ibid., quoted in P. S. H. Tang, *Russian and Soviet Policy in Manchuria and Outer Mongolia, 1911-31* (Durham, N.C., 1959) pp. 52-3; Jordan to Grey, 27 Feb 1908, no. 94, F.O. 371/428.

130. B. von Siebert, *Entente Diplomacy and the World, 1909-14* (London, 1921) pp. 25-7; G. F. Hudson, *The Far East in World Politics* (London, 1939) pp. 158-9.

131. C. Vevier, *The United States and China, 1906-13* (New Brunswick, N.J., 1955) pp. 143-4.

132. H. Coly, *Willard Straight* (New York, 1924) pp. 306-8; Vevier, *The United States and China*, pp. 32-4; Nicolson to Grey, 29 Nov 1909, no. 682, F.O. 371/842.

133. E. B. Price, *Russo-Japanese Treaties of 1907-16 concerning Manchuria and Mongolia* (Baltimore, 1933) p. 44.

134. Quoted in Zabriskie, *American–Russian Rivalry in the Far East,* p. 160.

135. Nicolson to Grey, 5 July 1906, Nicolson MSS., supp. vol.

136. *B.D.*, IV, no. 372.

137. Nicolson to Grey, 8 Jan 1909, no. 92, F.O. 371/727; annual report (1908) p. 25.

138. Quoted in Kazemzadeh, *Russia and Britain in Persia*, p. 517.

139. Isvolsky, *Correspondance diplomatique*, II 172-7.

140. Bestuzhev, *Bor'ba v Rossii*, p. 149; Kazemzadeh, *Russia and Britain in Persia*, p. 512.

141. 11/24 Aug 1907, *Krasny Arkhiv*, LXIX-LXX (1935) 36.

142. Ibid., pp. 5-18.

143. *B.D.*, IV, no. 507; Churchill, *The Anglo-Russian Convention of 1907*, pp. 302-3.

144. Rosental, *Diplomaticheskaya istoriya*, p. 239; Bestuzhev, *Bor'ba v Rossii*, pp. 142-3; Bompard, *Mon ambassade en Russie*, p. 273; Isvolsky, *Correspondance diplomatique*, I 293-5.

145. Martin, *German–Persian Diplomatic Relations*, pp. 143-6.

146. Isvolsky, *Correspondance diplomatique*, II 60-3, 64-5.

147. See F. Lindberg, *Scandinavia in Great Power Politics, 1905-8* (Stockholm, 1958) pp. 95-101.

148. Bestuzhev, in *Istoricheskie Zapiski*, pp. 174-7.

149. *Documents diplomatiques français*, X, no. 214, Barrère to Pichon, 30 Nov 1907.

150. Rosental, 'Frantsuskaya diplomatiya i anglo-russkoe sblizhenie v 1906-7 gg', *Istoriya SSSR*, V (1958) 136; Bestuzhev, in *Istoricheskie Zapiski*, p. 139; Isvolsky, *Correspondance diplomatique*, I 293-5.

151. Shatsillo, *Ruskii imperializm i razvitie flota*, pp. 59, 79-82.

152. See Sidorov, in *Istoricheskii Arkhiv*, for relevant documents; also Pokrovsky, *Vneshnyaya politika Rossii*, pp. 38-43; Shatsillo, *Russkii imperializm i razvitie flota*, p. 24.

153. Shatsillo, *Russkii imperializm i razvitie flota*, pp. 22, 57-8.

154. Shatsillo, in *Istoricheskie Zapiski*, pp. 128-9.
155. Nicolson to Grey, 8 Feb 1909, no. 92, F.O. 371/727.
156. Siebert, *Entente Diplomacy and the World*, p. 481.

124. Broglio in 1850, ibid. Vortrag, p. 25.
135. Aehrenthal to Graf, 4.7.6 (1906), no. 97, f. 1, f. 271.
136. Siebert to Grey, [illegible]

6 Brockdorff-Rantzau: The 'Wanderer between Two Worlds'

ELEONORE BREUNING

THE post of German Ambassador to Soviet Russia, which Brockdorff-Rantzau occupied from November 1922 until his death in September 1928, was by no means the first delicate and controversial task which he had undertaken. It was one of the Count's profoundest convictions that he was, more than most men, fitted by birth, breeding and experience to practise the art and craft of high diplomacy. Whether he lived up to his own conception of himself and his role, or fell short of it, or whether, at least during the Moscow period, his usefulness to his country consisted in his fulfilling a function quite other than that which he had envisaged for himself, has remained a matter of disagreement among historians. The present paper seeks only to indicate one or two possible new lines of approach; it does not claim completeness, let alone finality.

Born Ulrich Karl Christian, Count zu Rantzau, in 1869, scion of an ancient Holstein family and elder of twin brothers, he later added the surname Brockdorff on inheriting the estate of Annettenhöh near Schleswig from an uncle on his mother's side. He obtained a doctorate at Leipzig on the strength of a thesis on ecclesiastical law, and entered the German Foreign Ministry in 1894. From 1897 to 1901 he served as Secretary of Legation at the German Embassy in St Petersburg; from 1901 to 1910, with the rank of Counsellor of Legation, he was attached to the German Embassy in Vienna; from 1910 to 1912 he was German Consul-General at Budapest; then came his first major posting, as Ambassador to Denmark, where he remained until 1918.

During the course of the First World War, Rantzau at Copenhagen was drawn into two sets of secret policies towards Russia, which were set in train largely at the instance of Falkenhayn, who succeeded Moltke as Chief of the German General Staff after the defeat of the

Marne, and who envisaged retrieving the situation by means of what might be described as a diplomatic version of the Schlieffen Plan, namely getting Russia out of the war through a separate peace. The means employed in attempting to bring this about were, firstly, secret approaches to the Tsar via the Danish court or other intermediaries, and, secondly, the fostering of both subversion and the nationalism of minorities within Tsarist Russia. Rantzau, unlike his colleagues at other key diplomatic posts (Stockholm, Berne, etc.) became directly involved: he had his own special revolutionary contact in the person of Parvus-Helphand, but, as was to happen at other stages in his career, he was outshone in a sphere of activity which he had come to regard as peculiarly his own.[1] It was Romberg in Berne who was in touch with the super-revolutionary, Lenin, at the decisive moment, much as, during Rantzau's ambassadorship in Moscow, it was Seeckt who was virtually to monopolise contacts with the leading military men in Soviet Russia.

After the German collapse, and during the period of the German revolution, Brockdorff-Rantzau, having acquired some democratic notions in the course of the war,[2] seems to have seen himself somewhat in the role of a Philippe Égalité. In December 1918 he very willingly accepted the post of Foreign Secretary in the revolutionary Government, in succession to Solf. (In February 1919 he became Foreign Minister in the temporary Government which was formed after the elections for the National Assembly had been held, and pending the completion of the Weimar Constitution.) From this vantage-point he believed that he would be able to strike out on a policy of his own. Demanding the right to reject the Treaty of Versailles if he saw fit to do so, he proceeded to deal with matters after his own fashion. But, to adapt Professor Holborn's phrase, Rantzau was to find that he could not figure as a German Talleyrand.[3] He overestimated the extent to which he could exploit the differences between the Allies, and in fact succeeded in uniting them by his arrogant (or seemingly arrogant) bearing and the speech he made upon being handed the text of the peace terms.[4]

However we may judge Rantzau's subsequent achievements, it can scarcely be disputed that his efforts at Versailles ended in personal failure; resigning as Foreign Minister, he left it to others to sign the Treaty, and bear the odium for so doing, and himself retired into private life for a period of some three years, although he remained in contact with the world of affairs and of diplomacy.[5]

In 1922, when, under the Treaty of Rapallo of April of that year, full German–Soviet diplomatic relations were resumed, came Brockdorff-Rantzau's second chance to play an outstanding role, and that precisely in the area in which he had had a strong interest ever since his St Petersburg days.

Reference has already been made to the lack of unanimity in scholarly opinion as to Rantzau's role and importance. That opinion has indeed varied between wide extremes, ranging from the view of Herbert Helbig, who, ranking the Count above his enemy, Seeckt, and even above his master, Stresemann, claims that 'Brockdorff-Rantzau's image will remain unshaken in history',[6] through the judgement of Hajo Holborn that 'apart from a burning German patriotism Brockdorff-Rantzau was motivated by cool reason rather than sentiment' (though he does comment elsewhere that the Count could be 'a passionate hater'),[7] to the more recent assessment of Kurt Rosenbaum, who, though he does give some weight to the Ambassador's experience and professional competence, nevertheless misses no opportunity to advert to his weaknesses, for example his 'pathological fear' of a possible Russo-French alignment, his 'infinite egocentrism' which made him see Moscow as the centre of European politics simply because he was *en poste* there, and, in general, his tendency to engage in bitter quarrels with his colleagues and even his superiors.[8]

Although it can be argued that Rantzau's quirks of temperament added to, rather than detracted from, his importance to German–Soviet relations, it must be admitted that he can never have been a comfortable colleague or subordinate. Despite the democratic ideas which, as has been said, he adopted during the war, and especially after the February Revolution in Russia, he was essentially an elitist, proud of his rank and his intellect. He was also much concerned about his place in history. These considerations led him constantly to define and re-define on paper his policies and the powers which he would seek to have conferred upon himself in preparation for whatever task he was about to undertake. Similarly, after the event, he would engage freely in written reviews and justifications of the part he had played. For the historian, all this means that there is an abundance of material from Rantzau's own pen; but for his contemporaries, his passion for exactitude, combined with his *rechthaberisch* quality and his sense of what was due to his position, made him an uncertain quantity and one to be handled with caution.[9]

Although his experiences at Versailles in 1919 undoubtedly heightened these tendencies, which are always most evident in connection with that obsession about undoing the Treaty which remained with him until his death, his combativeness, like his interest in Russia, dated from long before that period. In November 1900, conscious that he was swimming against the prevailing current, he wrote from St Petersburg: 'But even ... if at present we should be intending to orient ourselves more strongly towards the West, it is in accordance with our traditional policy ... at least not to allow a profound troubling of our relations [with Russia] to occur.'[10] During the war he not only interested himself in initiating that liaison between the German authorities and the various revolutionary elements in Europe which led to Lenin's arrival at the Finland Station in Petrograd in April 1917 by courtesy of the German Government; he also concerned himself with the whole question as to what the future of German–Russian relations was to be. By a strange irony of fate Rantzau, who was later to condemn the Treaty of Brest-Litovsk because of its 'purely capitalist nature',[11] and who was to refuse to sign the Treaty of Versailles on the grounds that it was 'a subtle attempt designed to encompass the economic and political ruin of Germany',[12] was envisaging, in April 1917 (albeit as one of two alternatives, the other being a peace of reconciliation), the harshest possible treatment of Russia: first, a two months' pause to allow the process of disintegration resulting from the desertion by the 'peasants in uniform' to run its course, then a settlement involving the seizure of southern Russia, total disarmament of the Russian armed forces, dismantling of fortifications, destruction of the Russian Navy, prohibition of the manufacture of armaments, and extensive occupation. Anything short of this, such as 'depriving Russia of one province or another', argued Rantzau, would only be dangerous, for it would leave Russia able to make a rapid and inevitably vengeful recovery.[13]

The discrepancy (even allowing for changed circumstances) between Rantzau's advocacy of friendship with Russia in 1900 and his readiness to contemplate her almost total destruction in 1917 becomes less surprising when it is realised that, whilst he prided himself on his realism and his ability to subject important questions to cool appraisal, he was also (as he himself admitted) at heart a passionate, indeed a violent man.[14] This latter quality was quite often reflected in the almost Wagnerian language of his speeches and writings:

> [I said that] if the Entente wanted to make it impossible for the present German Government, which they themselves had described as fit to negotiate, to carry on, that was their affair, and it would be their responsibility if chaos became unavoidable in Germany ... but a nation of 70 million souls could not be destroyed, and if the Entente really carried out their intentions ..., Bolshevism would be inevitable in Germany.[15]

To make much, for public consumption, of the danger of Germany's succumbing to the Bolshevist infection if the Allies pressed her too hard was an obvious tactic for Rantzau to employ in his capacity as

Foreign Minister in the Versailles period. But the evidence indicates that at that time, desperate though he might consider his country's plight to be, he placed no faith in the possible expedient of aligning with Russia to defy the Entente.[16] His reason for rejecting this course was that he foresaw that, far from allowing themselves to be used for Germany's defence, the Bolsheviks would be likely to make use of Germany for their own purposes. Even in later years, when Rantzau *was* prepared to contemplate, indeed to press for, an improvement in German–Soviet relations, one of his reasons for so strenuously advocating a carefully gradualist approach was his fear lest the same contingency arise.[17]

Although in 1922 Brockdorff-Rantzau appeared to many to be the obvious candidate to head the Embassy in Moscow, the events of Versailles were to cast a cloud, not only upon the Count's equanimity, but also on his claim to the post. At Versailles he had clashed, not only with Seeckt, but also with Erzberger, the chairman of the German Armistice Commission, on the tactics to be adopted there.[18] By 1922, of course, Erzberger was dead, but Seeckt was very much alive and in a strong position to oppose Rantzau's appointment on the grounds that he had shown a lack of patriotism in 1919.[19] His views were shared by the Chancellor, Wirth, whom Rantzau regarded as 'the heir and political executor of the late Erzberger'.[20] As was his custom, Rantzau set about defining his policies with a view to obtaining the exceptionally wide powers which he considered their successful implementation would require, producing a considerable volume of notes and memoranda in the process.[21] In the course of numerous conversations and consultations he became aware, not only of the extent to which Wirth supported Seeckt in opposing his candidature, but also of the degree to which the Chancellor saw eye to eye with the General on the latter's plans for military co-operation with Soviet Russia.[22] In the months during which both his candidature and his programme were under debate, the Count, to his dismay, also learnt in some detail of the scope of the already existing military contacts with Soviet Russia.[23]

Thus, in the polemics of the summer and early autumn of 1922, we find Rantzau pursuing two aims at once: not only, as has already been said, the definition of, and acquisition of Government approval for, his proposed policies vis-à-vis Soviet Russia, but also the discrediting of Seeckt's policy of military contacts, which he saw as a threat both to Germany and to his own future control over German–Soviet relations as a whole.[24]

In now looking more closely at the documentary evidence relating to this episode, two sets of comparisons may usefully be made: firstly, between Rantzau's 'official' memoranda (that is to say, those intended for fairly wide circulation, and especially for submission to the President; the most important are those of 8 July and 15 August[25]) on the one hand, and on the other his 'unofficial' expressions of opinion, of which his memorandum of 17 July[26] is typical; and secondly, between Rantzau's line and Seeckt's.

In the 'official' papers, the Count's 'cool reason' is well to the fore. He stresses how narrow is the margin within which Germany's foreign policy must operate and how vulnerable her position, how undesirable are the Soviet Government as partners in any enterprise save the most innocuous, how easily an unwary German Ambassador might find himself being used in a Soviet game of promoting disunity among the capitalist-imperialist powers. The one advantage which Rantzau discerns in the situation is a negative one: both countries alike are in need of economic reconstruction, and they are in a position to assist each other in this task. (It was this shared economic need and the possibility of co-operating to meet it which Rantzau a few weeks later summed up in his famous phrase 'Community of Fate'.[27]) To this peaceful and non-provocative task must Germany confine herself, and, if possible, Russia too; above all, 'any appearance of a military tie between ourselves and the East would have the most unfavourable effects on our relations with the West',[28] because it would re-forge an Anglo-French solidarity which might otherwise be expected to decay, to Germany's benefit. The possibility that a Soviet attack on Poland might turn out advantageously for Germany, Rantzau scornfully dismissed; he was convinced that in such an event Germany would be invaded, not only by France but by France's Eastern European friends and by Denmark.

Summing up, Rantzau declared: 'What I advocate is not a policy of passive renunciation, but the sober consideration and planned, purposeful utilisation of the existing positive opportunities; admittedly, these are neither numerous nor attractive, and they may not be pleasing to the reckless daredevil. That is the truth. And to recognise it, in order to counter the danger – that requires the greater courage, the courage that dares.'

Despite the generally logical and sober tone of the 'public' memoranda, however, there are not lacking even in them some strongly emotional passages, though emotion is given much freer rein in the 'private' papers. In this context two themes predominate: on the one hand, if disaster supervenes, and Germany falls prey to Bolshevism, then the Entente will have only themselves to thank, and will have to bear the blame in the eyes of history; on the other hand, Rantzau stresses that no one (by implication, not even Seeckt) has been more zealous than he himself in seeking means of redressing the wrongs done to his country: 'Since Versailles I have been thinking of nothing but of how we can find, and if necessary exact, justice.' Plainly Rantzau wished (as he had at Versailles), by adherence to a rigidly 'correct' course of action and by the invocation of liberal principles, to clothe his country in the white garb of innocence. But, equally plainly (and this is most particularly apparent from the 'unofficial' papers), the bitterness of his feelings led him at times to contemplate revenge as the ultimate goal.

In his most eloquent moments, when he is torn between his feelings of injured innocence and unsatisfied vengefulness, Rantzau speaks to us almost in the tones of a modern Hamlet, even to the point of quotation from the Schlegel–Tieck translation of Shakespeare's play.[29] And, in Rantzau as in Hamlet, it seems to be the conflict of equally powerful, but opposing, emotions which makes recourse to decisive action and, in Rantzau's case, even the counselling of decisive action, impossible.

Perhaps it was the Hamlet in Rantzau which aroused Seeckt's ire, at Versailles as over the candidature question. Certainly, Seeckt opened his counter-blast[30] to the 15 August memorandum (the 'Promemoria') with the admonition that 'Germany must pursue an active policy', adding: 'He who takes his own powerlessness as the basis for his political thinking, who sees *only* dangers, who wants *only* to remain passive, is not making policy and should be kept far removed from the scene of action.' Not surprisingly, Seeckt regarded Rapallo, not as a burden, but as the source of 'the only increase in power which we have gained since peace was concluded'; the strength of the new German–Soviet bond lay 'in the fact that ... [it] offers the *possibility* of political and thus also of military ties'. In particular, the General took exception to Rantzau's whole chain of argument about doing nothing that might either arouse the wrath of France or drive France and Britain closer together; nothing, Seeckt maintained, could make France more vengeful than she already was; nothing could alter the fact that an inherent Anglo-French rivalry, and hence a latent Anglo-German attraction, existed. In the light of this interpretation, Seeckt implicitly dismissed Rantzau's fears of the dangers that a renewed Russo-Polish conflict might unleash, proclaiming that 'Poland's existence is intolerable, irreconcilable with the vital requirements of Germany. She must disappear, and she will disappear, through her own internal weakness, and through Russia – with our help.'

In so far as Seeckt's activism can be considered to be in the restless pre-war German tradition which held that failure to advance was tantamount to retreat, whilst the gradualism, almost quiescence, advocated by Brockdorff-Rantzau (at least in his calmer moments) can be seen as a new policy adapted to new circumstances, it could perhaps be argued that it was the diplomat who was making the better adjustment to post-war reality of the two. Certainly, the Ambassador-designate can be said to have 'won' the contest in that his appointment was eventually confirmed. Since, however, in the event neither his policy nor Seeckt's was put exclusively into effect, but rather an uneasy amalgam of the two, it is difficult to judge as to the efficacy of either. What can be said with certainty is that there hangs over the period between the appointment of Brockdorff-Rantzau and the advent to power of Chancellor, then Foreign Minister, Stresemann an air of directionlessness which is not explicable solely in terms of the Ruhr crisis.

Mention has already been made of Rantzau's aversion to decisive action. A good example of this is the fact that, despite his protestations to Wirth that the President, Ebert, must be informed of the doings of the military (activities which we may be certain Ebert would have opposed), Rantzau never, in the memoranda destined for Ebert's perusal, went beyond hints and allusions, and Ebert, his friend and supporter, was not put in full possession of facts which had an important bearing on the whole foreign policy of the Reich.

Strongly though Rantzau disliked the military relations (not least because he feared that they might enable Soviet Russia to exert a blackmailing pressure on Germany),[31] and energetically though he sought to hold the Reichswehr to their promise, repeatedly given and as often broken, that these relations should be channelled through the German Embassy in Moscow,[32] he nevertheless came to accept the fact of their existence[33] and, in July 1923, when A. P. Rosengolts, a member of Revvoen soviet, came to Berlin for an important round of negotiations,[34] tried, though without much success, to weave them into his own political system by demanding, in return for German technical and financial assistance, a virtual monopoly position for German business in the Russian armaments industry, plus a promise of help against Poland should the latter attack Germany.[35] This change of front was, of course, partly due to Rantzau's perfectly practical realisation of the harm that could be done by bringing the military contacts to an end, yet so marked a deviation from his declared plan would seem to lend support to doubts as to the correctness of a view of Rantzau as a moderate, content patiently to cherish a low-key relationship with rather dubious Soviet friends whilst awaiting the dawn of better days where the Versailles situation was concerned.

Certainly, he was no moderate in his constant stubborn condemnation of German moves towards reconciliation with the West, which he interpreted as voluntary reaffirmations of bondage as well as departures from the true gospel of German–Soviet friendship; in 1924 he opposed the Dawes Plan and the possibility, mooted that September, of Germany's entering the League of Nations;[36] in 1925 he fought most tenaciously against the conception and realisation of the Locarno idea;[37] in 1926, after what the Russians gleefully referred to as the 'Geneva fiasco' (the dispute over the allocation of permanent seats on the League Council which led to the postponement of Germany's admission to the League until the autumn), Rantzau continued to hope that the whole Locarno–League structure might collapse;[38] and in 1927, at the time of the Anglo-Soviet breach, he urged that Germany take her stand on the Treaty of Berlin, not on her League obligations.[39] Furthermore, the many cases of German–Soviet friction that arose in one way or another from the disparities between the political systems of the two countries (the Petrov affair in 1923, the Bozenhardt incident in 1924, the Kindermann–Wolscht trial in 1925, the repercussions in early 1926 of the 'Caucasus question' and the publication of the Red Army handbook *Foreign Armies*, the provocative speech by War Commissar Voroshilov and the ostentatious award by Revvoensoviet of the Order of the Red Banner to Max Hölz, at that time (1927) serving a prison sentence in Germany on criminal charges, and finally the Shakhty case in 1928[40]) – this long record of incident and reaction, invariably accompanied by lively press comment in both countries, finds the Ambassador, as often as not, putting aside his private feelings and striving to smoothe matters over, so as to preserve, if nothing else, at least the 'bluff value' of the relationship.[41] (Not that the Count was uniformly eirenic: bluff value or no bluff value, he could on occasion take a very sharp tone with the Russians, particularly on the propaganda issue or when he felt German honour to have been impugned – and on such occasions his anger was commonly only increased by the instructions that Stresemann would send him to continue at his post.[42])

There can be no doubt that the relationship between Rantzau and Stresemann was not a happy one. Apart from momentary differences as to tactics, the Ambassador disagreed fundamentally with the Foreign Minister over strategy. Of Rantzau, Dirksen cogently said: 'He wanted friendship with the Soviet Union in order to attain great political ends, but he often hesitated to make the requisite commitment in the form of political treaties.'[43] The latter part of this verdict was doubly true in regard to Rantzau's attitude to German–Western relations. In neither direction did he wish to see Germany tied; but, where obligations towards Russia already existed, he was prepared to make the best of them, whilst with the West he really wanted to see no treaties concluded at all.[44] On several occasions, most notably in the Locarno period, Rantzau expressed his disagreement with Stresemann's policies in terms that were less than temperate.[45] But there seems to be no record that Stresemann ever reacted other than patiently and with civility; he did not simply instruct his Ambassador on 'language to be held', but was at pains to make clear the logic of his moves. So it comes about that Stresemann's policies, especially in his heyday, the Locarno era, are exceptionally well documented; the more Rantzau resisted, the more Stresemann, or his faithful State Secretary, Schubert, explained and reasoned.

In terms of grasp, of a clearly formulated German foreign policy being programmatically put into effect, the contrast between the period up to August 1923 and the six years following is a striking one. Before the Stresemann period, there is hardly any sign of a general, broadly conceived policy at all; instead, there are particular policies on particular issues (the previously mentioned desire of Seeckt and Wirth to wipe out Poland; hand-to-mouth adjustments to recurrent Reparation crises; and a lack of overall control which made it possible for a German civil servant, albeit a prominent one, in the person of Ago von Maltzan,[46] to decide – at least by his own account – to torpedo an international conference – Genoa – more or less single-handed). Not surprisingly, this piecemeal approach produced nothing but disaster: not only directly, in the failure to reach an accommodation on the Reparation issue, but indirectly too, in that the German–Russian alignment signalised by the Treaty of Rapallo undoubtedly helped to decide Poincaré to take not only *gages productifs* but also a firmer hold on French security by occupying the Ruhr in January 1923.

By the manner in which Stresemann determinedly, and for some years at least successfully, set about achieving a reconciliation with the West, he brought his country to make the essential minimal concessions without which that reconciliation was not to be had, whilst at the same time extracting enough counter-concessions to avoid the label, and indeed the death, of an *Erfüllungspolitiker*. But a continued relationship with Soviet Russia was a part both of Stresemann's concept and of his tool-kit; whereas Rantzau, by his own admission, would have preferred no commitments in either direction, Stresemann developed a programme of balanced commitments, to achieve which he needed all his nerve and all his pertinacity, at home as well as abroad.[47]

The contrast between his and Rantzau's views emerges particularly clearly from what is perhaps Stresemann's single most comprehensive policy statement, his dispatch to Brockdorff-Rantzau of 19 March

1925,[48] sent at a moment when, the Security Pact offer having been made to both Britain and France, Stresemann wished to have the whole question set forth to the Russians in such a manner as to keep them in play until such time as matters would have reached a stage in the West where a German–Soviet treaty could safely be concluded. In this dispatch, Stresemann began by explaining why his first task lay in the West:

> France would of course be best pleased if, as a substitute for the earlier guarantee treaties and for the Geneva Protocol, a Franco-English-Belgian pact were to be concluded, whose effectiveness should be still further reinforced by precise military obligations on England's part. In itself, we might well have considered whether it would not have been best for Germany to leave the road open to these French wishes. But, apart from the fact that a pact between the Allies would have been directly aimed at Germany and would have perpetuated the Entente, this possibility was from the start ruled out because England categorically rejects the Three-Power pact. In these circumstances our active participation in the solution of the security question, which, the situation being what it is, is after all a precondition for the liberation of the Rhineland, was a matter of necessity. If we do not succeed in solving the security problem by these means either, France will undoubtedly see to it that the disarmament demands which are to be put to us are screwed up to such a pitch that in the foreseeable future neither the settlement of the disarmament question, nor the removal of the inter-Allied military control, nor the evacuation of the Cologne zone, is brought about. Even if, however, France, under pressure from England and perhaps also from America, were finally after all forced to evacuate the Cologne zone, she would make every effort, by invoking the provision in Article 213 of the Versailles Treaty for permanent League of Nations control, to ensure at least that permanent military control bodies were stationed in the evacuated territory. These control bodies would not only mean a perpetuation of the military control, but would also always offer a convenient starting-point for the further pursuit of French plans in the Rhineland.

In other words, the first aim must be to make it impossible for France, whether directly or indirectly through the League, to exert a repressive influence on Germany in the name of her own security. It need hardly be said that this unequivocal statement of Stresemann's priorities was not, despite the prospect of checkmating France, likely in itself to attract Rantzau. But in masterly fashion Stresemann moved on to one of the great issues that preoccupied Russia as much as it did Germany – Poland. Here, instead of Rantzau's rejection of the Seecktian idea of German–Russian military collaboration to destroy Poland, with all that such an attempt might mean in terms of reaction by France, Stresemann set himself the aim of establishing the right eventually to seek peaceful revision of the German–Polish frontiers, and meanwhile to subscribe to nothing that could curtail such a right:

... from the first diplomatic conversation onward, we have quite clearly attached to our co-operation in the security problem the *conditio sine qua non* that there might not be a solution which was in any way aimed at our recognising our frontiers in the East. Only in order to afford the French Government a façade behind which they would be able to drop their desire to have Poland included in the Security Pact ..., we have attached to our proposals a declaration that we are prepared to conclude arbitration treaties with all states who are our neighbours. In fact such arbitration treaties, however much they may proclaim a will to peace, are no real obstacle to our maintaining the political aims which we must pursue in regard to our eastern frontiers.

Leaving in the air the implication that, where Poland was concerned, an advantage gained for Germany would be one gained also for Soviet Russia, Stresemann passed on to the question on which the Russians had been objecting most violently, namely, the prospect of German entry into the League of Nations.[49] Here he deployed quite overtly the tactic which underlay his references to Poland: concessions gained by Germany in respect of the terms of the Covenant would, argued Stresemann, prove of benefit to the U.S.S.R., whilst Germany's very presence in the League would be more advantageous to Russia than her absence:

From the first moment when there became apparent the Allies' desire to bring about our entry into the League on this occasion, we have stated quite candidly in diplomatic conversations that we are neither able nor willing to sacrifice our relations with Russia to the League. We have even put this in writing in a memorandum which we communicated to Lord D'Abernon and which Your Excellency received enclosed in Herr von Schubert's private letter of 26 February.[50] Our familiar representations, too, against the unrestricted application of Article 16 of the League Covenant to Germany were nothing but an underlining of the view that we did not intend to allow ourselves to be drawn into a bloc of powers directed against Russia.

... the only really decisive question seems to me to be whether

our membership of the League would of necessity render more difficult or perhaps even impossible the flowering of German–Russian
relations. I do not think it correct simply to dismiss this question
with the general answer that our entry would mean final resignation
in regard to the Versailles Treaty or a swerve in German policy to
the West. It is, rather, essential to visualise quite concretely the
different repercussions which our entry would have in regard to
Russia, and thus to obtain the right standard by which to measure
each question. Here one must first of all take into account the fact
that, according to the replies of the Council Powers to our memorandum and according to the reply from the League Council itself,
which has now reached us, it may be taken as certain that we shall
be accorded a permanent seat on the League Council. Since, under
the Covenant, all Council resolutions of any importance, particularly resolutions concerning the sanctions measures provided for in
Article 16, must be passed unanimously, Germany, as a League
member, would be able to prevent any action of the League which
was directed against Russia.

On the question of what freedoms Germany stood to lose by joining
the League, Stresemann neatly turned Rantzau's own arguments
against him:

... it is clear that, in certain circumstances, our membership of the
League could considerably restrict our general political freedom. If,
for instance, I visualise the case of events occurring which bring the
reduction of Poland to her ethnographic frontiers directly within
the bounds of the possible, then one could very well conceive that
any active intervention on Germany's part would be greatly
restricted by her membership of the League. This is undoubtedly a
very important factor. Nevertheless, its scope is reduced by the
consideration that in such a case, even were we not a League
member, we would have to reckon with the certain hostility of the
Entente Powers, or at least of France, Belgium and Czechoslovakia.
There would really only be a difference if Germany and Russia were
strong enough and had the resolution to meet any coalition with
force of arms. As a member of the League we would only be able
to do this by a flagrant breach of the Covenant, and, therefore, only
by offending opinion all over the world. Moreover, I believe I am at
one with Your Excellency in saying that an overt or covert German–
Russian military alliance such as would then be required cannot
be part of our political aims for the foreseeable future.

Lastly, Stresemann discussed how best to tackle the negotiations for which the Russians were pressing: the best method would be to take up with them the very same material that was currently under discussion with Britain and France:

Although we therefore are agreed in proceeding from the assumption that general treaty arrangements with Russia are impossible, yet this is not, and I assume you will agree with me, to say that an expansion or concretisation of German–Russian relations is out of the question altogether. I believe that it would be expedient now to approach this question of the expansion or concretisation of relations, not in general or in the abstract, but by discussing, both internally and with the Soviet Government, the circumstances, briefly outlined above, which would arise were we to join the League. It would be important to convince the Soviet Government that our entry would not in the slightest degree mean a basic shift in our policy, but that rather, just like the London negotiations on the Dawes Report or the offer of a regional Western pact, it would be nothing but a defensive action against the threatened encroachments of French policy. It would, further, be important to make it clear to the Soviet Government that any limitation of our freedom of action would, precisely from the Russian standpoint, probably even be outweighed by the opportunity which we would gain of strongly counteracting all anti-Russian tendencies within the League of Nations once we were a Council member. If the Soviet Government prove accessible to this line of argument, we would at the same time be coming closer to clearing up the question of whether and in what manner a positive understanding on general political aims would be possible.

Recalcitrant though both Brockdorff-Rantzau and the Russians proved in the long negotiations that led, first to the conclusion of the German–Soviet trade treaty of 12 October 1925, and then to the signature of the Treaty of Berlin on 24 April 1926, the programme laid down by Stresemann was carried out. Germany not only became a signatory of the Locarno Treaties and a member of the League; she also retained the friendship of Soviet Russia, with all that this implied in terms both of the relationship itself and of its leverage value in the West. So little did the German–Western rapprochement weaken that friendship, that it was able to survive both Stresemann's death and the repercussions of the first Five-Year Plan, and would have survived even Hitler's advent to power had not Hitler himself willed otherwise.

But although the continuance of this ambiguous friendship was due in large part to the efforts of Stresemann, one may doubt whether he would have been able to carry out his Eastern policy without

Brockdorff-Rantzau as his Ambassador in Moscow. Ironically, however, this was so despite, rather than because of, the Count's own
efforts at shaping policy. The picture as it would now seem to be
taking shape is of a man who believed himself to be close to the
centres of power both in his own country and in that to which he was
accredited, and who thought that his importance lay in his own ability
judiciously to wield power, but who in reality was valuable to the
German Foreign Ministry, and valued by Narkomindel, not as a
formulator and implementer of policy but as a figurehead, an out-
ward and visible sign of the continuity of German–Soviet relations.
His early biographer, Stern-Rubarth, came closer to the truth than
he himself realised in describing Rantzau as a 'wanderer between two
worlds'.[51] Moreover, Rantzau's very pride, sensitivity and intransig-
ence, qualities which in anything else but moderation are not normally
an asset to a diplomatist, were useful to Stresemann at times when the
latter needed to employ delaying tactics in the East, whilst the uncon-
ventional frankness with which the Count expressed to the Russians
his doubts about his master's westward-looking policies served as a
constant assurance to his chronically suspicious interlocutors that they
had among the German leadership at least one whole-hearted advocate
of their cause.[52]

APPENDIX I

9101/H223176-80   Berlin, 8 July 1922
Secret

Political Directives for the German Ambassador in Moscow

The few illusions with which I was born I have, I believe, lost, and
lost thoroughly, during the course of the last ten years.

I therefore approach the task in Russia entirely without illusions
and almost sceptically. None the less I am prepared to undertake
it, under conditions which I reserve the right to define more precisely,
in order first of all to find out for myself whether, under the present
regime in Russia, there exists for German policy any opportunity for
positive activity, and in order to ascertain what prospects exist for
the future.

As things are today, the clarification of our relationship with Russia
and co-operation between the German and Russian peoples represents
the honourable solution for us, and, not only for Europe, but for the
world, the beginning of tranquillisation and of peaceful reconstruction.

The obstacles which stand in the way of this problem consist, on the German side, in the weakness of our foreign policy position, in the disorder of our domestic circumstances and not least in the impotence of our economic situation.

On the Russian side, albeit on a different scale, virtually the same difficulties exist. Russia's foreign policy position is, admittedly, much more favourable than Germany's. Russia has not been defeated and remains a force, not only in Europe, but in relation to the whole world.

From the domestic and economic viewpoints, Russia has, certainly, been more markedly weakened than Germany; she is governed by a group of unscrupulous fanatics who are only keeping themselves in power by means of terror and who shrink from *no* expedients in order to remain in power; in practice the Soviet Government are supported mainly by the urban factory workers and the Red Army, which is primarily recruited from among them; ideologically, they maintain power in virtue of the iron discipline of the Communist Party and, of late, in virtue of an ever more strongly sounded note of nationalism. Over the years the Soviet Government have considerably modified their political programme both internally and externally. That, under their leadership, the Russian Revolution could gradually be transformed into an evolution, is none the less scarcely to be assumed. The great aim of world revolution continues to be the Soviet Government's ultimate objective, and the changes in both their domestic and foreign policy activities are only tactical manœuvres. What is more, the leaders are not agreed among themselves as to the manner in which to proceed; Lenin exerts a moderating influence vis-à-vis the chauvinist elements.

That, in the present transitional phase, which is a critical one for them, the Soviet Government should be obliged to attach more importance to coming to an understanding with the Entente than with Germany, is as clear as it is understandable; that for the sake of this prize they would at any time be prepared to sacrifice us, is therefore obvious. The German representative in Moscow must therefore in no circumstances allow himself to be played off against the Allies.

He must, without offending them, and without getting caught up in the wake of the Entente or of any of its members, conduct an independent policy with the Soviet Government. In his contacts with the Soviet Government, he must always bear in mind that, both officially and unofficially, anything which might provide fresh nourishment for their deep-rooted suspicion towards the representative of any bourgeois government must be avoided. In addition to this, however, it will be one of the most important tasks of the German Ambassador to induce in *all* circles of the Russian people the conviction that the German *people* wishes to co-operate with the Russian *people*, that it is resolved to help the Russian people as much as its strength permits, and, regardless of the *form* of government which the Russian people has adopted, jointly, through all the years to come, to lighten the common burden through peaceful labour, and to coexist in true friendship and good-neighbourly relations. The community of economic and cultural interests should here be emphatically stressed.

Since, as far as the situation can be assessed from here, a change of government and system in Russia does not appear out of the question, it is absolutely necessary for the German mission to proceed in the direction indicated above; it would, on the other hand, be unsafe and unwise to count on, let alone work towards, the fall of the Soviet Government.

The German Ambassador must maintain the greatest reserve and tactful moderation in both domestic and foreign politics. In no case should he allow even the remotest suspicion to arise that he wishes to interfere in the internal situation. Such an attitude would, of course, in no sense preclude the most energetic action, if necessary even *against* the Soviet Government, once German interests were at stake.

Fateful as unjustified intervention in domestic affairs would be, for the German representative to allow himself to be used for military or foreign policy experiments, for instance in the sense of promoting anti-British propaganda, would be equally fateful. He will undoubtedly be subjected to numerous temptations of this kind; he must be able to avoid them, which is by no means to say that he should neglect to follow any tendencies in the above-mentioned direction with care and to study them attentively with an eye to their potential for development. For, when all is said and done, our relationship with Russia can only become the factor which we require for our foreign policy and for Germany's world position if the Entente realise that there exists a link between Germany and Russia, not aimed at *revanche*, but yet a force which will promote reconstruction and inspire respect.

If it should prove possible to achieve this end, then the world will take another tone with us than that which we have been accustomed to hear since the collapse.

The attempt to initiate a truly friendly relationship with Russia, despite all the objections and difficulties which stand in its way, *must* therefore be made; that an earlier point in time would have been more favourable for this step than the present, need not be mentioned here.

It will now be the duty of the German Ambassador in Moscow to test, with unshakeable patience and without illusions, but also without sceptical pessimism, the present situation in Russia to see what opportunities it offers for realising this aim. Close co-operation with Russia is today made greatly easier for us owing to the fact that, after the dissolution of Austria–Hungary and the decay of Turkey, Pan-Slavism is no longer a hindrance to us.

As regards, finally, the oft-invoked danger of Bolshevist infection, it is by no means a matter of certainty that this will be substantially increased by the resumption of diplomatic relations. As it is, it has not proved possible effectively to close our frontiers to Russian gold and Russian emissaries.

The healthy majority of the German people is not susceptible to Russo-Asiatic Bolshevism; an autochthonous Bolshevism in Germany, however, will be inevitable and will be bound to appear if, in foreign policy too, we continue to be denied a way out of the present hopeless situation, if the unhappy, tormented and oppressed, deceived and deluded German people, constantly subjected to the educational methods of its self-righteous, haughty rivals of yesterday and to the vengefulness of cowardly, megalomaniac sadists, is driven to ultimate desperation.

Brockdorff-Rantzau

APPENDIX II

9101/H223225-32   Berlin, 17 July 1922
Top Secret

The political guidelines for the German Ambassador in Moscow have been deliberately kept to general terms; he who cares to read between the lines can nevertheless discern my programme. 'Our debts to the Allies cannot be paid in gold and silver; the account between us and the Entente can only be settled with iron.' These words of the Majority Socialist Minister Dr Landsberg (of 8 July), in that they express the mood which has even reached deeply into Socialist circles, have proved to me that the policy which I am pursuing is the right one and one which, should it come to the final decision, will enjoy the support of the broad masses of the people.

The crime of Versailles presses for a decision; the article by Nitti (*Berliner Tageblatt* of yesterday, 16 July) affords proof that the most far-sighted statesmen of the Entente are themselves convinced of the untenability of the situation. Nitti bases his view almost word for word on the arguments contained in the Notes which I addressed to the Entente at Versailles; he has understood that Clemenceau's senile vengefulness is a pathological symptom and not a factor by means of which a world which has been put out of joint [*aus den Fugen*] can be brought back to normal courses. The former Italian Minister-President has realised that Clemenceau's policy desires nothing less than the dismemberment of the German Reich and the destruction of the German people. If a member of the Entente can come to this conviction, then the German people, which is, after all, the victim of the French experiments in sadism, should at long last attain to the recognition that it is a matter of being or non-being [*Sein oder Nichtsein*]. Slogans about the impossibility of destroying a people of 60 millions are today of little use. Such phrases are only dangerous because they paralyse the ability to act. If the, regrettably apolitical, majority of the German people, with – and to our shame we must say it – its servile characteristics which in misfortune are openly displayed and in happier times took the form of *parvenu* ambition, blindly or cynically – the question of motives does not matter in terms of the ultimate outcome – allows its doom to overtake it, it will have deserved its fate.

The only way out that remains to us leads eastward. Britain's attitude has been sufficiently discussed. London will only take us into account politically if they respect us. France is at present out of the question as far as a direct effort to reach an understanding is concerned. Italy, despite her traditional unreliability, might, if occasion arose, be of use as an opportunistic intermediary. America is dissociating herself [*desinteressiert sich*] from Europe and is, above all, refusing absolutely to have any contact, direct or indirect, with the Socialist movement.

These are the international conditions under which we must conduct a policy in the East. These conditions are being made considerably more difficult by our partners, the Soviet Government.

The Treaty of Rapallo undoubtedly represents a political burden for us, for, whether we wish it or no, we will appear to the outside world as the allies of Soviet Russia in consequence of it. After the failure of the negotiations at The Hague this political burden weighs all the heavier, for the possibility undeniably exists that the Soviet Government, having been denied the economic aid which they have demanded of the Entente and which we shall not be able to afford them in anything like the necessary measure, will have recourse to the last resort of all bankrupt governments, namely, to war. This expedient, in any case, fits excellently well into the Bolshevik programme of world revolution.

We must, therefore, make absolutely sure that we are not drawn into the catastrophe which is now impending. Germany, in her present state of impotence, could only figure as the field of battle in any conflict between East and West.

Our vital interests therefore incontestably demand that this conflict be delayed as long as possible in order that, in the meanwhile, an economic cure may take place in Germany and Russia. Any precipitancy, any urgency, or even any attempt on our part to bring about a military conflict would at present be criminal. We should begin by making every effort to strengthen Russia in the *economic* respect.

Should it become apparent that the Soviet Government despaired of economic reconstruction and intended to take military action, then we would have to avoid even the slightest suspicion of wishing to support them in these proclivities. Incautious conduct on our part would afford France the desired pretext for attacking us, and Britain would then scarcely be in a position to bid France desist. Moreover, we should have to allow for the fact that France would take any attack by Russia upon Poland as an occasion for invading Germany. In such an event, and if it proved possible somehow to avoid civil war in Germany, we should, whilst refraining from useless military resistance, have to wait and see whether England would permit the occupation of the Ruhr, etc. This is unlikely, if only in view of Italy.

Should it prove possible to avoid disaster now, our primary aim should, as has already been said, be to strengthen Russia in the economic sense, and this not only by supplying industrial products and agricultural machinery, but also by making intellectual aid available. We should place at Russia's disposal manual workers and white-collar workers, academics, businessmen and, in particular, organisers in all fields. [Even to organise the Russian Army will represent no danger for us, if England and America are in any case going to hand us over to the destructive rage of France.

A military alliance with the Soviet Government should today, of course, be rejected.]* German policy must seek, by actively promoting reconstruction, to strengthen the Russian Government – assuming that they do not intend to resort to arms in the near future – in the conviction that Germany is indispensable for the restoration of Russia, and that Russia has an incontrovertible interest in not seeing Germany weakened. This conviction should be caused to become so rooted in Moscow that, even without being allied to us, Russia would at once take military action if France or her monstrous political offspring, Poland, were to attack us.

A military *alliance* with the Soviet Government should today, of course, be rejected; were we to commit even the slightest indiscretion

---

* The square brackets occur in the original, presumably to indicate deletion of the passage therein enclosed.

in the form of verbal agreements in the military sphere, we should be placing ourselves irretrievably at the mercy of the Soviet Government, who would at any time have it in their power, and would not hesitate for a moment, to blackmail us by threatening to betray the military arrangements to the Entente.

Should Britain leave us to our fate – and this possibility too must be taken into account – then we must weigh up the possibility of threatening Britain in India through Russia as a last means of exerting pressure; we must therefore not begin by putting this expedient completely out of court.

If the conscienceless statesmen of the Entente really believe that they can treat the German people as a *quantité négligeable* and as a herd of docile helots, then the *furor teutonicus* will show them that there are still men in Germany who know how to rally the healthy, unexhausted strength of this misguided people and to prevent the suicide of a nation of 60 million souls. If the gentlemen in Paris and London nevertheless desire the *destruction of Germany*, then they shall have *chaos*, and they themselves will be engulfed in it too!

NOTES

1. See Werner Hahlweg (ed.), *Lenins Rückkehr nach Russland 1917* (Leiden, 1957); Z. A. B. Zeman (ed.), *Germany and the Revolution in Russia, 1915-1918* (London, 1958); Michael Futrell, *Northern Underground* (New York, 1963); W. B. Scharlau and Z. A. B. Zeman, *Freibeuter der Revolution: Parvus-Helphand. Eine politische Biographie* (Cologne, 1964).

2. In connection with his work during the war to ensure the continued exchange of Danish foodstuffs for German coal, Rantzau came into frequent contact with leading German social democrats and became convinced that political co-operation with the Social Democratic Party was possible.

3. See Hajo Holborn, 'Diplomats and Diplomacy in the Early Weimar Republic', in Gordon A. Craig and Felix Gilbert (eds.), *The Diplomats, 1919-1939* (first published Princeton, 1953; paperback ed., 1968, used for references here) p. 133.

4. There is no need to discuss here once again whether Rantzau's failure to stand whilst making his speech of 7 May 1919, in reply to Clemenceau, was the result of nerves or deliberate calculation; what is clear is that the text of the speech itself was the reverse of conciliatory. For the text, see Brockdorff-Rantzau, *Dokumente und Gedanken um Versailles*, 3rd ed. (Berlin, 1925) pp. 70 ff.

5. For Rantzau's contacts with, e.g., President Ebert, and Baron Ago von Maltzan of the German Foreign Ministry, see Herbert Helbig, *Die Träger der Rapallo-Politik* (Göttingen, 1958) pt I, sect. iii, pp. 38-53. In April 1921 the Count, who opposed 'fulfilment', suggested to Ebert that economic and political relations should be entered into with Soviet Russia as a means of resisting Entente, and especially French, pressure.

6. See ibid., especially his Conclusion, pp. 208-10.

7. See Holborn, in Craig and Gilbert (eds.), *The Diplomats*, pp. 133, 170.

8. Kurt Rosenbaum, *Community of Fate: German–Soviet Diplomatic Relations, 1922-1928* (New York, 1965) esp. pp. 94-5.

9. The unpublished sources chiefly drawn on here are the files of the German Foreign Ministry, which include the Brockdorff-Rantzau *Nachlass*. Individual documents cited below are identified by the microfilm serial and frame numbers allotted to them by the German War Documents project, or by other similar reference numbers. (Details of file titles, etc., may be found in *A Catalogue of German Foreign Ministry Files and Microfilms, 1867-1920* (1959) and *A Catalogue of Files and Microfilms of the German Foreign Ministry Archives, 1920-1945*, Hoover Institution–Stanford University, vol. I (1962), vol. II (1964) (in progress).) Not all relevant material, however, was microfilmed; nor are the German Foreign Ministry archives, extensive though they are, the only relevant source: much that is of interest has been, or may yet be, found in, e.g., the holdings of the Militärgeschichtliches Forschungsamt, Freiburg im Breisgau, the Bundesarchiv, Koblenz, and the Deutsches Zentralarchiv, Potsdam.

10. Cited in the unpublished draft biography by Professor Erich Brandenburg which forms part of the German Foreign Ministry collection of Brockdorff-Rantzau papers (1689/396927.

11. See Brockdorff-Rantzau, *Dokumente* (Charlottenburg, 1920) pp. 37 ff.

12. Draft of June 1919 for a speech to the Cabinet (1690/397186-7).

13. Rantzau memorandum, 1 Apr 1917 (1689/396920 ff.).

14. Rantzau memorandum, 27 Apr 1919, on conversation with Ebert (1690/397107).

15. Rantzau record of conversation with Colonel Conger in the train *en route* to Paris as head of the German peace delegation (1690/397112).

16. Rantzau memorandum, [?] Apr 1919 (9105/235177-85).

17. See, e.g., Rantzau's memorandum of 8 July 1922, 'Political Directives for the German Ambassador in Moscow', a translation of which is printed as Appendix I to this paper.

18. 1690/397006 ff.

19. Seeckt had been appointed Head of the *Heeresleitung* early in 1920. For the accusation of lack of patriotism, a Rantzau memorandum of 1 Aug 1922 (6812/E517765-76) is especially important.

20. Rantzau memorandum, 11 July 1922 (9101/H223182-8). Wirth had taken personal charge of the Foreign Ministry after the assassination of Rathenau on 24 June.

21. Relevant material may be found especially in Serials 9101, Pt 1, and 6812. Among others, Rantzau called on Chicherin, the Soviet Foreign Commissar, who happened to be in Berlin at the time, doing so before he had been officially offered the post of Ambassador (Rantzau memorandum, 23 June 1922, 9101/H223125-38).

22. Rantzau memorandum of a conversation with Wirth on 24 July 1922, quoted in Helbig, *Die Träger der Rapallo-Politik*, p. 119 (6812/E517743-4).

23. For details, see J. Erickson, *The Soviet High Command: A Military-Political History, 1918-1941* (London, 1962), and Francis L. Carsten, *Reichswehr und Politik 1918-1933* (Cologne, 1964).

24. The present writer must venture to disagree with E. H. Carr's assertion, in *The Bolshevik Revolution, 1917-1923*, III (London, 1961) 439, that Seeckt's

and Rantzau's 'views on the essentials of German policy became indistinguish-able'. Rantzau's dislike of the military links and his efforts to control, and if possible to de-emphasise or even dismantle them, continued throughout his tenure of the Moscow post, as, at a more generalised level of policy formula-tion, did his advocacy of caution as opposed to Seeckt's activism.

25. The memorandum of 8 July 1922 is printed in translation as Appendix I to this paper. That of 15 Aug, the 'Promemoria' (9101/223321-36), was published in part by Julius Epstein, 'Der Seeckt-Plan', in *Der Monat* of Nov 1948, pp. 42-50 (where, however, it is wrongly dated 15 July); it was published in full by H. Helbig, 'Die Moskauer Mission des Grafen Brockdorff-Rantzau', in *Forschungen zur ost-europäischen Geschichte*, II (1955) 286-344, and an English translation, with some cuts, appears in Gerald Freund, *Unholy Alliance* (London, 1957) pp. 131-5.

26. Printed in translation as Appendix II to this paper.

27. Rantzau Political Report No. 11, dated Moscow, 6 Dec 1922 (K1905/482396-408). Headed 'Germany's and Russia's Community of Fate', it contains the following passage, which well illustrates both the strengths and the weak-nesses of the Ambassador's grasp of the situation: 'Among many of the bourgeois, who are already once again co-operating positively, there obtains even today the conviction that Russia's association with the Entente and the breach with Germany is primarily to blame for the disaster. From such political considerations stems the readiness, despite a precise knowledge of Germany's economic straits, to proceed together in the community of fate of the work for national renewal.'

28. Apart from the 'military apprehensions' to which he feared it had given rise, one of Rantzau's chief reasons for disliking the Treaty of Rapallo was his view that it had been badly timed. He considered that an agreement with Soviet Russia could have been more opportunely concluded in the spring of the previous year, when it would have helped to counteract Allied pressure over Reparation (1691/397303 ff., and Rantzau notes of conversation with Ebert on 10 May 1922, 9105/H223115-21). This notion of the cardinal importance of timing had first figured largely, not in connection with Russia, but at Versailles, where Rantzau had wanted to delay matters somehow until the differences between the Allies began to make themselves felt, thus opening up for the Germans the chance of obtaining a negotiated peace (1690/397197).

29. August Wilhelm Schlegel and Ludwig Tieck (translators), *Shakespeare's dramatische Werke*, 6. Band (Berlin, 1844): *Hamlet*, Act I, scene v (p. 40), and Act III, scene I (p. 74). Cf. Appendix II.

30. 'Germany's Attitude towards the Russian Problem', memorandum of 11 Sep 1922 (Seeckt *Nachlass*, Stück Nr. 213; original at Militärgeschichtliches Forschungsamt, Freiburg im Breisgau); the text was published by Epstein, op. cit. Lengthy extracts are printed in Freund, *Unholy Alliance*, pp. 135-8. See also Carsten, *Reichswehr und Politik*, pp. 146 ff.

31. e.g. Rantzau memorandum, 3 Aug 1922 (6812/E517777-8, 799-807).

32. When, on 21 Feb 1925, Rykov, Chairman of the Council of People's Commissars, made a proposal for a German–Soviet treaty of alliance (Rantzau report of 24 Feb, 4562/E155006-9), the Ambassador was not equipped to make any constructive response, because he was unaware of discussions along similar lines which had taken place the previous month in Berlin between Seeckt, Stomoniakov (the Head of the Soviet Trade Delegation in Berlin), Krestinsky

(the Soviet Ambassador) and Rosengolts (see Carsten, *Reichswehr und Politik*, pp. 256-7).

33. He subsequently went so far as to describe them as 'one of the most important binding agents of our common policy' (in a letter of 8 Apr 1928 to Stresemann, quoted in Rosenbaum, *Community of Fate*, p. 261).

34. On 30 July 1923 a meeting was held between Rosengolts and Chancellor Cuno at the flat of Ernst zu Rantzau, the Ambassador's twin brother (Rantzau memorandum, 31 July, 4564/E162550-5). See also Carsten, *Reichswehr und Politik*, pp. 153-4.

35. Rantzau memoranda, 16 July 1923 (L340/L101210-13), undated (L340/L101221-8) and 29 July (4564/E162539-49).

36. See Rosenbaum, *Community of Fate*, pp. 114-15.

37. See K. D. Erdmann, 'Das Problem der Ost- oder Westorientierung in der Locarno-Politik Stresemanns', *Geschichte in Wissenschaft und Unterricht*, VI 3 (Mar 1955), and Rosenbaum, *Community of Fate*, chaps. iv and v.

38. Rantzau report to President Hindenburg, 8 July 1926 (9101/H224038-46), quoted in Helbig, *Die Träger der Rapallo-Politik*, pp. 187-8. For Soviet reactions to the events of March 1926 at Geneva, see *Dokumenty vneshnei politiki SSSR* (Moscow, 1957 ff.; in progress) (hereinafter cited as *D.V.P.S.*) IX (1964) nos. 102, 109 and 113, and memorandum by Dirksen (Head of the Eastern Department of the German Foreign Ministry) dated 30 Mar 1926 (4562/E156713-16).

39. See Rosenbaum, *Community of Fate*, p. 242.

40. Petrov, an attaché at the Soviet Embassy in Berlin, was discovered in the autumn of 1923 to have been purchasing arms for use by German Communists (see Carsten, *Reichswehr und Politik*, pp. 156-7, Rosenbaum, *Community of Fate*, pp. 72-3, and Stresemann letter to Rantzau, 1 Dec 1923, L337/L100880-6). Bozenhardt was a German Communist who, when being escorted through Berlin in May 1924 whilst under arrest in connection with his activities during the abortive Communist uprising the previous year, succeeded in taking refuge in the Soviet Trade Delegation, thus precipitating a search of the premises by the Berlin police and a virtual cessation of German–Soviet dealings at various levels until the end of July (see Rosenbaum, *Community of Fate*, chap. iii). Kindermann and Wolscht were two German students who had been arrested in October 1924, whilst on a fact-finding visit to the Soviet Union, on charges of political and economic espionage. They were not brought to trial until June 1925, after death sentences had been pronounced at Leipzig on certain leading Russian and German participants in the attempted Communist uprising of 1923. An exchange was eventually arranged (see Rosenbaum, *Community of Fate*, pp. 146-9, 151-5). The Caucasus question arose from the arrest in December 1925 of a number of 'locally employed' German consular agents in Baku, Poti and Batum on charges of military espionage. The matter was settled by an expression of regret by Narkomindel (see Rosenbaum, *Community of Fate*, pp. 200-2). For the appearance towards the end of 1925 of *Foreign Armies*, which contained references to clandestine German rearmament, see E. H. Carr, *Socialism in One Country, 1924-1926*, III, pt i (London, 1964) 434. For Voroshilov's speech of 12 Nov 1927, in which he forecast an early spread of the revolution, and for the Hölz incident, see G. Hilger and A. G. Meyer, *The Incompatible Allies* (New York, 1953) p. 157. For the arrest in March 1928, and subsequent trial, of three German engineers employed in the Donbas, on charges of industrial espionage

and sabotage, see Rosenbaum, *Community of Fate*, pp. 253 ff., and 'The German Involvement in the Shakhty Trial', *Russian Review*, XXIII (July 1962) 238-60.

41. Rantzau report to Hindenburg (see note 38 above): 'Our relationship with Soviet Russia will, as I have held since I took up my post here, always to a certain extent be based on bluff, that is to say that it will be useful outwardly, vis-à-vis our so-called *former* enemies, to give the impression of a greater intimacy with Russia than in fact exists.'

42. One occasion was when the charges against Kindermann and Wolscht appeared to implicate Hilger, Counsellor of Legation at the German Embassy in Moscow; Rantzau did not hesitate to follow Stresemann's instructions to take a high line with Chicherin (Rantzau report to the German Foreign Ministry, 1 July 1925, 2860/555366-8). Another occasion was the Max Hölz affair, when Rantzau wished to leave Moscow as a mark of displeasure but was told by Stresemann to remain (see Rosenbaum, *Community of Fate*, pp. 252-3).

43. See Helbig, *Die Träger der Rapallo-Politik*, p. 141.

44. Rantzau memorandum for Stresemann, 13 Apr 1925 (3123/646102-17).

45. e.g. Rantzau telegram to Stresemann, 7 Aug 1925 (6698/H106479-81), in which Rantzau bade the Foreign Minister 'to be so good as to take a personal interest in the critical state of German–Russian relations'. Rantzau contemplated resignation twice in 1925, in April and in November (3123/642935-41 and 9101/H224015-18, 24 ff.).

46. Maltzan was appointed Head of the Eastern Department of the German Foreign Ministry after the formation of the second Wirth Cabinet in October 1921. Maltzan's own, highly tendentious, account of the events at Genoa leading up to the signature of the Treaty of Rapallo is filmed as L309/L096110-26. What appears to be a shortened version is printed in Edgar Vincent, Lord D'Abernon, *An Ambassador of Peace*, 3 vols. (London, 1929-30) I 298-303. See also Theodor Schieder, *Die Probleme des Rapallo-Vertrags* (Cologne, 1956).

47. Early in June 1925 the Chancellor, Luther, himself took fright and tried to dissociate himself from Stresemann's Security Pact policy; see Gustav Stresemann, *Vermächtnis*, 3 vols. (Berlin, 1932-33) II 134.

For an admirably balanced assessment of Stresemann's policy of balance, see the pioneering work of E. H. Carr, *German–Soviet Relations between the Two World Wars, 1919-1939* (Baltimore, 1951) esp. pp. 88-90.

48. 4562/E155068-90. This dispatch is printed, in the original German, in the collection *Locarno-Konferenz 1925* ([East] Berlin, 1962) no. 9, and in Russian translation in the collection by A. F. Dobrov *et al.* (eds.), *Lokarnskaya Konferentsiya 1925g.* (Moscow, 1959) no. 7. This document is far more informative than Stresemann's better-known letter of 7 Sep 1925 to the German Crown Prince (7318/H159871-5), which is printed, but with some cuts, in *Vermächtnis*, II 555 ff.

49. From the time (29 Sep 1924) when Germany made her first, conditional, application for League membership, the matter was the subject of close Soviet attention. At first the Russians hoped for an agreement that neither power would join before consulting the other (Litvinov in conversation with Radowitz of the German Embassy in Moscow, reported by the latter in telegram of 18 Oct, 2860/554419-20). When it became apparent that no such German commitment would be forthcoming, the Soviet attitude towards prospective German membership hardened (see *D.V.P.S.*, VIII, no. 124 and n. 67). The introduction to the East German collection of documents, *Locarno-Konferenz 1925* (see note 48 above), observes (p. 12): 'A suitable means for binding Germany to the

imperialist West was seen by British diplomacy in the inclusion of Germany in the anti-Soviet League of Nations....'

50. 4562/E154993-5003.

51. Edgar Stern-Rubarth, *Graf Brockdorff-Rantzau: Wanderer zwischen zwei Welten* (Berlin, 1929).

52. *D.V.P.S.*, VIII, no. 105 (Chicherin record, dated 8 Apr 1925, of conversation): 'Rantzau spoke, above all, of his departure, and said that he might perhaps not return at all if it turned out that the German Government really were following a new course. I told him that, in the sruggle for the well-known line, he must not, so to speak, abandon a strategic position, and his presence at his post here amounted to [taking] a position upon the line as laid down. To this he replied that for him there was a point to remaining at this post if he had any sort of importance and influence; if, however, he was to be here only for form's sake, and if his views were not to have any significance for Berlin, then his presence here would only be harmful. He exclaimed with pathos: "I am prepared to play a tragic role, but I will not play a comic part." He said several times, with great emphasis, that as an official he must not criticise his Government. Thus he gave me very clearly to understand that in reality he is very much at odds with his Government.' This interview took place during the early stages of the development of Stresemann's Security Pact policy; Rantzau was about to travel to Berlin, where he was to remain for a period of some two months, continually voicing his opposition to a rapprochement with the Western Powers.

7 The Initiation of the Negotiations Leading to the Nazi–Soviet Pact: A Historical Problem

D. C. WATT

IN no problem are historians as apt to befuddle themselves with ambiguity and excessive zeal than in their search for the 'origins' of a particular set of causal processes from which a key event or set of events appears to have eventuated. Normally, professional historians are most careful not to isolate separate sets of developments from the general background of time and space in which they occur. One is reminded over and over again that events do not occur nor are decisions taken *in vacuo*. Those who take decisions or initiate events do not wear blinkers or separate their mental processes into individual compartments entirely isolated from one another. Historical events can only be understood in the total context of time and space within which they occur.

Yet these caveats are almost always forgotten when the historian starts on the trail of origins. The scent of novelty in his nostrils, he plunges into the past, wrenching events from their context, to create an intellectual construction often so complete and convincing in itself that even his professional colleagues are beguiled into forgetting their own principles and mistaking the historian's categorisation of events for the living actuality of history.

An excellent case in point is provided by the historiography of the Nazi–Soviet non-aggression pact of 24 August 1939. Its signature was for the contemporary world an event of traumatic effect. At one stroke of the pen the certainties and the categories in which current political analysis and debate had been carried on were revealed to be baseless. Long-standing loyalties were revealed to have been based on delusion. Thousands of supporters of the Soviet Union were shocked into abandoning the Communist movement for ever. In Japan the Cabinet discovered that its long debate over an alliance with Germany had been conducted on entirely false premises. Germany was prepared to move into close relations with the Soviet Union despite the Anti-Comintern Pact, signed only three years earlier, despite the fact that Japanese forces were at that very moment locked in combat with the Soviet Far Eastern Army under Marshal Zhukov around Nomonhan. The Japanese Ambassador in Berlin, General Oshima, was particularly hard hit. Small wonder that both he and the Cabinet felt in honour bound to resign.

The subjective impact of the non-aggression pact was matched by its objective significance. Hitler was freed to obliterate Poland and to drive to victory in the West, liberated from any fear of a war on two fronts. Britain's attempt to construct a diplomatic deterrent was destroyed. The Second World War was rendered inevitable. Europe was surrendered to enforced unity under the New Order. Any exertion of economic pressure on Germany by British sea power was severely limited by Russia's benevolent neutrality. Soviet power advanced to the whole of the Baltic coast north-east of the Russian border and moved a hundred miles or more westwards into Central Europe. Strategically, politically, and in terms of the balance of economic power, the Nazi–Soviet pact was almost as significant an event as it was in subjective terms. Never was there a more obvious target for origin-hunters.

It is this which makes it so suitable a case for study – especially as, since the initial burst of interest, in the period 1948-54,[1] so much new evidence has become available.

The problems the historian has to face are twofold, partly concerned with Russia, partly with Germany. In each case they can be resolved into a single question: when did those responsible for the direction of external policy in each country decide to embark on negotiations with a view to the signature of the political agreement that was, in fact, concluded on 24 August 1939? The formulation of the question is itself important. It carries four implications. Firstly, the question distinguishes between those who *advocate* a policy, and those who decide upon it. Secondly, it distinguishes between the general idea of improving relations and the specific point of negotiations leading to the non-aggression pact. Thirdly, it distinguishes between the negotiation of an economic agreement and the negotiation of a political agreement.[2] Fourthly, it is concerned not with the final moment of decision to sign the agreement, but with the decision to embark on negotiations.

It may be thought that the formulation of this question in fact begs the more general issue raised in the opening paragraphs of this essay.

I hope the argument which follows will show that this is not in fact the case. The question was formulated in this way not only so that attention might be precisely focused on what the author regards as the crucial set of events, but also so that alternative interpretations hitherto accepted may be examined in the light of this formulation and shown by examination of the general historical context to be mistaken.

German–Soviet negotiations can be said to have begun formally on the German side with the interview granted at German request by Molotov, who had succeeded Maxim Litvinov as Soviet Foreign Minister on 4 May, to the German Ambassador to Moscow, Werner von Schulenburg, on 20 May 1939. The interview was to be followed by ten days of dithering, if that is not too strong a word, in Berlin, dithering that was in some sense resolved by the speech given by Molotov to the Supreme Soviet on 31 May.[3] Schulenberg's report on this was in a sense crucial.[4] From that point the Germans were embarked on the economic and commercial negotiations, the success of which nerved Ribbentrop to the conviction that when Soviet support was wanted it would be forthcoming. He may well have been reinforced in this conviction by the very accurate and speedy information which was supplied to the German Embassy in London on the content of the exchanges between London and Moscow – information which, in the light of our present knowledge as to the inadequacies of the German intelligence network in Britain, it is not beyond reason to believe was supplied from Soviet sources in London.

In the existing literature on the Nazi–Soviet pact one can distinguish perhaps three schools of thought as to the moment when the decision to encourage, if not to solicit, German advances was taken on the Soviet side: one may refer to them for purposes of identification as the 'Molotov', 'Potemkin' and 'Stalin's speech' hypotheses. One may equally distinguish three schools of thought as to the moment of German decision: the 'Hitler's New Year reception' theory, the 'reaction to Stalin's speech' theory and the 'reaction to Litinov's dismissal' theory. Let us consider these in order.

What has been, for purposes of identification, called the 'Molotov' hypothesis tends to go back to Molotov's speech to the Central Executive Committee of the Soviet Communist Party on 10 January 1936.[5] This, it is felt, shows that Molotov was always in favour of a Soviet–German rapprochement. The well-known conversations between David Kandelaki, the Soviet Trade Commissioner in Berlin, and Neurath, Blomberg and Schacht in December 1936–January 1937 are adduced as marking a new stage in the same policy,[6] that of presenting the Soviet Union as a continuous suitor *à la* Rapallo for the favours of Nazi Germany. Not much attention needs to be paid to this line of argument since, if accepted, it at best indicates an inclination among the Soviet leadership, presumably also in Stalin's mind itself, to treat Nazi Germany as a possible associate despite the current Soviet propaganda line. Interpretations of Molotov's speech differ. And the theory itself is too general to explain the how and the why of the decisions which resulted in the Nazi–Soviet pact.

The 'Potemkin' theory has a lot more to be said for it. According to this line of argument, the Soviet exclusion from Munich had a traumatic effect. It marked the total defeat of Litvinov's policy of collective security. It left the Soviet Union entirely isolated. Britain and France had rejected any idea of a 'Grand Alliance' with the Soviets against Germany and Italy in favour of a measure of appeasement so far-reaching as to imply the virtually total abandonment of Eastern Europe to Germany. Nothing seemed to stand in the way of a German drive against Russia except Poland, herself anti-Russian and linked with Germany both by the non-aggression pact of 1934 and complicity in the dismemberment of Czechoslovakia. Faced with this and with Japanese pressure on her eastern frontiers, the pressure on the Soviet authorities to try to turn Germany westwards was obvious. It was voiced by the Soviet Deputy Foreign Minister, Vladimir Potemkin, to Robert Coulondre, then French Ambassador in Moscow, shortly after Munich: 'Mon pauvre ami, qu'avez-vous fait? Pour nous je n'aperçois plus d'autre issue qu'un quatrième partage de la Pologne.'[7] There is a good deal of supporting evidence to fit this theory, some of it quite crucial.

To begin with, it is clear that the Soviet authorities were more than adequately informed of the progress of the German–Japanese negotiations for a tripartite alliance, which had moved into a new and active stage after Munich. They must certainly have been aware that the sticking-point in these negotiations was the German desire that the alliance be not restricted to its operation against the Soviet Union, the implication of which was clearly that Germany's next target was Britain. Seen in this light, the Soviet–Polish agreement of November 1938 was intended to encourage the Poles in their policy of balance between their two neighbours and consequently of resistance to Ribbentrop's blandishments.[8] The Soviet withdrawal from involvement in Spain the same month was only common sense. The evidence that the Soviet press and propaganda was beginning to play down its denunciations of Fascist aggression in favour of attacks on the advocates of appeasement agrees equally with the view that the Soviet authorities, feeling that the idea of a common crusade against aggression and Fascism was failing in its purpose, were drawing in their horns for the time being.[9]

More positive evidence can be found in the eagerness with which the Soviet authorities took up the idea of a trade settlement with Germany. Whether or not they were aware of the arguments of the German Ambassador in Moscow that advantage should be taken of Soviet isolation to bring about general agreement with the Soviet Government, of which a trade agreement and a newer and larger credit agreement should be the first stages,[10] is unclear. We know very little of Soviet intelligence operations against Germany at this time. But the German initiative was taken up with alacrity and a trade agreement signed in Berlin on 19 December 1938.[11] The Soviet authorities had then proposed that the credit negotiations be transferred to Moscow, a proposal that the Germans had resisted, although they did agree to send the Foreign Ministry's financial expert, Julius Schnurre, to Moscow for conversations.[12] Schnurre's mission was cancelled by Ribbentrop in his anger at its effect on his visit to Warsaw, and the German–Soviet negotiations then faded. But on this view the speech that Stalin made on 10 March 1939 to the 18th Congress of the Soviet Communist Party represented an attempt to revive these negotiations.

There is a good deal of plausibility in this theory at first sight, but it falls down on two points. In the first place, if the Soviet authorities had been intent on anything more than simply mending their fences with Germany, they would certainly have removed Litvinov from office. As it was, there were frequent rumours of his impending dismissal,[13] but they remained rumours. They were to be revived in February 1939,[14] but again were not to be confirmed by events. Litvinov remained to experiment with collective pacts with Russia's neighbours, a Black Sea pact in February,[15] and non-aggression pacts with her Baltic neighbours in March.

The second major objection to this theory lies in its interpretation of Soviet views of German policy. Here the theory attaches far too much significance to a single remark made to Coulondre in October 1938 by a Soviet Deputy Foreign Minister, a remark which, but for the events of 1939, events which took place in quite different circumstances, would have probably passed into the limbo of history. To envisage a Soviet–German agreement on the partition of Poland in November 1938 would have been totally out of keeping with contemporary circumstances. While the actual contents of the German proposals made to the Poles may well have remained as secret to the Soviet authorities as they did to the British and French, there was no overt evidence of German–Polish hostility and much to suggest that the old amity continued – most notably the continuing failure of the German press to protest against the active policy of de-Germanisation being pursued by the Polish authorities in Pomorze and Silesia.

The Soviet authorities indeed seem to have feared that the British and French were inciting the Germans to act against the Soviet Ukraine. British and French anxieties over this eventuality, based as they were on knowledge of the subversive activities being organised by the S.S. *Volksdeutsche Mittelstelle* in the Carpatho-Ukrainian appendix to post-Munich Czechoslovakia, and voiced in the Western press, were taken by the Soviets as evidence not of Western anxiety but of Western desire to incite Germany to an attack eastwards. This was despite the British step of warning the Soviet Union against the German danger.[16] Thus, early in January 1939 Litinov remarked to Grzybowski, the Polish Ambassador in Moscow (who repeated it to his Italian colleague, Augusto Rossi): 'Paris and London are making great efforts to persuade Berlin that her road is signposted towards the East. Hitler, however, is less convinced of this than the French and British believe.'[17] And shortly after the visit paid in mid-January by Chamberlain and Halifax to Rome, Litvinov again told Grzybowski that the Soviets had information 'from a reliable source that in his conversations in Rome Chamberlain had sought to raise the Ukrainian question, allowing it to be understood that Britain would not view German aspirations in this direction with disfavour'.[18] Potemkin was to repeat the same story directly to Rossi on 5 April,[19] which would tend to suggest that the Soviet authorities really believed the story. It is in fact, as both the Italian and the British records of the Chamberlain–Mussolini meetings attest, quite untrue.[20]

There is, however, one other piece of evidence which needs assessment. On 27 January 1939, shortly after reports of an imminent German attack on Britain and the Netherlands had filled the British press and alarmed the British and American Governments, the *News Chronicle*, which was widely believed to be in close touch with the Soviet Embassy in London, published a sensational article on the possibilities of a Nazi–Soviet rapprochement. The article is said to have been written as 'pure speculation';[21] it was, however, reprinted without comment by the Soviet press and used to prepare the party faithful for a possible realisation of its prophecies.[22]

This evidence would appear to controvert the arguments advanced in the previous paragraphs against the 'Potemkin' hypothesis. It should, however, be noted that it points at best towards the idea that *some* pact link with Germany was being considered in Moscow. Despite Litvinov's conviction that Germany was planning a westward attack, and despite the confident echoes of this conviction in the Soviet press, it remains clear that as long as the possibility remained of an Anglo-German agreement designed to turn Germany eastwards, the Soviet

Union was at risk and any agreement with Germany would necessarily be entered into from a defensive posture. What made the agreement of 24 August 1939 so unique was that its conclusion was from the Soviet viewpoint not a Soviet concession of Danegeld to Germany but a German offer to the Soviet Union, concluded at German initiative and at whatever price Germany was prepared to pay. In January 1939 the Soviet Union was the wooer; in August she was the wooed.

Which brings us to the third hypothesis, that in his speech of 10 March 1939 to the 18th Congress of the Soviet Communist Party, Joseph Stalin held out an offer to the Germans which they recognised.[23] This hypothesis has much to support it, notably the toast made on the occasion of the signature of the Nazi–Soviet pact by Molotov[24] and in Ribbentrop's evidence at Nuremberg.[25] Most, though not all, writers on Nazi–Soviet relations have accepted it. E. H. Carr, it should be noted, is not one of them.[26]

It is perhaps unnecessary to quote Stalin's speech at length in the course of this essay.[27] What should be noted is that the speech as such was a declaration of non-involvement in inter-capitalist quarrels; that Stalin specifically denounced the Western discussion of a possible German attack on the Ukraine as a plan to provoke a Russo-German conflict; that he alleged that Britain and France had abandoned collective security for a position of neutrality; that he said that the Soviet Union would continue to support victims of aggression. The Soviet Union, however, he concluded, would not allow herself to be 'drawn into conflict by warmongers who are accustomed to have others pull their chestnuts out of the fire'.

As a declaration of intent to remain neutral in a war against the West, this speech did of course anticipate the policy the Soviet Union was to follow in September 1939. It did not, however, anticipate those clauses of the Nazi–Soviet pact which embodied the mutual recognition by the two signatories of their respective spheres of influence. It was not followed by Litvinov's dismissal. On the contrary, it was followed by the German march into Prague and by a British reaction which seemed to open the door finally to Litvinov's long-standing efforts to promote the doctrine of collective security.

Moreover, the speech was delivered at a time when German–Soviet relations were at a very low ebb. Schnurre's mission to Moscow had been called off by Ribbentrop. Subsequent negotiations in Moscow had run into the sand when the German Ministry of Economics had ruled a German credit to the Soviet Union completely out of court on the grounds that Germany's rearmament left her without the surplus capacity adequate to produce deliveries on the scale of the proposed credit.[28]

These passages in Stalin's speech in fact represented a Soviet reaction to the unprecedented efforts which the British had been making to mend their fences with the Soviets. With the substituion of Sir William Seeds for Viscount Chilston as British Ambassador to Moscow, Lord Halifax had overcome Chamberlain's deep-rooted distrust of the Soviet Union to the point of obtaining his agreement to an attempt to improve Anglo-Soviet relations. Seed's efforts provoked considerable demonstration of Soviet distrust.[29] Nevertheless the British persisted. On 20 February Lord Halifax dined at the Soviet Embassy in London. On 1 March Chamberlain himself was Maisky's guest, with four other Cabinet Ministers, the first visit paid by a British Prime Minister to the Soviet Embassy since its establishment.[30] Stalin's speech, immediately before the visit to be paid to Moscow by Robert Hudson, Parliamentary Under-Secretary to the Department of Overseas Trade, simply echoed the warnings given in London and Moscow by Maisky and Litvinov over the previous three weeks.

Very few diplomatists saw the speech in any other light. Neither the British nor the German Ambassadors submitted reports which foreshadowed a German–Soviet agreement.[31] The Italian Ambassador commented shrewdly on Soviet suspicions of the West, but otherwise echoed the views of his British and German colleagues.[32] Only the American Chargé d'Affaires noted the views of some of the junior members of the German Embassy staff in Moscow that if Stalin's remarks could be put to Hitler in the proper light, then something might be done to improve German–Soviet relations.[33] No reflection of this was to be found on the German side, however, until after Litvinov's dismissal.

So much for the 'Stalin speech' hypothesis on the Soviet side. The foregoing will show too that there is little to be said for the 'reactions to Stalin's speech' hypothesis as an explanation of the German decision to explore the possibilities of a rapprochement with the Soviet Union. Two alternative hypotheses remain: the first relates to Hitler's New Year reception at the Reichskanzlei on 12 January 1939. On that most public of occasions, at which the diplomatic corps in Berlin assembled to convey New Year's greetings to the Führer, Hitler chose to spend three-quarters of an hour in deep conversation with the Russian Ambassador.[34] What he said remains a mystery. Some historians have referred to this meeting as the first stage in the Nazi approach to the Nazi–Soviet pact. But the evidence on the German side conclusively refutes this. Not only were the German–Soviet economic negotiations, as already described, on the road to failure, but Ribbentrop was still in the midst of his courtship of Poland. Having failed with Colonel Beck's visit to Berlin on 6 January 1939, he was pinning his hopes on his own forthcoming visit to Warsaw. Whatever Hitler's motives at this point, they bore little or no relation to a non-aggression pact. This would only begin to make sense once an attack on Poland and the consequent establishment of a common German–Soviet frontier was decided upon. Until that point the main qualification to be made on Hitler's attitude to the possible enmity of the Soviet Union is that there is no evidence that he took the military threat of the Soviet armed forces at all seriously.

What changed everything was the diplomatic consequences of his annexation of Bohemia and Moravia on 15 March, and of Memel a week later. The atmosphere of imminent European war it produced led directly to the final breakdown of German–Polish negotiations, the issue of the British invitation to the Soviet Union to discuss the security of Romania, and the British guarantee for Poland. Indirectly, the Italian annexation of Albania and the consequent British (and French) guarantees for Romania, Turkey and Greece followed. A final consequence was the revival of Litvinov's proposals for collective security in his call for a Six-Power conference in Bucharest on 19 March and the proposal for a treaty of mutual assistance between Britain, France and the Soviet Union of 18 April 1939.

It is at this point that one has to turn to the third hypothesis as to the timing of the German decision, that which ascribes it to the reactions to Litvinov's dismissal. The evidence here comes mainly from three sources: the archives of the Foreign Ministry, which show the approaches made in the last eleven days of May, beginning with Schulenburg's interview with Molotov on 20 May; the memoirs of Gustav Hilger, the German Commercial Attaché in Moscow;[35] and the memoirs and papers of General Ernst Koestring, his colleague as Military Attaché in Moscow.[36] Both paint roughly the same picture. The news of Litvinov's dismissal apparently struck the Nazi leadership like a bolt from the blue. Hilger was recalled from Moscow, Schulenberg from Teheran where he was representing the German Government at an official celebration, Koestring from a tour of duty he was making in the Far East. Hilger saw Hitler and Ribbentrop first at the Berghof. Koestring saw Ribbentrop in Berlin and was flown out to see Hitler at the Berghof on the initiative of General Keitel, Hitler's Chief of Staff. Schulenberg saw Ribbentrop in Berlin. Julius Schnurre was also called into consultation. Both Koestring and Hilger depict Ribbentrop as intensely upset by the news and equally ignorant of conditions in Russia. Both depict Hitler as equally ignorant but intensely interested in their reportage, though somewhat sceptical as to their views on the strength of Stalin's position. Hilger says that neither Hitler nor Ribbentrop were at all aware of the contents of

Stalin's speech of 10 March or its possible implications. Both are themselves so convinced as to the importance of the role they played in swaying Hitler and Ribbentrop into undertaking the exploratory initiative constituted by Schulenburg's interview with Molotov on 20 May that the temptation to accept their testimony at face value is very strong. It must nevertheless be resisted.

There are two important arguments and a whole string of events which do not fit their convictions. The first is that neither was in Berlin in April 1939; their assumption that their information and arguments were new to the Nazi leaders remains therefore an assumption. The second is that their evidence bears much more strongly on Ribbentrop's reluctance to accept their arguments than on that of Hitler. Their picture of surprise and unpreparedness in Berlin fails entirely to fit the evidence available of German–Soviet contacts and the discussion in various official circles of the possibility of a German approach to the Soviet Union in April. In particular, it does not fit three events. The first is Ribbentrop's warning to Oshima and Shiratori, the Japanese Ambassadors in Berlin and Rome, given on the occasion of Hitler's birthday celebrations on 20 April, that Germany would be compelled to sound the Soviet Union on the prospects of a non-aggression pact, if the negotiations for an alliance with Japan were not speedily concluded.[37] The second is the omission of any attack on the Soviet Union from Hitler's speech of 28 April denouncing the German–Polish non-aggression pact and the Anglo-German naval agreement of 1935,[38] and the concurrent cessation of all attacks on the Soviet Union in the German press.[39] The third is the warning given to Colonel Paul Stehlin, the French Military Attaché in Berlin, on 3 May, the day before Litvinov's dismissal, by Goering's personal liaison officer with Hitler, General Bodenschatz. Bodenschatz told Stehlin that Ribbentrop had seen the Soviet Ambassador in Berlin, Alexei Merekalov, in mid-April, before the latter's recall to Moscow. He warned that a fourth partition of Poland was in preparation. 'Etwas im Osten im Gange ist', he said.[40] He repeated his warning that same day to the Polish Military Attaché.[41]

Clearly then, the 'reaction to Litvinov's dismissal' hypothesis requires extensive emendation in the light of the events and evidence of April 1939. It is to this that we must now turn. The first indication that anyone in Berlin was thinking of a pact with the Soviet Union is contained in a letter General Koestring wrote to Colonel von Tippelskirch, head of the *Abteilung Fremde Heere (Ost)* in the Army staff, on 17 April.[42] In this he refers to a letter from Tippelskirch dated 29 March in which the latter apparently voiced the belief that Stalin might think an alliance with Hitler possible, a belief which Koestring himself refused to accept. The second piece of evidence is difficult to date but seems to have occurred early in April 1939. The Italian Consul-General in Berlin, in the course of a conversation with Erich Koch, Gauleiter of East Prussia, referred to the possibility of a German–Soviet agreement in the not very distant future, only to hear Koch, visibly taken aback, exclaim: 'But how did you learn that Germany intends to reach an agreement with Russia?'[43]

The third piece of evidence has to do with the Soviet Embassy in Berlin. On 7 April Ribbentrop suddenly ordered Dr Peter Kleist of his private office, the *Dienststelle Ribbentrop*, to improve his relations with the Soviet Embassy. Kleist contacted Georgi Astakhov, the Counsellor to the Soviet Embassy. His report on the conversation, in which Astakhov showed the greatest of interest in the possibility of improving German–Soviet relations, was too enthusiastic and Ribbentrop ordered him to drop the matter.[44] The next evidence comes on 16 April. Field-Marshal Goering, to Ribbentrop's fury, who was ostensibly on a private visit to the Italian colony in Libya, suddenly arrived in Rome on an obviously official visit, in the course of which he had two lengthy meetings with Mussolini and Count Ciano. During the second meeting he told Mussolini that he intended to ask Hitler whether it would not be possible to 'put out feelers cautiously to Russia through certain intermediaries with a view to a rapprochement so as to cause Poland anxiety over Russia as well . . .'.[45] The two, Mussolini and Goering agreed that 'Germany and Italy ought to play the so-called *petit jeu* with this country [Russia]'.

Further evidence was to come the following day. The Soviet Ambassador to Berlin, Alexei Merekalov, called on Ernst von Weizsäcker, Ribbentrop's professional deputy in the Foreign Ministry. Apparently Emil Wiehl, Head of the Economic Policy Department in the Foreign Ministry, had recently expressed to him Germany's desire to cultivate and extend German economic relations with Russia. Merekalov, in Weizsäcker's version of these remarks,[45] deliberately used this to steer the conversation towards a quasi-formal statement that there was no reason why German–Soviet relations should not be put on a normal footing and 'out of normal relations could grow increasingly improved relations'. With that parting shot Merekalov returned to Moscow. There are no direct records of any other German–Soviet contacts until after Litvinov's replacement by Molotov. On 5 May Schnurre met Astakhov to tell him of Germany's intention to fulfil the outstanding contracts between the Czech Skoda armaments factory, which had passed into German control as a result of the occupation of Bohemia and Moravia, and the Soviet Government. Inquiry on this matter had been the ostensible reason for Merekalov's meeting with Weizsäcker on 17 April. Astakhov used the occasion to stress Molotov's importance.

The Germans took one other step as a preliminary to improving relations with Russia. This was to press the Italians to abandon their claims on seven Soviet sailors, prisoners of the Franco Government in Spain, so that they might be employed in an exchange with the Soviet authorities.[47] The German Embassy in Moscow was informed of this on 29 April.

This evidence is obviously imperfect. It does, however, call attention to three very obvious possibilities. The first is that the pressure on the German side for an approach to the Soviet Union came not from Ribbentrop, who was still doing his utmost to obtain a tripartite agreement with Italy and Japan, but from his old rival, Goering, among whose allies should be counted Erich Koch, elements of the German General Staff and the German Foreign Ministry. Koch and Goering had done their best in November and December to thwart Ribbentrop's encouragement of Hitler's violent anti-British plans. They had temporarily buried the hatchet with Ribbentrop in January 1939;[48] but the breakdown of the German–Polish negotiations and the issue of the British guarantee for Poland had again faced them with the prospect of an Anglo-German war. Against this they wanted the *petit jeu*, a manœuvre designed to deflate Polish bellicosity and lead Britain to the negotiating table. Hence the open warnings to both the Poles and the French from General Bodenschatz. Ribbentrop by contrast was still clinging desperately to the tripartite alliance with Japan. Early in May Hitler was to overrule him and order the conclusion of a bilateral alliance with Italy.

The second point to emerge from the fragmentary evidence we have of German–Soviet contacts in April indicates that from the Soviet side signals of German good intentions were asked for and received. One was the fulfilment of deliveries from the Skoda works asked for by Merekalov on 17 April and conceded on 5 May. Another, it would seem, was the cessation of German press attacks on the Soviet Union. We have no record of its being requested, only of its concession. It was so obvious as to be the subject of open comment by Astakhov on 9 May, when he introduced the new Tass representative to the press office of the German Foreign Ministry.[49] It is possible that the German action in the question of the Soviet sailors imprisoned in Spain was another.

Following this hypothesis of the exchange of signals, it would seem that the Soviet reply, the dismissal of Litvinov, was on a far larger scale than anyone in Hitler's entourage had anticipated. The evidence as to the surprise and astonishment the news created in Berlin cannot be doubted, even where doubt is cast on Hilger's and Koestring's assumption as to its explanation. Unfortunately, we have no account as to its effect on Goering or Koch, so we cannot tell whether it came as much of a surprise to them as it did to Hitler or Ribbentrop. It could be hypothesised that the Soviet move was greatly in excess of what Goering's *petit jeu* demanded. Unfortunately, we are left in the realms of speculation.

The third point, and a natural corollary to its two predecessors, is that there must have been contact between the Soviets and Goering, especially in the latter part of April, of which we are still ignorant. Something must have prompted Ribbentrop to send Kleist to see Astakhov; something other than Goering's conversation with Mussolini (the details of which only reached him much later) must have prompted his warning to Oshima and Shiratori. To Mussolini, Goering spoke of 'certain intermediaries'. Who they were is still unclear. The only clue we have is a report that General Syrovy, Czech Premier in the last days of September 1938 and Minister of Defence in the Czech Cabinet at the time of the German march into Prague, was acting as a go-between in Moscow shortly before Litvinov's fall.[50]

Let us pass now to the Soviet side of the relationship. It has been argued that the Soviet intention to explore the possibility of a rapprochement with Germany may have existed before the German entry into Prague; but the diplomatic consequences of that action were such that a decision to seek such a rapprochement carried quite different implications once both Hitler and Britain had shown their hands than it did before 15 March. The immediate Soviet reaction to the events of 15–19 March was to return to the old policy of collective security – though not in any very well-chosen form. Litvinov's proposal for a Six-Power conference struck the British as time-wasting and vague. The alternative, the offer of an alliance, went far further than they were, at the time, prepared to accept. It must have been in that last fortnight of April that the Soviet decision was taken. Ivan Maisky, the Soviet Ambassador in London, had been recalled to Moscow on 15 April.[51] Alexei Merekalov was recalled on 19 April. In his memoirs, Maisky has recorded his side of the conferences which followed.[52] Merekalov never returned to Berlin and left no memoirs. We know nothing of what he said. But his reports clearly won the day. Litvinov's dismissal and Molotov's accession were followed by a series of visits to the German Foreign Ministry by Georgi Astakhov on 5 May and 9 May, as already mentioned, and then again on 17 May for a further conversation with Schnurre. The Soviet decision had clearly been taken.

The German decision, however, was still outstanding. It was

delayed by Ribbentrop's last desperate attempts to secure a Japanese signature to the German–Italian alliance. In the course of this he finally accepted the Japanese demand that they should be allowed to make statements playing down the wider scope of the pact and limit its operation to the Soviet Union.[53] His offer must inevitably have become known to the Russians. Taken with the opening of the Japanese assault on Soviet territory in Mongolia at Nomonhan, this may have accounted for some of the asperity with which Molotov dealt with Schulenburg on 20 May. This asperity in turn afforded Ribbentrop further grounds for procrastination. Not until the end of May was his opposition finally overcome; not until the end of July did he throw himself whole-heartedly into the task of securing an agreement. By then the Nazi–Soviet pact was an essential element in his continuing reassurances to Hitler that there would be no British implementation of the guarantee to Poland.

The foregoing analysis leaves much to be investigated. Who, for example, were the unknown go-betweens? And with whom did they make contact in Moscow? It would be difficult to believe that Litvinov was directly involved, and there is a complete lack of any indication impugning Molotov. What became of Merekalov and Syrovy? Was the decisive factor in leading the Soviets to explore German willingness to combine against Poland the British guarantee of Poland, which was received so very badly in Moscow? What it is hoped this essay has shown is that the Nazi-Soviet pact was born out of the breakdown of German–Polish relations at the end of March 1939; that its German protagonists intended it as a *petit jeu*, a diplomatic form of pressure on Poland and Britain. It became a licence to Hitler to make war in the West, as a result of the vigour with which the Soviets were themselves attracted to the German alternative to an alliance with the West. Its worst victim, after France, was the Soviet Union itself, forced to fight for two years alone on the European continent, clamouring for the second front it had thrown away in 1939.

NOTES

1. Which produced the works of Angelo Rossi, *The Russo-German Alliance, August 1939-June 1941* (London, 1950); Gerhard L. Weinberg, *Germany and the Soviet Union, 1939-1941* (Leiden, 1954); Max Beloff, *The Foreign Policy of Soviet Russia*, vol. II (Oxford, 1949); J. B. Duroselle (ed.), *Les Relations germano-soviétiques de 1933 à 1939* (Paris, 1954).

2. As Molotov did in his interview with Ambassador von Schulenburg on 20 May 1939; for Schulenburg's report on this, see *Documents on German*

Foreign Policy, series D, vol. vi, no. 424 (hereafter cited as *D.G.F.P.*).

3. Jane Degras (ed.), *Documents on Soviet Foreign Policy* (Oxford, 1953) iii 332-40.

4. *D.G.F.P.*, D, vi, no. 463.

5. Degras, *Documents on Soviet Foreign Policy*, iii 151-8.

6. John Erickson, *The Soviet High Command* (London, 1962) p. 432 and n. 79 (p. 731), citing *German Foreign Ministry Photostats*, Foreign and Commonwealth Office Library, 1907/429298-9, Schacht memorandum of 6 Feb 1937. (Hereafter cited as *G.F.M.P.*)

7. Robert Coulondre, *De Staline à Hitler* (Paris, 1950) p. 165.

8. *Izvestiya*, 28 Nov 1938, commented: 'each land that wants to take care of its security must reckon with the Soviet Union and can count on its support'.

9. See *Foreign Relations of the United States: The Soviet Union, 1933-1939*, pp. 750-3, Kirk to Washington, 6 Apr 1939. (Hereafter cited as *F.R.U.S.*)

10. *D.G.F.P.*, D, iv, no. 478, Schulenburg to Berlin, 26 Oct 1938.

11. The German–Soviet trade treaty of 1 Mar 1938 (*D.G.F.P.*, D, vii, Appendix III G (i)), was extended for one year by an exchange of letters signed in Berlin on 19 Dec 1938 (*G.F.M.P.*, 3781/E041374-5).

12. *D.G.F.P.*, D, iv, no. 3, Wiehl memorandum, 11 Jan 1939.

13. *Documents on British Foreign Policy*, 3rd series, vol. iii, no. 217, Chilston to London, 18 Oct 1938 (hereafter cited as *D.B.F.P.*); *D.G.F.P.*, D, iv, nos. 476, 477, Tippelskirch to Berlin, 3 and 10 Oct 1938; *F.R.U.S.*, *Soviet Union*, pp. 591-2, Kirk to Washington, 31 Oct 1938.

14. *F.R.U.S.*, *Soviet Union*, p. 737, Kirk to Washington, 22 Feb 1939.

15. On this largely unknown episode, see *G.F.M.P.*, Kroll (Ankara) to Berlin, 23 Feb 1939, 257/202527; Heeren (Belgrade) to Berlin, 24 Feb 1939, 257/202525; Fabricius (Bucharest) to Berlin, 27 Feb 1939, 257/202526.

16. V. I. Popov, *SSSR i Angliya* (Moscow, 1965) p. 375, citing Soviet archival reports. I am grateful to Dr Sidney Aster for this information.

17. Rossi to Rome, 13 Jan 1939, cited in Mario Toscano, 'L'Italia e gli accordi tedesco-sovietici dell' Agosto '39', *Rivista di Studi Politici Internazionali*, xviii 4 (Oct-Dec 1951) 556 (hereafter cited as Toscano, 'L'Italia'). For an English translation, see Mario Toscano, *Designs in Diplomacy: Pages from European Diplomatic History in the Twentieth Century*, translated and ed. George A. Carbone (Baltimore, 1970) pp. 48-123.

18. Rossi to Rome, 12 Mar 1939, cited in Toscano, 'L'Italia', p. 557.

19. Ibid., p. 562, Rossi to Rome, 5 Apr 1939.

20. *D.B.F.P.*, 3rd ser., iii, nos. 500, 502; M. Muggeridge (ed.), *Ciano's Diplomatic Papers* (London, 1948) pp. 259-66.

21. Franklin Reid Gannon, *The British Press and Germany, 1936-1939* (Oxford, 1971) p. 40.

22. I owe this information to Mr Wolfgang Leonhard. See also *F.R.U.S.*, *1939*, i 313-14, Kirk to Washington, 31 Jan 1939.

23. Cf. Rossi, *The Russo-German Alliance*, pp. 8-10; Beloff, *The Foreign Policy of Soviet Russia*, ii 227; Toscano, L'Italia', p. 555.

24. *D.G.F.P.*, D, vii, no. 213, Henke memorandum of 24 Aug 1939. See also Molotov's speech of 31 Aug to the Supreme Soviet in Degras, *Documents on Soviet Foreign Policy*, iii 363-71.

25. International Military Tribunal, *Trial of the Major War Criminals*, x 267.

26. E. H. Carr, 'From Munich to Moscow', *Soviet Studies*, i 1 (June 1949) 3-17.

27. For the text, see Degras, *Documents on Soviet Foreign Policy*, iii 315-21.

28. *D.G.F.P.*, D, iv, no. 495, Wiehl memorandum, 11 Mar 1939.

29. *D.B.F.P.*, 3rd ser., iv, nos. 24, 46, 103, 121, 194.

30. George Bilainkin, *Maisky: Ten Years Ambassador* (London, 1942) pp. 228, 232.

31. For Sir William Seeds's reports, see *D.B.F.P.*, 3rd ser., iv, no. 452; for those of Schulenberg, see *G.F.M.P.*, 357/202529 of 11 Mar and 357/202530-4 of 13 Mar 1939.

32. Cited in Toscano, 'L'Italia', pp. 556-8.

33. *F.R.U.S., Soviet Union*, pp. 744-5, Kirk to Washington, 14 March 1939. One of the American sources was Hans von Henwath, later Federal German Ambassador in London; see Charles E. Bohlen, *Witness to History, 1929-1969* (New York, 1973) pp. 67-87.

34. For accounts of the occasion, see Max Domarus (ed.), *Hitler, Reden und Proklamationen 1932-1945* (Würzburg, 1963), ii 1030-7; Fritz Wiedemann, *Der Mann der Feldherr werden wollte* (Dortmund, 1964) pp. 229-32.

35. Gustav Hilger and Alfred G. Meyer, *The Incompatible Allies* (New York, 1953) pp. 293-7.

36. Hermann Teske (ed.), *Profile bedeutender Soldaten*, Band i: *General Ernst Koestring, Der militärische Mittler zwischen dem deutschen Reich und der Sowjetunion, 1921-1941* (Frankfurt am Main, 1969) pp. 133-6.

37. *D.G.F.P.*, D, vi, no. 270, Ribbentrop to Ott, 26 Apr 1939; testimony of Oshima and Shiratori, *International Military Tribunal (Far East) Record of Proceedings*, pp. 6079 ff., 35042 ff.; Attolico to Ciano, 25 Apr 1939, cited in Mario Toscano, *Le Origine diplomatiche del Patto d'Acciaio* (Florence, 1956) p. 125.

38. Domarus, *Hitler, Reden und Proklamationen*, ii 1148-79.

39. The last such attack appeared in the S.S. journal, *Das Schwarze Korps*, on 28 Apr 1939.

40. Paul Stehlin, *Témoignage pour l'histoire* (Paris, 1966) pp. 147-52; *French Yellow Book*, p. 123, Coulondre to Paris, 7 May 1939.

41. *D.B.F.P.*, 3rd ser., v, no. 377, Henderson to London, 5 May 1939; Anton Szymanski, 'Das deutsch-polnische Verhältnis vor dem Kriege', *Politische Studien*, xiii 141-4 (1962).

42. Teske, *Ernst Koestring*, pp. 231-3.

43. Renzetti to Attolico, 7 May 1939, cited in Toscano, 'L'Italia', pp. 577-9, n. 34 *bis*.

44. Peter Kleist, *Zwischen Hitler und Stalin. Aufzeichnungen 1939-1945* (Bonn, 1950) pp. 26-30.

45. *D.G.F.P.*, D, vi, no. 211, memorandum of 18 Apr 1939.

46. *D.G.F.P.*, D, vi, no. 215.

47. *D.G.F.P.*, D, vi, no. 293, Woermann to German Embassy, Rome, 29 Apr 1939.

48. See speech by Ribbentrop to General Staff officers of the Wehrmacht, as reported on the Czech memorandum of 22 Jan 1939. Václav Král (ed.), *Das Abkommen von München 1938. Tschechoslowakische diplomatische Dokumente, 1937-1939* (Prague, 1964) no. 286.

49. *D.G.F.P.*, D, vi, no. 351, memorandum of Braun von Stumm, 9 May 1939.

50. *D.B.F.P.*, 3rd ser., v, no. 552, Henderson to London, 17 May 1939, enclosing report by General Mason-Macfarlane, British Military Attaché in Berlin. A similar report reached Colonel Christie, organiser of a private intelligence service for Sir Robert Vansittart from German army sources; Christie Papers, Churchill College Library.

51. *D.B.F.P.*, 3rd ser., v, no. 182, Seeds to London, 15 Apr 1939.

52. I. Maisky, *Who Helped Hitler?* (London, 1964) pp. 119-23; Bilainkin, *Maisky*, p. 246.

53. *D.G.F.P.*, D, vi, nos. 382, 383, Ribbentrop to Tokyo, 15 May 1939.

SELECT BIBLIOGRAPHY

DOCUMENTS

(i) *Published*

Great Britain, *Documents on British Foreign Policy, 1919-1939*, 3rd series (H.M.S.O.).
——, *Documents on German Foreign Policy, 1918-1945*, series D (H.M.S.O.).
United States, *Foreign Relations of the United States: The Soviet Union, 1933-1939* (U.S. Government Printing Office).
——, *Foreign Relations of the United States, 1939*, vol. i.
U.S.S.R., *Documents and Materials Relating to the Origins of World War II*, 2 vols. (Moscow: Ministry of Foreign Affairs, 1948).
France, *Livre Jaune Française. Documents diplomatiques, 1935-1939* (Paris: Ministère des Affairs Étrangères, 1939).
Czechoslovakia: Václav Král (ed.), *Das Abkommen von München 1938. Tschechoslowakische diplomatische Dokumente, 1937-1939* (Prague, 1964).
Italy, *I Documenti diplomatici italiani*, 8th series, vols. xii xiii (Ministro degli Affari Esteri).
Jane Degras (ed.), *Documents on Soviet Foreign Policy* (Oxford, 1953) vol. iii.
Max Domarus (ed.), *Hitler, Reden und Proklamationen 1932-1945*, 2 vols. (Würzburg, 1963).

(ii) *Unpublished*

Public Record Office, London, Foreign Office Records, F.O. 371.
Foreign Office Library, London, German Foreign Ministry Archives (photostat collection).
National Archives, Washington, German Army Records (microfilm).

MEMOIRS

Robert Coulondre, *De Staline à Hitler* (Paris, 1950).
Joseph E. Davies, *Mission to Moscow* (London, 1942).
Gustav Hilger and Alfred G. Meyer, *The Incompatible Allies: A Memoir History of German–Soviet Relations, 1918-1941* (New York, 1953).

Peter Kleist, *Zwischen Hitler und Stalin. Aufzeichnungen 1939-1945* (Bonn, 1950).

I. Maisky, *Who Helped Hitler?* (London, 1964).

Augusto Rosso, 'Politica estera sovietica: obietive e metodi', *Rivista di Studi Politici Internazionali*, I 1 (1946).

Paul Otto Schmidt, *Statist auf diplomatischer Bühne, 1923-45* (Bonn, 1949).

Paul Stehlin, *Témoignage pour l'histoire* (Paris, 1966).

Anton Szymanski, 'Als polnischer Militärattaché in Berlin, 1932-1939', *Politische Studien*, XIII 141-4 (1962).

Herman Teske (ed.), *Profile bedeutender Soldaten*, Band I: *General Ernst Koestring. Der militärische Mittler zwischen den deutschen Reich und der Sowjetunion, 1921-1941* (Frankfurt am Main, 1969).

Fritz Wiedemann, *Der Mann der Feldherr werden wollte* (Dortmund, 1964).

BIOGRAPHIES

George Bilainkin, *Maisky: Ten Years Ambassador* (London, 1942).

F. W. Deakin and G. R. Storry, *The Case of Richard Sorge* (London, 1966).

Keith Feiling, *The Life of Neville Chamberlain* (London, 1946).

STUDIES

Max Beloff, *The Foreign Policy of Soviet Russia, 1929-1941* (Oxford, 1949) vol. II.

Seweryn Bialer, *Stalin and his Generals* (London, 1970).

Bohdan Budorowycz, *Polish–Soviet Relations, 1932-1939* (New York, 1963).

J. B. Duroselle (ed.), *Les Frontières européennes de l'U.R.S.S., 1917-41* (Paris, 1957).

—— (ed.), *Les Relations germano-soviétiques de 1933 à 1939* (Paris, 1954).

John Erickson, *The Soviet High Command: A Military-Political History 1918-1941* (London, 1962).

P. W. Fabry, *Der Hitler–Stalin Pakt, 1939-1941: Ein Beitrag zwei Methoden sowjetischer Aussenpolitik* (Darmstadt, 1962).

Anne M. Cienciala, *Poland and the Western Powers, 1938-1939* (London, 1968).

Trumbull Higgins, *Hitler and Russia: The Third Reich in a Two-front War* (New York, 1966).

Walter Laqueur, *Russia and Germany: A Century of Conflict* (London, 1965).

Ivo J. Lederer (ed.), *Russian Foreign Policy: Essays in Historical Perspective* (New Haven, 1962).

Hubertus Lüpke, *Japans Russland-Politik von 1939 bis 1941* (Frankfurt, 1962).

A. D. Nikonov, *The Origins of World War II and the pre-war Political Crisis of 1939* (Moscow, 1955).

N. Potemkine, *Histoire de la diplomatie* (Paris, 1947) vol. III.

Angelo Rossi, *The Russo-German Alliance, August 1939-June 1941* (London, 1950).

Bernad Rula, *Deutsche Botschaft Moskau. 50 Jahre Schicksal zwischen Ost und West* (Bayreuth, 1964).

Theo Sommer, *Deutschland und Japan zwischen den Mächten 1935-1940* (Tübingen, 1962).

Mario Toscano, *Le Origine diplomatiche del Patto d'Acciaio* (Florence, 1956).
——, *The Origins of the Pact of Steel* (Baltimore, 1967).
Vladimir Truchonowski (ed.), *Geschichte der internazionalen Beziehungen 1917-1939*, trans. Peter Hoffmann *et al.* (Berlin, 1963).
Gerhard L. Weinberg, *Germany and the Soviet Union, 1939-1941* (Leiden, 1954).

ARTICLES

Kurt Assmann, 'Stalin and Hitler, Part I: The Pact with Moscow', *U.S. Naval Institute Proceedings*, LXXV (June 1949).
Max Beloff, 'Soviet Foreign Policy, 1929-1941: Some Roles', *Soviet Studies*, II 2 (Oct 1950).
E. H. Carr, 'From Munich to Moscow', *Soviet Studies*, I 1-2 (June-Oct 1949).
Eberhard Jäckel, 'Über eine angebliche Rede Stalins vom 19 August 1939', *Vierteljahresheft für Zeitgeschichte*, IV 3 (Oct 1958).
A. Nikonov, 'The Western Powers and the Outbreak of War in Europe', *International Affairs* (Moscow), Sep 1959.
Otto Pick, 'Who Pulled the trigger?: Soviet Historians and the Origins of World War II', *Problems of Communism*, IX 5 (Sep 1960).
André Scherer, 'La Problème des "Mains Libres" à l'Est', *Revue d'Histoire de la Deuxième Guerre Mondiale*, VIII 32 (Oct 1958).
Mario Toscano, 'La Politique russe de l'Italie au printemps 1939', *Revue d'Histoire de la Deuxième Guerre Mondiale*, II 6 (Apr 1952).
——, 'L'Italia e gli accordi tedesco-sovietici dell' Agosto '39', *Rivista di Studi Politici Internazionali*, XVIII 4 (Oct-Dec 1951).
——, 'Italy and the German–Soviet Agreements of August 1939', in *Designs in Diplomacy: Pages from European Diplomatic History in the Twentieth Century*, trans. and ed. George A. Carbone (Baltimore, 1970).

8 E. H. Carr and the Study of International Relations

ROGER MORGAN

The Twenty Years' Crisis, 1919-1939, appeared just as the period it analysed came to its end in the Second World War. The book's sub-title – *An Introduction to the Study of International Relations* – still stands as a challenge to the present-day reader, more than thirty years later. How far can this assessment of twenty years of international politics – a time abnormally crisis-ridden by any standards, even if we suspend judgement on Carr's own view of it as a single crisis two decades long – illuminate the nature of the international political process in general? It must be noted as a preliminary that this earliest major work by Carr on international relations continues to stand the test of time rather better than his subsequent writings on contemporary affairs. Even though much profit may still be gained from a reading of *Conditions of Peace* (1942), *Nationalism and After* (1945), or *The Soviet Impact on the Western World* (1947), they bear unmistakable traces of their dates of origin, and of their author's hopes and judgements at the time. *The Twenty Years' Crisis* undertakes a deeper level of analysis, and retains an enduring value despite the author's use of current events (and even his subsequently controversial approval of the Munich Agreement) as illustrations of his thesis.[1]

It is appropriate to give a brief summary of this thesis. After subjecting the Wilsonian or Benthamite doctrine of an international harmony of interests to an unsparing critique – he reveals it as the ideology of the haves, resisting the demands of the have-nots – Carr advances the 'realist' argument that international peace can only be based on the frank acceptance of hard bargaining between conflicting interests. Peace cannot result from the imposition of international law by a revived League of Nations or world government – these goals, sought by such thinkers as Arnold Toynbee and Sir Alfred Zimmern, he dismisses as utopian – but only by the adoption of a process analogous to that of collective bargaining in industry. Here the exist-

ence of conflicting interests and the importance of their respective
power in the outcome is plainly recognised by all parties, and no
attempt is made to apply a solution that contradicts these realities.
True, Carr insists that an element of moral consensus must also be
present in the international agreements that are to mark the progress
of international conciliation, but his main concern is to destroy the
illusion of the 1930s that moral consensus could achieve anything
without effective power.

The most obvious way in which Carr's interpretation of international relations is still accurate, and possesses general explanatory
validity, is that the international system is still mainly composed of
sovereign states, acting essentially in pursuance of their own interests
as defined by themselves. Although – as will be argued below – there
are ways in which sovereignty no longer means what it did before
1939, and the processes of international negotiation have undergone
corresponding changes, the basic ingredients of international relations
remain as Carr described them.

Taking the world political system as a whole, the history of the
United Nations Organisation confirms the correctness of Carr's
diagnosis: peace between the major powers has not been preserved
by any process of international legislation, i.e. an extension of the
rule of law between nations, but by the traditional procedures of
diplomacy, based on the calculation and manipulation of the balance
of power. At the level of relations between the two super-powers,
accommodation of interests is being and will continue to be sought
through a bargaining process of this kind. The same is true of the
evolving relationship between Eastern and Western Europe, and of
the mechanisms whereby Japan and China are gradually being fitted
once more into both the Asian and the global systems.

At the level of the forces that motivate individual states, again,
many lessons of general validity may be learnt from Carr's analysis
of the inter-war years. Take, for instance, his characteristically
penetrating dissection of the Locarno Treaty as 'a simple and reveal-
ing illustration of the working of power politics':

> [By 1925] the Ruhr invasion had brought little profit to France,
> and had left her perplexed as to the next step. Germany might one
> day be powerful again. Germany, on the other hand, still feared
> the military supremacy of France, and hankered after a guarantee.
> It was the psychological moment when French fear of Germany
> was about equally balanced by Germany's fear of France; and a
> treaty which had not been possible two years before, and would

not have been possible five years later, was now welcome to both. (pp. 135-6)

This analysis of the process of international bargaining has very wide application. It could well be argued, for instance, that the Franco-German agreement to establish the European Coal and Steel Community, exactly a quarter of a century after Locarno, reflected a very similar convergence of interests and fears: Robert Schuman, like Herriot or Briand, saw the need to abandon national control of France's coal and steel industries as the price for tying down the potential strength of Germany, while Adenauer, like a latter-day Stresemann, accepted an apparently constraining agreement which in fact put an end to France's unilateral restrictions on Germany's industrial growth. In 1925 as in 1950, the broader international constellation – particularly the attitudes of Britain and the United States – formed a critical factor influencing French and German decisions.

Carr's analysis of the reasons why negotiations for Mediterranean and Eastern European 'Locarnos' failed in the 1930s – that they did not correspond to 'the power politics of a particular period and locality' – applies precisely to the abortive proposals for a 'new Locarno' launched by Winston Churchill after Stalin's death in 1953, and it also has an unmistakable relevance to the projects for a 'European Security Conference' current in the later 1960s and the early 1970s: unless the participants in such a conference are really in accord about the regulation of certain of their basic interests by an international agreement establishing a new system of European security, no such system will emerge.

Another example of a seemingly perennial truth, which Carr rightly stresses, is that the use or the threat of force is often the only way for states or other groups to attain their aims in international affairs. His use of the case of Ireland's independence and partition to illustrate this process of peaceful change by 'yielding to threats of force' is particularly poignant when read against the background of the Ulster situation of 1971-2: when he describes the Anglo-Irish treaty of 1921 as a successful compromise based on a mixture of 'yielding to threats of force' and finding a moral basis for agreement on what was reasonable (p. 280), the reader of thirty years later is reminded that it is the same mixture which has brought politicians to consider how to achieve a compromise between the rival factions in Ulster today.

Again, the current dilemma of reconciling the trend towards supranational groupings with the demand for regional autonomy within states is admirably summarised by a passage in *The Twenty Years' Crisis*: 'There is some evidence that, while technical, industrial and economic development within the last hundred years has dictated a progressive increase in the size of the effective political unit, there may be a size which cannot be exceeded without provoking a recrudescence of disintegrating tendencies' (p. 295).

For a further example of topicality, one has only to point to Carr's observation (pp. 77-80) that, while the Benthamite doctrine of the harmony of interests could claim to interpret international relations so long as the world possessed sufficient uncolonised land and raw materials to satisfy all demands, it is revealed as illusory once the limits of these resources come into sight. The world of the 1970s is likely to appreciate this lesson more acutely than that of the 1930s.

Turning to the 'study' of international relations, as pursued by academics, Carr enunciates – and his book illustrates – two general principles which are still not fully accepted: that the analysis of international politics cannot sensibly be separated from that of economics, and that the field of work now known as 'strategic studies' also forms a vital dimension of the study of relations between states. On the former point, as he says, 'economic forces are in fact political forces.... Much confusion would be saved by a general return to the term "political economy", which was given the new science by Adam Smith himself and not abandoned in favour of the abstract "economics", even in Great Britain itself, till the closing years of the nineteenth century' (p. 149). On strategy (p. 142): 'if every prospective writer on international affairs in the last twenty years had taken a compulsory course in elementary strategy, reams of nonsense would have remained unwritten'. This is hardly less true of the fifties and sixties than of the twenties and thirties.[2]

There is thus much that is still highly relevant, both for the practice and for the theory of international relations, in the pages of *The Twenty Years' Crisis*; the book justifies and lives up to its subtitle. The instances of topicality cited above, however, do not answer the question whether Carr's central thesis is still valid. The nature of the question needs clarification. Other commentators have answered it in different ways: Hans Morgenthau, for instance, has criticised Carr's basic philosophical position on the grounds that his emphasis on power leaves no room for any political objective beyond power itself;[3] Hedley Bull, while maintaining that Carr's main thesis is still valid, argues that his fundamental distinction between have and have-not countries must today be interpreted in radically new ways, in terms of the dichotomies between developed and underdeveloped, and between the nuclear and the non-nuclear.[4]

The approach to the question of Carr's relevance to be adopted here is rather different: there are many ideas in *The Twenty Years' Crisis* that deserve explanation at considerable length, but the one whose implications appear the most fruitful of all is Carr's comparison between the processes of bargaining in international and in industrial relations.

In his analysis of the problems of peaceful change in relations between states, he dismisses, as we have noted, the view that the amicable adjustment of international disputes can be expected to result from processes analogous to the judicial or legislative ones within nation-states – the development of international law or world government.

After going on to argue that 'it may be unnecessarily pessimistic to rush into the conclusion that the absence of an international legislature rules out any international procedure of peaceful change', Carr suggests that a parallel within the national community to the turbulence characteristic of inter-state relations may be found

> in the relations of those group-entities within the state whose conflicts have not been in the past, and still in large measure are not, settled by any legislative process. Of these group-entities, by far the most important, and by far the most instructive for our purpose, are those representing capital and labour respectively. Here we have the same recurrent conflict between 'haves' and 'have-nots', between 'satisfied' and 'dissatisfied'; the same reluctance, on the part of one or both sides, to accept the principle of 'all-in arbitration' ...; the same recognition of the inapplicability or inadequacy of the legislative process; the same appeals to 'law and order' by the satisfied group; and the same use, or threatened use, of violence by the dissatisfied in order to assert their claims. (pp. 269-70)

The last point is of course a reference to strike action, and Carr spells out the analogy between this and the international use or threat of military force in interesting and persuasive detail:

> The statesman, the trade union leader or the company director is a trustee for those whose interests he represents; and in order to justify extensive concessions at their expense, he must generally be in a position to plead that he has yielded to *force majeure*. When the change is effected by legislation [i.e. not in the case of industrial relations], the compulsion is that of the state. But where the change is effected by the bargaining procedure, the *force majeure* can only be that of the stronger party. The employer who concedes the strikers' demands pleads inability to resist. The trade union leader who calls off an unsuccessful strike pleads that the union was too weak to continue. 'Yielding to threats of force', which is sometimes

used as a term of reproach, is therefore a normal part of the process. (pp. 272-3)

The analogy between international and industrial relations is still worth considering in some detail today, not only because these two types of bargaining are dominant features of the life of modern societies, but also because both are in fact undergoing subtle but important changes. In the field of industrial relations, many states have attempted, in the thirty years since Carr wrote, to subject the bargaining process to a greater degree of legal control, so that wage agreements are more subject to judicial sanctions and hence the *force majeure* of the state is ultimately substituted for that of the parties engaged in the process. The Industrial Relations Bill proposed and then withdrawn by the British Labour Government in 1969, and the Conservative Government's Industrial Relations Act of 1971, are only the latest examples of numerous attempts to bring wage determination under legislative control. The change is of course only one of degree, but is none the less of considerable significance.

At the same time when the nature of industrial bargaining is undergoing an unmistakable change, it may be argued that this also applies to bargaining at the international level. It is true, as was remarked above, that the central mechanisms of the balance of power are still clearly at work in the relations between the super-powers: indeed, the emerging triangular balance between the United States, the Soviet Union and China shows distinct resemblances to the classical balance of the nineteenth century.[5] It is also true that force is still very widely used between states outside the central power balance – the Indo-Pakistani war of December 1971 is only one recent example – and the threat of force remains all-pervasive throughout the so-called 'Third World'. Indeed, the peace-keeping capacities of the United Nations Organisation appear to have declined quite radically since the Congo operation of the early 1960s, to a point where the most the Organisation was ever expected to do in the Indo-Pakistani war was to carry out some part of the relief of the victims. Much of the 'Third World', in fact, appears likely to remain in a condition of instability and latent or actual conflict.

It is thus not in the field of peace-keeping, or the control of international violence by law, that a parallel to the increasing legislative control of industrial relations must be sought: it is rather to be found in the development of a new quality of relations between the advanced countries of the Western world. National capitals of course remain the principal centres of power, and decisions are made, as noted above, in terms of each Government's definition of its 'national interest': the

United States decision of August 1971 to suspend convertibility and impose an import surcharge was unilaterally announced to the world, and the responses of America's main partners varied markedly from one capital to another. It remains true, nevertheless – and this is confirmed by the means whereby the immediate monetary problems of late 1971 were resolved – that the main industrial states of the world are now subject to a variety of constraints on their decision-making power, amounting almost to subjection to a quasi-legislative procedure. In monetary, commercial and general economic policy, the member-states of the I.M.F. and O.E.C.D. have undertaken to submit their decisions to the informed scrutiny of their fellow members, and to accept rules of conduct decided in common.

This is, of course, particularly true of the member-states of the European Economic Community, who have agreed to place increasing areas of hitherto national sovereign decision-making authority under central control; but even the United States is not fully able to take decisions on economic policy without reference to the policies agreed in international institutions, as the monetary compromise agreed in December 1971 by the Group of Ten fully demonstrated.

The underlying reality which makes previously autonomous decisions inevitably subject to a degree of external control is the fact of economic interdependence. Just as within the nation-state the vulnerability of the entire economy to strike action leads to demands for more legal control over industrial relations, so the increasing interdependence of the international economy makes the condition of any major state a concern of the whole system. No state can be permitted, or permit itself, to persist in a chronic payments imbalance or an excessive rate of inflation, and the whole system, for the general good and that of each of the members, provides mechanisms – however defective – to promote general alignment of policies and to manage crises.

States which are still formally sovereign are thus in reality subject to a wide variety of limitations, defining the framework within which international bargaining can take place. Much of the bargaining still occurs between national governments – as suggested in the earlier reference to the convergence of French and German interests in the establishment of the European Coal and Steel Community – but the network of constraints on these governments is now so intense that conflicts can no longer be pushed to anything like the *ultima ratio* of war. Although the relations between Schuman and Adenauer, or Pompidou and Brandt, offer *some* analogies to those between Briand and Stresemann, the 'national interests' of Western countries in the 1950s and 1970s must be pursued by much more circumscribed methods than were available to the same countries in the 1930s.[6]

A further dimension of the new situation is the number of different issues now at stake in relations between industrialised states at any given moment. The bargaining of 1970, which gave satisfaction to Italy on the European Community's wine regulations, to France on the financing of the Agricultural Guarantee and Guidance Fund, and to Britain on the principle of entry into the Community, is only one obvious example. The kinds of bargaining packages that may be assembled, as increasing areas of national activity can potentially benefit from international agreements, are limitless in number and immensely varied in scope. It appears certain that the bargaining techniques developed in the 1960s, not only in the European Community but more generally throughout the group of advanced capitalist economies, will be the forerunners of much more complex arrangements in the future.

The distinction between foreign policy and domestic policy will thus become even more blurred than it is already – a blurring foreshadowed not only in Carr's analogy between industrial and international bargaining, but also in many other parts of *The Twenty Years' Crisis* and his other writings. The distinction between foreign and domestic policy is breaking down in two senses: firstly, many of the issues traditionally regarded as belonging to home affairs – agricultural, financial, social and economic policy – now have external implications which make them inescapably part of foreign relations; secondly, a large part of foreign policy – at least among the advanced countries – now consists of attempts to establish systems of relationships designed to last, providing a framework for the flow of policy processes for a considerable period ahead, in the manner previously thought more characteristic of domestic policy. The first point is familiar – it permeates much of E. H. Carr's writing on international affairs[7] – but the latter requires further analysis.

One of the traditional divergences between foreign and domestic policy was that whereas the latter aimed at creating institutions whose results would be predictable and lasting – educational systems, health services or penal codes – foreign policy was thought to consist largely of actions and decisions whose 'output' was much less readily calculable: much of it was either concerned with the management of crises when they blew up, or with their prevention by the timely application of the great Lord Salisbury's proverbial boat-hook as the punt of state drifted downstream.[8]

Today, even though a large part of diplomacy – even between advanced Western nations, and certainly in the rest of the world – may still be concerned with crisis management, an increasing part of it is closer to domestic policy, as traditionally conceived. The concern of foreign policy with the establishment of instutions and systems designed to produce foreseeable results is in itself nothing new: all the treaties known to diplomatic history, in a sense, were intended to commit their signatories to certain future courses of action, and the same was of course true of the League Covenant and the United Nations Charter. What is a peculiar characteristic of the last twenty years, however, is the very strong emphasis, in the foreign policy of Western countries, on the establishment of systems designed either to *obviate* certain eventualities (for instance NATO, intended to prevent war) or to *facilitate* certain other developments (one is thinking here of the I.M.F., GATT, O.E.C.D. and the various European organisations, designed to promote economic growth). In other words, international bargaining is nowadays not only conducted *within* a system: it is very often *about* the system, like bargaining about issues of domestic policy.

The very fact that states, recognising their mutual interdependence, now devote increasing efforts to setting up structures intended to define the future limits of their autonomous power, not only indicates a convergence between domestic and foreign policy; it marks a very real degree of withering-away of the external powers of the state.

Of course, states will for long remain the most powerful actors in the international system. E. H. Carr might be the first to insist that even the degree of constraint apparently accepted by the member-states of E.E.C. may be revealed in a crisis as illusory: he once wrote to a young man about to take up an Assistant Lectureship in International Politics, 'I hope you will be able to continue your work along historical lines, and steer clear of SUNFED, ECOSOC and all these other horrors which have no substance in them, and are merely front organisations'.[9]

However, his own writings, not least by directing our attention to the new content and the new framework of bargaining between states, remain a powerful and lasting stimulus for students of international relations.

NOTES

1. Another example of the continuing relevance of Carr's thinking occurred in the early 1950s, when his *German–Soviet Relations between the Two World Wars, 1919-1939* (1951), by reminding policy-makers that Germany's isolation in 1919 had led to Rapallo, helped to influence the decision to bring the Federal Republic into full partnership with the West.

2. For a further discussion of the importance of the strategic factor, see the author's essay 'The Study of International Politics', in Roger Morgan (ed.),

The Study of International Affairs (Oxford U.P., for R.I.I.A., 1972).

3. 'The Surrender to the Immanence of Power: E. H. Carr', reprinted in Morgenthau's volume of essays *The Restoration of American Politics* (Chicago, 1962) pp. 36-43.

4. Hedley Bull, '*The Twenty Years' Crisis* Thirty Years On', *International Journal*, XXIV 4 (autumn 1969) 625-38.

5. Some of these parallels are elaborated in the writings of Coral Bell, notably *The Asian Balance of Power: A Comparison with European Precedents*, Adelphi Paper No. 44 (Institute for Strategic Studies, 1968) and *The Conventions of Crisis* (Oxford U.P., for R.I.I.A., 1971).

6. A discussion of the contemporary meaning of 'national interest' will be found in K. Kaiser and R. Morgan (eds.), *Britain and West Germany* (Oxford U.P., for R.I.I.A., 1971) pp. 10-15.

7. Both *The Twenty Years' Crisis* and *Conditions of Peace* insist heavily on the economic and social tasks of diplomacy. For a discussion of some contemporary aspects of this theme, cf. Kaiser and Morgan, *Britain and West Germany*.

8. Lord Salisbury's classic dictum about occasionally 'putting out a diplomatic boat-hook to avoid collisions' is quoted by James Joll in *Britain and Europe: Pitt to Churchill, 1793-1940* (London, 1950) p. 3.

9. Letter in private possession. For a more extended discussion see the author's *High Politics, Low Politics: Towards a Foreign Policy for Western Europe* (The Washington Papers, vol. I, No. 11. Beverley Hills and London. Sage Publications, 1973).

PART THREE
Soviet Studies

9 Some Observations on Bukharin and His Ideas

ALEC NOVE

A FULL-LENGTH political biography of Bukharin is long overdue. A good bibliography exists,[1] and some major work is in preparation.[2] I shall not try in this paper to cover all the ground. He was a prolific writer, in economics, sociology and philosophy, and he was also an active politician, with views on the nature of Russia's revolution, views that altered over time. He was also a journalist, a brilliant and witty speaker, a populariser of complex doctrines, and no mean caricaturist. All I can do is to set out some of his ideas on some matters which seem to me to be of interest. There are aspects of his thought which will not be touched on at all. For example, he argued at length with Rosa Luxemburg, in 1912-14, on the question of whether capitalism needs a non-capitalist sector for its survival, and I hear that an English translation of this controversy has appeared. He criticised Böhm-Bawerk, Tugan-Baranovsky, Struve, Trotsky, Skvortsov-Stepanov. All these things are well worth studying and analysing, but will hardly be mentioned here. I shall also have little to say about Bukharin the politician. This is a paper, not a large book.

Bukharin was born in 1888. Thus he was only twenty-nine when the Revolution happened. This may help to explain a certain basic inconsistency between his youthful 'Left' enthusiasm of 1918, when he was all for revolutionary wars and instant leaps into full communism, and the cautious, statesmanlike acceptance of the logic of N.E.P. after 1921. One question we can ask ourselves is: how great was the inconsistency? Peter Knirsch, the author of a survey of Bukharin's economic ideas,[3] virtually ignored those of the N.E.P. period, and justified this by asserting (in conversation) that after 1921 Bukharin subordinated his economics to political exigencies. Rudolf Schlesinger, who had known Bukharin, told me that in his view he was a genuine enthusiast in 1918-20, but that he was so shocked ('heart-broken') by the failures of war-communism that he went to the opposite extreme of moderation. Schlesinger interpreted Bukharin's political position in the 1920s as objectively pro-peasant, and he believed that Stalin was right to drive him out of politics (though not to shoot him), so he may have been a prejudiced witness.

Let us look at some of Bukharin's economic ideas, in and after the war-communism period. It must be noted that he had had some solid training in the subject, when he was at Vienna from 1912 to 1914. He read Western languages and was familiar with the literature; thus he was quoting from Keynes's *Economic Consequences of the Peace* within a year of its publication. He had worked on problems of imperialism, and many of Lenin's ideas on this subject could well have been influenced by Bukharin, whose writings[4] antedated Lenin's *Imperialism*.

What original contribution did Bukharin make to the economic ideas of the war-communism period? (We must bear in mind that his enthusiasms of the period were shared by other comrades: Larin, Obolensky-Osinski and many more.

There is, first, the concept of 'negative expanded reproduction', i.e. of the destruction of the means of production. This is a cost of revolution. What was happening was logical, *zakonomerno*. The possessing classes must resist revolution. There would then be civil war. There would be sabotage. Relations between the proletarian vanguard and the intelligentsia and also the peasantry would be strained, the one because they will fail to see or sympathise with the coercive necessities of a proletarian revolution, the other because the towns will be unable to supply the country and will try to collect food by administrative means, supplanting the market. Class war in the village, the breaking of customary links between village and urban markets, cause adverse effects on production. The proletariat, unlike the bourgeoisie, cannot learn to govern *before* the revolution. Its culture is low, it is likely to be crude and to make mistakes, all of which contributes to economic disruption. This seems to be a fair description of Russian war-communism experience, extended to proletarian revolutions in general.

At this stage of his development, Bukharin thought in terms of an inevitable 'open or concealed' conflict between the dictatorship of the proletariat and a peasantry attached to anarchic commodity (market) relations.[5] He clearly supported requisitioning (*razverstka*) and was not one of those who pressed Lenin to introduce N.E.P.

Nor can he be readily identified as a supporter of the extremes of nationalisation. Let us recall that by mid-1920 even the pettiest enterprises, even windmills employing one person, were (in the main) nationalised. Yet Bukharin, co-author with Preobrazhensky of the *A.B.C. of Communism*, had written in 1919:

We must remember that we do not expropriate petty property. Its nationalisation is absolutely out of the question, firstly because we would be unable ourselves to organise the scattered small-scale production, and secondly because the Communist Party does not wish to, and must not, offend the many millions of petty proprietors. Their conversion to socialism must take place voluntarily, by their own decision, and not by means of compulsory expropriation. It is particularly important to remember this in areas where small-scale production is predominant.[6]

Yet this popular book was certainly written in a 'Left' spirit.

He also took the position that, in the 'transition period' to socialism, Marxian value categories had almost as little place as Böhm-Bawerkian Western economics. 'The basic categories of the whole system of political economy were such concepts as commodity, value, price.' But these ceased to mean what once they meant. Bukharin believed that, under socialism, economics as the study of commodity exchange relations would wither away, being replaced by *administration* of a planned economy. In the transition period these relations, he wrote, are dying out. Value categories in capitalist as in Marxist economics are equilibrium categories. But there is no equilibrium during the transition period. Goods cease to be available. 'It is evident that in the period of transition, in the process of eliminating commodity production as such, there takes place a process of the "self-denial" (*samootritsanie*) of money. Money ceases to be a universal equivalent, becoming a nominal and highly imperfect denomination for the circulation of products.' These 'products' are no longer 'commodities'. Similarly, wages are no longer wages, both because a worker is no longer an 'employee' and because 'under a proletarian dictatorship the worker receives a ration and not wages'.[7] 'One of the basic tendencies of the transition period is the breaking of commodity-fetishistic disguises.... Economic theory must move towards thinking in natural units.' The process of production will be based on plans for use.

Bukharin was very open and frank in his ideas on coercion, and not only as applied to enemies of his revolution. The workers are to be the organisers of production, but 'all proletarian organisation must be under the most all-inclusive organisation, i.e. the state organs of the working class'. Hence the need for state control (*ogosudarstvlenie*) over trade unions. Hence the necessity of 'universal labour service'. He boldly faces the logic of 'eliminating freedom of labour', fearing that groups of workers will counterpose their sectional interests to the general interest, 'will fail to understand all-proletarian tasks'. In the name of 'the real liberation of labour' it is necessary to introduce labour conscription and direction of labour. Then, ultimately, all coercion will end, when real socialism is achieved, through the 'concentrated coercion' of the proletarian dictatorship.[8] Meanwhile, however, one needs maximum business sense (*delovitost'*), the concentration of control in few hands, the militarisation of economic command functions, the replacement of elections by 'careful selection' (*podbor*), by the proletarian dictatorial organs, of competent people.

This emphasis contrasts not only with his later criticism of selection as against election, but also his association in 1918 with those who opposed Lenin's attempts to introduce discipline and one-man management in industry. It led him briefly into Trotsky's camp on the issue of the militarisation of labour.

Of course Bukharin did look forward to the renewal of productive forces. He was vague about the organisational forms of this, though clearly he envisaged the replacement of requisitions by 'commodity exchange' in relations with the peasants. Capital assets would have to be rebuilt. It is noteworthy, in view of subsequent argument, that in 1920 Bukharin quoted approvingly the term 'primitive socialist accumulation', with acknowledgements to the inventor of the term, V. M. Smirnov. Only he interpreted it differently from Preobrazhensky's later version. He chose to stress that the capitalists accumulated capital by exploiting labour, and that therefore a socialist reconstruction would require the conscription of labour, including here the non-proletarians, the peasantry in particular. This is a kind of primitive accumulation via forced labour. Then 'the productive forces of society will be distributed between different areas according to natural conditions, such as proximity of fuel and raw material supplies. The question of industrial standards will be solved without capitalist barriers, and the development of productive forces will proceed in giant strides....'[9]

Lenin was fond of Bukharin, but made some sharp criticisms in his marginal notes on *Ekonomika perekhodnogo perioda*. These marginal notes were published in *Leninskii sbornik* in 1929, as part of the campaign to discredit Bukharin, though he was himself at that time one of the editors of that publication. It may be of interest briefly to summarise Lenin's reactions.

In many instances Lenin was pleased, even delighted ('Excellent', 'absolutely right', etc.). Indeed, he was delighted with almost all the *economic* statements in the book. True, he did not agree that economics disappear under socialism, since even under full communism there will be $c+v+m$. Another 'economic' exception, perhaps, was 'primitive socialist accumulation', a term which Lenin underlined and commented : 'ugh!' But this might have been not an objection of substance but an example of Lenin's many protests against 'excessive scholasticism of terminology'. Examples of this are many. Thus Bukharin spoke of 'horizontal competition', 'vertical competition' and 'combined [monopolistic?] competition', and Lenin's comment was: 'Ugh; playing at definitions.'

But Lenin's chief objections were of a more abstract-theoretical kind. One category was philosophical. He clearly suspected Bukharin of being too influenced by Bogdanov. For example, Bukharin wrote: 'It is further clear that the dialectical-historical viewpoint ...', and Lenin reacted as follows:[10] 'Spoiled by the eclecticism of Bogdanov, the dialectical "point of view" becomes just one of many equally legitimate "points of view". Wrong!' And again, Bukharin wrote that 'social-productive processes' may be 'examined' from a 'point of view' and be 'theoretically interesting'. Lenin scribbled: 'Wrong words. Errors of Bogdanov terminology clearly visible: subjectivism, solipsism. It is not a matter of who "examines", or who is "interested", but of what exists independently of the human consciousness.' He seems to suspect Bukharin of not being consistently dialectical, and indeed said this also in his testament. Bukharin is also taken to task for a phrase about 'the theoretical proof of the impossibility of the reconstitution of capitalist relations'. Lenin retorted: ' "Impossibility" can only be proved by practice. The author does not probe the relationship between theory and practice *dialectically*.' Lenin may have had in mind the active or voluntaristic aspect of Marxism, which had been so strikingly demonstrated in the successful seizure of power in Russia, under (theoretically) unripe, i.e. 'impossible', conditions.

Lenin's hackles are also raised wherever the word 'sociology' appears. Phrases recur: 'Bukharin worsened Marx with sociological scholastics', or 'Marx spoke without elaborate "terms" and "systems" and "sociologies"'. When Bukharin used an unhappy phrase about 'exploding relationships' (*lopayushchikhsya otnosheniyakh*), Lenin exclaimed: 'What language, what "sociology".' When Bukharin writes a phrase about 'sociological definition of productive forces', Lenin at once underlines the word 'sociological' and comments: 'Ha, ha.' Finally, Bukharin has a footnote mocking the 'sociologist' Kautsky, and Lenin comments: 'That's great. On page 84 the "sociologist" Bukharin puts the word "sociology" into ironical quotation-marks. Bravo!' Why did Lenin so hate this word?

But we shall return to Bukharin's sociology later. Let us briefly continue to discuss the 'transition period' and the evolution of Bukharin's ideas.

How did Bukharin look at his own ideas later on? Certainly, he admitted to 'illusions'. Thus in a work published as early as 1921 we find him insisting that the struggle to retain power *compelled* total control and heavy losses of productive capacity ('We did not needlessly smash crockery'). However, 'it became clear in 1921 that the Russian economy was still more obstinate [than we thought], and that the state machine had sufficient power only to keep large-scale industry socialised, and not all of that'.[11] He came to emphasise the vital importance, for survival, of 'raising up the productive forces', and for this 'requisitions and the ban on private trade were useless'. War-communism combined necessities and illusions. 'We thought that we could, at a blow and swiftly, abolish market relations. Yet it turns out that we shall reach socialism through market relations.'[12] The same ideas were expressed in 1924 in *Bolshevik*:

> The adoption of N.E.P. was a collapse of our illusions.... This does not mean that the war-communism system was basically wrong for its time.... War and blockade compelled us to act thus. But we thought then that our peacetime policy would be a *continuation* of the centralised planning system of that period.... In other words war-communism was seen by us not as military, i.e. as needed at a given stage of civil war, but as a universal, general, so to speak 'normal' form of economic policy of a victorious proletariat. The illusions of war-communism burst at the very hour when the proletarian army stormed Perekop.[13]

So it was to be a long, strong haul. Short-cuts were out. This Bukharin learnt by bitter experience.

Before returning to his economic ideas in the N.E.P. period, let us pass to a completely different strand of his thought, which found expression long before he himself became a victim of party-machine politics. This is the issue of possible degeneration of the so-called proletarian dictatorship.

As already noted, Bukharin stressed that proletarian cadres could not develop before the revolution. They need training. The intelligentsia and other non-proletarian elements must play a leading role. In his major work published in 1921 he referred to 'the ancient Inca state', in which 'there was a regulated and organised economy, in the hands of a gentry-priesthood class, an intelligentsia of a kind, which controlled everything, ran everything, and operated the state economy as a dominant class, sitting over the top of all the others'.[14]

Here Bukharin had had in mind a group of rulers of non-proletarian origin. (This was certainly Lenin's fear.) Bukharin expressed *this* fear in 1923. But in that year he made it clear that his thoughts ran deeper. He wrote the following:

> Even proletarian origin, even the most calloused hands, ... is no guarantee against turning into a new class. For if we imagine that a section of those who have risen out of the working class becomes detached from the mass of the workers, and congeals into a monopoly position in its capacity of ex-workers, they too can become a species of caste, which could also become a new class. ...
> After the revolution the old order collapses, the old [ruling] class is scattered and deformed, and out of it can arise a new class. ...
> How can we struggle against it? The answer will lie in the quantitative balance of cultural forces. ... But it is possible that the first battalions which the working class sends into higher education will become a close corporation which ... though of worker origin, will dominate through its monopoly of education.

This would be a new class. So it is 'vital not to let the cadres become a monopoly caste'.[15]

In the same pamphlet, Bukharin exclaims: 'We need Marxism plus Americanism', so that 'things are done efficiently'.[16]

In 1922, in another article, Bukharin was again concerned with the question of administrative cadres. 'The workers cannot be other than a class culturally deeply suppressed by the whole capitalist regime.' Consequently, this 'culturally oppressed class cannot develop [its culture] so as to prepare itself for the organisation of all society. It can be ready to prepare itself for the destruction of the old world. It must "remake its nature" and ripen ... only in the period of its dictatorship. Hence additional costs (*izderzhki*) of the proletarian revolution, ... unknown in general to the bourgeois revolution.'[17] But then 'how does the proletariat none the less create its cadres of political ideologues and leaders?' Inevitably, the leaders tend to come from 'the bourgeois intelligentsia', and he notes that the cultural gap between such leaders and the proletarian masses is very wide, much wider than between the bourgeoisie and *its* leaders. But he sees also the existence or emergence of a whole stratum of 'worker bureaucrats', such as exist in British trade unions or in the German unions and social democracy.

When the proletariat seizes power, it must inevitably utilise specialists who are hostile to it. The idea that this can be avoided is utopian and impracticable. However, this situation 'contains within it a major danger, inevitable in a proletarian revolution, ... *the danger of the degeneration of the proletarian state and the proletarian party*' (emphasis his).[18]

Thus far Bukharin seems to see, as Lenin did in 1921, the danger in the form of the uncultured proletariat losing out to the culturally superior alien classes, or adopting their ways ('like a barbarian victor adopting the way of life and habits, even the tongue, of the conquered people'). But he did see further than this: 'The cultural backwardness of the worker masses, especially in conditions of general misery, when *nolens volens* the administrative and leadership apparatus has to receive many more consumers' goods than the ordinary worker, gives rise to *the danger of a very substantial divorce from the masses even of that part of the cadres which emerged from the working masses themselves.*'[19] He went on: 'An appeal to working-class origin and proletarian goodness is not by itself an argument against the existence of this danger....' Classes become deformed by the revolution. Cut off from the masses, cadres *could* (though they need not) join their more cultured colleagues and together make 'the germ of a new ruling class'. Economic backwardness and the conditions of N.E.P. add to the danger. (Bukharin did not see that the ex-proletarian cadres could eventually turn on their 'cultured' colleagues and kill them. This happened to many a bourgeois specialist, and also to Bukharin himself.)

In 1926, when he himself was at his political apogee, he made a speech in Leningrad which was part of the campaign to destroy the Zinoviev power-centre there. The speech was mostly devoted to discrediting various criticisms of the then party line. Thus we can regard the allegation about the 'sergeant-like methods' (*feldfebelskie metody*) of party rule in Leningrad as normal factional-struggle language, since very similar methods were used elsewhere by Bukharin's then allies. However, he did make a significant point of general application. He deplored 'the replacement of elected functionaries by commanders appointed from above'. This, he said, can lead to excessive ' "hardness" of the apparatus, which, taken to absurd lengths, would lead to fossilisation (*okamenelost*) of the apparatus'.[20]

And finally, on the tenth anniversary of the October Revolution, Bukharin referred to 'former workers, who ceased to be members of a revolutionary class, linked by many threads with new bourgeois strata, with the new service-officialdom, [*sluzhilym chinovnichestvom*: note the deliberately archaic words, to remind readers of tradition] as distant from the needs and concerns of the masses as the earth is from the sky'.[21]

So no one can say that Bukharin was unaware of certain dangers to the party and the revolution. Yet he could not see, until too late, the dangers to himself from the Stalin group. Or rather, he must have considered the policies and personalities of the Trotsky group to be intolerable, and fought them with all his skill and cunning, considering them a graver danger than Stalin, until the latter turned on him.

Let us now go back to Bukharin the theoretician, or rather the populariser of sociological-philosophical theories. His *Teoriya istoricheskogo materializma* must be regarded as a very fine essay in popularisation, and this is in no sense a criticism. It certainly was one of the duties of the few educated leader-intellectuals to reach the less educated party members, and Bukharin did this job with a vivid language and without simplifying the issues. This is quite unlike the catechism of Stalinist indoctrination. The readers were compelled to think.

Let us see, for instance, how he discusses regularities or social laws (*pravil'nost'*, *zakonomernost'*). He gives examples. Under capitalism the number of wage-earners shows a tendency to increase, and cyclical fluctuations occur. There are also statistical regularities, such as enable us to predict the number of births next year, or the consumption of beer in Bavaria.

Man, unlike things or spiders, has conscious aims. He seeks causes. He is also caused, part of nature, part of society. Men's aims and actions depend on something, i.e. are in some sense determined. Men are subject to necessities yet there is free will. Men choose, they are neither pawns nor marionettes, but their choices are circumscribed. To assert the total freedom of human will leads either to nonsense or to religion. Man feels free. Thus an orator is free to drink water, and also to dance the *trepak*, but he drinks and does not dance, because his throat is dry. Men make the law of supply and demand by buying and selling freely. 'Society is composed of men, each social event is made up of a multitude of individual feelings, attitudes, wills, actions.' The net result, e.g. a market price, is independent of human will, in that many would have willed a quite different result. A price so arrived at is the basis of individual valuations of the product. So men's wills cause things to happen, but what happens is different from what men have willed – until communism comes. *Then* one will have collectively organised will, with no anarchy of production and no contradiction between the individual and society. Individual will, of course, would still exist, but men will act together in pursuit of aims determined by their situation and environment.

What about accident? Bukharin quotes Spinoza: 'a thing is called accidental because of lack of knowledge'. 'If, in the intersection of two or more causal chains, we know only one of them, then the event which follows this intersection will *seem* to us to be accidental, though in fact it is *zakonomerno*.'

'Accident' should be eliminated from social science. Necessity is a concept independent of moral judgement. Necessity and inevitability are not the same. Stammler argued: 'If socialism is inevitable, why struggle to attain it? No one strives to organise an eclipse of the moon.' Bukharin replies: 'Social events are made by men, otherwise we would have square circles and fried ice. Marxism does not deny the will, it explains it.'

Of course men make history, but the will of humans is itself determined. *Ex officio*, a general's will matters more than a corporal's, and it is the same with politicians. Social interconnections give power to an individual.

Bukharin emphatically denies that Marxists treat art or ideology as mere superstructure on a material base. These, and other elements of the superstructure, do have a feedback effect on the base.

He returns elsewhere to the necessity of distinguishing causal rationality from moral judgements. He rejects 'tout comprendre, c'est tout pardonner'. 'It is said that to understand is to forgive. Nonsense. We can only assess an event if we understand it. To understand a historical event is to present it as a consequence of a particular historical cause or causes, in other words *not* as an accidental unconditioned magnitude, but as something necessarily flowing from the totality of pre-existing conditions, i.e. causal necessity.' This is *not* fatalism. Men act. Hegel's 'all that is real is rational' should not be misunderstood. 'For Marx the "rationality" of reality was only the causal connection between past and present, while for apologists this rationality is an argument for justifying the event.'[22]

In his sociology, and especially in *Teoriya istoricheskogo materializma*, the term perhaps most frequently used is *ravnovesie*, 'equilibrium'. Indeed, this word occurs frequently in many of his works. Few Bolsheviks were fond of it. Let us see what he meant by it.

In his capacity as an economist, Bukharin stressed, quite logically, that economic theories, value theories, relate to and describe equilibrium situations. And indeed this is plainly true both of Böhm-Bawerk and of Marx. In fact all economists, whatever their persuasions, assume a tendency for profits to be equal in all sectors, and, as all must surely recognise, this is not so in reality, but would be so in equilibrium. For Bukharin, however, this concept has a wider connotation, and is extended far beyond economics.

Perhaps it would be correct to define it as follows. All systems, all social relationships, are to be defined and studied in their pure form, bringing out their essence, shape, interconnections, though of course recognising that in the real world there are many complicating factors *and* that all things change. Thus Bukharin would argue that Marx studied the basic features of capitalism, abstracting for the sake of clarity from, for instance, the survival of elements of feudalism in capitalist states. *Ravnovesie* could be a way of analysing capitalist market relations. It could also be a way of looking at the social structure, at governments, indeed at any social phenomena. Bukharin was well read in Western sociology, and no doubt sought to influence his colleagues, some of whom, Lenin especially, had little patience with it. Anyhow, 'equilibrium' as he used it brought Bukharin some way towards the structuralist or functionalist school. This, according to some critics, is an approach inherently conservative. Bukharin would disagree vehemently, no doubt. He would use against such critics the arguments already developed against 'tout comprendre, c'est tout pardonner': if we understand the interrelationships that make up a system, then we understand. This does not mean that we approve. But his enemies later attacked him for not being dialectical, for 'mechanism', and for all sorts of sins, of which 'sociology' was one. The very word became anathema for a generation after the political defeat of Bukharin.

Bukharin's name is also associated with two highly practical applications of equilibrium-type thinking. One was his striving for the maintenance of market equilibrium during N.E.P. The other – in the famous *Zametki ekonomista* – concerned his plea for what would now be called input–output balance, i.e. you cannot make bricks without straw, or build factories with bricks that are not there. However, these were political-economic issues on which, it seems to me, his judgement was based on considerations of a quite non-philosophical order.

But back to N.E.P. and to political economy. How did Bukharin understand N.E.P.? Having decisively abandoned 'illusions', what did he see?

First, his views on world revolution. In an article he wrote at the time of the seizure of power, he saw world revolution as 'providing reinforcements' for the Russian economy. 'The victory of the Western proletariat will make it possible to heal in a planned way the economic wounds of Russia with highly developed West European techniques. The economic backwardness of Russia will be offset by the high technical level of Europe.'[23] But the revolution had not spread. So what were they to do? In 1925 (in *Put' k sotsializmu*), and again in the following year in his address to the Leningrad party conference, he argued that it was wrong to assert that Soviet Russia in its isolation was doomed by its own internal contradictions. If imperialists attack, then the U.S.S.R. could be defeated, yes. The only guarantee against this is victory of the revolution in other countries.[24] But 'can we conclude from this that our technical and economic backwardness will destroy us?' No. 'If we do not have confidence in the sufficiency of

our internal forces for building socialism, then there was no reason
for us to go to the barricades in October, then the Mensheviks were
right, that in such a backward country as Russia it was pointless to
attempt a socialist revolution, then Comrade Trotsky was right in
asserting that without the help of a victorious West European proletariat we shall necessarily face a conflict with the peasants which we
must lose.'[25]

How did Bukharin see the peasants? He was certainly aware of
the existence of strata among them, and by 1927 he was, from his
point of view rather illogically, calling for 'pressure on the kulak and
bourgeois elements', but even then he emphasised that 'it would be a
mortal sin to break up or threaten the alliance with the middle peasant'.
None the less, 'together with the middle peasant, with the support of
the poor peasant, basing ourselves on the growing economic and
political force of our Union and our party, we should and we must
go over to a stronger offensive against the capitalist elements, first and
foremost against the kulaks'.[26]

Earlier in the decade the emphasis was different. While certainly
aware that 'the working class is an oasis in the peasant desert',[28] and
that this argument could be used to enforce the ban on fractions,
Bukharin wrote: 'Lenin taught that a conflict between the working
class and the peasantry is by no means inevitable. Trotsky teaches: it
is unavoidable. Lenin taught: our salvation comes from coexisting
(*uzhitsa*) with the peasant. Trotsky says it will all be fatal without
a world revolution. Hence Lenin's unique theory of agrarian–
co-operative socialism.'

Of course Bukharin was president of the Comintern after Zinoviev,
and can be credited with sincerity in rejecting 'national exclusiveness'.
However, he saw powerful political reasons for asserting that, despite
the peasant problem, Russia would be building socialism, and he
generalised this into a strategy for backward countries. His mind was
dominated by the experience of war-communism, when it became
abundantly clear – as already mentioned – that the peasant mass
would not tolerate the ban on market relations once the civil war
was over. Very well, said a maturing Bukharin, we must take this
reality into account, we cannot base policy upon illusions. Thus we
must generalise about reality. In doing this, Bukharin was certainly
influenced not only by events but also by Lenin, the Lenin of the 11th
Party Congress (1922) and of his semi-coherent article 'On Co-operation', written in his last lucid days. There is much evidence to support
the proposition that Bukharin thought that he was carrying out
Lenin's personal line, as indeed one can see by textual comparisons.
All this being so, I do not think that either Knirsch or Schlesinger were

being fair to the Bukharin of the 1920s in denying to his other ideas the 'theoretical' status which they accord to the extremist thought of the 1918-20 period.

In his pamphlet *The Road to Socialism and the Worker–Peasant Alliance*[28] one sees his view of peasants and of N.E.P. most clearly developed. For him, party rule represented, and had to represent, the dominance of the working class in the worker–peasant alliance. Thus, in a speech in the same year (1926), he rejected a naïve suggestion that a peasant party be legalised; the peasant would support it against the Bolsheviks, and it is in their own interest ('hard as it is to explain to them') that the working-class dictatorship exercised by the party be maintained.[29]

But back to 'the road to socialism'. Naturally, he wrote, there are some differences between peasants and workers, e.g. over food prices. There are differences also between poor and rich peasants, but Bukharin could see that the problem concerned the *bulk* of the peasants taken as a whole.

Lenin spoke of a link, the *smychka*, with the peasantry. Its economic aspect was *competition*, i.e. the competition of state industry and state trade with the 'privateer'. The NEPmen try to make their *smychka*, and can succeed if the state provides goods and services badly. If 'the state economy can meet peasant needs better than the private trader, capitalist, middleman, then the *smychka* is safe'.[30] Under war-communism it was proper to confiscate and smash the privateers. Now times are different. Such methods are out.

He looked forward to the gradual squeezing-out of the private sector by competition, using the economies of scale which represented a great and yet unused potential of socialist industry. This industry will gradually move towards overall planning (*obyedinena obshchinim planom*), but 'this sort of planning is not conceivable by itself, since our industry produces to a great extent for the peasant market'.[31] Peasant demand must be studied, the peasant economy must grow and be modernised. The peasants will gradually see the advantage of join-ing together. 'It is evident that we cannot persuade, or even try to persuade, the peasants to go over at once to uniting their landholdings. Old habits have so impregnated the people that to break these habits is not possible. Yet nevertheless the peasants will inevitably travel the road towards unity' – and this will be 'through co-operation', by stages: first marketing and purchasing co-operatives, then such joint production as butter-making and other processing. These peasant co-operatives will, as a whole, 'grow into (*vrastat'*) the system of economic organs of the proletarian state, and this will mean that we take large steps on the road to socialism'.[32] The parallel with the

Lenin of 1922-3 is very clear. Indeed, Bukharin spoke of Lenin's 'state trade and co-operative line' and asserted: 'We shall achieve socialism here through the process of circulation, not directly through production. We shall reach it through co-operation.'[33] He clearly did not have producers' co-operatives in mind, but then, despite Stalin, neither did Lenin.

What would Lenin have said? Bukharin's speech on Lenin, made soon after Lenin's death in 1924, emphasised his flexibility and tactical ingenuity as far as slogans of the moment were concerned. Bukharin noted that he could advocate the Constituent Assembly, and then destroy it, because both actions were right in the circumstances. He could launch crude slogans like *'grab' nagrablennoe'* if this was what moved the masses. Lenin understood well that, before the seizure of power, the task is 'destructive', to identify all those contradictions which it is the task of party policy to deepen, so as to destroy. But 'now we must not destroy, we must build'. What was Marxism, a methodology or a certain number of ideas in their concrete applica-tion? If the latter, then Lenin, facing a new situation, went beyond Marxism (*za gran' marksizma*). But this, said Bukharin, is wrong. Leninism is a synthesis of Marx's methods and basic principles with revolutionary experience. 'Lenin possessed Marxism, Marxism did not possess Lenin.'[34] He quoted Lenin (in italics): 'Many of our mistakes are due to the mechanical use of slogans which were correct in one historical situation ... in a completely different situation.' Was Bukharin uneasily aware that his former master would have taken a more 'offensive' line had he been alive at the end of the 1920s?

It may be necessary to remind some readers just how 'gradualist' and cautious was Lenin's position in 1922-3. Lenin's co-operatives were above all to be concerned with trade. The whole population, he argued, should become so 'civilised' as to participate in co-operatives and learn to calculate. This is 'all' that is needed to move on to socialism, but Lenin put 'all' in inverted commas, because the low level of culture made it a huge task, 'immeasurably difficult', 'requiring a cultural revolution'. 'Russians now trade in the Asiatic manner, they must learn how to trade as Europeans.' Co-operatives he saw primarily as a means of ensuring the participation of the people in retail distribu-tion, as a way of limiting private trade. State control over industry and land nationalisation would ensure that Soviet co-operatives would be unlike those existing in capitalist countries.[35] Lenin, in his speech to the 11th Party Congress (1922), insisted that the *smychka* required the communists to learn to trade, to satisfy peasant needs better than the 'capitalist-NEPman'. He exclaimed: 'As for you, your principles are communist, your ideas are excellent, you resemble saints qualified for instant transfer to paradise, but can you run a business?' This is all quite consistent with Bukharin's mid-1920s concept of competition between the private and the state economy through the market, and the substitution of economic for administrative means of waging the class struggle. This, however, still leaves open the question of what Lenin might have thought in the circumstances of the second half of the 1920s. For him N.E.P. was at once a necessary retreat (*reculer pour mieux sauter?*), and the right path to be followed 'seriously and for a long time'. When would he have resumed the advance? And in what direction? We can never know.

Bukharin, anyhow, followed fairly consistently the logic of N.E.P. Prices, the market, is the connecting link between town and country. 'Our industry will develop the more rapidly, the higher is effective demand from the peasantry. Accumulation in our industry will be the more rapid as accumulation speeds up in the peasant economy.'[36] If someone says: 'Charge more for industrial goods, raise wages, down with concessions to the rural petty-bourgeoisie', then Bukharin replies: 'Nonsense, industry would then impoverish the peasantry and will itself be deprived of its market.'[37]

What of class war in the villages? Bukharin would see richer peasants striving for influence in the villages, and in co-operatives too. But, he insisted, now is not the time to rob the kulaks to give to the poor. The days of confiscation and requisitions are over. The middle peasant will become better off, will 'catch up the prosperous' by better methods and via co-operation. Even kulaks can 'grow into' (*vrastat'*) socialism via co-operation, by putting their money into state banks, etc. True, they would be a species of foreign body in the system (like foreign concessions), but kulaks could only be a menace if they grow faster than state industry.

Bukharin returned again to the theme of peaceful competition, indeed coexistence, with the NEPman. Greater freedom for bourgeois elements is not dangerous now (1925) because we are stronger, he said. (Contrast this with the argument that because we are stronger we can pass to the offensive.) He denied that they were abandoning the poor, who will become less poor in a developing economy. 'Against the village money-lender and petty trader we shall use not coercion but credit co-operatives and efficient shops.'[38]

Bukharin's 'growing into' concept attracted some hostile comment at the time. He denied that his policy was based on the prosperous peasant, or that it was a form of degeneration of party policy: N.E.P., he asserted, strengthened the forces of socialism, 'it is not treason to the proletarian line, but the only correct proletarian policy'.[39]

Bukharin's formulations were made in the face of attack from

Trotsky and his friends. Bukharin would occasionally agree that N.E.P. was 'only a *peredyshka*' (temporary halt), and that there will be battles and offensives to come.[40] But Bukharin, unlike Trotsky, was willing to be a gradualist, and accepted the logic of N.E.P. – coexistence and competition with the private sector and a species of equilibrium relations between them – this being contrasted with Preobrazhensky's view that one must 'eat up' (*pozhirat'*) the other. The Leninist idea of a bloc or *smychka* with the peasants means a gradual and slow progress. 'We shall proceed forward slowly and bit by bit, dragging the peasant cart behind us.'[41] Elsewhere he spoke of moving towards socialism 'at the pace of a tortoise'. Some comrades would not be so patient.

One must ask oneself if Bukharin's ideas of 1927, with phrases about 'passing to the offensive against the kulaks', were consistent with his own ideas of 1925, or indeed with the growth of the peasant economy and of marketing of food at which he was aiming. Probably not. Probably by 1927 he was already under political pressure to recant his ideas on *vrastanie*. There is an odd phrase in his Leningrad speech of 1926: 'When we shall be sufficiently strong ... then we shall be able decisively and sharply to turn the basic masses of the peasantry on to the socialist road. But this is a matter for the future, though not a particularly distant future.'[42] This was surely in line with Stalin's ideas of the time. Did he mean it? Probably not in Stalin's way. A few minutes earlier he had said that the kulak's economic grip was due to his value to his fellow-peasants: 'The co-operative trades badly, the kulak trades better. The co-operative has no galoshes, the kulak has. We cannot feed the peasant with good decrees and speeches about Chamberlain.'[43]

As already noted, Bukharin used the term 'equilibrium' very frequently. N.E.P. was, of course, based on market relations, and Bukharin became a most fervent supporter of measures to achieve and maintain equilibrium in the market. A resumption of the offensive for socialism seemed, for him, consistent with market relations, for this would be an *economic* offensive, not based on coercion and police measures vis-à-vis the petty-bourgeois elements. So the 'goods famine' of the period after 1926 seemed to him to threaten a dangerous disequilibrium, and Stalin's coercive measures in the first months of 1928 put the final seal on a split which was to destroy Bukharin politically and, in the end, physically.

But his allegiance to N.E.P. should not be taken as evidence that he is a kind of prophet of market socialism. This is to misunderstand his economics. It is not only the Bukharin of 1920 who saw socialism as a non-market system. Writing in 1927, Bukharin asserted: 'Despite the existence of the market and of capitalist forms of management, we are already moving from a type of economy based on profit to one based on the requirements of the masses (*pokrytiem podrebnostei mass*).'[44] An eminent Soviet scholar who had known both men said to me: 'Bukharin and Preobrazhensky, however much they differ on other matters, were both agreed that the law of value would have no place under socialism.' (In his opinion they were both wrong.) Bukharin accepted the 'market' logic of a mixed economy such as that of N.E.P. He was for building socialism *using* the market. But socialism for him would *not* be any species of market economy, and none of his writings can be cited to support a contrary view. My own belief is that experience has proved him to have been mistaken, but that is hardly the point.

Bukharin did not oppose industrialisation and was aware of the need to accumulate. 'The transfer of value into the accumulation fund at the expense of the petty producers must occur.' But this, he insisted, was *not* exploitation, was *not* any kind of internal colonialism.[45] He had opposed Trotsky's demand, made in his letter of 8 October 1923, for planned industrial expansion. It was, in his view, absurd for its time, threatening the hard-won 'equilibrium' (that word again!) of political and economic forces. But he insisted even then that a plan will be needed, and industrialisation too. Either that, 'or we shall degenerate' (*pererodimsya*).[46] Then again: 'We are sometimes reproached for wishing to obtain the missing capital at the cost of the people (*za shchyot naroda*). But there is no other "cost"! (*shcheta drugogo nyet!*).'[47]

Bukharin's line, therefore, should certainly not be so presented as to make him an opponent of planning and industrialisation. The essential point was that he wished to advance as fast as possible *within N.E.P.*, and this meant advancing rather slowly. His willingness to go along with anti-kulak measures (stopping, it is true, far short of expropriation and deportation) seemed, however, to be basically inconsistent with his 'N.E.P.' premises: increased agricultural marketings were vital, and those peasants who were successful were, or would become, kulaks, to the extent to which they expanded marketings. But I have not the space here to pursue this fascinating problem of the viability of Bukharin's policies in the late 1920s, except perhaps to refer briefly to one important dimension of the discussion. Part of Bukharin's 'line' of the late 1920s was, in a sense, negative: do *not* try to build factories with bricks which are not there, do *not* make unbalanced plans, do *not* antagonise the peasantry, do *not* return to requisitions and confiscations. Yet, as any economic adviser knows, sound recommendations can well take the form of urging that the wrong things be not done. This is not really 'negative' advice either.

While he was unable to say so publicly, we may be sure that Bukharin in the 1930s must have thought: 'If those who accepted the unbalanced and excessive First Plan, and launched the offensive against the peasants, had known the huge cost which would be incurred, which *was* incurred, would they have persisted in their policies?' After all, even the agricultural surplus might have been mobilised at less cost if there had not been a decline in output, mass slaughtering of live-stock, famine, sabotage, etc., all these being direct consequences of the policies Bukharin had opposed. A possible answer to this would invoke Lenin's 'Port Arthur' analogy: the Japanese (in 1904) had launched an assault which failed, but learnt from this failure how to succeed; Stalin's assault led to vast mistakes and heavy losses, but in the end they broke through and built a mighty industry. Yes, but warnings which, if heeded, might have reduced the losses, must still be regarded as having been justified. It seems to me that the argu-ments in, for instance, *Zametki ekonomista*, about excesses in planning, were well founded and were abundantly supported by subsequent events. The man whose work we are honouring in this volume has put us all in his debt by his truly immense contribution to our knowledge of Soviet Russia, and I yield to none in my admiration. But, as he knows, in this particular area of discussion my view remains obstinately different from his.

Finally, some concluding thoughts. Bukharin was a strikingly original thinker, and it is a tragedy that he was for all practical pur-poses silenced at the end of the 1920s. The attacks on him, made by little men when he was forbidden to reply, make painful reading. True, he was himself a vigorous polemicist, not averse to both demagogy and 'organisational measures' in his own attacks on the Trotskyists. But argument, however fierce, is not the same as calling in the police. Bukharin himself was no administrator. He at no time headed a commissariat, nor was he a party secretary at any level. Indeed, he had grave weaknesses as a practical politician. He was a brilliant journalist and populariser, but also a man who had made important contributions to Marxian economics and was something of a pioneer in Marxian sociology. It was a great blow to this subject in particular that Bukharin's association with sociology led to the virtual banishment of the subject as well as the word from Russian academic life after his fall. It is only now slowly coming back to life. His concept of equilibrium and system, involving a kind of functionalism or institutionalism, was open to attack from those Marxists who emphasised change: he could be accused of an un-dialectical approach, mechanism, Bogdanovism even. Yet the study of the interaction of the parts of a system, indeed the concept of system, seems to me so obviously useful that the accusations hang in the air. The 'system' could be a market, a general staff, a planned centralised economy, a relationship between state, workers and peasants, a bureaucratic apparatus. True, it is a kind of instantaneous photograph, not a moving picture. A system changes. One may wish to overthrow it. But it has an inner logic, or essence, which are worth bringing out in analysis. (Lenin, it is true, would take exception to both 'logic' and 'essence', as evidenced by his marginal notes.)

To cite an example, Bettelheim uses a phrase: 'analyser les formations sociales en transition comme des structures complexes, dans lesquelles "tous les rapports coexistent simultanément et se supportent les uns les autres", selon l'expression de Marx....'[48] Bukharin would have approved. I cannot see how one can disapprove in the name of Marxism.

However, those who silenced Bukharin the social scientist were not really interested in these philosophical distinctions, even if they really understood them. For some, philosophy or social theory was merely incidental to the real issues. ('*Kto kogo, vot nasha filosofiya*', to cite a fictional but not untypical local functionary.) For others, what was needed was simplicity, a catechism, which provides answers which do not raise awkward questions, and which establishes unquestioned authorities and axioms. Typical of this was Stalin's well-known letter to the editor of *Proletarskaya Revolutsiya* in 1931, when an unfortunate historian, Slutsky, was castigated for daring to suggest that Lenin underestimated the extent to which the German social democrats had abandoned the revolutionary path before 1914. Stalin was not interested in the substance of the case, but he assaulted author and editors alike for daring to discuss the undiscussable. Bukharin was never this kind of populariser. He was far too much the erudite intellectual. This quality, which perhaps limited his political effectiveness, he shared with many Bolshevik intellectual victims of the Purges.[49] Maybe, it could be argued, dissident voices had to be silenced if Russia was to get through the crises and cataclysms of the 1930s. But we are a generation and more removed from this period. Surely the time has come for a free and open discussion of his ideas in the U.S.S.R.?

NOTES

Notes on sources: All quotations are translated by the author. References followed by the letter (H) are taken from the very useful compendium, edited by S. Heitman, *Put' k sotsializmu v Rossii* (New York, 1970), this being a selection of Bukharin's works.

1. Sidney Heitman, *A Bibliography with Annotations* (Stanford University Press; California, 1967).
2. Stephen Cohen's *Bukharin and the Bolshevik Revolution* (Knopf), has now appeared.
3. Peter Knirsch, *Die ökonomische Anschauungen Nikolai Bucharins* (Berlin, 1959).
4. *Mirovoe khozyaistvo i imperializm*, 3rd ed. (Moscow, 1925), written in 1915.
5. *Ekonomika perekhodnogo perioda* (Moscow, 1920) p. 83.
6. Bukharin and Preobrazhensky, *Azbuka kommunizma* (Petrograd, 1919) pp. 195-6.
7. *Ek. per. perioda*, pp. 110-12.
8. Ibid., p. 147.
9. Ibid., p. 95.
10. *Leninskii sbornik*, XI (Moscow, 1929) 387.
11. *Teoriya istoricheskogo materializma* (Moscow, 1921) pp. 306-7.
12. *Put' k sotsializmu i rabochi-krestyanski soyuz* (Moscow, 1925) pp. 62, 64.
13. 'O likvidatorstve nashikh idei' (1924) (H) pp. 177-8.
14. *Teoriya ist. mat.*, p. 69.
15. *Proletarskaya revolutsiya i kultura* (Petrograd, 1923) pp. 44-7.
16. Ibid., p. 49.
17. 'Burzhuaznaya revolutsiya i revolutsiya proletarskaya' (1922) (H) p. 168.
18. Ibid., p. 171.
19. Ibid., p. 172. Emphasis his again.
20. Speech at the 23rd Special Provisional Conference (Leningrad, 1926) (H) p. 352.
21. *K desyatiletiyu oktyabrskoi revolyutsii* (Moscow, 1927) p. 5.
22. *Mirovoe khozyaistvo i imperializm*, pp. 126-7.
23. *Sotsial-demokrat*, no. 5, 9 Nov 1917, reprinted in *Na podstupakh k oktyabryu* (Moscow, 1926) pp. 146-7.
24. *Put' k sotsializmu* (H) p. 313, and speech to the Leningrad Conference (1926) (H) p. 340.
25. Leningrad Conference (H) p. 340.
26. *K desyatiletiyu ...*, p. 70.
27. *K voprosu o trotskizme* (Moscow, 1925) p. 17.
28. *Put' k sotsializmu i rabochi-krestyanski soyuz*, 3rd ed. (Moscow and Leningrad, 1926).
29. Leningrad Conference (H) p. 348.
30. *Put' k sotsializmu*, p. 26.
31. Ibid., p. 30.
32. Ibid., p. 37.
33. *K voprosu o trotskizme*, p. 73.
34. *Lenin kak marksist* (H) pp. 229, 226.
35. Lenin, *Sochineniya*, 5th ed., XLV 371-6.
36. *Put' k sotsializmu*, p. 41.
37. Ibid., p. 44.
38. Ibid., p. 55.
39. Ibid., p. 66.
40. *K voprosu o trotskizme*, p. 25.
41. Ibid., p. 64.
42. Leningrad Conference (H) p. 339.

43. Ibid., p. 335.
44. *K desyatiletiyu* . . . , p. 87.
45. *K voprosu o trotskizme*, p. 68.
46. Ibid.
47. *K desyatiletiyu* . . . , p. 66.
48. C. Bettelheim, *Calcul économique et formes de propriété* (Paris : Maspers, 1970) p. 9.
49. Even Dr Schlesinger had it. He once told me that he was expelled for being, in the words of the official who expelled him, 'an incurable *Privatdozent*'.

10 Some Military and Political Aspects of the 'Militia Army' Controversy, 1919-1920

JOHN ERICKSON

FOR many months in 1917 the Bolsheviks worked assiduously to cripple an army rather than labouring to create one. The party's specialists in 'military affairs', the propagandists and agitators of the 'Military Organisation', were bent on paralysing the Imperial Army which otherwise might have been used against them, but once in power these same Bolsheviks, practised as they were in demolition and demoralisation, faced a fight for survival which demanded nothing less than the raising of a military force – an army – which would be capable of defending their new-found regime. It was a task for which, as Lenin himself subsequently admitted, neither ideological nor political preparation of any kind had been made.[1] Though rejecting the idea of using the prevailing military machine in the service of a revolutionary regime and propounding in turn the idea of a class-based revolutionary force, Marx and Engels had perforce little, if anything, to say about the form and function of the armed forces in post-revolutionary society; emotionalism filled the gap left by defective theorising and expressed itself in the radicals' loathing of the standing army, the idealisation of the *levée en masse* and the yearning to establish a wholly 'new' type of army.

The nature of the armed force at the disposal of the Bolsheviks on the morrow of the seizure of power furnished further complications: it was as variegated as it was miniscule, comprising an urban 'Red Guard' whose equipment, training and proficiency were negligible, the tough but ungovernable sailor squads of the Baltic fleet, a few thousand dour but indomitable Lettish riflemen, scattered 'fighting detachments' of armed workers, the bulk of them poorly fitted out and devoid of even rudimentary military skill, and a vast, demoralised, decaying army the best elements of which were avowedly anti-Bolshevik. Having assumed state power, the Bolshevik leadership quickly discovered that 'military affairs' were taking on aspects both novel and urgent as the threat of civil war at home and armed intervention from abroad impelled 'the revolution' to think of arming itself, and that with some speed. The Left, imbued as it was with a deep-seated hatred of the 'standing army' and repelled by the whole notion of *l'idée militaire* and the trappings of 'the barracks and bivouac, sabre and musket, moustache and uniform', resolved to try for a radical solution which would eliminate the 'bourgeois' army. In this design they were assisted by the inexperience, the conceit and the military ineptitude of the managers of the November *coup*, who rested extravagant hopes in utopian schemes for 'popular forces', for proletarian militias or locally raised 'revolutionary guards', which promised to be at once both democratic and socialist.[2] Unfortunately, they quickly proved to be anarchic and inefficient.

The debates over the type of armed force to be raised by the Soviet state, which reflected with cruel precision an unavoidable collision between principle and practicality, were carried on with varying degrees of passion, conviction and bitterness over the ensuing three years and then into one further stage (which persisted until the 'military reform' of 1924-5). From the outset the idea of using the 'old' army to protect the Soviet state was rejected, and sensibly so, but thereafter few could agree over what was involved in a 'militia army', or a 'National Socialist Guard', or yet again a 'Socialist Army', to mention but a few of the profusion of designations, schemes and organisations. In this very early stage Lenin seemed to favour a militia system, a preference based on 'economic' reasoning, but growing military threats brought him to accept a 'trained and disciplined Red Army', avowedly a class-based force designed to defend 'the revolution'; to those who pleaded for a war of national resistance or a 'revolutionary war' against the advancing Germans, Lenin returned the uncompromising answer that the first meant arming the opponents of the regime and the second was a military fantasy. Though the 'worker–peasant' link was stamped into the name of the new army, few of Lenin's earlier preconceptions survived. In the spring of 1918 he was demanding an army of 1 million men, quickly expanding this to 3 million, and with similar dispatch put Trotsky in charge of raising, training, administering and supervising this force. For officers and for the requisite military expertise he called on Tsarist military experience in the form of the *voenspets*, the 'military specialists', most of whom were anathema to

the party. The opposition raised a hue and cry almost at once: on
25 March 1918, in what proved to be a dress rehearsal for the great
encounter exactly one year later at the 8th Congress, Lenin faced the
anger and outraged feelings of party workers who protested that this
'new' army was even now slipping from their grasp and sliding into
odious bourgeois orthodoxy with its noxious discipline, alien
'specialists' and dangerous centralisation.[3] The protagonists of a
militia, with Podvoisky much to the fore, tried once more to win
acceptance of their plans for a 'militia army', decentralised and
democratic, but the crisis on the battlefronts demanded men and
divisions rather than paper plans and 'detachments' (*otryady*).[4]
Decentralisation gave way to centralisation, the volunteer principle
was abandoned in favour of systematic mobilisation and obligatory
military service, and 'elective command' was replaced by a formal
military hierarchy.

At the 8th Congress in March 1919, as the fighting in the civil war
reached a fierce crescendo, the 'military question' brought fresh bouts
of dissent, though the grievances were by no means new. The 'military
opposition', which took a stand against the prevailing policy, combined genuine idealism with vengeful politicking, not to mention
frustration and sheer pique. The more utopian fancies over military
organisation Lenin dismissed along with much else as sheer 'phrase-
mongering'; as for the notion that the army and military affairs had
either got out of control or into the wrong hands, he insisted that the
Defence Council (*Soviet Oborony*) and the Revolutionary Military
Council of the Republic (*Revvoensoviet Respubliki*, R.V.S.R.) were
both essential bodies, that strategy was under the general supervision
of the Central Committee and that discipline there had to be, whatever the ideological plaints or personal lamentations on this score.[5]
For all practical purposes the 'military opposition' was drummed off
the floor of the Congress, the advocates of centralisation and military
efficiency (with Trotsky and Stalin seemingly enjoined here, though
actually riven by the deadliest vendetta) seemed to have won the day,
but the victory rang a little hollow. For all the thrust of his counter-
stroke and the power of his logic, Lenin had not succeeded in reconciling socialism with this new-found militarisation – or was it
militarism? To Chicherin's assertion that here was 'a Red Army of
state capitalism' and never 'an army of communism', Lenin returned
only a dogged denial: 'This is altogether untrue.'[6] Doubts and mis-
givings, however, were widely spread. The final resolution of the 8th
Congress on 'the military question' affirmed specifically that the Red
Army as it then stood was purely 'transitional' (*perekhodnyi*) in form
and represented only a stage in the progress towards a 'territorial-

militia army', which 'responsible organs of the military apparatus' were even now actively seeking to implement.[7]

The prospect of disaster had triggered off the first furious debates about the form and function of the armed forces of the Soviet state; presently it was anticipation of victory which provided fresh relevance to what was simultaneously a dispute and a dilemma, both tautly summarised by Bukharin and Preobrazhensky in *Azbuka kommunizma*. They admitted that war-time exigencies forced the party to use 'the old methods of organisation', but the present Red Army was professedly 'provisional' in form and 'the essential aspiration' still remained the creation of *'something utterly different'*, namely an army in which 'artificial military unity' must give way to that induced by 'the natural productive unity of the workers' and where 'proletarian divisions' would learn discipline 'through the very methods of production' as opposed to having it imposed on them 'from above'.[8] This view of the symbiosis of soldier and worker largely corresponded with Trotsky's prescriptions for the second stage of the development of the Red Army; to field an army capable of fighting and winning, he had abandoned ideological formulas in favour of practical measures promoting military efficiency, but with victory in sight economic problems loomed larger than military commitments. Military methods were to be employed on the economic front and economic solutions applied to the military establishment in what appeared to be an abrupt transmigration of Trotsky's pragmatism: the vast Red armies would be run down, the centralised apparatus pruned and a 'class-based militia army' would enable the worker to produce and to train in a decentralised and democratic system. The urgency of laying plans for the demobilisation of the war-time Red Army provided the ideal opportunity to consider the features of a 'new' system – indeed, one was inconceivable without the other – and at the end of July 1919 Trotsky issued orders to the All-Russian Supreme Staff (*Vserosglavshtab*) to prepare such a plan.[9]

Trotsky lost no time in changing the direction of 'military affairs'. In the directive of 27 July 1919 issued by the R.V.S.R., he indicated that victory over Kolchak and Denikin was in sight and accordingly instructed *Vserosglavshtab* to prepare plans for the demobilisation of the multi-million-man Red Army; such a step, however, was not to be construed as a means of weakening or winding up the Soviet armed forces, which must remain in being so long as capitalist encirclement existed, and the attention of *Vserosglavshtab* was drawn specifically to the need to preserve 'the cadres' of the regular Red Army. These, however, should be so deployed and distributed throughout the country that they would form the core of military units to be raised by the 'administration for universal military training', *Vsevobuch*, presently under Podvoisky's command.[10] In effect, this was a prescription for a militia-based defence system and signalled Podvoisky's long-awaited opportunity, if not his actual triumph. Hot on the heels of this order, Trotsky embarked straightaway on a programme to cut the size of the central military administration, setting up a special commission (*Komissiya po Sokrashcheniyu Shtatov Voennogo Vedomstva*) in August to supervise these reductions; by mid-September several of the main military administrations – Command Staff (officers), Mobilisation, Organisation, the Central Administration of *Vsevobuch* and the Council of *Vserosglavshtab* itself – had been substantially reduced, by which time the Field Staff (*Polevoi Shtab*) of the R.V.S.R. was working on a review of the establishment of the field armies and the Inspector of Infantry, the ex-Tsarist General D. N. Nadezhnyi, received instructions to prepare reductions in the establishment of units.[11]

The officers of *Vserosglavshtab*, having set up their own working commission, presented their report to the R.V.S.R. on 3 September 1919. In spite of the original directive, *Vserosglavshtab* chose to ignore the militia issue and concentrated on the problems of demobilisation and calculations of post-war strength, defined by delineating the basic tasks of the Soviet military establishment, with four such tasks or roles being identified: garrison service and guard duties, supporting civil order, securing the state frontiers and training the civilian population for military services. Such tasks could be discharged by internal security and frontier defence troops, the territorial cadres of *Vsevobuch* and guard troops (*karaulnye voiska*), with the remainder of the Red Army being disbanded. In terms of figures, this meant demobilising 80 per cent of the 'command staff' (that is, 58,000 officers) and 1,400,000 Red Army soldiers (or some 75 per cent of the field armies), giving a peace-time 'establishment' of 342,500 officers and men, though for some six months after the ending of military operations certain regular Red Army divisions would be retained to defend the state frontiers during this transitional phase. Not surprisingly, the R.V.S.R. threw this plan out on 18 September and decided to set up a broader inquiry drawing in 'military and political workers'.[12]

The savage burst of fighting in the autumn of 1919, with Denikin driving on Moscow and Yudenich lunging at Petrograd, seemed to belie Trotsky's earlier optimism and imparted a slightly academic air to discussions of demobilisation. But Denikin was first deflected and then destroyed, Yudenich was dispersed and on 29 November a plenary session of the Central Committee assembled to discuss demobilisation, having first approved the measures taken with regard to the central military apparatus; the R.V.S.R. was instructed to investigate the demobilisation problem and 'the introduction of a militia system based on labour conscription'. From now on the commissions flourished apace. On 30 November the R.V.S.R. set up a commission on the militia system under I. I. Vatsetis (until 8 July the C.-in-C., when he was replaced by S. S. Kamenev), followed by a commission to work out details of the central military administration under the ex-Tsarist General P. S. Baluyev and a commission to review the establishments of field units under D. N. Nadezhnyi.[13] The first of these reports was not ready until mid-January 1920, but already one important step had been taken to prepare *Vsevobuch* for the 'new' system: during the course of the summer of 1919 the 'territorial cadres' of *Vsevobuch* had been much weakened and diluted, drawn as they were into the heavy fighting, but the R.V.S.R. laboured to reinforce the party presence during the autumn and also resolved to combine these 'territorial cadres' with the 'special detachments' – *otryady osobogo naznacheniya* – first raised from worker-communists in the latter half of 1918.[14] On 12 November the R.V.S.R. held a special conference to discuss this merger and for all practical purposes the process was pushed through during the remainder of the month; by the end of the year 'special detachments' were set up in all towns, industrial centres and larger populated localities.

On 3 December 1919 Podvoisky, in full charge of *Vsevobuch*, seized the occasion of a Komsomol congress to propound his ideas about the transition to a militia system in a document entitled 'Perekhod k klassovoi militsionnoi systeme'. It was in many respects a moderate and sensible paper, which insisted that the only proper military instrument for the defence of a socialist republic, one which broke decisively with the traditions of bourgeois militarism, was 'the class-based militia army'; but facts, and especially the facts of a difficult transitional phase, could not be denied – the Soviet republic was searching for the best method to accomplish that transition from a 'standing Red Army' to a 'Red Army of a militia type'. Podvoisky recommended, therefore, that two lines should be followed, the first involving the gradual utilisation of the most effective elements of the Red Army – 'effective' in both the communist and the military sense – to build up a militia army (otherwise undue haste might leave the Soviet republic virtually defenceless), and the second exploiting the Red Army as a vast reserve of organised labour, a disciplined workforce which should be employed to assist that vital economic recovery from the aftermath of war, blockade, famine and the physical devastation brought to the country. As for the mechanics of a shift to a militia system, Podvoisky argued that this could be managed by using the network of territorial cadres in *Vsevobuch*, which would be appreciably strengthened by the infusion of the *otryady osobogo naznacheniya*, while the Red Army would also retain hand-picked elements of its 'command and communist staff' to remain in their posts during the period of the disbanding of regular units.[15]

If Podvoisky was cautious, the soldiers were downright conservative, an attitude exemplified in the official report submitted by Vatsetis on 18 January 1920 to the R.V.S.R. under the title of 'Variant reformy vooruzhennoi sily R.S.F.S.R. s perekhodom k militisionnoi systeme'. As head of the commission on implementing a militia system of defence and as a recently displaced C.-in-C., Vatsetis's opinion carried some considerable weight, for all his irascibility and his ex-Imperial Army background. From the outset he was sceptical about the durability of any 'truce' between the Soviet republic and the capitalist states, for which reason it was essential to maintain a powerful military force in a high state of combat-readiness. It was essential to recognise that the European segments of the Soviet republic formed the most likely targets of attack, thus making it only prudent to consider shifting the 'military-administrative centre' from west to east, into the region of the Urals, the Kama and the Volga, and setting up a unified 'state military-technical base' in the area of Vyatka–Perm–Ekaterinburg–Chelyabinsk–Ufa–Simbirsk. Apart from this plan for strategic dispersal, Vatsetis recommended the retention of a strong force of regular units of the Red Army, basing his figures on the number of divisions which Poland and Romania could field in combination against the Soviet republic – 20 divisions; hence the Red Army must retain not fewer than 20 regular divisions at full war strength, 10 divisions forming the core of the regular army as first-echelon formations and the other 10 providing a second echelon to be fully mobilised in the event of war.[16] Assuming that these divisions were maintained under Establishment Table No. 220, Vatsetis calculated that this would provide up to 1 million men for any front in a very short period of time.[17] Artillery, engineer troops and aviation units should be maintained at full strength and at full combat-readiness; cavalry formations must come within the regular army establishment, with infantry units cut to half strength in second-echelon establishments, though this must depend on economic factors.

Vatsetis did not equivocate. The introduction of a militia system must be regarded as 'only an experiment of a temporary nature; the military situation of the Soviet republic demands continuous combat-readiness, which only a regular army can guarantee'. If anything, a militia system could lead to the weakening of the Soviet state, since it would cost four or five times as much as a regular army. Thus, from the strategic and the economic point of view, there was little to recommend a militia system.[18] Cogent though the Vatsetis report was, it could scarcely be regarded as the final word since the C.-in-C. (*Glavkom*) and the Field Staff had yet to submit their own findings, an occasion which promised to be interesting, to say the least, in view of the rivalry between the new *Glavkom* (Kamenev) and his predecessor, Vatsetis. In the event no one was disappointed. On 21 January 1920 *Glavkom* Kamenev, the Chief of the Field Staff P. P. Lebedev and the commissar to the Field Staff D. I. Kursky (who was also a member of the R.V.S.R.) presented their report under the title 'Ob organizatsii vooruzhennykh sil strany'. Though concerned with the details of the transition to a militia system, the Field Staff report concentrated largely on preserving the military capability of the Red Army, an approach which was hardly unexpected from these ex-Imperial officers. The basis of this plan involved splitting the Red Army into formations held in a high state of mobilisational readiness with the remainder of the divisions being used to build a militia system; the latter would draw on the 'toiling masses' who would be liable for military service between the ages of twenty and fifty. The number of regular troops to be retained was fixed against the strength of the Red Army at the beginning of 1920, namely, 66 rifle divisions and 15 cavalry divisions divided into two groups: 21 rifle and 9 cavalry divisions kept fully mobilised and deployed along the frontiers as well as in 'suspect' areas, with the remaining 45 rifle and 6 cavalry divisions assigned to the role of acting as cadres for the militia system. All supporting troops such as the railway troops and internal security units should be disbanded, but to secure internal order and to carry out garrison duties the Field Staff suggested deploying one rifle regiment to a *guberniya* (with three regiments in Moscow), giving a grand total of 43 regiments. The divisions assigned to the militia system should be known as *potentsial'nye voiska*. In terms of numbers, *Glavkom* and the Field Staff estimated that the formations held at readiness and the *potentsial'nye voiska*, plus their administrative apparatus, would mean a peace-time establishment of 1 million men, with 12 regular rifle divisions maintained with a two-brigade structure and a third brigade held in the *potentsial'nye* category; the cavalry divisions of the first-line troops would be kept at full three-brigade strength. Refining the figures, this gave a ceiling of 900,000 men, with 200,000 at mobilisational readiness, 700,000 men with the *potentsial'nye voiska*, administrative units and rear services. The annual intake required to sustain this force would be in the region of 360,000 men, though the mobilisation of one select age-group could furnish 450,000 men and thus satisfy the needs of the formations at full readiness, if the occasion should arise.[19]

Glavkom and the Field Staff also presented specific proposals about the organisation of a militia army: the whole country should be divided into 'divisional districts' (*divizionnye okruga*), which would be divided in turn into brigade, regimental and battalion districts, taking account not only of the administrative-territorial subdivisions but also the industrial locations which already existed; each military district and subdistrict would have its own administration and mobilisation plan, the 45 rifle and 6 cavalry divisions would be deployed into the main 'divisional districts', with men moving from the regular Red Army into these formations on an annual basis and then proceeding to the reserve. The whole system should be supervised by a 'Main Administration of the General Staff', or a 'Greater General Staff' (*Bol'shoi Generalnyi Shtab*), with a People's Commissar for War and the R.V.S.R. – assisted by the Chief of the General Staff, the Chief of the Supreme Staff and the Chief of Supply Services – at the head of this 'popular army'. The Main Administration of the General Staff could be assembled from the Field Staff and *Vserosglavshtab*; two types of local military administrative organs would be required, comprising the military commissariats and the administrations of the 'militia districts'.[20]

The Field Staff had flung a spanner well and truly into the works with their report of 21 January. Two days later the R.V.S.R. considered it in a formal session but could reach no conclusion, save for the bureaucratic response of calling for more reports, taking the form of written submissions from the *voenspets*. Vatsetis volunteered with alacrity and Podvoisky also asked for the opportunity to present his observations. At the end of the month, on 29 January, a full session of the R.V.S.R., with Sklyansky, Kamenev, Lebedev, Kursky, Podvoisky, Rattel', Vatsetis, Baranov, Sharmanov and Egoriev also in attendance, assembled to consider the problem formally tabled as 'Ob organizatsii armii na militsionnykh nachalakh'.[21] Vatsetis had already submitted his written criticisms on 28 January, the better to launch his attack the following day on his old rival Kamenev. The ex-C.-in-C., in assailing the present C.-in-C., stated categorically that the plans drawn up by the Field Staff for a militia system were wholly unsuitable for the Soviet republic, the chief weakness lying with the delineation of the 'divisional districts' which were nothing but a copy of the French system of divisional territorial districts prevailing at the time of the Franco-Prussian War; in addition, the idea of aligning the militia system with the military-administrative map of the country was mistaken, since such administrative divisions did not correspond to strategic entities but were based on economic considerations. This pale copy of a foreign system, in which a standing army existed along-side cadres subsisting on minimum strengths, simply could not be accepted. Nor was Podvoisky inclined to accept the proposals of the Field Staff, his principal objection being that the 'mixed' system (a regular army and a militia) under this type of arrangement would mean for a lengthy period of time that 'regular troops will form the basis of our armed forces, whereas the militia troops – in the eyes of the regular cadres – will more or less occupy the position of reserves'.[22]

Faced with this deadlock, the R.V.S.R. could do little more than start again from the beginning and duly instructed the participants in the meeting of 29 January – together with *Vserosglavshtab* – to submit their proposals bearing on 'the implementation of a militia system' within three days and in the most concise form: submissions were to go to all members of the *Revvoensoviet Respubliki* and must take the form of either a draft decree or an instruction from the *Soviet Oborony*. Promptly on 1 February Vatsetis, Podvoisky and the Field Staff all presented their 'draft decrees', which refined but did not alter their previous propositions and arguments. Vatsetis concentrated on the relationship between the 'military-administrative structure' of the country and the distribution of forces, suggesting that the 'military district' should be the basic unit (with one army to each district and nine districts in all: Petrograd, Moscow, Kiev, Perm, Tsaritsyn, Omsk, Krasnoyarsk, Turkestan and the Caucasus); he repeated his injunction to maintain strong regular forces and proposed that certain divisions be located in the frontier regions to act in these specific military districts as the 'forces-in-being' of the militia army, though no such provision need be made for the interior districts. This would provide up to 30 divisions, which in turn would mean an army of 1,800,000 men with less than all-out mobilisation. To run this system Vatsetis proposed two bodies, the administration of a 'Greater General Staff' and the 'Main Staff of the Militia Army' (*Glavnyi Shtab Militsionnoi Armii*).[23]

Podvoisky again took exception both to Vatsetis and to the Field Staff, on the grounds that a 'mixed' military system was wholly unacceptable. Since both stressed the 'inopportune' nature of the transition to a militia army, Podvoisky was impelled to propose changes which would make the system work: he suggested the reorganisation of *Vsevobuch* and the transfer of 'reserve units' (Podvoisky was referring to the *Krasnye rezervnye chastei* raised through *Vserosglavshtab*) to a 'Main Administration of Militia Troops' which would be directly subordinated to the R.V.S.R. As for experience and competence, Podvoisky suggested that *Vsevobuch* had already acquired enough of both. Undeterred by this onslaught, the

Field Staff repeated that any move to a militia army must be made 'only by degrees', that it was essential to retain between one-third and one-quarter of the regular Red Army, with provisions for keeping the best division intact; to run this militia army, the Field Staff submitted that a 'Greater General Staff' must be organised and directly subordinated to the People's Commissar for War, but until that time came the Field Staff itself should assume the responsibility.[24]

It was time also for *Vserosglavshtab* to redeem its reputation. At the end of January Rattel' (Chief of the Supreme Staff) had submitted three important documents dealing with the reduction of Red Army strength, the implementation of a militia system and the central administrative system of a militia army. On 21 March Rattel' presented the R.V.S.R. with a composite report entitled 'Osnovnye polozheniya dlya perekhoda k militsionnoi systeme', which advanced practical proposals for setting up a militia system in the Soviet republic. Aligning itself from the outset with the C.-in-C. and the Field Staff, the Supreme Staff insisted that any move to a militia system must depend on the 'political situation' and that in any event the security of the frontiers could only be ensured by 'special covering units drawn from the personnel of the present field armies'. None of this was new, but what made (and still makes) interesting reading was the provision of a series of definitions of a 'militia system' and a 'militia army', a prerequisite of purposeful discussion conspicuously lacking in the other papers (though March 1920 witnessed a flurry of publication devoted to the militia idea: *Vestnik militsionnoi armii* appeared once every two weeks in Petrograd, where the results of a conference on introducing the militia system also appeared in print as a booklet entitled *Militsionnaya systema i tekhnika provedeniya eë v zhizn' v RSFSR*). The *Vserosglavshtab* plan envisaged the adoption of the territorial system of recruitment based on universal military service, with a structure built much as the Field Staff suggested, incorporating divisional, brigade and regimental districts: the actual transition to a militia army would depend on the readiness state of the various districts and their cadres (drawn from the regular Red Army), with the most likely start being made at the regimental level and then culminating in brigade and divisional districts.[25]

Meanwhile General Nadezhnyi's special commission, charged with reviewing the establishments of the field armies and units, had worked in less spectacular style but much more positively, for on 19 March the report on the revised establishments for the rifle formations and units of the Red Army was ready for presentation to the *Glavkom* and the Field Staff. Ironically, this one report which was ready and acceptable could not be implemented, because within a matter of days the

Red Army was fighting furiously against Polish divisions in the first exchanges of the Soviet–Polish war, a collision which gave Vatsetis's earlier observations a curiously prophetic cast. On the political front the 'military question' turned somewhat dramatically on the militarisation of labour and the advent of the 'labour armies', for both of which Trotsky displayed an unqualified enthusiasm and paraded it at the 9th Congress. With the workers transformed into 'soldiers of labour' and subject to the methods of military compulsion, in the whole transition from *voennaya mobilizatsiya* to *trudovaya mobilizatsiya*, Trotsky saw an effective transplantation of the military mode which had brought victory in the Civil War, but it produced a strange juxtaposition in his ideas about military and economic organisation.[26] He was willing to see a Red 'barrack-regime' fastened on worker-soldiers to win the production battle, but loath to countenance a barrack-regime – a regular military establishment – to produce Red canon-fodder. He was not, after all, an arbiter of armies but rather an organiser of victory; the distinction may be a fine one, but it explains his espousal of the militia system after his spirited defence of the regular Red Army not so many months before at the 8th Congress.

In a spirit of rising optimism, though still impressed with the gravity of the dangers so recently passed, the delegates to the 9th Party Congress unanimously adopted Trotsky's resolution presented on 4 April 1920 for the establishment of a 'Worker–Peasant Red Militia' and the implementation of a territorial-militia system, defined in the Congress document as 'that organisation of armed forces by which the working masses will receive the necessary military training with the minimum disruption of their productive labour' – a fusion of defence and economic functions which had recommended itself to Trotsky for some time. The decisive battles were to be waged henceforth on the 'bloodless front' (*beskrovnyi front*, in Lenin's phrase) of production, reconstruction and rehabilitation of a shattered economy, demanding not only the 'militarisation of labour' but also the 'demilitarising' of the military, whose skills, habits of discipline, collective labour potential and organisation were needed for peaceful purposes, exemplified in the conversion of several front-line Red armies into 'labour armies' (the first being 3rd Army in the Urals which became the '1st Labour Army' at the beginning of 1920).

The 9th Congress resolution – 'Rezolutsiya o perekhode k militsionnoi systeme' (the 'theses' for the Congress were published on 28 February) – proposed refashioning the Soviet military system along the lines of a territorial militia, stiffened with a core of select Red Army units, organised to correspond with the location of industrial regions and their 'agrarian peripheries' and arranged to provide the closest collaboration between local economic enterprises, the trade unions and the particular militia units in a given area; the 'best elements' of the industrial, administrative and urban cadres would be turned into a military cadre by passing through the requisite command courses.[27] (Yet another transmogrification canvassed at this time took the military institution of the *kommandnyi sostav* – the euphemism of 'command staff' used to cloak the officer corps of the Red Army – and suggested that skilled workers be turned into the *kommandnyi sostav* of the entire labour force, exercising 'command functions' within it.)[28] It was generally accepted that the basis of the new militia must be the working classes, much as it was in the Red Army, and the new system would embody the 'dictatorship of the proletariat' in the most literal sense, with worker-soldier cadres spreading party control throughout the country – admirable in theory, but somewhat suspect in practice, as critics of the scheme were not slow to stress, pointing to the uneven distribution of the worker elements in the Soviet republic and the thinness of this true 'proletarian' crust.

Though intended to be a 'practical' measure (as opposed to the rider on the militia incorporated in the 8th Congress resolution, which has been explained away as a purely 'theoretical' injunction), the 9th Congress enactment accomplished little or nothing. For all the fervour of its assertion of the militia principle, the resolution affirmed quite plainly that the transition to a militia system would have to be gradual and related to the military and diplomatic position of the Soviet republic, with the *indispensable* condition being the maintenance of a high degree of military capability. This, to many minds, was the great *non sequitur*, though already in August 1919 Trotsky had fought off one assault on the militia idea by a senior 'military specialist' – General Svechin – who somewhat snidely suggested that the scheme merely repeated the errors of the Second International and the notion of the 'nation in arms', as well as reproducing all the drawbacks of what was improvisation rather than military efficiency as such. Trotsky rebuffed the general with some heat, rebuking him for his 'political blindness' in suggesting the creation of a national army – nothing more than the *damnosa hereditas* of the former Imperial regime – and rejecting the argument that the militia was an inherently weaker form of military organisation. As for the historical evidence adduced by General Svechin to support his case, this could be turned against him without much difficulty and exploited to prove the military worth of a militia system as much as demonstrating its drawbacks.[29]

Trotsky identified General Svechin as one of the 'academic critics' of the militia programme, but by the early spring of 1920 the issue had ceased to be in any way academic. The 'debate', if it can be called that, was but a barely concealed struggle for control of the military establishment, disputed by several factions and given a disturbingly provocative aspect in view of the proposed application of the military mode of centralised political control to party affairs in particular and civilian life at large. It is possible that one motive for Trotsky's advocacy of a militia system lay in his grasp of the compelling need to implement the hegemony of the industrial worker over the peasant; clearly, the proposed plan for a 'Worker–Peasant Militia' had social control, political regulation and economic rationalisation prominently built into it, and what needs no elucidation is Trotsky's insistence on the absolute necessity for retaining centralised control in both political and administrative matters. This was how he had set a vagabond army to fight; with the same method he was determined to make a 'vagabond Russia' – *brodyachaya Rossiya* – work for its survival. The shape of things to come was shown, if in experimental and improvised style, in the emergence of the 'labour army', with Trotsky exhibiting unconcealed delight at the action of 3rd Army turning itself into a 'regional economic centre' in the guise of the '1st Revolutionary Labour Army' and about to assert its authority over the local civilian administrative bodies (an attempt which met with little or no success in the end).

No one, however, not even Trotsky, could square the circle of discipline versus decentralisation. Amid all the talk about merging military obligations and economic activity, there was a striking (and ominous) convergence between the uneasiness displayed over Gol'tsman's ideas about a 'command staff' or officer corps within the labour force and the dissension over the 'military question'; much as leading trade unionists (other than Gol'tsman himself) feared for their own positions under such an arrangement, while communist workers tended to complain that it made the prospect of their control over industry even more remote, so the senior military specialists (and latterly a swelling group of 'Red commanders', successful soldier-communists) feared the loss of 'their' army with the advent of a militia even as the more fervid protagonists of the militia saw their military dream-world still far from being realised. Trotsky's authority appeared to many to be the chief obstacle to the attainment of their goals. Once again, in the name of the 'democratisation' of political work in the Red Army, local party committees, such as that of Saratov, tried at the 9th Congress to break the centralised direction of political work in the armed forces by demanding that local party bodies be given control of the Red Army's political sections (*politotdel*), which was vested in the P.U.R. (the Political Administration attached to the

R.V.S.R.) and designed expressly to exclude the interference of these local organisations.[30] Though this pale imitation of the furore at the 8th Congress was easily stifled, the principle of the centralised direction of political work was already being successfully undermined by Zinoviev, and not in the Red Army, but in the turbulent enclaves of the Baltic fleet, where the sailors had no love for the centralisation imposed by *Pubalt* (the Political Administration of the Baltic fleet); in November Zinoviev succeeded in bringing political work in the Baltic fleet under the Petrograd party committee.[31]

Even that most abstract of military undertakings, the formulation of military doctrine, was increasingly pressed into service as part of this same struggle for a more decisive voice in military policy. If one segment of the party burned to bring military organisation into line with their socialist ideals, yet another sought to align military doctrine with Marxist principles (and thereby strike a blow at the *voenspets* and Trotsky, who were abused for implementing an 'orthodox' strategy in an 'orthodox' army). The prospect of a militia, however, brought a number of these erstwhile opponents of the military specialists and the *voenspets* themselves into a curious conjunction, if not actual alliance; the ambitious and vastly more confident 'Red commanders', with men like Frunze in their ranks, were as unwilling to see the dismantling of the Red Army as many a die-hard *voenspets*, for here lay their future as they discerned it, though it must be within their new class-based army committed to the principles and practice of a 'unitary military doctrine' – *edinaya voennaya doktrina* – which fused political objectives and military capabilities as one.[32] This was, in many respects, as imperfectly thought out and imprecise as the grandiose plans for a militia establishment, leaving much to the imagination and appealing to an ideal future, but the sudden drastic impact of full-scale war with Poland brought the Soviet command face to face with the day-to-day realities of fighting fierce defensive actions and trying to plug a sagging line with more Red divisions. The pamphleteers had once again to take up their battle stations.

For all its previous triumphs, or rather precisely because of these selfsame victories, the Red Army was ill prepared for full-scale war with Poland in the spring of 1920, by which time five well-drilled Polish armies overshadowed the three bedraggled and depleted Soviet armies (15th, 16th and 14th, the latter in the Ukraine) covering the western frontiers; nor did the conversion of elements of these field armies into 'labour armies' do much for their military effectiveness. Other Soviet armies, including the crack 1st Cavalry Army, were still engaged far to the south-east in eliminating the remaining White divisions, or were strewn over the Ukraine in the hunting down of

Makhno, or were laying siege to Wrangel in the Crimea, the last White redoubt. The Soviet command embarked on some precautionary moves north of the Pripet marshes, only to be taken unawares when Pilsudski launched his attack in the south, where Soviet defences crumpled late in April and Kiev itself fell to the Poles on 6 May.[33] The Red Army was caught in considerable disarray, simultaneously mobilising and demobilising: between January and April the R.V.S.R. had been disbanding battle-worn divisions and two field armies (4th and 6th), replacing them with seven newly-raised divisions, all of which gave the Red Army a strength of 11 rifle armies and one cavalry army in April 1920. Demobilisation of the 1885-79 age-classes was authorised for certain regions, but a selective mobilisation of the 1901 age-class was begun in mid-March, bringing in some 200,000 recruits. Hurried orders were also issued to turn the 'labour armies' back into fighting formations.[34]

War with Poland inevitably pushed the planning for a militia into the background. From labouring to devise ways to cut the Red Army, the command now found itself working frantically to reorganise and to redeploy Red divisions to strike back at the Poles. It was not all disaster: as the Soviet armies concentrated and the 'drive on Warsaw' transformed a counter-attack into the 'export of revolution', all against the advice of Trotsky, the soldier-communists believed that their hour had struck. Writing from his forward H.Q., Tukhachevsky in July urged the adoption of far-ranging plans for this new 'revolutionary army' which would take the offensive against armed *Weltkapital*.[35] These bloody visions were brutally curtailed by Soviet defeat at the approaches to Warsaw, the Red Army fell back in pell-mell retreat, and a chastened, if not wholly repentant, command turned its attention once again to the demobilisation of the Red Army and the militia controversy. In February an important and influential commission had begun work on considering the form of central military organisation best suited to a militia establishment, working under P. S. Baluyev who was a member of the *Osoboe Soveshchanie pri Glavkom* (a standing committee attached to the C.-in-C., with A. A. Brusilov as president, Podvoisky as a civilian member and ex-Imperial Generals Baluyev, Verkhovsky, Gutor, Danilov, Zaionchkovsky, Parsky and Samoilo as the military component). Throughout the summer the *Osoboe Soveshchanie* gave all its attention to raising fighting troops and cutting 'the tail' of Red Army divisions, but by November its report was finally ready. It proved to be a further demonstration of how difficult it was to plan – definitely and in workable terms – for a militia establishment.

The 'Baluyev plan' called for the unification of the army and the navy within a 'People's Commissariat for the Army and the Navy' (the commission used its own designation of 'People's Commissariat for State Defence'); supreme authority over the Soviet armed forces would be vested in *V.Ts.I.K.* (Central Executive Committee), control in a 'Soviet for State Defence' (*Soviet Gosudarstvennoi Oborony*) assisted by a People's Commissar, and the actual direction of military affairs in a newly-created 'All-Russian Army–Navy General Staff' and an 'All-Russian Army–Navy Supreme Staff' (*Glavnyi Shtab*), supported by an 'All-Russian Supply Administration', a military-legal branch, a higher Army–Navy tribunal and a secretariat. The 'All-Russian General Staff' was conceived as an operational organ of the armed forces, responsible for collecting that information essential for the conduct of military operations and issuing operational directives to the various administrations; the Supreme Staff would be charged with managerial functions including supervision of the rear services. These proposals adroitly advertised themselves as being applicable either to a regular army establishment or a militia system, but their fundamental importance lay in the reaffirmation of the principle of unified command and reflected in the 'All-Russian' emphasis the military centralisation carried through in 1919. The most glaring omission, however, lay in the failure of the commission to mention the place of the political administration under this new dispensation.[36]

By comparison, the commission appointed by the R.V.S.R. on 20 October under the chairmanship of General Brusilov to work out a plan for the 'sectioning' of the Soviet republic, thereby providing the basis for a militia administration, fared far worse. It proved quite impossible to arrive at an answer by the stipulated deadline (15 November), and in fact the commission presented five possible variants in its final report 'O raionirovanii Rossii dlya provedeniya militsionnoi systeme'. Brusilov's officers proceeded from the assumption that regular Red Army forces would cover the frontiers and thus provide time for the mobilisation and concentration of the militia army. Working on the Field Staff estimates that the Soviet republic would require 'in moments of danger' not fewer than 70 rifle divisions, the commission therefore sought to demarcate 25 'divisional districts', with each district contributing three divisions. Difficult as this task proved to be, the commission was quite unable to establish a satisfactory solution for the further subdivisions into brigade, regimental and battalion districts, that is, without disrupting the existing administrative map. The Brusilov commission decided at that juncture to work out a scheme for European Russia, but to leave the delineation of militia districts for Asiatic Russia to future discussions.[37]

While the soldiers compiled their reports and struggled with man-

power figures or administrative details, all in preparation for a series
of conferences to be held in December, Podvoisky took matters into
his own hands and organised his own meetings, the first in Moscow
at the end of October and the second in Petrograd on 4 November.
Both these assemblies publicly supported Podvoisky's platform that
Vsevobuch had a prior claim when it came to setting up a militia
system and that *Vsevobuch* should be charged with managing the
transition; the militia should be based on *Vsevobuch*'s existing
territorial cadres, the local military commissariats should be closed
down and the *Vsevobuch* local apparatus strengthened. The time was
ripe for that gradual transition to a militia system and the process
should begin in the three 'proletarian centres', Moscow, Petrograd, and
the Urals–Volga region – shades of the old 1918 plan. On 4 November
1920, fresh from these triumphs, Podvoisky addressed a letter to the
Central Committee in which he insisted that *Vsevobuch* had occupied
itself with matters pertaining to a militia system for some considerable
period and that practical details related to the actual transition to a
militia system must come within the competence of *Vsevobuch*; he
suggested, therefore, that *Vsevobuch* should emerge from under the
wing of *Vserosglavshtab* and be reconstituted as the 'Supreme Staff
for Militia Troops' (*Glavnyi Shtab Militisionnykh Voisk*), directly
subordinated to the R.V.S.R.

Proceeding with its own heavy bureaucratic tread, the R.V.S.R.
meanwhile charged C.-in-C. S. S. Kamenev and the Field Staff to
prepare a 'general plan' for the transitional and demobilisational
period, a military *tour d'horizon* which took a wider view than the
several specialist reports and which was ready on 5 December 1920,
submitted under the title 'O zadachakh perevoda Krasnoi Armii na
mirnoe polozhenie' (and augmented by a paper on the form of the
central military administration, the latter formally presented on 13
December). The Kamenev–Lebedev draft plan asserted bluntly that the
Red Army needed strengthening rather than being cut or disbanded,
and suggested raising combat strength by reducing the rear service
units, separating the 'labour armies' from the Red Army proper and
improvising combat training; the organisation of fronts, field armies
and military districts should be retained, together with specific commands (Western, Caucasus and Turkestan fronts, the Ukraine, the
Crimea and Siberia), and out of 13 infantry armies and one cavalry
army, it was necessary to keep 9 infantry armies and the 1st Cavalry
Army. As for actual troop strength, this was set at 1,489,000, giving a
divisional strength of 45 rifle divisions, plus 4 independent rifle
brigades with the requisite cadres to bring them up to divisional status;
in round figures, the plan envisaged 1,362,900 rifle troops and 21

cavalry divisions (with a strength of 126,000 men). The total manpower of the Red Army would be brought down from over 5 million to 3,298,500 men, including administrative personnel, internal security forces, support and reserve troops and *Vsevobuch*. On 6 December the R.V.S.R. considered the plan, adopted it in general terms and gave Kamenev as C.-in-C. and Lebedev of the Field Staff until 25 December to cut the administrative staff, until 15 January 1921 to reduce the support troop strength and until 1 January 1921 to reorganise the field divisions. Demobilisation of select age-classes would begin on 1 January 1921.[38]

It was also apparent that neither the C.-in-C. nor the Field Staff had much use for the proposed reform of the central administration contained in the 'Baluyev plan': this, rather than vague talk about the suitability or otherwise of a militia, formed the very heart of the issue, for everything turned on the retention or the dismantling of the centralised apparatus and a unified command. Both opponents and protagonists of a militia were not slow to see this, for which reason the special meeting held by the R.V.S.R. on 13 December 1920 assumed a singular, if not decisive, significance. With some sixty-eight participants, including prominent commanders such as Tukhachevsky and leading civilian party members connected with the military, the meeting convened to consider the report on the central military administrative system submitted under Lebedev's name. Not surprisingly, the sessions proved to be stormy, with the proposal to establish two staffs for the Red Army (*Generalnyi Shtab* and *Glavnyi Shtab*, as in the 'Baluyev report') producing bitter controversy; in the end, the idea of a single staff for the Red Army won the day with 35 votes cast in favour, 16 against. The delegates approved the retention of the R.V.S.R. itself, only to fall out over its composition, finally voting by 46 in favour, 12 against and 6 abstentions to recommend a membership of chairman, deputy chairman, *Glavkom* (chief of a unified staff), chief of the political administration and members concerned with matters of supply. Next came the turn of P.U.R., the political administration. The majority voted to retain the P.U.R. as an independent administration under the aegis of the R.V.S.R. – 45 votes cast in favour – rather than setting up a new administration which would combine political work with military training; similarly, a proposal to bring military training under the R.V.S.R. was defeated by an overwhelming vote (47 against), the decision being to leave training under the requisite section of the Red Army staff. The assembly also rejected proposals to modify the local military administrative apparatus by restricting military commissariats at *guberniya* and *uezd'* level to simple statistical and mobilisational functions.[39]

After two days' respite the R.V.S.R. convened a second meeting, this time with more than 130 participants. It was time for Podvoisky to fight the final round, though already it was clear that opinion was hardening against any general transition to a militia, however attractive the idea was in principle; principles of themselves, however, did not dispose of the deterioration in the relationship between the workers and the peasantry, the prevalence of 'banditry', the ruination of the transport system and the famine conditions in many areas. None of this favoured a resort to a territorial militia. The very *fundament* of territoriality was suspect, the proletarian leaven too thin, the strategic viability questionable and the much-vaunted saving in cost open to doubt. Nor did the extremism – or the sheer lack of practicality – on the part of the militia lobbyists help to assuage doubts: for example, in advocating in *Vestnik militsionnoi armii* the 'militia-isation' of all arms and services in the army (including technical branches), a militia navy, and the winding-up of all political organs in the armed forces, as well as military schools, for the population would receive all the necessary political instruction in general schools, with training establishments becoming redundant as the 'command staff' became redundant as the regular army was dissolved.[40] Trotsky never shared these harum-scarum ideas: in his speech of 28 November 1920, perhaps his most closely reasoned exposition of the case for a militia, he pointed out that the Soviet republic could simply not afford to maintain a huge Red Army – no state could afford to maintain a standing army geared to meet every possible contingency – whereas a militia army which systematically (*planomerno*) utilised Red Army resources, the system of the militarisation of labour and the schools would mean a rationalisation of the total effort, where 'each would feel himself part of one colossal collective'. 'We shall unite education and work with the army', and sport with all three, but for all the idyll and the ideal there were, Trotsky emphasised, practical questions to be answered: mobilisation, concentration, the size of the regular force to cover the frontiers, the distribution of military schools and the location of barracks, to cite but a few.[41]

The R.V.S.R. meeting of 16 December, which proved to be a stormy affair, convened with few, if any, of these questions ready for answer, though this scarcely deterred Podvoisky who was determined to press the claims of *Vsevobuch* for a commanding position in implementing a militia system. Tukhachevsky and Smilga (head of the P.U.R.) took up the cudgels on behalf of the regular army. The delegates rejected a motion to discuss the whole party programme on a militia system, but approved a motion (with only 11 votes against and 6 abstentions) that the time had come to take 'the first practical step' towards implementing such a system. Trouble flared at once when practicality intervened, and the strength of the opposition was shown by the voting on the resolution as to what proportion of the Red Army's resources in men and equipment should be allocated to setting up a militia – one-third or one-fifteenth? 58 votes were cast for the option of a third, but 72 for the much reduced allocation of one-fifteenth; it was thereupon decided to confine the 'first practical step' to a few select industrial areas.

The decisive question followed straightway: should *Vsevobuch* territorial cadres or those drawn from regular Red Army units be used to form the militia army? Fewer than half the delegates (only 50) voted for *Vsevobuch* and 86 for using the Red Army. Podvoisky tried to suggest that both systems could be run in tandem, but the assembly threw this idea out lock, stock and barrel, going on to recommend the subordination of the territorial organisation of *Vsevobuch* – in which Podvoisky's hopes rested – to the military commissariats (using the *guberniya* commissariats, *gubvoenkomaty*, as the base for this forced amalgamation). *Vsevobuch* would be charged with pre-military service training, physical education and sport. To complete the rout, the delegates also rejected the idea of two separate staffs, one for the Red Army and another for the militia: only 22 votes were cast in favour.[42] To rub in the lesson the assembly adopted a resolution for public circulation, which stated unequivocally that

> new steps in the matter of setting up a militia army can only be undertaken successfully under conditions of the active and conscious participation of all experienced elements of the Red Army and under conditions of the utilisation of the accumulated experience of commissariats, commanders and conscientious Red Army soldiers....[43]

Completely unabashed, Podvoisky on 18 December was pressing for the adoption of a militia system at a conference of military district commanders; he continued to do so until the onset of the 10th Party Congress.

The militia idea was many things to many men, to Tukhachevsky 'the crucifixion of Soviet Russia', to Trotsky a 'historical necessity', to Podvoisky the realisation of the full potential of *Vsevobuch* and thus a genuine alternative system, to others the fulfilment of a long-cherished ideal or the expression of radical opposition to an oppressive centralisation. In Trotsky's scheme of things for a militia army, ideas which underwent subtle but significant modification as time went on, a certain element of decentralisation was foreshadowed by his advocacy of the idea of voluntary enlistment, but even at this distance of time it is difficult to reconcile the centralised direction necessary to realise the order, discipline and productivity of the *kolossal'nyi kollektiv* with the yearnings for effective decentralisation which inspired so many in the militia lobby, or even the proponents of 'army syndicalism'. Inevitably, the historian's eye has been caught by the lectures, the debates, the lusty polemics and the paraphernalia of Party Congress resolutions dealing with the transition to this *militsionnoe stroitel'stvo*, or 'military organisation on the basis of militia principles' and similar synonyms, but the planning documents not only throw a new light on the role of the senior 'military specialists' but also demonstrate the complexity of the problems inherent in setting up a militia system, all woefully underestimated or else ignored by the militia enthusiasts. The sudden fury of the Soviet–Polish war eclipsed the pallid resolution of the 9th Congress: in the winter of 1920-1 the very economic conditions which a militia was intended to ameliorate militated against its being adopted on any scale, with the Tambov insurrection and the Kronstadt rebellion sealing the fate of any ambitious plans to rely on a militia. It needed the therapy of N.E.P. to repair the worst ravages in the peasant–worker relationship, and only then was it at all practical to think once more of a militia.

For all the buffetings and pressure, the central military machine had emerged unscathed, with its operational, administrative and 'political administration' competences unimpaired. For the hermaphrodite thing that it was, this was in many respects quite remarkable: the militia was not thus far allowed to escape from under the thumb of the Red Army. It was plain, nevertheless, that the Red Army would have to be reduced, a decision endorsed by the Central Committee plenum of 10 November 1920 and implemented by the Demobilisation Commission operating under Sklyansky, which early in December produced a plan to cut the army by at least 2 million men, leaving the Red Army with 59 rifle divisions, 22 rifle brigades and 21 cavalry divisions; the South-western and Southern fronts were stood down (though the Western, Caucasus and Turkestan fronts remained operational), four armies were disbanded and half a dozen rifle divisions reduced immediately to brigade status.[44] This was accompanied by a start on the reduction of local, front and central military-administrative personnel, part of the programme presented to the 8th Congress of Soviets at the end of 1920 under the provisions of the enactment 'O sokrashchenii armii'. Military organisations by their very nature exist, function and perform by the clockwork of command, so that it is no abrupt simplification to say that the new Soviet military establishment – that is, the post-war environment – became effective on 29 December 1920. It was ushered in with a stern lecture from Lenin, who had emphasised at the 8th Congress of Soviets that both state and party could not dispense with the good right arm of the Red Army, smaller perhaps, but of improved quality, and in no way diminishing the military effectiveness of the Soviet republic.[45] Lenin took a less sanguine view of the *novaya peredyshka* which the militia lobby espied as one of economic recovery and cultural recuperation: the threat, in Lenin's view, was not removed and the need for a standing army, albeit reduced in size, no less compelling.

Three years elapsed before the protracted process of demobilisation, complicated by poor planning and insufficient preparation, was completed; Red Army strength then stoood at a little over half a million men. In 1923 Trotsky was able at last to launch the 'mixed' military system consisting of a small regular army backed by a territorial militia, an arrangement which served the Soviet Union well enough for more than a decade. But in the end, with the development of a powerful military-industrial base and the steady expansion of the regular Red Army, it was General Svechin rather than Trotsky who had lighted even in 1919 on the brutally correct solution to the 'military question'. For all the radicals' loathing of 'bivouac and barrack' and the party's ingrained mistrust of the professional military, neither could survive without an army at their backs.

NOTES

1. The military/regular army controversy, and Lenin's early views in particular, has recently been revived in Soviet writing. For the 'regular army' view, see Yu. I. Korablev, 'Sovetskaya istoriografiya o roli V. I. Lenina v stanovlenii i razvitii vooruzhennykh sil Sovetskogo gosudarstva', *Voprosy Istorii*, no. 3 (1970) pp. 12-29; also his major monograph *V. I. Lenin i sozdanie Krasnoi Armii* (Moscow: Nauka, 1970) esp. chaps. 2 and 3. For a more balanced view, see the important study by E. N. Gorodetsky, *Rozhdenie Sovetskogo gosudarstva 1917-1918 gg.* (Moscow: Nauka, 1965) chap. 5. See also V. I. Lenin, *Polnoe sobranie sochinenii*, XXXVIII 139-40.

2. See the original and indispensable work by S. M. Klyatskin, *Na zashchite oktyabrya. Organizatsiya regularnoi armii i militsionnoe stroitel'stvo v Sovetskoi respubliki* (Moscow: Nauka, 1965) chap. 1, pts. 1-2.

3. Apparently no formal record of this meeting was kept. See A. F. Myasnikov, 'Moi vstrechi s tovarishchem Leninym', in *Vospominaniya o V. I. Lenine*, II (Moscow, 1957) 149, and S. I. Aralov, *V. I. Lenin i Krasnaya Armiya* (Moscow, 1959) pp. 7-11.

4. For details, see Klyatskin, *Na zashchite oktyabrya*, p. 149 (on the 'militia

commission' under Al'tfater, Aledogsky and Danilov) and also the 'Trifonov plan', pp. 165-6.

5. See L. Trotsky, *Kak vooruzhalas' revolutsiya*, vol. II, bk i (Moscow, 1924): 'K VIII S'ezdu RKP', pp. 46-50; Lenin, *Pol. sob. soch.*, XXXVIII 53-4; also A. F. Danilevsky, *V. I. Lenin i voprosy voennogo stroitel'stva na VIII s'ezde RKP (B)* (Moscow: Voenizdat, 1964).

6. See *Leninskii sbornik*, XXXV 78.

7. *KPSS v rezolutsiyakh* ..., pt I, pp. 430-41, under 'Rezolutsiya po voennomu voprosu' (8th Congress).

8. N. Bukharin and E. Preobrazhensky, *The A.B.C. of Communism*, Introduction by E. H. Carr (Harmondsworth: Penguin Books, 1969) p. 264.

9. See P. I. Yakir, 'Iz istorii perekhoda Krasnoi Armii na mirnoe polozhenie', in *Oktyabr' i grazhdanskaya voina v SSSR* (Moscow: Nauka, 1966) p. 446. This is an important essay, based on many original sources.

10. Cf. Klyatskin, *Na zashchite oktyabrya*, p. 424.

11. Ibid.

12. Ibid., p. 426.

13. Ibid.

14. On these special units or hand-picked shock-troops (also referred to as *chastei osobogo naznacheniya, ChON*), see *Grazhdanskaya Voina. Materialy po istorii Krasnoi Armii*, I (Moscow, 1923) 267-8.

15. See Klyatskin, *Na zashchite oktyabrya*, p. 427.

16. Ibid., p. 429.

17. Establishment Table No. 220 was the war-strength of a Soviet rifle division, fixed in 1918.

18. Klyatskin, *Na zashchite oktyabrya*, pp. 429-30.

19. Ibid., pp. 430-1.

20. Ibid., p. 432.

21. Ibid., p. 433.

22. Ibid., quoting an archival source.

23. Ibid., p. 434; also Yakir, op. cit., pp. 451-2.

24. Yakir, op. cit., p. 452.

25. Ibid., pp. 452-3.

26. Cf. discussion in D. Fedotoff White, *The Growth of the Red Army* (Princeton U.P., 1944) chap. vii, pp. 188-93.

27. Trotsky, *K.V.R.*, III i 134-5; also *Rossiiskaya Kommunisticheskaya Partiya (B): IX S'ezd. Stenograficheskii otchet* (Moscow, 1920) pp. 350-1.

28. Cf. E. H. Carr, *The Bolshevik Revolution, 1917-1923*, vol. II (London: Macmillan, 1952) on 'War Communism', pp. 214-15, also n. 4.

29. See Trotsky, *K.V.R.*, III i, 'Programma militsii i eë akademicheskii kritik', pp. 115-21; also printed in *Voennoe Delo*, no. 25 (1919).

30. See A. A. Geronimus, *Partiya i Krasnaya Armiya* (Moscow, 1928) p. 115; see also chap. v, 'Novaya peredyshka', pp. 89-98, for background.

31. Cf. Leonard Schapiro, *The Origin of the Communist Autocracy* (New York: Praeger, 1965) pp. 258-9.

32. See M. V. Frunze, 'Edinaya voennaya doktrina i Krasnaya Armiya', in *Izbrannye proizvedeniya*, II (Moscow: Voenizdat, 1957) 4-22; also Fedotoff White, *The Growth of the Red Army*, chap. vi, 'The Birth of a Doctrine', pp. 160-3.

33. For Polish and Soviet accounts, see my own study (chap. iv) in *The Soviet High Command: A Military-Political History, 1918-1941* (London:

Macmillan, 1962) pp. 84-9. See also N. E. Kakurin and V. A. Melikov, *Voina s belopolyakami 1920 g.* (Moscow: Voenizdat, 1925), which is still of great value.

34. See Trotsky, *K.V.R.*, II ii 93-178, on the Polish war; cf. Klyatskin, *Na zashchite oktyabrya*, p. 442.

35. Text in M. N. Tukhachevsky, *Voina klassov. Stat'; 1919-1920 g.* (Moscow: Gosizdat, 1921) pp. 138-40.

36. Klyatskin, *Na zashchite oktyabrya*, pp. 451-2.

37. Ibid., pp. 453-4.

38. For detailed summary, see Yakir, op. cit., pp. 458-9.

39. Klyatskin, *Na zashchite oktyabrya*, p. 455.

40. For a recent denunciation of the militia scheme, see A. Gromakov, 'Politika Kommunisticheskoi partii v oblasti voennogo stroitel'stva (1920-1923 gg.)', in *Voenno-istoricheskii Zhurnal*, no. 6 (1970) pp. 4-9.

41. Trotsky, 'Stroitel'stvo Krasnoi Vooruzhennoi sily' (28 Nov 1920), in *K.V.R.*, III i 122-32.

42. Klyatskin, *Na zashchite oktyabrya*, p. 458.

43. Yakir, op. cit., pp. 462-3.

44. See S. Klyatskin, 'Problemy voennogo stroitel'stva na zavershayushchem etape grazhdanskoi voiny', in *Voenno-istoricheskii Zhurnal*, no. 6 (1964) p. 15.

45. V. I. Lenin, *Pol. sob. soch.*, XLII, esp. pp. 130-1.

11 Education in Tsarist and Soviet Development

MICHAEL KASER

I. THE PROGRAMME FOR MASS EDUCATION

IN their *A.B.C. of Communism*, Bukharin and Preobrazhensky observed that 'the transference of power to the proletariat was immediately followed by a nearly tenfold increase in the expenditure upon popular education'.[1] They cited, as reliable statisticians, state outlay in Russia as 340 million roubles in 1917 and 2,914 million in 1918; as misleading economists, they failed to deflate current outlays by any index of prices, which rose half as fast, but even so real outlay must have doubled.[2] Such an expansion – sufficient for any propogandist – is borne out by the education share of the budget, which rose from 1·2 per cent in 1917 to 6·4 per cent in 1918.[3]

The 1919 Programme of the Communist Party listed the Bolshevik platform on education immediately after the initial sections 'Politics', 'Nationalities' and 'Justice', and well ahead of 'Economic Affairs', 'Agriculture' and other material topics. It declared that 'the first step' in educational reform should be 'the introduction of gratuitous, compulsory, general and technical instruction for all children of both sexes up to the age of 17'. A mention of 'technical schools' and a paragraph towards the end on 'polytechnic education' were the most that were advanced on the economic gains to be derived from teaching; all the other references and the preamble were concerned with what analysis later came to call the 'private demand' for education.

The ranking of educational objectives in the Programme closely followed Marx's own instructions to delegates at the founding Congress of the First International at Geneva in 1866: 'First, intellectual education; second, physical education, such as is given in schools of gymnastics and in military exercises; third, technical education which acquaints the child with the basic principles of all processes of production and at the same time gives the child and the adolescent the

habits of dealing with the most simple instruments of all production.'
Engels had previously sketched the concept of 'polytechnical education' embodied in that third objective, but had considered education
itself to be primarily a matter of 'the complete development of abilities'
(1845). For Marx, 'technological instruction', after 'the inevitable
conquest of power by the working class', would only 'win its place',[4]
viz. in such proportion as it advanced industry or technology.

Earlier leaders of Russia had twice conformed to Marx's advocacy
of the private demand for education, though fleetingly and under the
stress of revolution. It was again to be accepted when the Soviet
Government was in flux, on the second occasion to implement after
fifty years the promises of the October Revolution. Until the recent
introduction of ten years' free and compulsory schooling, however,
the moves towards provision for the masses have been superseded by
a specifically defined need of the state as the criterion for the provision
of education. The structure of the education furnished to meet this
requirement is a high ratio of secondary students to primary enrolments – one, that is, which is geared to the comprehensive training of
the few for administrative and business management and for scientific-
technical development. Because the state, from Peter the Great to
Khrushchev, has been the prime mover in economic dynamism, the
interest of the state in education has been that conducive also to
material growth. The coincidence does not obtain when the hierarchy
of government plays a much more exiguous part, as in a market
economy or even, it would seem, under Kosygin's partial adoption of
Liberman's 'profit motive' for state factories.

The obverse for the individual of these alternatives is that, where
Government service monopolises labour, recruitment to the posts from
which the higher echelons are selected is by education. The more
extensive the opportunities for private enterprise, the wider are those
for the self-made man. These observations[5] do not controvert the
correlation of earnings with education under both systems, but make
upward socio-economic mobility in the U.S.S.R. harder to achieve
without higher education than it can be under a market mechanism.

II. THE PRACTICE OF SELECTIVE EDUCATION

One of the statistical conclusions of this paper is that for something like
a century Russia (chiefly from official funds) has paid out more for each
student than do individuals and the Government combined in the
market economies (both calculations relative to per capita G.N.P. in
comparable valuations). Such an allocation was logical while access
to education was restricted and when those who completed the full

course were destined for the administration of the state and the economy. *Mutatis mutandis*, Soviet policy followed Peter the Great's call that the educated 'go forth into the church or the civil service, be prepared to wage war or to practise engineering or medicine'.[6] Soviet outlays per pupil have been falling since the mid-1960s when policy changed on both the supply and the demand side, viz. the opening of complete secondary education to all aged from 7 to 17 and the devolution of economic management under something of a profit motive. Until the recent concurrence of the trends in the allocation of resources for education, in the access to schooling and in the running of the economy, divergences from a conjunction of controlled entry and generous spending were few and transient. The 1803 'Rules for Enlightenment', the school and university legislation after the 1905 and the February 1917 revolutions, the 1919 Party Programme, the 1952 Party Directives and the reforms of 1964-6 are linked by an actual or expected overthrow of government: for the first it was the French Revolution and the Napoleonic danger, and for the two latest it was *coups* within the Kremlin.

Speransky's attempt was liquidated, with the Decembrists, by the adage of Nicholas I that 'the police were to educate the public and the schools to discipline them'.[7] The Duma never enacted its Law on Education, but the Provisional Government took up where it had left off. The People's Commissariat of Enlightenment began to implement the 1919 Programme, but, as Lunacharsky put it in 1922, 'N.E.P. completely destroyed those gains'.[8] Khrushchev's educational reform of 1958 checked the trend which Stalin had belatedly started.

In capitalist economies the demand for education commonly distinguishes between that for consumption and for investment[9] or on a private and a social rate of return.[10] In the administered society of Russia, which, in educational provision at least, largely survived the 1861 emancipation, and in the U.S.S.R. until very recently, it is proper to distinguish a specific 'state demand' for education. The school and university enrolment, its distribution between levels or content of teaching and the resources devoted to educational services can, on this view, be seen as provided by virtue of the needs of the state. Gerschenkron has argued on a more general level that the question as to why state intervention was needed to industrialise Russia 'can at least partly be answered in terms of absence or presence of certain prerequisites'.[11] Lacking the prerequisite of adequate literacy or of educational standards, Russia found some substitute in foreign technicians and the technology embodied in capital-good imports, a solution which interlocked with other strategies for circumstances of deep backwardness, such as 'stress in industrialisation on bigness of both plans and enterprise' and special institutions to supply capital to nascent industries.[12]

III. THE HISTORICAL INTERPRETATION

The statistics compiled in this paper may help to fill a gap between the historical analyses of Gerschenkron and of Carr. It is now a commonplace that the expansion of educational facilities is not directly associated with economic growth, but the presentation here shows that the substitute for general literacy and technical knowledge which Gerschenkron sought may perhaps be found within the Russian and Soviet educational system, namely, in a narrow-based but high-quality provision. The eleven books that thus far constitute Carr's monumental history culminate in the acceptance in the U.S.S.R. of the 'belief in a strengthening of state power for the achievement of economic ends.... The original concept, inherited by Lenin from Marx, of a proletarian or socialist revolution from below, was insensibly merged, and submerged, in the Stalinist industrial revolution from above. The conception, embodied in the Communist International, of leadership offered by the weak and backward Russian proletariat to the more prosperous and more sophisticated working classes of the West was foredoomed to failure.'[13]

Engels, he points out, had stressed that a revolution from above must be completed and extended 'from below',[14] and it is implicit in Carr's interpretation that the latter would have required mass education. Since it is the leaders of the party who implement the revolution, one would expect him to find that their education only is significant: he reserves his references to the People's Commissariat of Enlightenment to political features, viz. to subsidies for the Komsomol and work among Party organs, or to the teaching institutes of the party.[15] The analysis of strictly economic developments required some reference to worker training,[16] but in politics the first Commissar of Education, Lunacharsky, is assigned a negligible role. Carr puts him as little more than a bystander during the campaign of 1926-8 to coerce writers into conformity with party dictates;[17] he emerges as party spokesman only on atheism[18] and elsewhere appears almost as a figure of fun.[19] Lunacharsky's estrangement from any revolution from above is evident from a recent biography: as soon as he took office he affirmed that his Commissariat 'is certainly not a central power directing educational institutions. On the contrary all school affairs must be handed over to organs of local self-government.'[20]

IV. THE STATE'S OBJECTIVES

Lunacharsky might be seen as continuing a process of devolution (though with different objectives) begun in 1905 (see below, pp. 236-7), but he was at variance not only with the contemporary movement in the other main field of Soviet social administration, public health,[21] but also with that underlying state centripetalism, which originated with the Petrine reforms. The majority of the factories established in the first half of the reign of Peter the Great were state enterprises. 'Peter needed foreign technicians, but he did not want his factories in foreign hands.'[22] The managers of these plants, or the domestic property-owners he later began to force into manufacturing enterprise, needed technical education, and Russia can claim 'the first non-classical school in the world', the School of Mathematical and Navigation Sciences in Moscow, antedating by five years the Mathematische und Mechanische Realschule of Halle (1706);[23] other technical colleges followed, but his expectations for 'numeracy schools' (*tsifirnye uchilishcha*)[24] established from 1714 onwards were not met: ten years later they held only 2,000 pupils in a population of 13 million and were gradually merged with the still fewer schools of the Holy Synod, which remained the only general schools from 1721 to 1786, having a mere 1,491 pupils at their peak in 1785. The narrower interest of the post-Petrine state in an elite of administrative ability was epitomised in the creation from 1721 of state boarding (*kadet*) schools to facilitate access to Government posts by the provincial nobility and gentry on the same terms as the metropolitan. By 1917 the 29 boarding schools for boys (from 1764 there were also some for girls) catered for only one in every thousand schoolchildren.

With the same perspective, Catherine's people's schools (*narodnye uchilishcha*) resumed state support for day classes: from 1786, 'minor' schools with a two-year course were set up in district seats, with 'major' schools with a four-year course in each provincial capital. Thus concentrated in the centres of government, they reached within five years an annual enrolment of some 17,000, at which recruitment then levelled off. By forming a constrained base for a still smaller higher-education structure – Moscow University (founded in 1755), the Institute of Mining (1773) and the Military-Medical Academy (1799) – they are the prototype of the restriction of education to those needed for administration: state penetration of the economy meant that an economic objective was thereby served, but formal education was provided at a level well below that which capitalist economies furnished at corresponding levels of development.

The crucial change proposed to Alexander I in the wake of the French Revolution was expressed by one of the advisers who drew up the 'Rules for National Enlightenment' of 1803:[25] 'We do not need universities, especially universities on the German model, when there is no one to study at them, but primary and secondary schools ... the [French] system of *lycées* is the best that Russia can adopt.'[26] The Rules of 1803, whereby 'national enlightenment in the Russian Empire is a special function of the state',[27] principally followed the new French practice of secondary schools organised into six educational regions, each topped by a territorial university as soon as such could be established.

The effects are shown in Table 1: the ratio of secondary to primary schoolchildren increased, while the opening of new universities (Vilnius 1802, Kazan and Kharkov 1804, and St Petersburg 1819[28]) and other higher educational institutions[29] brought the ratio of tertiary to primary students to a peak it did not regain for exactly a century. By the Education Act of 1809, Speransky hoped to enforce the entry of all qualified primary leavers into secondary and higher education, but when he fell from power aristocratic self-interest reappeared, gaining potency after the defeat of the French invasion. Thus in 1813 the admission of a serf into a gymnasium was made dependent on the express consent of the Ministry of Education, and in 1827 serfs were totally excluded from gymnasiums and universities; tuition fees began to be introduced in 1819; the Ministry was combined with that of Religious Affairs in 1817 (with a consequent slimming of coverage of the syllabus); and the new Minister of 1824, Shishkov, took office with the statement 'to teach the whole nation to read and write would do more harm than good'.[30] New statutes of 1828 effected a separation between primary and secondary education: the three-year district school led nowhere, while the seven-year gymnasium became strictly a course for university entrance. The combined enrolment remained below 1 per cent of the population (see Table 1), but although the ratios of university and of secondary enrolments to primary decreased until the emancipation, they stayed far higher than in other countries. Thus even the Russian nadir of 61 secondary per 1,000 primary pupils was not bettered in Germany, Italy, Scandinavia and the United States until the beginning of the twentieth century, and after the First World War in Western Europe generally and in Canada; that of 9 university students per 1,000 primary was also achieved in Western Europe only after that war, although Germany and Italy (like North America) reached such a ratio a little earlier.

In the four decades after the 1864 reforms the overall enrolment rose, though it reached barely to one in twenty of the population and

Table 1

Indicators of Enrolment Structure, 1801-1970

	Total population	All pupils and students[a]	Secondary pupils	Vocational pupils	Higher education students
	(millions)	(% of population)		(per 1,000 primary pupils)	

Tsarist Empire (excluding Finland)

1801	37·5	0·04	0·1	92	—	9
1825	52·3	0·2	0·4	113	—	21
1835	60·2	0·2	0·4	106	—	14
1845	65·2	0·3	0·5	89	—	12
1855	71·1	0·4	0·6	72	—	16
1865	75·1	0·8	1·1	61	—	9
1875	90·2	1·2	1·3	93	—	9
1885	108·8	1·9	1·7	93	—	9
1895	123·9	2·8	2·3	63	—	6
1905	144·0	5·6	3·9	67	—	10
1914	175·1	9·5	5·5	72	—	15

Soviet Union: (A) pre-1939 territory; (B) present territory

1914(A)	139·3	8·1	5·8	68	—	15
1914(B)	159·2	9·9	6·2	69	17	14
1927(A)	147·1	12·4[b]	8·4	147	38	29
1940(B)	194·1	38·1[c]	19·4	64	78	37
1950(B)	178·5	38·2[d]	21·4	73	108	62
1960(B)	212·4	41·8	19·7	98	104	128
1970(B)	241·6	60·8	25·2	139	328	222

(a) Excluding on-the-job training for adults.
(b) 1928 from same sources: 13·4 (for use in Table 8).
(c) 1937 from same sources: 32·3 (for use in Table 8).
(d) 1955 from same sources: 34·7 (for use in Table 8).

Sources:
   Tsarist period: N. Hans, *History of Russian Educational Policy* (London, 1931) p. 242.
   Soviet period: N. de Witt, *Education and Professional Employment in the U.S.S.R.* (Washington, D.C., 1961) pp. 577, 580, 634, 638.

was supplemented by informal education (see below, pp. 245-6); the ratio of secondary and higher enrolments was nevertheless remarkably stable, with a low point during Witte's industrialisation drive of the 1890s.

Johnson describes the 1864 reforms bluntly as for 'Russification, nationalism and clericalism'[31] in the wake of serf emancipation,[32] and Alston characterises the district school boards established by the State School Statute of that year as 'a fixed arena within which the partisans of ecclesiastical traditionalism, bureaucratic Westernism and gentry paternalism could struggle among themselves for the minds and loyalties of the people they had neglected for centuries'.[33] The boards included representatives of each zemstvo,[34] which was authorised to open schools but over the curriculum or teachers of which it had no control. In rural areas the local peasant commune found all accommodation, equipment and fuel; the zemstvo supplied the funds; and the Ministry of Education (through the district board) decided the curriculum. The arrangement is paralleled in the U.S.S.R. today, where the collective farm provides school buildings and teacher accommodation, the local authority the money and the Ministry of Education the curriculum; textbooks and uniforms are, as ever, at the parents' expense.

It is fair to say that there are somewhat more favourable interpretations showing Ushinsky, in promoting the 1864 reforms, to be inspired by a concept of *narodnost'*, such that while the Russians must have a Russian education, other nationalities should have the same facilities for their own concept of 'nationality'. There is in Ushinsky's last published work (1870) caution against the entrusting of tuition to the clergy, though he himself was 'deeply religious and understood Christianity in its Orthodox interpretation'.[35] But, by and large, in the second half of the nineteenth century outlay on education, whether by the Ministry, by the zemstvo or by parents, remained modest and central control severely restrictive.[36] Tuition charges were raised substantially in 184, and a circular of 1887 comprised provisions which in effect closed gymnasiums to the children of the lower classes.[37]

The 1905 revolution began a radical break with this trend and the proportion of pupils in the population not only doubled (as Table 1 shows) but brought nearly half the appropriate age-groups into primary schools;[38] two of every five schools existing in 1916 had been established in the preceding decade, over which period the budget of the Ministry of Education rose from 8·8 to 72·3 million roubles.[39] Although the Duma did not succeed in enacting its comprehensive Education Bill, it authorised large grants to local authorities for primary schools and by 1915 definitive schemes for universal primary education had been established in 421 out of the 441 district zemstva and in 376 out of 789 municipalities; 15 of the former and 33 of the latter had already set up the required number of schools. By a law of 1912 the Duma transformed the urban schools into four-year 'intermediate' schools, and under a Liberal Minister of Education, Ignatiev, the curriculum of secondary schools for girls was aligned with that for boys. Enrolment in schools of the Holy Synod was being run down in favour of state schools (see Table 4), but it was not until after the February Revolution that a law (of 20 June 1917) provided for their transfer to the Ministry of Education 'for an actual and uniform realisation of universal instruction in primary schools'. A decree of 8 May 1917 abolished the provincial and district school boards, the powers of which passed to the local authorities, which also took over the school inspectorate (decree of 26 September 1917). Another bill for decentralising control of secondary schools was awaiting enactment when overtaken by the October Revolution.[40]

'Lenin reasserted the political domination of education that the most consistent exponents of the Enlightenment had hoped to end for ever.'[41] Lilge goes on to suggest two factors which reversed the trend of the pre-revolutionary decade and Lunacharsky's expectations, leaving, by 1922, school attendance at only one in twenty children in the age-group 12-17.[42] The first was the belief that Marx's idea of polytechnic education[43] could be implemented by no more than a communal environment;[44] this would explain the concern in the 1920s for adult literacy drives and the high reliance until the 1960s upon *praktiki* (i.e. those fulfilling a skilled function without the relevant formal qualification). The second was the stringency of resources, a rationing of which to a strictly calculated requirement became the essence of Stalin's policy on education. The school system and those of further and higher education were reshaped to the convenience of the planners under the First Five-Year Plan. The standard history of Soviet education in the 1920s divides the decade at 1921, when the 'first consolidation' of the school system began, and at 1928 when the transitional period of 'phasing-out' (*absterben*) began, to run until the 'second consolidation' of 1931.[45] The strategy of the 1930s allowed the enrolment ratio[46] to rise, after the introduction of compulsory primary education, but kept the rate of secondary and of higher enrolments to primary pupils well above that exhibited by market economies at comparable levels of production. By the end of the decade university recruitment had slackened relative to primary enrolment, and by 1940 its rate to the latter was only a little better than that of market economies at a similar per capita output. The maintenance of a higher rate of secondary to primary pupils formed part of a 'recycling' concept, whereby urban schools were allowed longer courses (seven years) than those in the countryside (to which the minimum of four years related), essentially because it was from the urban school-leavers that skilled personnel would be drawn. The Commissar for Foreign Affairs, Litvinov, is reported to have said to the United States Ambassador, Bullitt, in the presence of the Commissar for Education, Bubnov, 'We shall always educate in special schools and institutes enough chosen men to handle the affairs of the nation'.[47]

While Stalin still controlled the U.S.S.R., nevertheless, he authorised changes which made a clear break with his inter-war policy. Seven-year free and compulsory schooling was extended to rural areas in 1949 and a programme was announced at the 19th Party Congress (1952) to increase all schooling to ten years before 1960.[48] The reintroduction of polytechnical training also figured in the Congress Directives, but 'this brief pronouncement' undoubtedly left many Soviet educators puzzled about, and fearful of commenting on, the proposed plan; discussion did not begin until after Stalin's death[49] and it was only in 1954 that the Soviet State Planning Commission began to 'elaborate draft annual plans for training specialists by groups of specialities for every ministry, office and Union republic'.[50] The significance of this planning innovation lies in the shortfall in the number of secondary school-leavers qualified for university entry from the number of places in higher education which had previously ruled. Not only did numbers in secondary schooling increase rapidly, but fees were abolished for the top grades leading to university entry qualification and for universities themselves. In drawing attention to this change of ratio in qualified school-leavers to higher-education places, Schwartz and Keech by-pass the Government's motivation with the phrase 'the Soviet regime for reasons of its own', but show how an inevitable consequence was acceptance by school-leavers of quite unsuitable courses or their relegation to 'perennial college candidates'.[51] This was a misallocation of resources which Khrushchev countered, not by accepting the pressure of private demand as Stalin had begun to do, but by the drastic cuts of his 1958 reform.

There are so many obscure pointers – and contributors – to fundamental policy changes in 1949 as to defy codification in a paper such as this. The death of Zhdanov in 1948 and the execution of Voznesensky in 1950 set the terminal dates of changes in the leadership near Stalin. The political scene was marked by the 'Leningrad affair'; the economic, by the volte-face over subsidies to heavy industry and over wholesale-price reform. When the history of that time can be written, the changes in educational policy must be taken also into account.

The evidence is far more prolific on the educational retrenchment of 1958. The forces openly ranged against Khrushchev were sufficient greatly to modify his policy: 'if we compare Khrushchev's September memorandum with the actual law adopted in December 1958 we find that the two differ not only in detail but in basic principle ... the secondary day school was preserved more or less intact both in form and in content; ... the provision for admission to and study in higher education institutions likewise markedly deviated'.[52] The significance of the extended period of public discussion is relevant both in comparison with the secrecy over the 1949-52 policies and when set against the absence of preliminary general debate before the joint Party and Government Resolution of 13 August 1964,[53] the first major break with the 1958 enactment and consummated in the 1966 reform.

This reform reduced the length of 'complete secondary education' from eleven to ten years (except in the Baltic Republics where the longer period was retained[54]), eliminating a year added at the time of Khrushchev's changes to maintain the previous curricular content. Its central effect was to extend schooling to the ten-year cohort beyond the seventh birthday, and it is this culmination which may best introduce the analysis of school-enrolment patterns focused on Tables 1 and 2.[55] As the quantitative review in the following section shows, the volume of secondary education in relation to primary entry was by 1970 lower than that of market economies at corresponding income levels, but that of vocational and university enrolments was well above them.[56] It is not without significance to the content of Soviet education in relation to the needs of the state that its products have been described as 'less anti-adult, rebellious, aggressive and delinquent' than those of the United States systems.[57] That much of the variation in child attitudes can be explained by infant, pre-school and extra-curricular influences, as Bronfenbrenner goes on to show, is a consequence partly of a fundamental continuity in Russian adult-to-child relationships. The constants characterising the Soviet period, which in some regards extend back to Tsarist times, underlie the statistical examination which occupies the remainder of this paper.

V. THE EVIDENCE OF ENROLMENT

No complete statistics on education were officially published until the appearance of the Empire's first *Statistichesky ezhegodnik* in 1900, just when the first comprehensive demographic data had been collected in the 1897 census. All information on the enrolment structure (Table 1) and on its relation to the population of school age (Table 2) suffers from certain deficiencies, for which the Soviet authorities also must accept some responsibility. Thus the 1959 and 1970 censuses grouped age-cohorts differently from each other and into generations which did not correspond with the data published on school grades; as Table 3 shows, an estimated breakdown of the censuses is a preliminary to assessing the percentage of a given age in school. For the nineteenth century, the problem is of estimation from incomplete data. Johnson, drawing chiefly from Hans's careful compilation of primary sources,[58] presents the most substantial array of statistics on enrolments, but he offers them without comment on their mutual inconsistencies. Thus, as Table 4 shows, only at the start of the general

Table 2

Relationship of School Enrolments with Approximately Relevant Age-groups at Censuses, 1926-70

(millions)

	1926	1939(a)	1939(b)	1959	1970
Primary enrolment:					
Grades 1-4	9·46	21·20	21·38	17·78	20·68
Population aged 8-11	11·23	16·48	20·04	14·98	19·69
Per cent in school	84·3	128·6	106·6	118·7	105·0
Junior secondary enrolment:					
Grades 5-7	1·06	8·78	10·77	8·94	15·83
Population aged 12-14	11·52	13·39	17·02	8·57	14·57
Per cent in school	9·2	65·6	63·3	104·3	109·4
Senior secondary enrolment:					
Grades 8-10	0·14	1·40	2·37	4·66	12·86a
Population aged 15-17	10·68	9·12	11·21	10·19	13·83b
Per cent in school	1·3	15·4	21·1	45·7	93·0
Per cent enrolled of above ages	31·9	80·5	71·4	93·0	102·7

Note: The grouping of junior and senior secondary education follows the 1966 change in Soviet practice. Enrolments are at the nearest September, population is at the census date (but corrected to September for 1970).

(a) Grades 8-10 plus grade 11 in the Baltic Republics.
(b) Ages 15 to 17 and to 18 in the Baltic Republics.

Sources:
1926-59: de Witt, *Education and Professional Employment in the U.S.S.R.,* p. 138 (with 1958-9 school year enrolments enlarged to include all except special schools – those for children with physical defects, enrolment of 0·12m.), from *Narodnoe khozyaistvo SSSR v 1958 godu* (Moscow, 1959) p. 809; 1970 enrolments from *SSSR v tsifrakh v 1970 godu* (Moscow, 1971) p. 185; 1970 population from Table 3; the similar adjustment of census age-groups to those for published grade enrolments for 1959 is in de Witt, p. 582.

Table 3

Estimated Age Breakdown of 1970 Census
(*thousands*)

	(1)	(2)	(3)	(4)
0-7		—		
8		4,705		44,966
9	19,690	4,910		
10		5,065		
11		5,010		
12		4,947	29,724	29,299
13	14,565	4,872		
14		4,746		
15		4,659		
16	13,727	4,649		
17		4,419		17,263
18-19		—		

Source:
Col. (2) is estimates made by Dr E. Csocsan de Varallja (Institute of Agricultural Economics, Oxford) from published numbers of births (adjusted to years beginning 1 Sep) annually from 1953-4 to 1962-3, reduced by published infantile mortality and age-specific probabilities of death on basis of 1958-9 published Soviet life-table, adjusted in proportion to the published infantile mortality for subsequent years (according to Finnish, U.K. and U.S. experience) at each level of infantile mortality as appropriate. Col. (4) is published age-groupings from the preliminary results of the 1970 census; the small difference in the comparable years is attributable to the shift of the estimates in col. (2) to a school-year basis. By difference from the census, the ages 18 and 19 would comprise approx. 4·2m. and 4·0m. and the Baltic Republics (at 2·3 per cent of total school enrolment in 1970) would hence represent an addition of 0·096m. to yield the relevant age-group for Table 2.

time series (1800) is it possible to sum the total from the parts; deficiency grows through the century.

Two contrasting magnitudes are not, however, at issue. Firstly, the Speransky reforms did not at any one time bring into schools more than one in every 200 of the total population: applying as an age breakdown the 1821 census of Great Britain, this would represent under 3 per cent of children aged 7 to 11. Secondly, the ratios of secondary to primary and of tertiary to primary corresponded to a far higher level of social and economic development than that which Russia had then reached. The enrolment structure has its importance. Denison attributed for the United States[59] three-fifths of the earnings differential between primary and secondary and between secondary and tertiary to the effect of additional schooling, when parental circumstances and I.Q. at an early age are held constant. These shares of the differential do not appear unreasonable in other countries, developed and underdeveloped.[60]

Table 4

Shortfall in Constituent Data on Estimates of Aggregate Enrolment
(thousands)

Reference in Johnson	1800	1835	1855	1885	1900	1914
Table 1, p. 263						
Minor and major schools	19·9	—	—	—	—	—
Table 12, p. 270						
Universities and higher education	—	3·9	4·0	—	—	—
Gymnasiums	—	19·0[a]	17·8	—	—	—
Table 13, p. 271						
District, parish and private schools:	—	73·0[b]	94·3	—	—	—
of which district[c]	—	25·0	27·0	(19·0)	24	18[d]
Table 25, p. 282						
Church schools	24·2[e]	12·0[f]	100·0[g]	202·4	1,634[c]	1,900[c]
Urban schools	0	0	0	27·5[h]	87	154[d]
Table 32, p. 287						
Universities	0·1[e]	2·0	3·7	11·5	16	35[i]
Table 33, pp. 288-9						
Other higher education	—	—	—	(3·5)[j]	10[k]	42[l]
Text table, p. 196						
Secondary schools	—	—	—	—	—	685
Primary schools:	—	—	—	—	—	8,000
of which zemstva (p. 204)	—	—	—	—	—	(3,000)
Other higher education	—	—	—	—	—	115
Total above	44	110	220	—	—	8,880[m]
Table 33	45	240	400	1,900	4,500	9,500
Shortfall below Table 33 total	1	130	180	—	—	720

(a) 6·5 in 1825 and 19·4 in 1837 (Alston, p. 27).
(b) 73·3 in 1837 (ibid.).
(c) Hans, pp. 233-5.
(d) In 1911 (Hans, loc. cit.).
(e) Alston, pp. 19 and 11 respectively.
(f) 1·9 in 1831 and 19·0 in 1840.
(g) 98·3 in 1853 and 133·7 in 1860.
(h) In 1881 (Hans, loc. cit.).
(i) 34·5 in 1912 and 36·7 in 1916.
(j) Seminaries (Johnson, p. 171).
(k) 9·64 in 1899.
(l) 38·99 in 1912-13.
(m) 'Close to 9m.' (Johnson, p. 196).

Although attention has been drawn above to the distinctive structure of early nineteenth-century Russia in comparison with other industrialised countries,[61] it is worth stressing that the 1825 enrolment of one secondary to ten primary was not achieved in the United States and Germany until after the First World War (though at the turn of the century in Japan), by Belgium, the Netherlands, Italy, Sweden, Norway and Canada in the 1930s and by England and Wales[62] and France after the Second World War. The foundation of the universities at the start of the nineteenth century gave Russia a ratio of university students to primary pupils that, Japan again apart, was only reached by the United States (with a wider definition of a university student) after the First World War, and by most other industrialised countries after the Second World War (e.g. Australia, Canada, England and Wales, France, Italy, Norway).

But it is perhaps more significant to relate such enrolment structures to the levels of per capita income with which they were associated. This involves the use of Sweden and Japan as yardsticks more often than might be desirable, because time series on income and education are in both countries better documented than elsewhere. Throughout the discussion, dollar values are in prices of the mid-1960s.[63]

When G.N.P. was $200 per head at the turn of the century, Russia had an enrolment ratio of only $3\frac{1}{2}$ per cent of its population as students compared with 8 per cent in Japan at the same level (1890) and 15 per cent in Sweden (1880), but had more secondary and university students in relation to primary than had Japan or Sweden at the corresponding level of G.N.P. (65 against 9 and 23 in the first group and 8 against 4 in the two other countries in the second group). The margins were relatively narrower by the outbreak of the Second World War: when per capita G.N.P. was of the order of $250-$300 Russia showed an enrolment ratio of $5\frac{1}{2}$ per cent against an unchanged Swedish ratio for 1890 and 11 in Japan (1900). The 1914 Russian educational structure showed 70 secondary pupils for every 1,000 primary against 26 and 29 in Sweden and Japan; Italy, at around $300 per capita in 1870, had 40 secondary pupils per 1,000 primary; Russia had, however, bettered its ratio of university students per 1,000 primary pupils at the $250-$300 level, viz. 15 in Russia against 4 both in Japan and in Sweden and 7 in Italy. In the U.S.S.R. of 1927, on the eve of the First Five-Year Plan, but four years before the introduction of primary compulsory education, G.N.P. per capita was in the same range as at the outbreak of the First World War, viz. $250-$300, and – in the area of the time – the enrolment ratio had only slightly increased (to 8 per cent); but there were almost 150 secondary pupils and 29 university students per 1,000 primary enrolments.

The pre-war Five-Year Plans brought the U.S.S.R. (within its present boundaries) to the $500-$550 G.N.P. range per capita and, after the primary school recruitment of the 1930s, at last to an overall enrolment ratio which was standard in market economies at a similar level of product per head, viz. to 19 per cent, which was above Italy's in 1921 (12), Sweden's in 1920 (13) and Norway's in 1910 (17) and only a little below Australia's in 1921 (20) and Japan's in 1950 (23). Similarly, its secondary to primary ratio of 74 was above that of Sweden (47) and Norway (65), although below Italy (78) and Japan (649) which had at that G.N.P. per head far outdistanced the other market economies in this respect; the corresponding university student ratios, however, had become remarkably closer: 37 per 1,000 primary in the U.S.S.R. against 27 in Sweden, 29 in Australia, 34 in Japan and 36 in Italy and Norway. When reconstruction after the Second World War had been completed, the Soviet enrolment ratio and its secondary to primary relationship were almost unchanged; university numbers were rather higher than before. By 1960 Soviet per capita G.N.P. was almost $1,200, and its enrolment ratio corresponded closely to those of the countries of the West at that level of product (though it was well above the Swedish ratio); its secondary to primary rate was, however, generally lower than that ruling in the comparable states, though its university rate remained higher.[64]

Finally, by 1970, when Soviet G.N.P. was nearly $1,750 per head, its enrolment ratio was rather above that of the developed West (25 against 16 to 24 elsewhere, though the United States in 1960, at $2,350 per head, was at 27 pupils per 100 population), while it had relatively fewer secondary but more university to primary pupils. Since by that date vocational schooling was everywhere widespread, the data are for convenience set out in Table 5.

Table 5

*Soviet Enrolments per 1,000 Primary Pupils in 1970
Compared to Other Countries at Similar Per Capita G.N.P.*

	Secondary	Vocational	Higher
U.S.S.R.	139	328	222
England and Wales	517	504	20
United States	350	122	79
Canada	172	—	32
Germany	230	414	41
Norway	183	142	15

Source:
Table 1 and Kaser, op. cit., p. 115.

VI. INFORMAL EDUCATION AND LITERACY

Enrolment statistics by definition treat of formal training. Reference has already briefly been made to the contribution of informal education, which must be considered before turning from the coverage of education to the resources allocated.

As Table 1 indicates, the school enrolment rose from about $1\frac{1}{2}$ to $2\frac{1}{2}$ per cent of the population during the last quarter of the nineteenth century, whereas literacy among army recruits rose from 21 to 49 per cent.[65] The paradox is to be explained by the growing availability of learning opportunities outside the school system. Thus in the Bogorodsk district in Moscow guberniya in 1883-4, of a total of 7,123 literate factory workers only 38 per cent had learnt in general schools; 10 per cent had learnt in factory schools (the number of which was increasing with industrialisation), 7 per cent had learn with the clergy, in military service (a source which presumably did not change in relation to total population), and the remaining 36 per cent had learnt from unspecified sources.[66]

The improvement of literacy was especially rapid in the final five years of the century – the peak of Witte's industrialisation drive – for among recruits it rose from 32 in 1890 to 39 in 1895 but, as just noted, to 49 in 1900. Although the sample may not be stable in composition,[67] literacy among immigrants from Russia (excluding Poland and Finland) into the United States rose from 66 per cent in 1895 to 76 per cent in 1898.[68] The census of 1897 showed literacy rates of 29 per cent among males and 13 per cent among females, or 21 per cent for both sexes. The rate of literacy decreased towards the eastern periphery of the Empire, but even in the capital, St Petersburg, it was no more than 69 (for both sexes) and 61 in Moscow; its average in Poland was 31 and in European Russia 23, and sank to 12 in Siberia and the Transcaucasus and a mere 5 in Turkestan.

The speed at which Russian national income expanded between 1885 and 1913 (2·8 per cent annually according to Goldsmith[69]) demonstrates that Russia at least was an exception to a 40 per cent literacy rate and a 10 per cent primary enrolment rate being a necessary (though not sufficient) condition for rapid economic growth.[70] When Witte launched the industrialisation drive of the 1890s, literacy was 20 per cent and the primary enrolment ratio 2 per cent.

Certainly, almost as many were learning to read without going to school as those that did attend, and it was doubtless an encouragement that there were attractive posts going for as many literate workers as could apply. Blaug reads the 'lesson of the Soviet experience [as] to

provide literacy campaigns within the framework of a total development effort in order to insure the creation of jobs for literates in step
with the issue of literacy certificates',[71] but Government strategy
appears to have been the same before the October Revolution. Kahan
has shown good correlation between the percentages of literate and
of 'hereditary' workers (i.e. those whose fathers had also worked in
factories) not only in the late nineteenth but in the mid-eighteenth
century.[72] Vaizey argues strongly for the importance of 'on-the-job'
training in the development process: 'skill acquisition properly understood therefore *follows* investment rather than precedes it. In other
words, education is not a necessary prior condition of a skilled labour
force.'[73]

VII. THE REGIONAL PATTERN

The fact that literacy, however gained, can be mapped in direct
proportion to the intensity of economic development suggests an extension of Gerschenkron's hypotheses and a link with the 'infrastructure'
approach to development.

On national averages, the Russian economy accelerated in the late
nineteenth century with the minima neither of literacy nor of primary
education which other countries seem to have needed at corresponding
phases. The literacy threshold had, however, been passed in certain
regions: as early as 1835 two-thirds of craftsmen-proprietors could
sign their names in St Petersburg, where – as just noted from the 1897
census – general literacy was to touch 70 per cent by the end of the
century. Yet throughout the first half of the century the number of
primary schools had remained constant at a mere ten.[74] The experience
of the capital city confirms the view that opportunities for use encourage
the informal acquisition of literacy.

Public education beyond the three Rs was, however, much more
evenly spread through the Empire with respect to the urban population. A concentration of secondary schooling in towns during the first
three Soviet Five-Year Plans (see above, pp. 237-8) is evident also during industrialisation. Urban literacy was 45 per cent for the Empire as
a whole (49 per cent in the European part except Poland, where it was
45, and 39 per cent in Siberia).[75] As Table 6 shows, the ratio of
gymnasium enrolment was more uniform in relation to urban population (in respect of which Kiev was 1·6 times Odessa or Moscow) than
to total (St Petersburg was 3 times the districts of Kharkov, Vilnius
and the Caucasus). But even the five Asian districts not covered by
Table 6 had 6 per cent of gymnasium enrolments with but 11 per cent
of the urban population.[76] Since gymnasiums were the channel to

university entry, their uniform distribution in relation to urban population implies a policy of providing infrastructure throughout the
Empire which was consistent with the generous supply of higher and
secondary education in relation to primary enrolment. The policy
corresponds to that on railway construction of the last quarter of the
nineteenth century which spread the potential for industrialisation
well ahead of actual demand. It also of course illustrates bureaucratic
centralism, which ordains equal local ratios for administrative
simplicity (or rigidity),[77] as well as one theme of this study, viz. the
state view of schools as training establishments for its service.

Table 6

*Gymnasium Enrolment Ratio in Selected School Districts in 1891
per 1,000 Population at 1897 Census*

	Urban	Total
Moscow	3·1	0·5
St Petersburg	4·6	1·2
Warsaw	3·9	0·9
Kiev	5·1	0·5
Odessa	3·1	0·6
Kharkov	3·7	0·4
Vilnius	3·4	0·4
Caucasus	3·5	0·4

Source:
Alston, pp. 253, 279.

It may be relevant to compare the regional situation with that of
Italy, which in 1860, still before unification, had an overall enrolment
that, in relation to population, Russia was not to reach until the First
World War. Both countries nevertheless enjoyed the same ratio of
secondary (60) and tertiary (9) per 1,000 primary enrolments. The
regional disparities in Italy were far wider than in Russia and it may
be surmised that the advantages of lateness in development accessible
through big and technically more advanced plant could be reaped in
effect only where educationally advanced entrepreneurs and staff were
available; the existence of intra-Italian frontiers precluded the
standardisation characteristic of Tsarist rule. In Russia, on the other
hand, secondary and higher education was more uniformly offered
throughout the country[78] and the regional spread of the country's
income has, during the ensuing century, been much less than in Italy.

Table 7

Finance of Education in Russia, 1885, and U.S.S.R., 1960
(million roubles)

	1885	1960
Local authorities	5	5,133
Ministry of Education	17	3,005
Other institutions	16	765
Households	13	350
Total	51	9,253

Sources:
1885: central and local authorities from Johnson, pp. 291-2; Holy Synod outlay (included with other ministries in 'other institutions') and household expenditure from proportion of church and private-school pupils to state enrolments.
1960: H. J. Noah, *Financing Soviet Schools* (New York, 1966) Table 6, pp. 78-9, with local authorities separated from Table 1, p. 53, on the assumption that virtually all 'culture and research' outlay in the budget classification is made at the central level. Noah shows values in 1960 roubles, but the above have been decimated in accordance with provisions of the 1961 monetary reform.

Table 8

Aliquots per Student in Russian and Soviet Educational Finace

	Aliquot to pupil fraction	Aliquots per pupil
1885	$\dfrac{680,000}{1,900,000}$	0·36
1928	$\dfrac{4,085,000}{13,400,000}$	0·30
1937	$\dfrac{10,006,000}{32,300,000}$	0·31
1950	$\dfrac{11,655,000}{38,200,000}$	0·31
1955	$\dfrac{11,479,000}{34,700,000}$	0·33
1960	$\dfrac{10,004,000}{41,800,000}$	0·24
1970	$\dfrac{13,454,000}{60,800,000}$	0·22

Note: For discussion of aliquots, see text.

VIII. RESOURCES FOR EDUCATION

The Russian G.N.P. in 1885 was about 7,500 million roubles, of which just over 50 million, or 0·7 per cent, was spent on education (see Table 7); Italy in 1883 spent 1·1 per cent, the same as in the United States, but above the proportion in the United Kingdom (0·9 per cent).[79] Three-quarters of a century later, the United States still ranked highest at 6·2 per cent of G.N.P., and Italy (at 5·2 per cent) was the same as the U.S.S.R.; the United Kingdom devoted 4·4 per cent of G.N.P.[80]

It is, however, of somewhat more interest to relate educational proportions of G.N.P. to the number of students and hence to the quality of education in terms of opportunity cost. The indicator elsewhere suggested by the present writer is the 'aliquot per pupil', where each 'aliquot' represents the G.N.P. per head of total population.[81]

Russian and Soviet 'aliquots per pupil' (Table 8) have been quite remarkably stable, but their magnitude compared with other countries is yet more prominent. At the beginning of the century the corresponding value for Germany was 0·12, for England and Wales 0·05 and for the Netherlands 0·09; it was probably of the order of 0·06 in the United States.[82] Under both Tsarist and Soviet regimes it was constant and above 0·30 while education was restricted; it declined when access was opened but even so is high in relation to market economies. At 0·24 per pupil in 1960 it compared with 0·25 in the United Kingdom at the same time, 0·22 in the Netherlands, 0·17 in Belgium and 0·19 in the United States; all these countries had a per capita G.N.P. well in excess of the Soviet, and no Western economy – let alone one as poor as the U.S.S.R. in the 1930s – has yet recorded a value of 0·30.

The Ministries of Education of St Petersburg and Moscow have both been lavishly treated in terms of resources at their country's disposition; the corollary was restricted access to the teaching provided, and only certain political circumstances induced them to respond to a wider private demand. The expectations of ten years of general schooling raised by initial Bolshevik pronouncements were half a century in coming, but, radical as the propositions then were, they are conservative by the Western standards of today. The United Kingdom requires a minimum of eleven years' education (5 to 16), but so many children stay beyond the official leaving age that its ratio of secondary to primary enrolments is much larger. On the other hand, Soviet provision of higher education remains very high in international comparison.

The inequality implicit in the provision of relatively large sums per person enrolled is being dissipated as spending per pupil moves closer to that typical of market economies. Enough studies have now been made on the economics of education to show that the causal relationship is probably from income to education rather than from education to growth. Russian and Soviet experience bears this out, but illustrates with special clarity the perennial dilemma of the sacrifice of equality for growth. While the country was poor, the state made education available on a selective basis, responsive to its own needs in administering society and the economy; the U.S.S.R. is still not yet a rich country, but the parity in schooling which it now affords its citizens is concomitant with a slower pace of economic development.

NOTES

1. N. Bukharin and E. Preobrazhensky, *The A.B.C. of Communism*, trans. E. and C. Paul, ed. with Introduction by E. H. Carr (Harmondsworth, 1969) p. 297.

2. Inflation was so rapid that a month-by-month adjustment of both 1917 and 1918 outlays would be necessary to make a precise calculation: no such expenditure breakdown is published today, still less in times as disturbed as those. R. W. Davies, *The Development of the Soviet Budgetary System* (Cambridge, 1958) Tables 3 and 5, shows, e.g., the price index (1914=1) at 7 in January 1917 and 12 in October 1917 and (1913=1) at 21 in January 1918 and 94 in October; a quintupling of prices may be estimated from one full year to another.

3. Appendix I (by R. W. Davies) to S. Fitzpatrick, *The Commissariat of Enlightenment: Soviet Organisation of Education and the Arts under Lunacharsky* (Cambridge, 1971) p. 291.

4. For a fuller discussion, see M. Shore, *Soviet Education: Its Psychology and Philosophy* (New York, 1947) chaps 3 and 4, from which the quotations above are taken.

5. Framed for the U.S.S.R. by J. S. Berliner, 'Managerial Incentives and Decision-Making', in *Comparisons of the United States and Soviet Economies* (Washington, D.C., 1959) p. 351; D. Granick, *The Red Executive* (London, 1960) p. 62; and R. Hutchings, *Soviet Economic Development* (Oxford, 1971) p. 102.

6. Quoted by L. Alston, *Education and the State in Tsarist Russia* (Stanford, 1969) p. 4.

7. Ibid., p. 31.

8. Fitzpatrick, *The Commissariat of Enlightenment*, p. 289.

9. e.g., M. Kaser, 'Needs and Resources for Social Investment', *International Social Science Journal*, no. 3 (1960) pp. 400-33.

10. See particularly M. Blaug, *An Introduction to the Economics of Education* (London, 1970) chap. 6, and J. Vaizey (with K. Norris and J. Sheehan) *The Political Economy of Education* (London, 1972) chaps 5, 6.

11. A. Gerschenkron, *Economic Backwardness in Historical Perspective* (Cambridge, Mass., 1962) p. 47.

12. Ibid., p. 354.

13. E. H. Carr, *Foundations of a Planned Economy, 1926-1929*, II (London, 1971) 446-50.

14. *Critique of the Erfurt Programme* (1891), cited ibid., p. 447.

15. E. H. Carr, *Socialism in One Country*, II (London, 1959) 89, 194; *Foundations of a Planned Economy*, II, chap. 44.

16. Ibid. (with R. W. Davies), I 475.

17. Ibid., II, chap. 55.

18. Ibid., II 390-2.

19. Ibid., I 592-3; II 399.

20. Fitzpatrick, *The Commissariat of Enlightenment*, p. 26.

21. The first Commissar of Public Health, Semashko (appointed in July 1918), pressed for centralisation because the health service had stronger links both with zemstvo and other local interests (notably through the Pirogov Society, eventually dissolved) and with enterprises (and hence with the *fabzavkomy*, whose influence was checked by the nationalisation of June 1918). For a brief account sympathetic to Semashko, see G. A. Batkis and L. G. Lekarev, *Teoriya i organizatsiya sovetskogo zdravookhraneniya* (Moscow, 1961) pp. 50-5. Carr, *Socialism in One Country*, II 250, notes Semashko's preference for centralisation in 1926, but sees him (like Lunacharsky) at other times as a spokesman without much prominence, until his eclipse in 1929 as a mild oppositionist (*Foundations of a Planned Economy*, II 27); Semashko remained, apparently unmolested, in academic posts until his death at the age of seventy-five in 1949.

22. W. L. Blackwell, *The Beginnings of Russian Industrialisation* (Princeton, 1968) p. 18.

23. W. H. E. Johnson, *Russia's Educational Heritage* (Pittsburgh, 1950) p. 34.

24. This translation perhaps better reflects the content of the curriculum than the more usual 'cipher schools' (Johnson, *Russia's Educational Heritage*, p. 34; Alston, *Education and the State in Tsarist Russia*, p. 5), or the present writer's 'arithmetic schools' (*Annuaire de l'U.R.S.S., 1968* (Paris, 1969 p. 131).

25. It was intensively discussed whether the Ministry of National Enlightenment (*narodnogo prosveshcheniya*) then set up should not be termed 'of Public Instruction' (*narodnogo obrazovaniya*); Kochubei, the adviser quoted in the text, disliked the former because 'it is dangerous to spread too much light' (quoted in Alston, *Education and the State in Tsarist Russia*, p. 21). The Soviet People's Commissariat began by use of the former, but later took the latter as the title of the Ministry.

26. Ibid., p. 22.

27. Quoted ibid., p. 23.

28. Dorpat (Tartu), founded in 1632, came under Russian control in 1802.

29. For detailed list, see Johnson, *Russia's Educational Heritage*, p. 288.

30. Quoted ibid., p. 32.

31. Ibid., pp. 172-3.

32. Schools for state peasants, which had been confirmed by decree of 1842, had 100,000 pupils by the emancipation of 1861, and the 1864 statutes opened state schools to everyone.

33. Alston, *Education and the State in Tsarist Russia*, pp. 61-2.

34. These had just been set up, but education was added to their responsibilities only as an afterthought.

35. N. Hans, *The Russian Tradition in Education* (London, 1963) pp. 73-7.

36. See Johnson, *Russia's Educational Heritage*, pp. 147, 152.

37. Ibid., p. 155.

38. N. Timasheff, *The Great Retreat* (New York, 1964) p. 34, cited by T. Shanin, *The Awkward Class* (Oxford, 1972) p. 10.

39. N. Hans and S. Hessen, *Educational Policy in Soviet Russia* (London, 1930) pp. 4, 7.

40. Ibid., pp. 9-13; university admission restrictions were lifted by decree of 13 June 1917 and university self-government introduced by another of 17 June (thereby confirming the frustrated intentions of the First Duma). According to N. Ivanov, 'The Training of Soviet Engineers', in G. L. Kline (ed.), *Soviet Education* (London, 1957) p. 160, one-third of the 150,000 students in institutions of higher education were women.

41. F. Lilge, 'Lenin and the Politics of Education', *Slavic Review* (June 1968) p. 231.

42. A. V. Lunacharsky, *O narodnom obrazovanii* (Moscow, 1958) p. 197.

43. In *Capital* he defined this as producing 'the fully developed individual fit for a variety of labours'.

44. For a brief survey on its application through the *shkola-kommuna* and the *shkola-goroda*, see Kaser, in *Annuaire de L'URSS*, p. 132, and A. V. Voronov, 'On the Fostering of Social Participation among Pupils in School Communes and Educational Settlements, 1918-25', *Sovetskaya Pedagogika*, no. 5 (1967).

45. O. Anweiler, *Geschichte der Schule und Pädagogik in Russland* (Heidelberg, 1964).

46. Blaug, *An Introduction to the Economics of Education*, p. 67, distinguishes this enrolment ratio (to total population) from the enrolment rate (viz. to the appropriate age-group), though is not entirely consistent in his own usage (e.g. pp. 64-5).

47. Quoted in H. H. Willis, *Sovietised Education* (New York, 1965), p. 8.

48. For a study of education during this consumer-oriented period, see D. Levin, *Soviet Education Today* (London, 1959); a postscript is added citing Khrushchev's 1958 thesis.

49. See R. V. Rapacz, 'Polytechnical Education and the New Soviet School Reforms', in G. F. Bereday and J. Pennar (eds), *The Politics of Soviet Education* (New York, 1960) p. 32.

50. L. A. Komarov, *Planirovanie podgotovki i raspredeleniya spetsialistov v SSSR* (Moscow, 1961), quoted by H. C. Rudman, *The School and State in the U.S.S.R.* (New York, 1967) p. 42.

51. J. J. Schwartz and W. R. Keech, 'Group Influence and the Policy Process in the Soviet Union', in F. J. Fleron, Jr (ed.), *Communist Studies and the Social Sciences* (Chicago, 1969) p. 300.

52. Ibid., pp. 302-3.

53. See P. D. Stewart, 'Soviet Interest Groups and the Policy Process: The Repeal of Production Education', *World Politics* (Oct 1969) p. 33. The last three months of Khrushchev's authority were notable for what can retrospectively be seen as his defeats: the main events in the economic sphere were the introduction of the Bolshevichka-Mayak experiment in July and the Gosplan conference of September on future planning policy.

54. The variation of legislation by Union republics is an insufficiently explored feature of Soviet political practice. On the divergences in the laws on the previous reform (enacted in all fifteen Union republics between 29 March and 2 June 1959), see J. Hough's appendix to de Witt, *Education and Professional Employment in the U.S.S.R.*, pp. 556-74.

55. An excess over 100 per cent is that of 'repeaters' over precocious children in any group of ages.

56. Except for vocational enrolments in Germany and England and Wales.

57. U. Bronfenbrenner, *Two Worlds of Childhood: U.S.A. and U.S.S.R.* (London, 1972). See also especially N. Grant, *Soviet Education* (London, 1964) chap. 3, and E. J. King (ed.), *Communist Education* (London, 1967) chap. 3.

58. N. Hans, *History of Russian Educational Policy* (London, 1931).

59. E. F. Denison, *The Sources of Economic Growth in the United States and the Alternatives before Us* (New York, 1962) pp. 69-70.

60. M. Blaug, 'The Correlation between Education and Earnings', *Higher Education*, ɪ 1 (1972) 53-70, and *An Introduction to the Economics of Education*, pp. 32-54.

61. The data are from Kaser, 'Education and Economic Progress: Experience in Industrialised Market Economies', in E. A. G. Robinson and J. Vaizey (eds), *The Economics of Education* (London, 1966) Table 13, pp. 110-15, supplemented for Italy in the nineteenth century by compilations of Vera Zamagni (doctoral student, St Antony's College, Oxford).

62. As observed, ibid., pp. 136-7, the Scots system differed considerably; it is certain that the threshold was passed much earlier in Scotland. See G. E. Davie, *The Democratic Intellect* (Edinburgh, 1961) pp. 4-9, and Blaug, *An Introduction to the Economics of Education*, p. 64.

63. For Japan the series with a higher yen valuation (JB rather than JA) is used from Kaser, in Robinson and Vaizey, op. cit., because A. Maddison, *Economic Growth in Japan and the U.S.S.R.* (London, 1969) p. 146, also uses a high 'agio of purchasing power over exchange rate' for the recent incomes per head from which both studies work back. His agio is 86 per cent, above all other countries in his survey.

64. The 98 secondary to 1,000 primary pupils compares with 91 in England and Wales (1937), 122 in Norway (1950), 132 in Canada (1941), 167 in France (1954) and 177 in Sweden (1950). University rates elsewhere ranged from 9 to 23 against 128 in the U.S.S.R.

65. The record of army literacy, which began in 1874, is quoted by C. M. Cipolla, *Literacy and Development in the West* (Harmondsworth, 1969) p. 118, from A. G. Rashin, *Formirovanie rabochego klassa Rossii* (Moscow, 1958) p. 582.

66. Statistics from Cipolla, *Literacy and Development in the West*, p. 25; his figures for elementary school attendance (though he may mean enrolment), p. 88, taken from E. Levasseur, *L'Enseignement primaire dans les pays civilisés* (Paris and Nancy, 1897) are confirmed by Hans, *History of Russian Educational Policy*, p. 233, at 0·9m. c. 1873 and 2·2m. c. 1895, but at 0·5m. must exaggerate for 1840 (for which Hans cites 125,000).

67. The ethnic composition may have changed, e.g., to comprise more Jews, for whom self-education was more important than among Russians. This was also a factor in the higher literacy rates shown in Poland.

68. *Annual Reports of the Commission-General of Immigration*, quoted by Cipolla, *Literacy and Development in the West*, p. 96.

69. R. Goldsmith, 'The Economic Growth of Tsarist Russia, 1860-1913', *Economic Development and Cultural Change* (April 1961) pp. 441-75; Maddison, *Economic Growth in Japan and the U.S.S.R.*, p. 155, shows 2·5 per cent for 1870-1913, faster than seven of the fourteen countries for which he gives corresponding data.

70. See Blaug, *An Introduction to the Economics of Education*, p. 64, citing Kahan, in C. A. Anderson and M. J. Bowman (eds), *Education and Economic Development* (Chicago, 1965); Anderson, ibid.; and A. L. Peeslea, 'Primary School Enrolments and Economic Growth', *Comparative Education Review* (Feb 1967) p. 67.

71. Blaug, *An Introduction to the Economics of Education*, p. 259.

72. Kahan, op. cit., pp. 291-7.

73. Vaizey, op. cit., p. 148.

74. *Ocherki istorii Leningrada*, vol. I: *1703-1861* (Moscow and Leningrad, 1955) pp. 808-9. At mid-century these were, however, supplemented by the many factory schools established (ibid., p. 801).

75. Johnson, *Russia's Educational Heritage*, p. 283.

76. Alston, *Education and the State in Tsarist Russia*, pp. 137, 279.

77. This inference may be corroborated by the experience of the deliberate contraction of gymnasium enrolments in 1887: the correlation is weak between the degree of zemstvo democracy and the closure to sons of 'townsmen' (as distinct from gentry, etc.), but strong between the local ratio of Jews and the exclusion of Jewish children (ibid., pp. 279-80).

78. Non-academic secondary education was less evenly distributed. Thus in mid-nineteenth-century St Petersburg there were four times as many pupils in military schools and three times as many in private schools as in the state gymnasia, and half as many under private tutors. *Ocherki istorii Leningrada*, I 796-800.

79. On G.N.P. see Kaser, in *Economic Journal* (Mar 1957) pp. 83-104; R. Goldsmith's estimate of 4,250m. roubles for fifty provinces of European Russia in 1885 on Prokopovicz's national income definition (excluding services); Prokopovicz allowed 39 per cent for Siberia and Asia in 1913, and Mulhall 35 per cent for services in 1895. Educational expenditure in Russia is from Table 7, in Italy from Zamagni thesis and in U.S. and U.K. from A. Fishlow, in *Journal of Economic History* (Dec 1966) pp. 418-36.

80. F. Edding, 'Expenditure on Education', in Robinson and Vaizey, *The Economics of Education*, Table 2, p. 40. The Italian figure he gives is 5·19, but his Soviet ratio of 7 per cent is based on estimate of the real purchasing power in U.S. dollars'; the estimated G.N.P. of 175,800m. used here shows that 5·26 per cent was spent on education.

81. See Kaser, in Robinson and Vaizey, op. cit., 90, 96.

82. Ibid., pp. 111-12.

12 The Soviet Rural Economy in 1929-1930: The Size of the Kolkhoz*

R. W. DAVIES

I. INTRODUCTION

'THE year of the great breakthrough', as Stalin described 1929 in November of that year,[1] marked the end of the New Economic Policy (N.E.P.). During N.E.P., a largely state-owned industry was linked with some 25 million private peasant households through a market system in which private as well as state and co-operative trade was permitted to operate. Within this framework both agriculture and industry first recovered to their pre-war levels of production and then expanded beyond them.

The New Economic Policy assumed that the state should abandon the forced requisitioning of agricultural products carried out during the civil war of 1918-20. Coercion should no longer be used in order to compel the peasants to yield up their products: the state would manipulate prices and employ taxation and other forms of economic pressure in order to improve its terms of trade, but in the last resort it would pay the prices the peasant was prepared to accept. When in the first few months of 1928 grain was exacted by force from the peasants, this marked the beginning of the end of N.E.P. By the summer of 1929 the majority of the Soviet leaders were convinced that the central planning of the whole national economy, including agriculture, was possible, and was essential if the industrialisation drive was to succeed. The behaviour of the peasant on the market was no longer seen as setting an upper limit to the possibilities of state capital investment in the urban sector. Agricultural activity was to be brought fully under the direct management of the state.

The new approach was rejected by the vast majority of the engineers,

economists and agricultural experts who advised the various commissariats and worked in their agencies. An *émigré* Russian economist
succinctly summed up their outlook:

> They were undeniably hostile to the existing system, which was
> purely political in its tendencies. They could not possibly connive
> at such cruel measures as the raising of monstrous levies, the
> enforced collectivity, the 'Dekulakisation' and others. They
> endeavoured to put a brake on these activities, relying for support
> on the Right wing's disaffection.[2]

From the spring of 1928, almost before these attitudes had a chance
to form, the Soviet authorities set out to destroy the influence of the
'bourgeois specialists' by public and secret trials, by purges in every
Soviet establishment, central and local, aimed at ejecting those of
doubtful loyalty, and by a vigorous press campaign. This drive against
the specialists continued until the summer of 1931. From the point of
view of the Soviet authorities, it was perhaps successful in preventing the onslaught of a cohesive open opposition of the specialists
and the Right wing of the party, potentially very dangerous in view of
the mass discontent evoked by the actions of the regime in the
countryside. But the campaign against the specialists also had the
harmful effect of depriving the authorities of their frank advice.[3]
Instead, in the crucial years 1929 and 1930 the Soviet Government in
every sphere had to rely on the handful of specialists who actively
supported the new policies, intermingled with a much larger number
of enthusiasts lacking in expertise and an unknown number of
careerists. With the removal of major experts in the State Planning
Commission (Gosplan) and in all the other Government departments
concerned with the economy, the People's Commissariat of Workers'
and Peasants' Inspection for the U.S.S.R. (Rabkrin), headed by
Ordzhonikidze until the autumn of 1930, moved to a central position in
policy-making in the state sector. Rabkrin was virtually a party organ,
having joint staff with the party Central Control Commission which was
also headed by Ordzhonikidze; its staff contained a higher proportion of
party members than any other commissariat, and it was dominated by
semi-trained enthusiasts for party policy. In agricultural policy Rabkrin
was less important, and major decisions in this crucial period were
made by a more or less *ad hoc* group of leading politicians and party
officials in which Stalin played a very active part; these leading
politicians and officials might also not unfairly be described as 'semi-
trained enthusiasts'.

The dominant group in the Politburo, backed by a relatively small
number of officials in each commissariat, by Rabkrin, and by an

unknown number of ordinary party members, had thus by the autumn of 1929 embarked, without expert advice and in an atmosphere of extreme confidence and optimism, on the construction of a new economic system, designed to force through rapid industrialisation; a system in which physical planning predominated and inflation was being allowed to develop. The effort to control the economic develop-ment of a major nation through a comprehensive state plan was a novelty in human history. What happened in the next five years may from one point of view be described as a learning process on a grand scale, in which the Bolshevik leaders and their supporters, at con-siderable economic and human cost, brought into being by trial and error a new economic and political system. The process was complex and uneven. In the course of 1929 and the early months of 1930, revised Five-Year Plan targets which proved to be utterly unachiev-able were adopted in all sectors of the economy. In the same period financial and other controls were swept aside, and for a short while a moneyless economy appeared to be emerging. Between the summer of 1930 and the spring of 1933 the economy passed through a profound economic crisis, while simultaneously a large-scale industrial invest-ment programme was pushed through, more modest than had been envisaged in the heady atmosphere of 1930, but unprecedented in its pace and scale. In this second period the main features of the Soviet planning system took shape; some financial and other controls were introduced or restored; and the party leaders moved towards the acceptance of more realistic targets. In a third period, roughly spanning the years 1934 to 1936, the planning system was consolidated and the large investment projects constructed between 1930 and 1933 were put into operation.[4]

The majority of the largely urban Bolshevik Party particularly lacked understanding of the peasant and his economy; the problems in agriculture were in any case more acute; the resulting crisis was more profound. The collectivisation drive, abruptly undertaken between October 1929 and the end of February 1930, aroused so much antagonism and resulted in such widespread destruction of horses and cattle that the authorities were impelled to retreat. By the summer of 1930, long before the ambitious industrial programmes had been cut down, they had abandoned many of their extravagant notions of organising agriculture on the model of large-scale industry and had incorporated into their daily practice some of the features of the eventual compromise, in the *artel* form of the collective farm (*kolkhoz*), between the private property instincts of the peasant and the insistence of the state on organising and controlling agriculture. Nevertheless, in our second period, between the autumn of 1930 and the spring of 1933, collectivisation was resumed, although at a slower pace; the state continued to exact very large amounts of agricultural produce; peasants left the villages in large numbers; the destruction of horses and livestock continued; and the supplies of tractors from the new factories were quite inadequate to replace the loss of horses. The harvest troubles of 1932 and the famine of 1932-3 ensued; and in 1934-6, although agricultural production improved, it remained below the pre-collectivisation level.

In this article I endeavour to illustrate some aspects of this process by considering Soviet policies and practice in relation to one important problem of agricultural organisation – the size of the kolkhoz. I have confined the discussion to the relatively short period from the middle of 1929 to the autumn of 1930 in which the issue was in principle resolved. Between the middle of 1929 and the end of February 1930, in this as in other matters, constraints were removed; wildly ambitious proposals for huge kolkhozy covering whole administrative districts replaced the earlier notions of relating the kolkhoz closely to the existing rural settlement. After the retreat signalled by Stalin's article 'Dizziness from Success' of 2 March 1930, these extravagant proposals were quickly abandoned, and it became clear that the kolkhoz system, at least for some time to come, would not eliminate the existing rural settlement but seek some kind of compromise with it.

II. THE RURAL SETTLEMENT, THE KOLKHOZ AND THE TRACTOR: MID-1929

The basic unit of rural organisation in the U.S.S.R. until the end of the 1920s continued to be the self-governing *mir* or commune, known officially as the 'land society', and controlled by meetings of all adults in the village, under an elected elder. One or more rural settlements (*seleniya*) formed a mir, and one or several mirs together formed an administrative village (*selo*), the lowest unit in the Soviet hierarchy: in the U.S.S.R. at the end of the 1920s there were approximately 599,000 rural settlements, 319,000 mirs and 72,163 village soviets, so there were on average 1·9 settlements per mir and 4·4 mirs per village soviet.[5] The size of these units varied considerably from one part of the country to another. The basic difference was between the small settlement of Central Industrial, north-western and western Russia and Belorussia, with an average of 16-20 households in each settlement, and the larger settlement of south-eastern Russia and the Ukraine, with an average of 100-150 households. The great grain-growing regions of European Russia and the Ukraine, which were at the core of the collectivisation programme, were all regions in which the average settlement was relatively large (100 or more households), and the settlements of the Ural and Siberian regions, although somewhat smaller, still contained more households than the non-grain areas.[6] The village soviet was an official rather than an economic unit, and its boundaries had undergone frequent changes during the 1920s. The basic unit of land holding was the mir, which was generally responsible for agricultural arrangements on its territory, above all for crop rotation and the distribution of land among its members; until 1929 it also controlled the greater part of rural finance.

The settlement and the mir were natural units for an agriculture in which the horse-drawn plough was the basic implement, and in which the peasant needed to be able to walk from his cottage and his household plot (*usad'ba*) to his allotments of land (*nadel*), usually in the form of strips, in the fields of the settlement. Within the framework of these agricultural techniques, the attention of the authorities was directed towards improving the boundary lines between settlements and consolidating strips within the settlement so as to facilitate improved crop rotation and use of land.[7]

The advent of the tractor challenged these assumptions. At first some efforts were made to incorporate mechanised farming within the existing land structure, and in the middle 1920s, when concessions to individual peasant agriculture were at their maximum, some peasants were permitted to buy their own tractors. But even at this time most tractors were allocated to sovkhozy and kolkhozy. This immediately raised the question of the size of the kolkhoz. Efforts were made to consolidate kolkhoz land to facilitate the efficient use of the tractor, but the crucial difficulty was that nearly all kolkhozy at this time were smaller than the mir from which they had split off. In the course of 1927 and 1928 the view became generally accepted that the existing kolkhoz was far too small to cope with mechanised agriculture. The study of agricultural developments in the United States, and the energetic experiments and calculations of Markevich, director of the Shevchenko sovkhoz which established the first machine-tractor station (M.T.S.), led to the acceptance of a new optimum for mechanised agriculture. Markevich argued that tractors could be most efficiently utilised and maintained if they were operated in groups of 200-250, which would enable them to cover an area of 40,000-50,000 hectares of arable land.[8] It was not, however, at first supposed that the unit appropriate for tractor maintenance was also appropriate for field work and other farming activities. Contracts were initially made by Shevchenko with individual households and then with mirs and kolkhozy. The new Traktorotsentr of the U.S.S.R., established in 1929 under the chairmanship of Markevich to administer all state-owned M.T.S.s, treated the village as the largest unit of agricultural organisation, even in conditions of unbroken collectivisation.[9] The conference of large (*krupnye*) kolkhozy in July 1929, attended by delegates strongly identified with the need to increase the size of the kolkhoz, was fairly modest in its aims; its organisation section resolved that 'the size of large kolkhozy is completely adequate for the rational organisation of collective production with high-productivity power and machine bases'.[10] At this time the average number of households in kolkhozy officially classified as 'large' was about 180, equivalent to the population of 4-5 rural settlements. The largest kolkhoz then in existence, the Digorskii kombinat, North Caucasus region, included only 13 settlements and 1,781 households.[11] It should be added that it was the unchallenged assumption of the large kolkhoz movement that the existence even of the typical large kolkhoz, embracing a few neighbouring settlements and 100-200 households, was justified only by the more or less immediate prospect of a substantial degree of mechanisation. 'We shall not travel far on horses', a delegate remarked at the conference of large kolkhozy; and the organisation section of the conference resolved that 'the main lever in developing large kolkhozy is the group supply of tractors and complex agricultural machines'.[12] At the conference, Kaminsky, chairman of Kolkhoztsentr, persuasively argued that for a long time to come large and small kolkhozy would develop simultaneously. In administrative districts with a high proportion of collectivised households, the large kolkhoz would form the nucleus, and would be supported by a surrounding 'self-acting mass of small kolkhozy of all kinds'. The large kolkhoz would be closely associated with the emergent machine-tractor stations and tractor columns, the 'foundation and the path to the establishment of mass collectivisation'; the small kolkhozy would for the moment develop 'not on the basis of large-scale machine technology, of tractor stations and combine harvesters, but around the collective utilisation of horses, of individual agricultural machines, and so on'.[13] The drastic changes in policy which were soon to come were heralded at the conference only by the reports from a couple of areas that 'giant' kolkhozy were to be established which would embrace a whole administrative district, even though mechanisation was almost absent; the most famous of these was the Gigant kolkhoz in the Urals, planned to include three administrative districts and some 10,000 households.[14] But even the ambitious organisers of Gigant, who proposed to go ahead with their plans in spite of the lack of tractors and agricultural machinery, treated this lack as a major – and a purely temporary – deficiency.[15]

III. THE DRIVE TOWARDS 'GIANT' KOLKHOZY:
JULY-DECEMBER 1929

From the middle of 1929 onwards, the question of the optimum size of kolkhozy was constantly under discussion, and before the end of the year the assumptions of the July conference of large kolkhozy were swept aside. The view became dominant that the large mechanised kolkhoz must include a number of settled points, several villages, possibly even a whole administrative district; the notion of a number of independent kolkhozy of 2,000 hectares or so being served by a common M.T.S. or tractor column was more or less rejected; the Digorskii kombinat and the Gigant kolkhoz, it was argued, must become typical rather than exceptional. This movement of policy towards 'giant' kolkhozy formed part of the drive towards a much increased pace of industrialisation, which in the opinion of the party leadership carried the corollary that the agricultural problem must be solved once and for all through forced collectivisation, which would facilitate control by the authorities over the production of the countryside and at the same time sweep aside the individual peasant units which stood in the way of increased production. The view that the methods of industry must prevail in agriculture became more and more prevalent. Meanwhile in the towns industrialisation was more and more coming to mean the implanting of very large new factories using the most advanced United States technology. In this general context, two circumstances seem, during the summer and autumn of 1929, to have been of particular importance in encouraging confidence in the viability of very large agricultural units. First, the achievements of the new giant grain state farms (*sovkhozy*), initiated by the party as an emergency measure in the summer of 1928, so far seemed satisfactory. With the support of its American advisers, Zernotrest, the state trust responsible for the new grain sovkhozy, had decided early in 1929 that the optimum sovkhoz should have a sown area of 20,000-50,000 hectares, later raised to 40,000-60,000 hectares; these figures were consistent with Markevich's proposals for the optimum size of an M.T.S.[16] In the meantime, Gigant sovkhoz, in the Salsk okrug, North Caucasus region, had already sown 60,000 hectares for the harvest of 1929,[17] and in September 1929, at a festival addressed by Maxim Gorky, a first harvest of 60,000 tons was announced;[18] this was respectable both in quantity and in yield. These practical successes greatly encouraged the supporters of giant sovkhozy. Kalmanovich, chairman of Zernotrest, declared on his return from the United States that he had found no farms there 'which on our understanding could be called large', praised the Gigant sovkhoz as showing that 'we have not only caught up but also overtaken the technically leading countries', and announced that the minimum sown area for a sovkhoz should be 30,000 hectares.[19] In his famous article published on 7 November 1929, Stalin, who had been a strong defender of the new grain sovkhozy during the discussions of 1928, now felt able to declare: 'The objections of "science" to the possibility and expediency of organising large grain factories of 50,000-100,000 hectares have been exploded and turned into ashes.'[20]

At the Conference of Agrarian Marxists in December 1929, the rapporteur on sovkhozy argued that the criterion for deciding the question of size should be the 'most rational organisation of the main means of production, which in grain farming are the internal combustion engine, the tractor and all the appropriate attachments, and the repair shops', and concluded that 500 tractors and 100,000-150,000 hectares (this evidently referred to sown area or arable land) was the correct size;[21] this was already something like twice the size recommended by Markevich for the M.T.S. Even if these recommendations were sensible in the case of the new grain sovkhozy, they should not have been regarded as necessarily appropriate for the kolkhoz movement: unlike the kolkhozy, the new sovkhozy were being established on virgin territory, and with the aid of very substantial supplies of imported large-size tractors and combine harvesters. However, during the summer and autumn of 1929 and after, the plans for the sovkhozy created a certain atmosphere in which the really successful agricultural unit was presumed to be a huge farm, larger than the biggest in the United States, and worked with modern machines and a small number of skilled technicians. In a mood of exuberance and thoughtlessness, the existing settlements and land structure could be seen as a mere obstacle to the technical revolution in agriculture; this was already the view taken of them when they got in the way of the provision of the sovkhozy with an uninterrupted land area. At the same conference, one speaker argued more generally from the experience of the sovkhozy that the agrarian economist Chayanov was advocating a 'biological and in a sense a private capitalist orientation' when he suggested that the structure and organisation of the farms should be determined by the territory and type of crop rather than by the needs of the most up-to-date means of production.[22]

The second circumstance encouraging the formation of very large kolkhozy was the belief, vigorously advocated at all levels of the kolkhoz system, that tractors and agricultural machinery should be brought under the control of the kolkhozy themselves, or at least of the kolkhoz system, rather than being managed by a separate state agency such as Traktorotsentr or by the agricultural co-operatives. At the conference of large kolkhozy in July 1929, Kaminsky, chairman of Kolkhoztsentr, strongly urged collective farmers to acquire resources to buy up machine-tractor stations, and many delegates strongly urged that the tractor columns of the agricultural co-operatives, which at this time were quantitatively far more important than the state M.T.S.s, should also be brought under kolkhoz control: 'the instruments of production', one speaker declared, 'cannot be in some-one else's hands'.[23] The proposal to transfer the tractor columns to the kolkhozy was strongly supported by Kolkhoztsentr in its report to the Party Central Committee dated 7 September 1929. According to this report, the separation of the tractor column from the kolkhoz enabled the collective farmers to use the horses and implements which were replaced by the tractor for other private activities rather than handing them over for common use.[24] But perhaps the most important argument persuading the authorities to favour ownership of tractors and other agricultural machines by the kolkhozy themselves was that this would result in the provision of substantial kolkhoz funds for purchase of the tractors; in practice, tractors had so far been made available both to columns and to M.T.S.s out of state funds. This approach continued to prevail throughout the vicissitudes of the next twelve months: as late as July 1930 Narkomzem intended 'to transfer tractors and the whole tractor economy to the kolkhoz system'.[25] In the light of the later development of a state-managed network of M.T.S.s as the sole provider of tractors to the kolkhozy, these proposals may seem surprising. It should be remembered, however, that in the summer of 1929 the vast majority of all tractors used by the kolkhozy had been bought by them in the course of N.E.P. (often, it is true, with the aid of state loans) and were under their direct management.[26] The problem was that almost all these existing kolkhozy were only large enough to need a single tractor, and that their scattered land holdings made it difficult to utilise tractors efficiently. The M.T.S.s and tractor columns could serve to spread the use of tractors more widely, and to encourage the formation of kolkhozy with continuous land masses. Once unbroken collectivisation was achieved, manage-ment of the tractors by the kolkhozy could be seen merely as the old arrangements writ large. The question was, how large? What was the appropriate size of unit for the management of the tractor economy and of farming generally? As far as the tractor economy itself was concerned, Markevich's calculations were almost unchallenged.[27] But there was of course no inherent reason why tractor stations and columns which formed part of the kolkhoz *system* should necessarily be managed by individual kolkhozy; the move towards kolkhoz ownership of tractors did not necessarily imply that each kolkhoz must be made sufficiently large to be capable of utilising a complete M.T.S. or column. At the conference of large kolkhozy in July 1929, some speakers advocated management of the tractor economy by the local agencies of Kolkhoztsentr, while others insisted that tractors should come directly under each individual large kolkhoz.[28] The advocates of the latter course presumably thought that it would increase the willingness of collective farmers to subscribe to the purchase of tractors. At any rate, the decision that tractors should not be managed by an agency external to the kolkhoz system made it easier to contemplate the fusion of tractor and other farm operations under the unified management of a giant kolkhoz.

Against this background, the rapid development of forced collectivisation in the autumn of 1929 was closely accompanied by growing enthusiasm for the giant multi-village kolkhoz. In September the grain co-operative organisation Khlebotsentr made a tentative move towards bringing together tractor and other farm operations under a single management. It arranged with Kolkhoztsentr that in three districts of the Central Black Earth region the M.T.S. should in 1929-30 cover the whole agricultural population. In these districts 'the transfer of the M.T.S. to direct management by the collectivised population' was to be accomplished through the establishment of a 'group co-operative union' of the kolkhozy of the district; the existing kolkhozy would, however, retain their individual identities.[29] Traktorotsentr was more cautious. At an all-Union conference of its local officials in September 1929, Markevich did envisage a future stage in which the optimum size of a kolkhoz, so as to enable the 'cheapest, most rational and most exact (*chetkii*) use of machinery', would be 'thousands or tens of thousands of hectares'; but he continued to presume that in the 'first period' of kolkhoz development, which was evidently to be a lengthy one, each of the group of villages served by an M.T.S. would continue to remain the basic economic unit, with its own economy and crop rotation.[30]

In this as in other questions of agricultural policy, a major shift in official attitude followed the session of the Party Central Committee in November 1929. The resolutions of the session made no specific reference to the size of kolkhozy or their relationship with the M.T.S.; and Molotov appears to have ignored the question in his wide-ranging reports. But Kaminsky, the chairman of Kolkhoztsentr, apparently argued, departing from his previous statements, that large kolkhozy should be established even when no M.T.S. existed. Declaring that 'life itself is pressing for unification and grouping around the stronger collectives and for a further development via group combines to large-scale production', he proposed the establishment of kolkhozy which included whole districts.[31] Moreover, Kaganovich, in his report on the Central Committee session to Moscow region party activists, pointed out that ten kolkhozy in the Urals had a total area amounting to a million hectares, and chose the famous Gigant kolkhoz, the largest in the U.S.S.R., and one which so far had relatively few tractors, as his principal example of successful kolkhoz development. He depicted – and predicted – in glowing phrases the setting-up of a telephone network and a bakery for the whole kolkhoz and of communal kitchens which would deliver food straight to the fields.[32] To say the least, the impression was given that the party leadership was not averse to the establishment of giant kolkhozy equal in size to an administrative district, and that such kolkhozy need not await the arrival of large numbers of tractors. This impression was assisted by the vigorous campaign conducted at this time against the once powerful group of ex-Socialist Revolutionary economists who had persistently defended small-scale agriculture as economically more viable. The pressure exercised on these men was such that in September 1929 their leading theoretician, Chayanov, repudiated as inappropriate to an age of technical revolution his earlier defence of the peasant family unit and vigorously advocated large-scale farming and the socialist reconstruction of agriculture.[33] This change of heart was criticised by official writers as insincere,[34] and the adherents or former adherents of small-scale agriculture were abused on all hands. At the Conference of Agrarian Marxists which met from 20 to 27 December 1929, for example, a work on agricultural settlements was denounced as propaganda for 'Belorussian national-democracy'. Particular scorn was directed at its argument that in the conditions of the Belorussian S.S.R. 'everything that is technically and economically progressive finds its maximum expression in settlements of 75-200 hectares' (some 8-16 households), put forward primarily on the grounds that all fields should be easily accessible on foot from the peasant's household plot.[35] A 'bourgeois specialist' who had recently recommended that the optimum area of a kolkhoz should be 1,600 hectares, so that the fields should not be more than 2 km. away from the peasant households, was equally repudiated.[36] In this atmosphere, the positive merits of the very large kolkhoz naturally if illogically seemed a necessary corollary. Shlikhter, People's Commissar for Agriculture of the Ukraine, objected to the 'almost dwarf-like character' of 80-90 per cent of kolkhozy, and called for the establishment of inter-village kolkhozy of 50,000-60,000 hectares; these would be appropriate to 'the optimum set or system of machines', would enable land utilisation to be adjusted to the needs of the M.T.S., and would carry the corollary that the land society (the mir) could be abolished. As alternatives to the giant kolkhoz, Shlikhter also advocated the establishment of 'large integrated agro-industrial kombinaty' and of 'sovkhoz-kolkhoz kombinaty'; the latter would be more appropriate when sovkhozy already existed, or were being established, in places where an M.T.S. was being set up. Both types of kombinat, according to Shlikhter, should, like the giant kolkhoz, cover an area of 50,000-60,000 hectares.[37]

The brakes were not quite off. In his report to the conference, the agrarian economist Lyashchenko called for central management in the kolkhoz to be 'differentiated' rather than 'integrated', so that the M.T.S., the processing plant, and so on, would each have different spans of control. He also warned that the transfer of the peasants' personal plots into new population centres, which was being 'inexpediently attempted' in some places, involved 'colossal difficulties' and would take a number of years.[38] And although the statements by prominent political figures such as Kaganovich and Shlikhter appear to have encouraged the formation of giant kolkhozy even when few tractors were available, some directives from the centre issued during the next few weeks continued to assume that the giant kolkhozy should be formed only when at least some degree of mechanisation was present. In a telegram to the Central Black Earth region on 18 January 1930, Khlebotsentr ruled that giant kolkhozy (i.e. those with 50,000-60,000 hectares of arable land) should be formed on the basis of its M.T.S.s and tractor columns only when these held more than twenty tractors (i.e. about 8-10 per cent of the full complement of tractors for an area of this size).[39] In the following month Khlebotsentr, developing a proposal by the Party Central Committee in its resolution of 5 January 1930,[40] called for the establishment of 3,790 M.K.S.s (*mashino–konnye stantsii*, machine–horse stations) within kolkhozy, stipulating that the area of each kolkhoz should be a minimum of 3,000 hectares;[41] this, though much larger than the average kolkhoz, was very roughly equal in area to the group of rural settlements covered by an average village soviet.

IV. GIGANTOMANIA AT ITS PEAK:
DECEMBER 1929 – FEBRUARY 1930

(a) Policy

In spite of these slight notes of caution, the heady atmosphere among the partisans of immediate collectivisation at the end of 1929 and the beginning of 1930 strongly influenced attitudes to the size of the kolkhoz. At the Conference of Agrarian Marxists, Larin firmly declared that there should be a single M.T.S. and kolkhoz in each district, with the district soviet executive committee replacing the land society; and he looked forward to a future in which electric vehicles and ploughs would have replaced petrol lorries and tractors, the kolkhozy would become sovkhozy or 'obkhozy' (*obshchestvennye khozyaistva*, public farms) and the peasants would move into agro-towns.[42] While the conference was still in progress, a meeting to discuss the 'agro-industrial kombinaty' (A.I.K.) was held under the auspices of the All-Union Council of Kolkhozy.[43] The kombinaty were intended as a grandiose development of the combination of farming with associated industrial activities, on a district scale, which had already been attempted by the Tiginskii kombinat.[44] Some ten reports were heard from districts with widely different agricultural profiles, and the chairman asserted that all districts of unbroken collectivisation were tending to become A.I.K. The meeting was reported to have looked with disfavour on kombinaty of a mere 30,000-40,000 hectares, and to have given its preference to what were described as 'future agricultural Dneprostrois', evidently on a multi-district basis, such as that proposed for Mineral'nye Vody in the North Caucasus, of 50,000 hectares. These would include 'dozens of dairy farms, oilseed and cheese factories, factories to rework all other agricultural products, cattle sheds for a thousand animals, electric ploughs, power stations, cultural settlements' and were to increase marketed output to ten to fifteen times its existing level. Most resources for these vast developments were to be provided by the peasants themselves, and the economic newspaper suggested that 'with insignificant help from the state the land in these districts will become a factory'. But even on the wildly optimistic calculations presented at the meeting, the cost of establishing these kombinaty would evidently have been some tens of milliards of roubles a year, with a substantial proportion of this to be borne by the state.[45] Proposals of this kind continued to appear for some weeks. The famous Khoper okrug in the Lower Volga announced that with the aid of the Sovkhoz and Kolkhoz Faculty of the Timiryazev Agricultural Academy in Moscow, working all out for three days and three nights, a plan had been prepared for a grain–livestock kombinat with a single population centre, a 'socialist agro-town', of 44,000 persons, divided into twenty-two blocks of flats, with communal eating as in the best flats in Europe, not to mention a reading-room, library, studies, gymnasium and solarium in each block. This would replace the present situation in which families were isolated from their neighbours and suffered 'boring loneliness under the dark smoky oil lamp in the long snowy winter evenings':

> Eight thousand separate, scattered economic cells, almost defence-less from fire, mass epidemics and other social evils. How much unnecessary waste of energy just to service and light the stoves, prepare eight thousand family dinners, heat baths, do the washing, etc.

The agricultural newspaper commented that in drawing up this plan, inspired by the spontaneous decision of a group of peasants at present scattered over a radius of 15-20 km., to move to the centre of their kolkhoz, the 'local party and soviet agencies, as in the whole development of the process of unbroken collectivisation, have proved far ahead of our centres, and this time have been the forerunners of a big revolution'.[46] In an article published in January 1930, Ya. Nikulikhin boldly declared that 'all our agriculture will gradually be reorganised along the lines of an A.I.K.' 'Some comrades', he reported, 'believe it fully possible to have only 50,000 agricultural enterprises by the end of the present Five-Year Plan'; and he envisaged that towards the end of the proposed 'general plan' (i.e. in ten to fifteen years) the whole of agriculture would be organised into some 5,000 A.I.K. of 100,000 hectares each.[47] The historian sympathetic to industrialisation is almost tempted, as he turns these yellowing pages, to forget elementary economics and common sense, and identify himself for a moment with these inexperienced urban enthusiasts in those grim January days of 1930, boldly dreaming about rapid progress towards giant mechanised factory farms, cajoling reluctant peasants into kolkhozy, denouncing recalcitrants and driving them out of the villages into the endless snow.

These fanciful programmes were only one strand, though a significant one, in the proposals about the optimum size of kolkhoz prepared in the last weeks of 1929 and the first few weeks of 1930. In the absence of any firm recommendations there were striking variations in the plans adopted in different regions, or even in different okrugs within the same region. In the Ukraine, as we have seen, there was a general commitment to a kolkhoz–M.T.S. unit of 50,000 hectares. In the Lower Volga region plans varied from okrug to okrug. Some okrugs, such as Balashov, appear to have favoured giant kolkhozy each covering a whole district: in the Lower Volga, each of these would have been several times as large as the M.T.S. optimum of 50,000 hectares. Others favoured smaller units: in Khoper okrug, the fantastic grain–livestock kombinat was planned as an experimental exception to the general pattern, and for the okrug as a whole it was proposed to set up 100 kolkhozy each with an area of 12,000 hectares. The view of the regional party committee in the Lower Volga appears to have been that a kolkhoz covering a whole district would be almost impossible to manage: in districts served by an M.T.S., Markevich's optimum was appropriate; for the other districts (which were of course the majority), the regional party committee did not apparently go further than stipulating that each kolkhoz should include at least one village.[48] In the Central Black Earth region, the regional soviet executive committee approved in one case the establishment of an agro-industrial kombinat, presumably covering a whole district, and embracing over 11,000 households.[49] In the Tambov okrug of the same region, the Kirsanov district endeavoured to establish a single giant commune for the whole district of 198,000 hectares and 23,700 households, explicitly on the model of the Gigant sovkhoz in the North Caucasus; the okrug authorities insisted, however, that the district should limit itself in 1930 to establishing a number of large kolkhozy, and postpone unification until an adequate technical basis was available.[50] In the North Caucasus itself, the authorities appear to have decided to establish one kolkhoz in each stanitsa (the stanitsa was the large Cossack village, usually containing a thousand households).[51]

At the beginning of 1930, then, policy – or rather policies – towards the size of the kolkhoz appear to fall into the following pattern. It was generally accepted that with the replacement of the horse by the tractor the criterion for determining the size of the kolkhoz should not be the existing land configuration and practices of the peasants but the needs of the machine; and these needs were held to involve the organisation of units of 50,000 hectares of arable land or more.[52] There was also a definite tendency to argue that in districts which were not yet mechanised, the size of kolkhoz should be determined not by the present but by the future level of mechanisation, though this tendency was resisted by some important local authorities. These policy decisions were made in an atmosphere, strongly encouraged by leading members of the Politburo, of 'big means best'; in this atmosphere, arguments against giant units were rarely heard, at any rate in public, and wild schemes were not publicly rebuffed.

(b) Gigantomania in practice

Much less was accomplished in practice than might have been inferred from these discussions and decisions. Certainly, a number of giant kolkhozy were established. At least two kolkhozy in the Ural region and three in the Lower Volga region included one or several entire districts. The famous Gigant kolkhoz in the Urals was extended to embrace five administrative districts with a population of some 13,000 households and a total area of 275,000 hectares. Land consolidation was said to have been carried out over the whole territory. All animals, farm buildings and even dwellings were declared to have been socialised and transferred to indivisible capital; substantial numbers of cattle were driven into temporary cattle-yards, and an unknown number of peasant households – in addition to those classified as kulaks – were resettled in the course of the effort to establish a single commune over the whole territory. However, even in the case of the highly publicised Gigant the process of forming a single commune was far from complete. As late as 25 January 1930, a report at a conference still referred to the continued separate existence of the 160 kolkhozy which were to be merged into Gigant. It was not apparently until the end of January or beginning of February that the constituent kolkhozy and their elected boards were replaced by 'production departments' (*uchastki*) of the commune with appointed managers.[53]

In addition to these 'super-giants', a number of other kolkhozy, although not including the whole of their district, approached Markevich's optimum of 50,000 hectares. In the Khoper okrug, Lower Volga region, the 423 kolkhozy, with a total collectivised population of 52,000 households, which existed by December 1929 were replaced by 81 kolkhozy covering 91,760 households, 90 per cent of the rural population of the okrug, as compared with the 100 kolkhozy planned in December 1929.[54] But although such examples can be multiplied, they were exceptions. A.I.K. were normally set up only in districts where more than 50 per cent of the rural population were collectivised. The maximum figure I have found for the number of A.I.K. is that early in 1930 some 300 A.I.K. had already then been set up (*voznikshie*); in the R.S.F.S.R. 36 of these were recognised as model combines.[55] Over most of Soviet territory, the general pattern of collectivisation seems to have been that some existing kolkhozy amalgamated, others expanded to include many more members of their settlement or their village, and many new kolkhozy were formed; in the U.S.S.R. the number of kolkhozy increased on paper from 57,000 with 1,008,000 households on 1 June 1929, to 110,200 with 14,260,000 households on 1 March 1930, so that the average number of households per kolkhoz rose from 18 to 127.[56] This means that the 'average' kolkhoz had a population somewhere between that of a settlement and that of a village. The only region in which the population of the average kolkhoz was larger than that of the average village was the Lower Volga, where there were 588 households per kolkhoz and only about 380 households per village.[57] Even in the Ukraine, where the formation of giant kolkhozy had explicit official approval, there were 25,000 kolkhozy for 12,000 village soviets.[58] These figures leave out of account the various arrangements for grouping (*kustovanie*) of kolkhozy in which the kolkhozy in the groups continued to retain their separate identity. Precise figures do not appear to be available. At least in the Ukraine a substantial proportion of the kolkhozy were members of groups.[59] In some cases the groups controlled tractors and other farm machinery, more rarely some horses as well, in others they were responsible for joint industrial enterprises, dairy farms, silos and so on.[60]

V. GIGANTOMANIA IN RETREAT: MARCH 1930 ONWARDS

From early March 1930, policy gradually moved towards the condemnation of giant kolkhozy. The size of the kolkhoz was not mentioned in Stalin's article of 2 March, nor in the Party Central Committee resolution of 14 March. Early in March, in fact, some measures were adopted which seemed to give further encouragement to the formation of large units. On 4 March, Sovkhoztsentr announced that it intended to form 12 sovkhoz-kolkhoz combines (*ob''edineniya*) in twelve regions, varying in area from 30,000 to 500,000 hectares and with an area of 1·5 million hectares in all.[61] A week later, a report on collectivisation in the Ukraine treated the village as the basic kolkhoz unit for the time being, but still argued that the village-kolkhozy should be unified, as the M.T.S. developed, into 700-1,000 groups (i.e. one or two groups per district) which would themselves in future become kolkhozy: Markevich's optimum for the M.T.S. thus still remained a goal for the size of the kolkhoz.[62] Meanwhile, on 9 March 1930, Odintsev, a deputy chairman of Kolkhoztsentr, published the first criticisms of the hasty formation of giant kolkhozy, giving as an example a giant in the Kursk okrug, Central Black Earth region, with only one telephone in its sixteen villages: 'Giants are often thought up from above without preliminary work among the masses and without taking into account organisation, technical and economic prerequisites.' He was careful, however, to exempt from criticism both carefully prepared and long-established kolkhozy such as Gigant in the Urals, even though they lacked tractors, and large inter-village kolkhozy in which each sub-unit corresponded to an existing settlement.[63] A week later, on 17 March, a telegram was published from Narkomzem of the U.S.S.R. and Kolkhoztsentr which asked local authorities what steps they had taken both to cease further amalgamation and to 'divide up kolkhozy larger than justified by existing machinery'.[64] On 24 March a conference held under the auspices of the agricultural newspaper 'decisively repudiated' uncritical or exclusive reliance either on giant kolkhozy of tens and hundreds of thousands of hectares or on small kolkhozy no bigger than a single settlement.[65] The policy of forming giant kolkhozy before a substantial number of tractors and other agricultural machines were available was henceforth generally abandoned.[66] A survey published at the time of the 16th Party Congress in July 1930 roundly condemned non-mechanised kolkhozy with a sown area of 10,000-15,000 hectares, or even 5,000 hectares, as 'not viable' owing to the separation of their boards from the collective farmers, the increase in centralised decision-making and hence in travel, and their tendency to put together working animals into large, badly maintained columns.[67] Long before the policy changes were complete, those giant kolkhozy which had come into existence during the collectivisation drive were rapidly breaking up. On 14 March 1930 *Pravda* reported that in the Borisogleb okrug 'all the "giants" created by proclamation in the past six to eight weeks are cracking up and disintegrating'. Gigant in the Urals broke up into separate kolkhozy in the course of March, and a district kolkhoz combine (*raikolkhozkombinat*) was established to handle some common activities including sales and supplies.[68] During March and April 1930 most of the giant kolkhozy were subdivided or fell apart, though as late as May there were still some 200 kolkhozy without tractors and with a sown area in excess of 5,110 hectares.[69] The total number of kolkhozy fell, from an estimated 110,000 on 1 March 1930 to 86,000 in May, and the number of households per kolkhoz fell from 127 to 70;[70] in the Lower Volga region the number of households per kolkhoz fell particularly rapidly, from 588 to 247.[71] Throughout the U.S.S.R. the population of the average kolkhoz was now the equivalent of that of one or two settlements. However, as a substantial number of peasants had left the kolkhozy in a vast number of settlements, the typical kolkhoz now tended to include *part* of the population of each of a number of settlements.

In July 1930 the more modest solution to the question of optimum size of kolkhoz was authorised by the 16th Party Congress, which roundly condemned 'the creation as so-called "giant" kolkhozy of lifeless bureaucratic organisations, designed on the principles of orders from above'.[72] The control figures for the economic year 1930-1, published on 27 July 1930, treated the kolkhoz-village as the basic unit for further development, and proposed to form 1,000 M.T.S.s, one per district, in the 900 districts of the grain-growing regions and in 100 districts in the consumer belt. Each M.T.S. was to have a sown area of 18,000 hectares, and the M.T.S.s would thus cover something like one-third of the total sown area.[73]

Much remained unresolved. In districts where agricultural machinery was relatively unimportant, the village was to remain the basic economic unit. But what was to be the effect of mechanisation? *Were* the M.T.S.s to be transferred to the kolkhozy, which was still the intention at the time of the 16th Congress? And how were the tractor and the existing land structure to be reconciled? Was the sole criterion for organisation to be the needs of the tractor and the machine, as was believed between the end of 1929 and the middle of 1930? In articles published in the summer of 1930, considerable differences of opinion about these matters may be found. An article published in the planning journal immediately before the 16th Party Congress continued to assume that giant kolkhozy of 50,000-60,000 hectares would be formed when enough modern machinery was available; on the other hand Grinko, deputy chairman of Gosplan, looked forward to the establishment of as many as 50,000 M.T.S.s (which would mean 10 or 15 per administrative district) and several hundred thousand kolkhozy (which would presumably mean one per settlement rather than one per village).[74]

The solution which was finally adopted in the course of 1930-2 was to concentrate all tractors under the authority of state-owned M.T.S.s, each of which served a 'substantial group of kolkhozy.'[75] Two important factors in the position of the kolkhozy themselves pressed in this direction. Firstly, the break-up of such giant kolkhozy as existed, and the withdrawal of peasants in large numbers from kolkhozy everywhere, eliminated almost all those kolkhozy which were of sufficient size, given the premises of Markevich, to control a group of tractors efficiently. In August 1930 some attempt was made in the Central Volga region to transfer tractors to kolkhozy large enough to be able to handle ten or more tractors, but this scheme failed.[76] Secondly, the authorities were unable, particularly once the pressures were relaxed in March 1930, to collect more than a minor part of the cost of the tractors either from kolkhozy or from the peasants direct. But it was perhaps the overwhelming pressure of the economic and political system as a whole towards centralised state control of the levers of authority in the countryside which was the decisive factor. The rise of the state-owned M.T.S. accompanied the final decline of the system of agricultural co-operation. While some ownership of tractors by co-operative M.T.S.s and by the kolkhozy themselves continued until 1932, the crucial decision was taken on 10 September 1930, when the Party Central Committee resolved that the management and construction of all M.T.S.s, including those belonging to the co-operative system, was to be concentrated in the hands of the state organisation Traktorotsentr.[77]

The concentration of mechanisation in M.T.S.s which each served a large area in turn almost automatically set general limits to the size of the kolkhoz. In conformity with Markevich's original intention, it separated, at least in part, the problems of the efficient unit for the management, maintenance and use of the tractor as such from the problem of the efficient management of the farm. All arguments, from the point of view of both management and production, now pointed in the direction of keeping the order of magnitude of the production unit the same as that of the traditional rural settlement.[78] The lure of giant agricultural units did not completely lose its savour in the summer and autumn of 1930. In 1931 and 1932 some giant kolkhozy re-emerged; but they were much more modest in scale than those of the early months of 1930, and were dissolved by the decision of the authorities.[79] After the Second World War, the campaign to amalgamate small kolkhozy was associated with Khrushchev's abortive proposals in 1950 to establish 'agro-towns' as the basis for giant multi-village kolkhozy.[80] But for a period of nearly twenty-eight years between the summer of 1930 and the abolition of the M.T.S.s in 1958, the compromise solution that the M.T.S. should serve many kolkhozy while the kolkhoz was based on the traditional rural settlement or village remained more or less intact.

NOTES

*I am grateful to my colleague Dr Moshe Lewin for valuable criticisms and suggestions.

1. *Pravda*, 7 Nov 1929.

2. B. Brutzkus, *Economic Planning in Soviet Russia* (1935) pp. 233-4.

3. As Strumilin, principal drafter of the Five-Year Plan, put it in a famous passage written at the beginning of 1929, specialists in the State Planning Commission (Gosplan) were 'already admitting in the corridors that they prefer to stand for high rates of expansion rather than to sit in jail for low ones'. *Planovoe Khozyaistvo*, no. 1 (1929) p. 109.

4. The first two of the three periods I have sketched here correspond to Jasny's 'All-out Drive' (Nov 1929–mid-1933); the third to his 'Three "Good" Years' (1934-6). N. Jasny, *Soviet Industrialisation, 1928-1952* (1961).

5. For the figure for mirs (referring to 1928), see D. J. Male, *Russian Peasant Organisation before Collectivisation* (1971) p. 11; for rural settlements (approximately equal to 'other inhabited points') and village soviets (referring to 1 Jan 1929), see *Administrativno-territorial'noe delenie Soyuza SSR i spisok vazhneishikh naselennykh punktov*, 8th ed. (1929) p. 12.

6. The following table sums up the situation (from ibid., pp. 24-31):

	No. of settlements per village soviet	No. of persons per village soviet	No. of persons per settlement
R.S.F.S.R.	9	1,540	180
of which:			
Leningrad region (excluding Murmansk okrug)	24	1,930	80
Lower Volga region	3	1,879	576
North Caucasus region	7	4,145	564
Central Volga region	2	1,666	747
Siberian region (excluding Krasnoyarsk okrug)	4	1,468	405
Ural region (excluding Tobolsk okrug)	8	2,163	257
Central Black Earth region	5	2,312	462
Ukrainian S.S.R.	5	2,300	c. 500
Belorussian S.S.R.	27	2,900	110
Transcaucasian S.S.R.	5	1,876	368
Uzbek S.S.R.	6	2,000	340
Turkmen S.S.R.	6	2,427	440

There is an unexplained discrepancy between the first two columns and the third. There were approximately 5 persons in each household. The hierarchy of local government normal in the R.S.F.S.R. in 1929 was: republic, region (oblast or krai), okrug, district (raion), village.

7. See E. H. Carr and R. W. Davies, *Foundations of a Planned Economy, 1926-1929*, I (1969) 227-36.

8. Ibid., pp. 190, 213; Markevich purported to show that costs per hectare ceased to fall substantially if the M.T.S. rose above this size.

9. A telegram from Markevich as head of Traktorotsentr to the Khoper okrug kolkhozsoyuz, which was urging its local M.T.S. to sign contracts with multi-village kolkhozy, read: *'The organisation of the station excludes inter-village kolkhozy*. Contracts must be *concluded with the production combines of villages'* (*Trudy Pervoi Vsesoyuznoi Konferentsii Agrarnikov-Marksistov, 20.XII-27.XII 1930 [sic 1929]* (1930) II [i] 161). The same practice appears to have been followed by co-operative M.T.S.s and tractor columns.

10. *Za krupnye kolkhozy* (1929) p. 141. At the conference the German expert Püschel argued that the basic unit should have an area of 1,500-2,000 hectares served by 10-15 tractors, which would provide the best possibility of precise supervision and would obviate unnecessary tractor journeys; but larger units would be required in order to maintain a cultural centre and industrial enterprises. This situation could be achieved either through setting up large communes divided into units or by grouping smaller kolkhozy for common purposes (ibid., pp. 99-100).

11. Ibid., pp. 91-5, 141, 470-7. In December 1928 the Council of People's Commissars (Sovnarkom) apparently defined a 'large' kolkhoz as one with a sown area of at least 2,000 hectares; but, presumably in order to boost the number of large kolkhozy, Kolkhoztsentr from the middle of 1929 onwards changed the minimum requirement from 2,000 hectares *sown area* to 2,000 hectares *total area*, and retained this definition in its statistics in spite of a

decision by the relevant Government departments to use the more restricted definition. See *Za krupnye kolkhozy*, pp. 123, 130-2, 140; *Materialy po Istorii S.S.S.R.*, VII (1959) 222, 229-33. The exaggeration of the success of the movement for large kolkhozy by this sleight of hand undoubtedly contributed to the atmosphere of over-confidence of the autumn of 1929, and appears to have been undertaken by Kolkhoztsentr on its own initiative. The figures given for what is translated as 'giant' kolkhozy in M. Lewin, *Russian Peasants and Soviet Power* (1968) p. 409, refer to 'large' (*krupnye*) kolkhozy in the wider definition of 2,000 hectares total area and above. For the 'giant' kolkhozy, see note 14 below.

12. *Za krupnye kolkhozy*, pp. 429, 142.

13. Ibid., p. 283.

14. Ibid., pp. 46-50, 421-32. The term 'giant kolkhoz' (*kolkhoz-gigant*) was at first used to describe kolkhozy which embraced the whole of a single village or a single settlement; see, for example, a document of September 1928 in *Kollektivizatsiya sel'skogo khozaistva v srednem povol'zhe (1927-1937 gg.)* (Kuibyshev, 1970) pp. 52, 636-7. By the autumn of 1929 the term was reserved for kolkhozy embracing a number of villages (see also note 11 above).

15. *Za krupnye kolkhozy*, p. 38.

16. M. Bogdenko, *Stroitel'stvo zernovykh sovkhozov v 1928-1932 gg.* (1958) p. 62.

17. Ibid., pp. 158-9; Carr and Davies, *Foundations of a Planned Economy*, 190-1 (12,000 hectares in the autumn of 1928; 48,500 in the spring of 1929). Gigant sovkhoz in the North Caucasus should not be confused with Gigant kolkhoz in the Urals.

18. *Pravda*, 3 Sep 1929.

19. *Ekonomicheskaya Zhizn'*, 3 and 13 Oct 1929.

20. *Pravda*, 7 Nov 1929. In the version of the speech published in Stalin, *Sochineniya*, XII (1949) 129, '50,000-100,000' is replaced by '40-50,000'. He did not indicate in either version whether he was referring to total land area, arable land or sown area.

21. *Trudy Pervoi Vsesoyuznoi Konferentsii Agrarnikov-Marksistov*, II [i] 201-3.

22. Ibid., pp. 229-30. Chayanov was apparently working at this time on sovkhoz problems, and was criticised at the conference for being guided by the norms of the American Campbell's capitalist farm (ibid., p. 221).

23. *Za krupnye kolkhozy*, pp. 284-5, 297-304, 312-16. For an account of the 1929 discussion about the relative merits of different forms of ownership and organisation of tractors and agricultural machinery, see Lewin, *Russian Peasants and Soviet Power*, pp. 362-6.

24. *Materialy po Istorii S.S.S.R.*, VII (1959) 227-8.

25. *XVI S''ezd VKP(B)* (1931) p. 623.

26. On 1 Oct 1929, 19,109 tractors came under kolkhozy and group combines of kolkhozy and 3,769 under agricultural producer co-operatives, a looser form of co-operative farm, as against 2,387 under co-operative and state M.T.S.s and tractor columns. *Narodnoe khozyaistvo S.S.S.R.* (1932) p. 145.

27. At the conference of large kolkhozy in July 1929, however, a speaker cautiously suggested that the concentration of tractors suggested by Markevich was inappropriate in many cases, for example in Bashkiria and the Urals, in view of 'the inconvenience of driving tractors large distances along our roads'.

Za krupnye kolkhozy, pp. 300-1; see also Lyashchenko's report, note 38 below.

28. *Za krupnye kolkhozy*, pp. 297-304.

29. N. V. Korol'kov, in *Istoriya S.S.S.R.*, no. 4 (July-Aug 1969) p. 32, citing the archives. This proposal was not out of line with Markevich's estimate of the optimum size of M.T.S.; two of the three districts for which information is available, Ilovai-Dmitrievskii and Talovskii, had arable land amounting to 49,200 and 68,800 hectares respectively (*Materialy po Istorii S.S.S.R.*, VII (1959) 232-3).

30. *Ekonomicheskaya Zhizn'*, 10 Sep 1929.

31. G. A. Chigrinov, *Bor'ba KPSS za organizatsionno-khozyaistvennoe ukreplenie Kolkhozov* (1970) p. 48.

32. *Pravda*, 26 Nov 1929 (report delivered on 21 Nov).

33. *Ekonomicheskoe Obozrenie*, no. 9 (1929) pp. 39-51; in a letter to *Sel'sko-khozyaistvennaya Gazeta*, 12 Dec 1929, he criticised his past defence of individual agriculture as a 'crude reactionary mistake' and announced that a substantial work was now in the press on *Organisation of the Large Economy in the Epoch of the Socialist Reconstruction of Agriculture* (his classic defence of the small farm was entitled *The Organisation of the Peasant Economy*).

34. See, for example, O. Targul'yan, *Ekonomicheskaya Zhizn'*, 21 Dec 1929; V. Milyutin, chairman of the Central Statistical Administration (Ts.S.U.), and G. Gordeev, in *Trudy Pervoi Vsesoyuznoi Konferentsii Agrarnikov-Marksistov*, I 38, 99-100.

35. Ibid., p. 176; the work in question was N. Kislyakov, *Poselki* (1928). (100 hectares = 1 sq. km.)

36. *Trudy Pervoi Vsesoyuznoi Konferentsii Agrarnikov-Marksistov* I 185. (1,600 hectares = an area of 4×4 km.)

37. Ibid., I 85-7. For these kombinaty, see p. 271 and note 61 below. Sovkhoz-kolkhoz kombinaty were sometimes known as combines (*ob''edineniya*); the terms appear to have been interchangeable.

38. Ibid., II [i] 56.

39. Cited from the archives in *Istoriya S.S.S.R.*, no. 4 (July-Aug 1969) p. 33.

40. *Resheniya partii i pravitel'stva po khozyaistvennym voprosam*, II (1967) 154.

41. *Sotsialisticheskoe Zemledelie*, 13 Feb 1930.

42. *Trudy Pervoi Vsesoyuznoi Konferentsii Agrarnikov-Marksistov*, I 65-72; he developed these thoughts in an article in *Ekonomicheskoe Obozrenie*, no. 1 (1930) pp. 41-50.

43. This was the co-ordinating committee for the kolkhoz agencies in the different Union republics; it was at this time in process of being superseded by the Kolkhoztsentr of the U.S.S.R. and the R.S.F.S.R.

44. See *Na Agrarnom Fronte*, no. 1 (1930) p. 40. A programme for the establishment of 'combine enterprises' or units 'of an agro-industrial type' was proposed in some detail by Professor V. R. Batyushkov in 1926, and was presented as a partial alternative to industrialisation via large-scale urban factory industry. He envisaged them as involving the collectivisation of agriculture and a considerable degree of mechanisation; they would vary in size from a few hundred to 30,000 hectares of arable land according to the type of production, with an average of 15,000 hectares and 3,000 households so that there would be 8,000 in the U.S.S.R. as a whole. *Planovoe Khozyaistvo*, no. 5 (1926) pp. 107-27; he also published a pamphlet *Postroenie agro-industrial'nykh kombinatov* (1929) which I have not seen; see also article by

N. Oganovsky in *Sel'sko-khozyaistvennaya Gazeta*, 19 Nov 1929.

45. *Ekonomicheskaya Zhizn'*, 26 and 27 Dec 1929; after a brief notice on 26 Dec, *Pravda* did not apparently report the meeting further. The following estimates were given in the reports of the conference and in *Na Agrarnom Fronte*, no. 1 (1930) p. 39, for particular districts, though, to judge from the area given, evidently sometimes covered several districts.

District	Total cost (in million roubles)	of which from local population	Cost per hectare	Area (in thousand hectares)
Balandinskii, Lower Volga	37	14	349	107–260
Mineral'nye Vody, North Caucasus	17	9	74	500
Volchanskii, Ukrainian S.S.R.	28	18	255	110
Mekhonskii, Ural	14	5	105	134
Chern. okrug, Crimean A.S.S.R.	9	3	300	30
Yendovishchenskii, Central Black Earth region	33	?	?	?
Yessatukovskii	22	11	?	?
Likhoslavl	60	35	150	400
Kashira	37	?	370	99
Petrovskii, Orenburg okrug	20–30	10	60–90	340
Gorodetskii, Belorussian S.S.R.	65	25	650	100

46. *Sel'sko-khozyaistvennaya Gazeta*, 9 Jan 1930. In an address to the Communist Academy on 22 Feb 1930, Larin also envisaged the future establishment, once electricity had become the main motive power for agriculture, of agro-towns with several tens of thousands of inhabitants serving an area of 200,000 hectares; the present villages would become stores on the outskirts of the kolkhoz (*Ekonomicheskoe Obozrenie*, no. 3 (1930) pp. 65-6).

47. *Na Agrarnom Fronte*, no. 1 (1930) pp. 39, 44; cf. Batyushkov's proposal in 1926 that 8,000 combines should be established with 15,000 hectares of arable land each (see note 44 above).

48. *Krest'yanskaya Gazeta*, no. 104, 30 Dec 1929; *Sel'sko-khozyaistvennaya Gazeta*, 4 Jan 1930.

49. Decision of 4 Jan 1930, cited in *Voprosy Istorii*, no. 3 (1965) p. 14.

50. *Sotsialisticheskoe Zemledelie*, 23 Feb 1930.

51. Ibid., 26 Mar 1930, describing the situation in the early part of February.

52. In *Na Agrarnom Fronte*, no. 2 (1930) p. 11, M. Golendo argued that the optimum territorial unit of management within the area served by an M.T.S., would not usually correspond to the rural settlement, so that the territory would have to be reorganised; he criticised Markevich for supposing that the size of each farm unit would be 'predetermined by the historically established dimensions of the villages'.

53. *Pravda*, 12 Jan 1930; *Na Agrarnom Fronte*, no. 5 (1930) pp. 31, 36-7; no. 7-8 (1930) pp. 86-7, 92, 95.

54. In the Ural region, in addition to Gigant the kolkhoz for the Shatrovskii district included 215,000 hectares before the end of 1929 (*Izvestiya*, 13 Jan

1930); in the Lower Volga region, one kolkhoz included 354,000 and another 259,000 hectares (*Sel'sko-khozyaistvennaya Gazeta*, 4 Jan 1930); for kolkhozy covering over 30,000 hectares in the North Caucasus and the Central Black Earth regions, see *Pravda*, 13 Dec 1929, *Sotsialisticheskoe Zemledelie*, 23 Feb 1930; for Khoper okrug, see *Krest'yanskaya Gazeta, Izdanie dlya Nizhne-Volzhskogo Kraya*, no. 98, 10 Dec 1929; no. 32, 23 Apr 1930. In Votsk region, although tractors were very scarce, dozens of giant kolkhozy were established, sometimes embracing as many as 300 settlements; these giants 'normally absorbed everything on this vast territory, turning into some kind of "great universal store"' (*Na Agrarnom Fronte*, no. 5 (1930) p. 35).

55. *Na Agrarnom Fronte*, no. 1 (1930) pp. 39, 41.

56. *Narodnoe khozyaistvo SSSR* (1932) pp. 130-1; *Izvestiya*, 9 Mar 1930. The figures for 1 Mar 1930 are certainly overestimates; the exaggeration presumably affected the number of households in kolkhozy rather than the number of kolkhozy, so that the size of the average kolkhoz on 1 Mar 1930 is likely to be overestimated.

57. For the number of households per kolkhoz, see S. Minaev (ed.), *Sotsialisticheskoe pereustroistvo sel'skogo khozyaistvo SSSR mezhdu XV i XVI S''ezdami VKP(B)* (1930) p. 280; for the number of households per village, see p. 270 above.

58. *Sotsialisticheskoe Zemledelie*, 12 Mar 1930.

59. 484 groups had apparently been formed in 22 of the 40 okrugs by the beginning of March, and in 15 of these more than 50 per cent of the kolkhozy belonged to groups (ibid.).

60. Minaev (ed.), *Sotsialisticheskoe pereustroistvo* . . . , pp. 239-41; many of the groups were said to have been a mere formality.

61. *Sotsialisticheskoe Zemledelie*, 4 Mar 1930. For these combines, see also p. 267 above. The Central Committee resolution of 5 Jan 1930 welcomed experiments, in areas with a considerable number of sovkhozy, in 'a type of combined economy' based on a sovkhoz and supplying tractor-ploughing, machine-harvesting and other services to kolkhozy by contract for payment (*Resheniya partii i pravitel'stva po khozyaistvennym voprosam*, II (1967) 154-5), and a conference was held on the subject later in the month. A Sovkhoztrest report of 6 Feb 1930 described the setting-up of a combine around the sovkhoz 'Khutorok' in the North Caucasus, with a total area of 150,000-200,000 hectares, in which in addition to tractor services the sovkhoz factories processed the products of the kolkhozy and used their unskilled labour; the report also condemned a sovkhoz in the Lower Volga region for having in effect completely absorbed the kolkhozy, and listed various other combines in process of formation (*Materialy po Istorii SSSR*, VI (1959) 311-21). Sovkhoz-kolkhoz combines were seen to be particularly important on the grounds that in many areas state virgin lands were scattered in plots of 2,000-3,000 hectares (in the Central Volga region, such lands amounted to 650,000 hectares in all); if sovkhozy were to be developed successfully in these areas, peasant lands must be included in the crop rotation (*Na Agrarnom Fronte*, no. 1 (1930) p. 43). A recent Soviet commentator drily remarked about all this that 'the directive on setting up kolkhoz-sovkhoz kombinaty was in practice hardly carried out at all' (*Materialy po Istorii SSSR* VII (1959) 316 n).

62. *Sotsialisticheskoe Zemledelie*, 12 Mar 1930.

63. Ibid., 9 Mar 1930.

64. *Izvestiya*, 17 Mar 1930.

65. *Sotsialisticheskoe Zemledelie*, 26 Mar 1930.

66. A circular from Narkomzem of the R.S.F.S.R. on breaking up the giants was issued early in April 1930 (*Istoricheskie Zapiski*, LXXVI 35); further articles condemning 'gigantomania' by Markevich and by Khataevich, secretary of the Central Volga regional party committee, appeared in *Pravda*, 8 Apr, *Izvestiya*, 6 May 1930; see also Gaister, in *Na Agrarnom Fronte*, no. 3 (1930) pp. 10-11, and Vareikis, secretary of the Central Black Earth regional party committee, ibid., no. 3 (1930) pp. 30-1.

67. Minaev (ed.), *Sotsialisticheskoe pereustroistvo* ..., pp. 237-8.

68. *Na Agrarnom Fronte*, no. 7-8 (1930) pp. 88, 100.

69. Minaev (ed.), *Sotsialisticheskoe pereustroistvo* ..., p. 238.

70. For the figures for 1 Mar 1930, see note 57 above; for the figures for May 1930, see *Narodnoe khozyaistvo SSSR* (1932) pp. 130-1.

71. Ibid., p. 133.

72. *KPSS v Rezolyutsiyakh*, III (1954) 53.

73. *Sotsialisticheskoe Zemledelie*, 27 July 1930.

74. *Planovoe Khozyaistvo*, no. 5 (1930) pp. 79, 16.

75. Developments after the summer of 1930 will be discussed in a book which this author is now writing.

76. *Istoriya SSSR*, no. 4 (July-Aug 1969) p. 35.

77. *Kollektivizatsiya sel'skogo khozyaistva. Vazhneishiye postanovleniya Kommunisticheskoi Partii i Sovetskogo pravitel'stva, 1927-1935* (1957) p. 322.

78. Between 1930 and 1932 the number of kolkhozy served in part or whole by M.T.S.s rose from 4,600 to 92,500 and the number of M.T.S.s from 462 to 2,916; thus the number of kolkhozy per M.T.S. rose from 10·0 to 49·5. See *Istoriya SSSR*, no. 4 (July-Aug 1969) p. 38.

79. See A. Baykov, *The Development of the Soviet Economic System* (1947) pp. 203-4; in July 1932, for example, a document of the Central Volga authorities described the revival of 'leftist gigantomania', in the form of giant kolkhozy with 1,000 and more households (*Kollektivizatsiya sel'skogo khozyaistva v srednem povol'zhe (1927-1937 gg.)*, pp. 315-21).

80. See the account by L. Richter in J. Degras and A. Nove (eds.), *Soviet Planning: Essays in Honour of Naum Jasny* (1964) pp. 32-42; the proposals made in 1950-1 strongly resembled those of January 1930, but were more modest: the agro-towns of 1950 were intended to have a few thousand inhabitants rather than tens of thousands, and to consist at least in part of individual dwellings rather than blocks of flats.

13 'Taking Grain': Soviet Policies of Agricultural Procurements before the War

MOSHE LEWIN

DURING the so-called era of the Five-Year Plans in the Soviet Union, and indeed during the whole of Stalin's rule, grain (and the ways of securing it) played a crucial role in the Soviet system. It was a strategic raw material indispensable to the process of running the state and of industrialising it. The term 'strategic', with its military connotations, is here quite appropriate; the grain, as leaders would constantly remind their subordinate administrations, 'would not come by itself' and had therefore to be literally extracted. Such extraction of grain from peasants could not proceed as a normal economic activity. In order to succeed, so the leaders felt, a state of mobilisation had to be declared for the duration of the campaign, with party cells and specially created shock-administrations mightily seconded by the state's punitive organs.

Not surprisingly, as the whole operation assumed the character of a semi-military requisitioning, it contributed towards shaping the Soviet economy as a *'sui generis* war economy'.[1] *Zagotovki* – the Russian term for procurement of agricultural produce which we shall be using here – was probably a linchpin of this war economy, as the single activity which required more large-scale mass coercion than any other state activity in those years. Year after year, the *zagotovki* campaign was a difficult affair taking up the energies of many agencies, including the Politburo itself which supervised closely all the stages of the campaign and constantly intervened in it. For a good quarter of a century, extracting grain from the peasants amounted to a permanent state of warfare against them and was understood as such by both sides. For the peasants, *zagotovki* became a symbol of arbitrariness and injustice and they employed all possible means of passive resistance and even sabotage against the squeeze. The state responded by devising counter-measures to outmanœuvre every subterfuge and to close every escape-valve which could be used by peasants – not to mention the crudest punishments whenever these were deemed necessary.

A campaign of this scope and character, naturally enough, became the central activity of the state in the countryside and moulded the state's relationship with the peasants. It became the essence of party policies in the countryside to which all the rest was subordinated. In this way, Soviet agriculture, the kolkhoz system and – in many aspects – the character of the whole polity, were shaped by this peculiar and simple procedure of 'taking grain'.[2]

It is therefore worth our while to sketch out, briefly, the main stages of the *zagotovki*, its methods and its features. As grain procurement was the crux of the matter, we shall devote most of our attention to it; the extraction of other farm products, like meat and milk, though important, can be dealt with only cursorily, for the methods applied in this sphere were borrowed from the grain front.[3]

I. TOWARDS A NEW PATTERN: 1928-30

During the N.E.P. period, from roughly 1924, when the tax-in-kind was replaced by a simple tax-in-cash, and up to 1928, the state resorted to grain procurements through its commercial agencies and Government-controlled co-operative organisations. But this was then, essentially, a commercial operation, consisting of buying grain from peasants at a market price. To be sure, some gradual changes were introduced during those years which favoured the state agencies and discriminated against the private dealers, such as denying to the latter credit by banks or putting obstacles in the way of their shipment arrangements. From 1925, governmental limit-prices were introduced which the state's agents were not supposed to overstep. But the private dealers were not eliminated, there was no state monopoly in grain, and sales to the state were not made compulsory. Furthermore, the numerous state and co-operative agencies engaged in those purchases conducted their businesses with the peasants exactly as any market operator would do it: they competed among themselves, disregarded the price-limits, bid up prices and collaborated with the skilful private traders by either buying grain from them, or by using them as their purchasing sub-agents. One should also be reminded that towards the end of the N.E.P. the state purchases managed to concentrate some

12-14 per cent of the gross harvest, and some 56-7 per cent of the marketable grain that the peasants were willing to part with. These figures will become more meaningful to the reader as we proceed.[4] But this NEPmen's near-idyll ended abruptly in the winter and spring of 1927-8, when such methods of procuring grain stumbled and ushered in the 'grain-procurement crisis', as peasants preferred to sell the better-priced animal products and technical crops rather than the relatively underpriced grain which could be put to better use in stock breeding, for personal consumption or for building up reserves.

The Government, alarmed by the dwindling procurements and the prospect of being starved out of power by the peasants' self-interested behaviour, resorted to so-called 'extraordinary measures' consisting of confiscating grain, though still paying a near-market price for it and even raising it quite considerably during the next campaign.[5] Such measures were presented as temporary and, at the beginning, sincerely so. In fact, normal market-procurement practices were never afterwards restored and the 'extraordinary' soon became ordinary practice – though not without dramatic upheavals.[6]

1928-9 was still a transition year in the history of the *zagotovki* campaigns; the private merchants were hard pressed and driven out of the markets, but many were still functioning and, obviously, preferred by the peasants as they were willing to pay them much more than the state. The numerous governmental agencies still kept competing with each other and, on the whole, coped badly with their task. The extraordinary measures, which were, as promised, eased at the beginning of the campaign, were soon restored, but the overall result was, nevertheless, weaker than in 1927-8, itself an emergency year: as only 10·7 million tons of grain were collected, against 11 million in the earlier campaign (but in this latter total, the share of food grain as against forage was then significantly higher).

Such facts definitively swung the Government into a complete reshaping of its relations with the peasantry. The First Five-Year Plan with its ambitious targets and insatiable pressures for ever more investment resources had just been launched and was becoming a huge national effort on an unprecedented scale. The countryside, if not properly controlled and mastered, was able to wreck the whole effort: such was clearly the conclusion drawn by some of the key leaders from the 'grain crisis' and the continuing difficulties thereafter. The two campaigns conducted by emergency methods in 1927-8 and 1928-9 gave the necessary experience, and preparations were made to meet the next challenge during 1929-30 on entirely new lines. The two major far-reaching innovations introduced in the autumn of 1929 were the launching of the collectivisation drive, and the abolition, *de facto*, of the whole N.E.P. framework. The single clearly discernible factor which triggered off these two interconnected changes was the transformation of the *zagotovki* into a compulsory state duty and, particularly, the set of means employed in imposing this new policy on the peasants. Critics of the Government charged its policies contemptuously with having 'slid into forced collectivisation on the wave of forced *zagotovki*' – and this was a substantially correct statement.[7] We shall show later the relevance of the methods of squeezing grain to the ways of forcing peasants into kolkhozy, and to the ways of running the kolkhoz system. But let us first outline the main stages through which the whole system passed before it evolved into a stable pattern.

The 1929-30 campaign should concern us, to begin with, because it exhibited many of the features of the framework which was to emerge in a definitive form by the end of 1933. The agencies which previously competed with each other were now unified, considerably streamlined and organised into a powerful apparatus led from the centre by specially designed bodies.[8] Instead of the numerous central, republic and local organisations, only a few were now allowed to operate, to ensure unity of policy, command and control of the entire campaign.

On the eve of the following year a method of contracts (*kontraktatsiya*) had been introduced into the grain-exchange sphere which was borrowed from the areas of technical crops. This method consisted of signing up individual peasants, whole peasant communities or kolkhozy before the sowing campaign on contracts for the supply of grain to the state. It was intended to be a bilateral agreement, freely signed, with obligations on both sides, as a deal with reciprocal advantages. The Government was supposed to advance money, to supply goods and means of production, and to help with grain loans when necessary. The peasant would agree to deliver a certain, not clearly specified, minimum of grain, and enjoy special premia for sales of grain above those minima. Initially, neither the signing-up nor the parting with surpluses above those stipulated by the contracts were compulsory.

The Government pinned great hopes on this method – and it stuck to this practice until the end of 1932. It was meant to be a powerful new tool for planning agricultural production which would introduce predictability to the thorny delivery process and ensure stability and security in the country's food supplies.

The idea was no doubt interesting, and it was many years later successfully applied by the Polish Government after they abolished the kolkhozy in 1957. But in the Soviet case this idea was killed before it came to be seriously tested and operated. The trouble was that already, in the autumn of 1929, signing up became compulsory, and the prices paid to producers – compulsory too – were by now beginning to lag seriously behind the market. Furthermore, the Government began evading its contractual obligations. Advance payments were soon to be abolished, and promises of supplies were not kept. Obviously, in these conditions both sides lost interest in the contracts, though – as mentioned – the Government stuck to the procedure and made it an obligation to sign, especially for the kolkhozy. But whatever the content of such a contract, the actual quantities of grain to be delivered were by now fixed by planned delivery quotas prepared by the Government, and handed down by local officials to every village. Kolkhozy became aware by now, as a special decree of April 1930 brought home to them, that they would have to deliver from one-quarter to one-third of their crop in grain-producing areas, and one-eighth in the other areas. Furthermore, the delivery was to be accompanied by a vociferous campaign enjoining kolkhozy and also private farmers to give up not just these or other legally prescribed quantities, but 'all surpluses', with the notion of 'surplus' becoming dangerously extendible, much at the discretion of local authorities.

For the well to do and the kulaks a special procedure was devised: they were not allowed to sign contracts, but had fixed (*tverdye*) quotas imposed on them independently of their sowings and output. By this token, thanks to the extendibility of categories like 'kulaks', and especially 'well to do' (*zazhitochnye*), many peasants were stripped in this campaign – and in the two previous ones – of all grain reserves they might have accumulated during past years.[9] For the stronger producers of the Soviet countryside the loss of reserves meant the beginning of the end for them as farmers. In fact, as the *zagotovki* were proceeding in the autumn and winter of 1929-30, they eventually grew into a full-fledged 'dekulakisation' of the well to do, whereas millions of the other peasants were forcibly driven into kolkhozy.

Unfortunately for the newly established kolkhozy, they were themselves handicapped at their birth by the same *zagotovki*, partly because of the tough delivery quotas and partly because of the extremely chaotic way in which these quotas were distributed. The method of central plans descending from above as an imperative command, being split into local quotas by intermediary echelons of the administration, and finally worked out into detailed assignments to kolkhozy, villages and private farmers by the *raion* and the *selsoviet*, had all the unavoidable features of 'mechanical' planning which have characterised all Soviet planning ever since. In the case of agriculture, with its infinite diversity of local conditions, such a method was particularly pernicious. Targets coming from above were accompanied by a power-ful pressure on lower echelons to meet those targets 'at any price' – an expression quite current in administrative orders, and coupled with a reminder of the appropriate paragraphs of the Criminal Code in store for the laggards. Such pressures did not leave much leeway to local officials to adapt the final quotas to the conditions and possibilities of kolkhozy and of the other farmers. A mechanical distribution of quotas resulted, mindful only that the sum total demanded from above be secured, though many experts were calling for a more sensible approach.[10]

For delivery quotas to be an economic proposition, or at least not to wreck the producing unit, such quotas had to be calculated on the basis of carefully composed grain and fodder balances (*khlebofurazhnyi balans*), which would consider in detail the needs and possibilities of every kolkhoz separately, and of whole raiony. Such balances by their very character could not be anything but a basically local affair, with data coming from below and made dependent on the estimates of the producers themselves, to a large measure. Producers would obviously be able to use such balances in order to defend their own interests – and this was the reason which determined the Government's attitude to the whole problem. It soon came out very strongly against all those who wanted balances to serve as the basis for *zagotovki* assessments, presenting such demands as a subterfuge for defending the peasants and for sabotaging the interests of the state.[11]

As the 'mechanical' assessment gained the upper hand during the 1929-30 campaign, its damaging influence on the economics of the kolkhozy became apparent immediately; and in later years, as we shall see, the sapping of production capabilities of the countryside resulting from this way of doing things was to acquire catastrophic proportions. But one instance of such a sapping effect can be quoted now, as observers were already pointing to it in 1930: with the reserves of the well to do entirely wiped out by 'extraordinary measures' and the delivery quotas becoming tougher, the *zagotovki* soon enfeebled, and later dried out almost entirely, the quantities of grain which used to circulate in the inter-village and inter-district grain markets.[12] Such inter-village commerce played an important role in helping out in case of a local crop deficiency or in some plans for modest improvements on the farm, but the deep inroad into this resource by voracious *zagotovki* contributed towards rendering the countryside extremely vulnerable to the slightest climatic setback.[13]

The Government seemed rewarded and pleased by the result of the *zagotovki*: towards the end of 1929, earlier than in any other campaign, the plan was met and an unprecedented 16 million tons gathered. But at the same time bread supply in the cities had to be rationed, and during 1930 rationing was to spread to all foodstuffs. The Government had only just begun building up some state reserves of grain, but much more than before was now needed for the growing cities, technical plant growers and for the non-grain-producing areas, and the Government was also keen to resume substantial exports of agricultural produce to obtain foreign currency for purchasing machinery. But as at the same time collectivisation was being forced on reluctant peasants, a new calamity befell the country, a quite predictable result of the policies of the Government in the winter and spring of 1930: as peasants saw their horses and cows herded into the collectivised stockades against their wish, they preferred to slaughter their animals and sell or eat them before they themselves joined the kolkhoz. The blow caused by this process to the national economy was even worse than the damage inflicted on Soviet stock breeding by the German invasion eleven years later. Such slaughtering was to go on for some time, but even when it stopped, the numbers of draught animals and cattle still continued to dwindle as the result of inadequate care and bad husbandry. A trend towards recovery in this branch, which became discernible from 1935 onwards would not be sufficient to make good the losses before the war.

In 1930, in any case, which interests us here, the slaughter of cattle produced at first a transitory abundance of meat, soon to be replaced by an acute shortage of animal products aggravating the already tense food situation.

The authorities tried feverishly to stop the damage by temporarily discontinuing the collectivisation drive at the end of the spring and by letting people leave kolkhozy; the kolkhozy that survived were now allowed to let their members keep a family cow and a small private plot – two measures which were previously refused by the leadership. Another step taken consisted of transforming the *zagotovki* of animal products, which were up to now a market operation, into a compulsory operation on the pattern of grain.[14]

Thus, when the time came to prepare for the next campaign, in 1930-1, i.e. the one to be conducted basically after the harvest in the second half of 1930, the authorities resolved that it was to be based on two pillars: firstly, the campaign would be centred on an exact delivery plan prepared beforehand and reaching every village well before the harvest; secondly, the campaign would have an emergency character and the entire party would be mobilised for that task as its central activity during the *zagotovki* season.[15]

The Commissar for Internal and Foreign Trade, A. Mikoyan, was the chief planner of the operation. Once the central targets were approved – or imposed – by the Politburo, his office had to prepare targets for the big national regions, whereas the Commissariats's local organs (in republics and oblasti) would break the general figures down into more differentiated norms (so many quintals per hectare per crop) for their appropriate areas. On the basis of such norms, specially con- stituted committees in the *raiispolkomy* finished the planning and assignment job by computing the amounts of grain to be imposed on every kolkhoz and (with the help of the *selsoviety*) on every private farmer. The same committee was also charged with the arduous task of assessing the prospects for the future crop in their district, which had, of course, to be dealt with before the quotas were distributed.

As already mentioned, according to existing decrees the amounts to be taken from kolkhozy had to fluctuate within the limits of one- quarter to one-third of their crops (one-eighth in the non-grain- producing areas) – a very high toll indeed, but in fact not the final word yet, as the propaganda was hammering into the kolkhozy that any *pud* of grain sold to anybody other than the state amounted to helping class enemies and to criminal anti-state action. This meant that the official limits were not to be taken too seriously as guidelines, but that 'all surplus' was the real target. But this was no longer any guide. It was never defined and almost undefinable. Therefore the laborious planning by Mikoyan's agencies, their norms and quotas, were only lower limits – as was made perfectly clear by Mikoyan's (and the party's) own propaganda and actions against sales of any grain on the markets.

During the new 1930-1 campaign the badly battered kulaks were to be taxed, as previously, with firm quantities of grain, and the other non-collectivised peasants – still a majority of the rural population at that time – were legally bound to deliver prescribed norms of grain per hectare of their sowings, but not less than the amounts per hectare which the kolkhozy would have to supply.[16]

Both kolkhozy and private farmers were promised premia in industrial goods for either accurate deliveries or over-fulfilment of quotas – but such promises were all too often broken. The supply of goods to the countryside was extremely badly organised, and in any case the quantity of goods assigned to rural areas fell towards the end of 1930, compared with previous years.[17] But whatever the quantities of industrial goods, they were now firmly welded to the *zagotovki* campaign: those who were promised goods would not necessarily be supplied, but those who failed to deliver their quotas would be punished by refusal of indispensable merchandise.

The crop that grew in 1930 was a gift from heaven. All the disorders and excesses of the spring notwithstanding, it came to the excellent figure of 83·5 million tons, the biggest crop since 1913 (by certain estimates even bigger than in 1913). It was in anticipation of such a bounty that the *zagotovki* plans were drawn aiming at new records in grain collecting. The amount actually gathered from the 1930 crop was a record indeed: 22·1 million tons, compared with 16 million the previous year.

Such a crop and such procurements should have helped in mitigating the food shortages and in normalising supplies. Paradoxically, this was not to be the case. On the contrary, a further aggravation of the country's situation was in store. One reason for this was that the crop figure was exaggerated and the real crop, though still respectable, was nevertheless much lower: 77·1 million tons according to one source.[18] This would mean that the *zagotovki* in fact mopped up about 30 per cent of the crop, against some 14 per cent in 1928 (see above, pp. 281 ff.). Other reasons for the ensuing aggravation will be given later.

The reaction of the peasants to this type of campaign was predictable: it became current practice for them to use any possible device, subterfuge and escape-valve to ease this burden, in fact to sabotage it wherever possible. Every ounce of peasant shrewdness was put into practice, including hiding data on real sowings, harvests and grain actually threshed; premeditated poor harvesting or threshing so that they could return later for a second go and use the returns for themselves; pilfering and hiding any grain they could put their hands on; somewhat later, during the hungry years of 1931-4, many would go out into the fields and cut off spikes before the harvests – the 'hairdressers' (*parikmakhery*), as the press called them.[19]

It very soon became clear to the authorities that there was no difference between the still uncollectivised peasants and the kolkhozniki, in so far as trying to defend their bread was concerned. Kolkhoz members would call – and the press would predictably dub them 'kulak slogans' – for using the grain 'first for ourselves'. Many peasants would hide grain in holes, and kolkhoz administrations all too often connived in such practices. And, the sum of irony, the allegedly proletarian sovkhozy, 'the people in leather jackets' as Mikoyan euphorically characterised them, who went out into the steppes and built the new grain factories, soon began to display a behaviour common to other producers.

So, despite the good harvest, the campaign in the autumn of 1930 proceeded with great difficulties. The Ukraine, for example, was so stubborn that it even at some stage put the entire plan in jeopardy. The harassed local authorities and *zagotovki* agents preferred to concentrate on the more easily controllable kolkhozy and weakened their attention towards the private peasants. These could thus sell certain amounts on the black markets and make money, whereas the strictly supervised kolkhozniki came out of the whole affair considerably worse off than the non-affiliated. This was in itself not a small ideological setback, because it made the kolkhoz even more unpalatable and discouraged potential new entrants.

To put things right, to make 'the economic superiority of the kolkhoz' over the private farmers convincing and to save the *zagotovki*, the authorities redoubled their energy: a special mobilisation of workers and party officials to be sent to the countryside was decreed; a deluge of heavy fines was hurled on the recalcitrant peasants and taxes and delivery quotas were increased to punish them; mass searches for hidden grain were conducted; finally, to crown the operation, mass arrests were conducted and numerous court cases brought against the dodgers of the grain quotas.[20]

It goes without saying that the battle was joined by the leadership in terms of warfare against class enemies, with the well-to-do peasants (by now dekulakised, deported, or in any case impoverished) serving as the main villains. The trouble with these slogans was that the opposition to *zagotovki* was a general and genuine mass affair. By implication, 'kulak' came to mean just any peasant who tried to evade the *zagotovki*. This fact was unintentionally acknowledged by the party, as its propagandists began to circulate additional epithets like *podkulachniki* ('kulak hirelings') or the still more unspecified *kulatskie podpevaly* ('kulak choirboys') – terms that relinquished any claim to a sociological content, but had a clear political intention: to attack any disobedient peasant or official.[21]

So, the *zagotovki* of 1930-1 became growingly violent and, as in the previous year, developed into a new wave of deportations and the renewal of the temporarily dormant (since the spring of 1930) pressure on more peasants to join kolkhozy. This sequence became by now an established pattern: a *zagotovki* campaign in the autumn, with governmental reprisals growing as peasants offered stubborn resistance; then a new wave of mass arrests and deportations, as a shock treatment to prepare the next stage; finally, in the last stage, inducing new millions of peasants to join kolkhozy.

The same pattern was to be repeated on a grand scale during the next two years, and on a lesser scale and with modifications in the ensuing years. Obviously, still more shattering blows had to be delivered to the peasants before a somewhat more regular kolkhoz system emerged, pointing to a certain degree, at least, of acceptance by peasants of the kolkhoz and of the *zagotovki* as an unavoidable reality. Events during the following two to three years amounted to precisely such 'education' of the peasants, to make them accept the new order.

II. ZAGOTOVKI AND FAMINE: 1931-3

Though some of the events of the ensuing years will look like a simple repetition of the pattern just alluded to, in fact, as they constantly gained in breadth and in gloom, they finally reached proportions of a major national catastrophe.

The *zagotovki* seemed to proceed smoothly at the beginning of the 1931 campaign, but towards the end of the summer grain suddenly 'stopped' flowing in. Immediately, 50,000 emissaries were sent from the cities to help the local officials. As crops in the eastern regions (the Urals and Siberia) were poor, the Government, however reluctantly, had to reduce the quotas for these regions, but pressed harder on the others to secure the overall target. The Ukraine and other areas had their initial targets raised, so that the Ukraine, though its crop was mediocre, was finally forced to give up more grain than in the bountiful previous year. Once more, no grain came from the peasants spontaneously. As peasants kept resisting and numerous local administrations claimed that the targets were too big, the central authorities reacted by more of the same: demotion of local administrations, dispersal of whole kolkhozy, mass arrests and numerous expulsions from the party.[22] The Government knew that peasants would not become more co-operative, especially because it did not intend to, or could not, keep its own promises. The anticipated plan of supplies to rural areas was fulfilled only by half, and the goods shortage in the countryside became an additional, strong disincentive for peasants to part with their grain. In fact, many rural areas, as an authoritative source put it, 'became entirely stripped of manufactured goods'.[23] It was a reflection of an overall economic crisis which the country was plunged into; the inadequacy and ineptitude of the state's trade networks was a further aggravating factor. These networks, created hastily to replace the destroyed private and co-operative circuits of the N.E.P. period, could barely cope with their tasks.

The familiar feature of the previous campaigns – the inability to distribute the quotas to fit the real possibilities of districts and kolkhozy – became by now a real scourge for the countryside. Some kolkhozy and villages were over-taxed and nothing more could be taken from them whatever the repressions. As a way out, the numerous professional and voluntary 'plenipotentiaries' (*upolnomochenny* – a familiar figure of the emergency methods of those years), backed by repressive legislation and G.P.U. squads, returned with renewed demands to those who had already fulfilled their quotas. Such reimposition was a breach of promise and of legality which matched the worst of what the 'kulak propaganda' was anticipating, and as these practices went on, the countryside was squeezed dry, especially the numerous regions in which the crop that year was very poor. Kolkhozy suffered probably more than other farmers. Many of the kolkhozy saw all their fodder taken away, and much of their seed as well, and the authorities kept coming back, sometimes three or four times, and demanding ever more, of extra (*vstrechnye*) plans.[24] No wonder that the passive resistance grew into serious political trouble in the Ukraine, the Northern Caucasus and Kazakhstan,[25] where 'anti-Soviet demonstrations' were reported – a term meaning different forms of rioting, protesting and attacking officials.

Nevertheless, the planned quantities of grain were forthcoming – and they were bigger than in the previous campaigns – but by now the central authorities had become worried about the effects of the orgy of violence to which peasants were submitted. A kind of cooling-off operation was begun, announcing a drive against excesses and the illegal treatment of peasants which was committed – so the centre claimed – in breach of the Government's 'line'. Such temporary halts on the over-zealous local executors of central policies were not new. They probably resulted from some internal pressure and criticisms of the policies in the upper leadership and amounted to putting the blame on local officials for their 'illegal' repressions. There was in fact hardly any problem in locating the real culprit: it would suffice to read the central press and numerous decrees of those days, with their shrill appeals to get the grain and to suppress any 'kulak' talk, or the attacks against the criminal 'reductionist tendencies' (*skidochnye nastroeniya*, demands to reduce the unfeasible quotas), to find out. But suddenly, when the bulk of the expected grain was already in the governmental granaries, the leadership became liberal and interested in legality. On this occasion the Ukrainian Central Committee thought fit to disclose that many local administrations were engaged in something amounting to 'kulak-inspired provocative abuses' against the peasants.[26]

The same Ukrainian C.C. was somewhat later to admit that the chaotic onslaughts of the *zagotoviteli* during the 1931 campaign caused difficulties in sowings in the autumn and following spring, which implied that people had no seeds or no energy to sow. In a fit of honesty, this C.C. declared that the 'excesses' of the *zagotovki* caused a complete disorganisation of the numerous kolkhozy; we can easily gather that these badly mauled and harassed organisations could not cope with such a routine peasant activity as sowing.

But more was looming behind it all. A great and growing trouble had by now emerged in the Ukraine and other grain-producing areas (elsewhere too, as we learn from modern sources): the ugly spectre of famine made its appearance. The Ukrainian C.C. spoke of numerous regions, especially Vinnitsa and Kiev, in which 'many kolkhozy found themselves faced with a critical food situation' – an expression used as a euphemism for famine by this Central Committee and later by modern Soviet writers for the same purpose. The emerging picture was distressing: famine began to spread in grain-producing areas, though their crop, however poor, was not catastrophic and would not normally produce such calamity. The Government (Ukrainian in this case) blamed local officials for being blind to the signs of growing trouble until it was too late,[27] and the reader will by now be aware of the reason for the scapegoat operation 'against excesses' undertaken from Moscow after the *zagotovki* campaign was basically over. Moscow would not admit any responsibility for the disaster.

But it was impossible for the Government to claim that only local leaders were blindfolded, so soon after the vicious campaign against some of the same local leaders who were clamouring against excessive *zagotovki* and warning about impending difficulties. Mikoyan certainly anticipated no problems at all when, at the end of 1931, he fixed for the next campaign the fabulous target of 29·5 million tons; but later, when the situation in the countryside towards the beginning of the 1932 campaign became increasingly alarming,[28] he would have to lower his target for grain to 18 million and to half that for live-stock products.

But these reductions occurred later. In the meantime the preparations for squeezing what Mikoyan initially planned were as stringent as ever. The Ukrainian C.C., which had recently fulminated against 'abuses', was now again on the battle lines fulminating against the eventual 'enemies' who were preparing to sabotage the coming campaign by pretending that the targets were too big. The Ukrainians were thus inviting the unavoidable new wave of 'excesses' (*peregiby*) and imitating thereby the familiar manœuvre of the Moscow Politburo which consisted in alternating damaging pressures with accusations against lower officialdom for the damages done.[29]

As the new campaign was being deployed, the local agencies were still suffering from a relative torpor resulting from the very recent punishments meted out to some of them for those excesses, and it took some time to spur their energies into a new wave of the same – especially as many local officials were aware of the desperate situation of the peasants, with many of them already hungry and with prospects for the new harvest at best quite poor. In addition to unfavourable climatic conditions, the work badly done by the disoriented and demoralised kolkhozy could not promise anything better.

Peasants, whether members of kolkhozy or still on their own, after having endured the difficult winter and spring of 1931-2 and well aware of the gloomy prospects ahead, were desperately preparing to use every technique in order to retain some of their grain.

All these factors conduced to a very sluggish start of the 1932 *zagotovki*. As the new crop began to be threshed, kolkhozniki tried to divide among themselves as much of the fresh grain as possible, with the connivance, or under the direct leadership, of their managements. Grain was used to feed the peasants working in the fields, to create all kinds of seed and reserve funds, to advance payments on the *trudodni* earned by the members – all actions which were supposed to be taken only after the state had taken its share. Not before, as was made clear by a circular of the Commissariat of Justice, which assimilated 'consumption of foodstuffs and forage over and above the established norms' and 'consumption of grain and forage above the plans established by authoritative organs' with 'pillage and delapidation of national property'.

Naturally, this campaign in the by now desperately hungry countryside moved more slowly and worse than during the corresponding autumn of 1931.

But the Politburo would not relax its vigilance. A new offensive was launched – and first of all a terroristic wave against agencies and local authorities still too reluctant to re-engage in excesses. Thanks to powerful 'stimulants', new records of anti-peasant repression were to be beaten.[30] The local authorities had no other way out than to return the pressure downwards. Formerly attacked for their ruthlessness, they now saw themselves attacked for 'rotten liberalism' towards the laggards, especially in the three principal granaries, the Ukraine, the Northern Caucasus and the Lower Volga (responsible for some 60 per cent of all *zagotovki*). Officials understood well the meaning of the calls addressed to them to engage in a 'truly Bolshevik struggle for grain', to 'carry blows' against the squandering of grain (this aimed at the above-mentioned unauthorised distributions to field-workers and kolkhoz funds), and finally, to get the grain 'at any price' (*vo chto by to ni stalo*) – another of those rather vague directives with a clear meaning, but still easy to be disowned by the leadership when necessary.

Spurred by a flood of orders and pressures, the local agencies now veered sharply from their alleged 'rotten liberalism' into another batch of 'sharp measures of repression', as our source put it.[31] Though the physical limits of an exhausted countryside and low crops forced the

Government to lower its demands in many regions (the Ukraine and the Northern Caucasus had their quotas lowered consecutively four times[32]), it still needed a big battle to take the rest. The Ukraine, the Northern Caucasus, the two Volga regions and other grain-producing areas, according to archives quoted by a modern author, 'dropped out of the organised influence of Party and Government',[33] and the Government responded by transforming these areas into a vast arena of an unprecedented repressive operation. Stalin, who took over personal command and shaped these policies, called for 'a smashing blow' to be dealt on kolkhozniki, because 'whole squads of them', as he saw it, 'turned against the Soviet state'.[34] A special Central Committee meeting was held in January 1933 to endorse some of the old and to adopt new, severe measures to keep the countryside under control.

Some of the actions taken before and after this plenum can be mentioned here. An unspecified but large number of peasants were arrested, and often, especially in the Kuban district (Northern Caucasus), were deprived of most of their belongings and deported to the North. Mass arrests, purges and dismissals struck many party members for having been engaged in 'defending kulaks' and in 'anti-state sabotage of the *zagotovki*'. In many places the squads of *zagotoviteli* went berserk (with an unmistakable blessing from above: Kaganovich, Molotov and other top leaders were on the spot) and stripped the recalcitrant villages of any grain they could lay their hands on. This included grain the peasants had legitimately earned and been paid for their *trudodni*.[35] This was an obvious sentence to death by starvation, though an unknown number of straight shootings also probably took place.

As these events were unfolding, the grain-producing areas were by now, in the winter and spring of 1932-3, in the throes of a terrible famine. The Soviet Government never officially acknowledged this fact, though the *woolly* formula used by the Ukrainian C.C. ('the critical food situation in many kolkhozy') was the nearest to the mark. But publications in the post-Stalin period, especially *belles-lettres*, said much more, though without giving estimates of the scope of the disaster.[36]

Many factors contributed to the famine. The vagaries of climate and crops were this time not the central cause. The crops in 1931 and 1932, though poor, were not catastrophic. Collectivisation which played havoc with agricultural production was even more of a factor. The slaughter of stock dealt a shattering blow to Soviet agriculture, and the retreat the Government operated by allowing kolkhozniki to have a private plot and a family cow came too late to avoid the damage.

As to the surviving herds, the newly founded and hastily organised kolkhozy did not know how to cope with them – and the hæmorrhage continued for quite a time.

But the squeeze operated on the rural economy by the *zagotovki* was probably the main factor. 32 per cent from the 1931 crop (and an even higher percentage from kolkhozy) was a blood-letting. And this was a national average. In some regions – the Kiev district, for example – no more than one-fifth of the crop was left to the kolkhoz-niki.[37] Facing the dwindling cattle and the disappearing grain, the newly organised kolkhozy, caught in the *zagotovki* clutches, lacked both experience and interest in doing a proper job for ensuring the next crop.

Moreover, as if the cup was not yet full enough, the Government, fascinated by its heavy industry targets and mindless of minimal precautions, embarked upon an ambitious grain-exportation policy. During the N.E.P. only relatively modest amounts were exported, but in 1930 a massive 4·8 million tons, and the next year another huge 5·2 million tons, were shipped abroad. This turned out to be folly. In the spring of 1932 the situation in the countryside was so bad that the Government even had to import some grain, though it was only a trickle which could not do much to alleviate the situation. Prestige was probably the reason why more was not imported to help out the starving.

Economists can easily estimate how much this 10 million tons of exported grain in two years helped industrialisation, as against the losses in human lives and the economic potential of agriculture;[38] in any case these exports were soon stopped, and the unsoundness of this policy acknowledged in deeds if not in words.

III. 'HARD LINE', 'SOFT LINE'?: 1933-4

Against this background of tenuous battles for grain in a famine-stricken countryside (its repercussions were still being felt and seen well into 1934), the Government embarked upon a considerable over-hauling of its procurement policies and machinery, to meet the campaign of autumn 1933 in strength and to introduce some stability into the shattered rural economy. The essential ingredients of the new strategy were as follows: firstly, at the end of 1932, a new centralised administration was created, the Committee for Procurements (Komzag in Russian, which we shall be using), under the auspices of the inter-ministerial co-ordinating body for labour and defence (S.T.O.). But the centralised might bestowed upon this body was further under-lined by attaching it, somewhat later, directly to the Council of Commissars (Sovnarkom). At all administrative levels of the country special bodies (local *komzagi*) were created, down to every raion. Kuibyshev, former head of Gosplan, was put at the head of Komzag, soon to be replaced by M. A. Chernov.[39]

The main idea behind such a body was to secure unity of command and structure, and to give it enough power both to cope with the formidable *zagotovki* function, and to make its agents independent from local pressures and dedicated only to their own administration. The practice of creating such special bodies, endowed with emergency powers, to impose the state's will down to the remotest village and to make its agents, hopefully, immune to the all-dissolving mass and local influences, now became a standard way of the 'Bolshevik style of organisation'. The Civil War is the quite obvious source of inspiration for such methods.

Secondly, yet another special shock-administration was organised and sent to the raiony to serve as political departments in the machine-tractor stations. Reporting only to its own hierarchy directed from the centre, this administration was given superiority over the regular local party and soviet bodies and, significantly, included, in every station, a special G.P.U. deputy (himself rather independent from the rest as he had his own command line). 23,000 experienced cadres, with long-standing party affiliation and administrative, often military, careers behind them, were selected to staff these bodies (the *politotdely*), which were made responsible for managing the kolkhozy, the rural economy and much else besides.[40]

Thirdly, through a set of enactments, principles for grain deliveries were formulated and presented as a new and long-term policy; the chief piece of this legislation was the Government and Party decree of 19 January 1933.[41]

This law was a result of the tacit recognition by the Government – soon made explicit in the press commentaries – that the existing practice of target distribution and grain levying was faulty. It was chaotic in the extreme, and it fettered agricultural production. As delivery plans were in fact unpredictable and capriciously changing, it introduced instability into kolkhozy, and lack of security as to their future incomes and production possibilities. But its own incomes, which interested the Government above all, were also unstable and unpredictable, as experience had shown, and could not be secured without enormous efforts.

The innovation consisted in declaring that the *zagotovki* become a compulsory state tax. Compulsory they were, as we already know, but now, as a tax, they were supposed to become a regular and predictable norm, though it was to be a harsh norm, high and independent of the size of crops – as the decree made clear. Also it was not liable to changes, other than by the central Government; the local governments were forbidden under penal responsibility – so the law firmly promised – from changing the plans and engaging in those fatal repeated reimpositions which the peasants hated and the economy could not bear.

At present, the Government intended to create conditions for enhancing the interest of peasants in promoting kolkhoz production, by solemnly promising that the kolkhozy would know several years in advance what amounts of grain per hectare they would have to supply, and that the surpluses above the quotas would be entirely at the disposal of the kolkhozy, either for internal use or for sales on the kolkhoz market.

Such markets had already been legalised in the summer of 1932 – probably the gloomiest year of the Five-Year Plan crisis – in an effort to improve the country's desperate food situation as well as to provide some incentives to the kolkhozniki. Both the kolkhozy and their individual members were allowed to sell their surpluses on these markets at prices freely formed through supply and demand interplay. This was a retreat into some pale version of the N.E.P., and at first did not improve much; on the contrary, as this move raised hopes among peasants and some officials that compulsory deliveries would be abolished, the current state procurements suffered additional setbacks. But the error was soon to be corrected: any kolkhoz trade had to stop as soon as *zagotovki* began, and markets would be allowed to reopen, by special decree, only in those districts that fulfilled their quotas. Otherwise the culprits were promised to be pursued as speculators. The 1933 decree on *zagotovki* as a compulsory tax now put a special stress on the right to trade on kolkhoz markets any surpluses remaining after the deliveries. At least some in the Government seemed to be sincerely interested in discontinuing the devastating reimpositions and introducing some certainty both to the state's incomes and to the production process. In such a way the kolkhoz system would be offered minimal conditions for doing its job.

We shall see later whether such hopes were to materialise. For the moment, we should draw attention to one element, at least, in the whole strategy, which was undermining at the outset the promised predictability of the state's obligations. The new legislative package made it obligatory for the kolkhozy to pay the M.T.S.s in kind for their services. Hitherto the M.T.S.s were paid a fixed price in money per hectare for their ploughing or harvesting. The payment being independent from the results of their work (from the crops and yields), the M.T.S.s – as the Commissar for Agriculture, Yakovlev, bitterly complained – were interested in inflating in their reports the acreage dealt with by their machines, but they were indifferent as to whether they were sowing or harvesting grain or weeds.[42] The new law ordered the payment to be called henceforth *naturplata* (payment-in-kind, to distinguish it from the tax-in-kind, the *postavki*).

Consequently, all the talk about fixity of payments applied only to the part of deliveries called *postavki,* but the newly introduced category – the *naturplata* – was to be paid as a percentage of the crop, and thus only relatively fixed. The actual amount would become known only after the whole crop was gathered. The decrees on *naturplaty* were formulated in a harsh anti-peasant tone. They granted the M.T.S.s a decisive role in assessing the actual amounts of kolkhoz dues, and the right to collect it from the kolkhozy 'without demur' (*bezogovorochno*).[43]

At the beginning of 1933 when these decrees were promulgated, it might not have occurred to many what was involved in the *naturplaty*. But the M.T.S.s were increasingly relied upon by the Government as the key organ for securing the advancement of agricultural production and for controlling agriculture. The important special administration (*politotdely*) created to provide teeth for this M.T.S. as the new strategic lever has already been mentioned. The M.T.S., the sole state agency actually present on the fields of the kolkhozy, seemed well adapted to become also a major collector of *zagotovki*. In fact, in a few years' time, the *naturplaty* were going to become the main part in the state's overall grain collections;[44] but this part, as we know, was not a fixed figure, but a *pro rata*. The actual amount of grain to be supplied by kolkhozy became once more, by this bias, uncertain, quite contrary to the letter of the legislation which introduced this system.

This uncertainty was further deepened by a quite extraordinary device introduced formally in the same year of the great overhaul: the state took over full control and the last word over the assessment not only of the prospects of yields and crops, but also of the final figures. One more special administration was created for this purpose, centrally run, as all of them, and with the same pattern of local agencies made dependent on their special line from the centre. Some friction is reported to have taken place between the Commissar for Agriculture and the Sovnarkom, as the former wanted to give the kolkhozy themselves a say in assessing what their actual crops were, but the latter rejected this approach.[45] The final assessment of the figure, which was crucial for the fixing of the delivery quotas, especially of the payments to the M.T.S., was firmly lodged in the Government's hands, to the exclusion of the producers themselves.[46] It is not difficult to imagine how this method would influence the

Government's share in the real agricultural output.

Besides the assessment of the crop, the other key figure for the calculation of the delivery dues was the sowing acreage. The new decrees now legalised what had already been established practice for some time: the sowings were to be done according to governmental targets sent in from above to every village and made, like much else, compulsory and not open to reductions. Such reductions were explicitly forbidden[47] (though, one would guess, not increases of targets). The *zagotovki* dues would thus be calculated on the basis of the planned sowing targets, and peasants, or kolkhozy, would later have infinite trouble if they did not actually sow the prescribed acreage and crop.

In such a way, the main criteria for computing its imposition became wide open to the Government's wishful thinking. Once the targets were fixed, however, the problem of getting the grain from the peasants needed an additional lever: control over the threshing process. A decree therefore prescribed firmly (with appropriate penal clauses quoted in the text of the decree to warn transgressors) that 90 per cent of the proceeds of threshing had to go to the *zagotovki* and only 10 per cent distributed to peasants as advances for their labour, as long as the quotas were not fully met. It was clear that a fierce opposition was to be expected from the peasants against such a practice at a time when they themselves badly needed grain at a labour-intensive peak of the season, and when the reserves of food from the previous harvest would be all too often long exhausted. To ensure that the sensitive threshing operation suited the needs of *zagotovki*, the decree made it compulsory on kolkhozy to sell to the M.T.S. all their bigger threshing machines; if they had to do the job with smaller ones, the work had to be done on special grounds organised and supervised by the M.T.S.[48] In this way, the keys to the operation were transferred to the M.T.S. and another valve through which grain might have escaped the Government was hopefully closed.

From the middle of 1933, and until Kirov's death in December 1934, a relative lull seemed to have set in in many fields of Soviet policy. A set of more liberal measures could be discerned, beginning with more moderate targets of industrial growth and a promise of more attention to consumer needs during the next Five-Year Plan. Eventually, the cruder methods of mass repression, shootings and deportations were considerably curtailed. Behind the scenes, in the top leadership, pressures were exerted for a change of course and the adoption of different strategies in running the country. Stalin's policies might have been questioned and his removal contemplated among certain leaders. Observers link all these pressures and doubts to the emergence of a Kirov faction' or trend – though the existence of such a trend, however plausible, has never yet been convincingly proved.[49]

This problem cannot be dealt with here comprehensively, but for our central topic – the *zagotovki* – some proof can be given to substantiate the existence of pressures for rethinking agricultural policies. As the rural economy, now largely collectivised, continued to be a costly and largely disappointing affair, one would expect a tendency to arise to do something in order to make agriculture move. This could hardly be achieved without trying to improve the relations of the state with the mass of bitter, frustrated and hostile peasants. The press spoke freely about the fact that peasants distrusted any promise or pledge given by the Government; and one can surmise, as we just have, that stronger feelings than mere distrust must have been widespread.

And it was in fact a public speech by Kirov, though not, to my knowledge, in published speeches by any other leading figure, that a strong hint could be found of disappointment with the results of the current policies. In this speech, after having paid the ritual homage to the 'sacredness' of the *zagotovki*, Kirov objected to what was in fact, to use his own term, 'a squeeze' (*vykolachivanie*) – a term which very aptly characterised the whole procedure. Kirov by now knew very well, and said so, that such *vykolachivanie* was fraught with the danger of jeopardising the development of agriculture and of putting a brake 'on the further development of the kolkhozy and sovkhozy'.[50] More research is needed in order to discover what actual policy changes were proposed by Kirov or others; but the central thesis on which to base the changes, and a justification for such changes, is unmistakably present in this speech.

According to many sources, in the lower echelons of officialdom too a certain amount of opposition was present, in different forms, against the terroristic line towards agriculture and especially against the same *vykolachivanie* which Kirov criticised.

To be sure, the traditional tough-liners kept pressing for a harsh treatment of peasants, and the official legislation, as we shall see, followed suit, showing that these still had the upper hand. The fighting-slogan of hard-liners was the term 'sabotage' – and evidently appeals for treating recalcitrant peasants as saboteurs were tantamount to applying terror against them. Thus, for example, the militant journal of Komzag presented the situation in the following terms: 'Day in, day out, the central press keeps bringing a multitude of facts pointing to the existence, all too often, of an organised opposition to the deliveries of grain.'[51] The press material which this source had in mind consisted of numerous reports about peasants and managements of kolkhozy hiding grain, falsifying reports on sowings, preparing padded grain and fodder balances and a host of other subterfuges. From the severe pen of the General Procurator came appeals to the courts and other agencies to deal properly with such actions.

But the same journal and other sources allow one to infer that this time the peasants enjoyed a measure of support from sections of local state administrations, and the accusations of sabotage were directed against such people not less than against peasants. Many local officials seemed to be rather stubborn in demanding the lowering of the delivery quotas. Hard-liners would castigate such behaviour as 'reductionist tendencies', 'orientations on reduction' (of delivery quotas), though the translation of the Russian *skidochnye nastroeniya* does not render the flavour of this coinage. That these 'moods' were seen in the most sinister light by the hard-liners can be gathered from their accusations that such officials tend to 'put the interests of the kolkhozy above the interests of the state' – a charge which in the prevailing conditions was in fact easily reformulated as sabotage.[52]

All this was a serious affair in the eyes of the leadership. The 'reductionist' tendencies were strongly attacked during the July 1934 plenum of the Central Committee by leaders like Vareikis, Kossior and Postyshev,[53] though no source openly shows any top leader attempting to protect such moods of lower officials. In fact, even during those days of a relative relaxation of terror, many officials paid with their jobs or party cards, and sometimes were prosecuted in court, for their leniency towards peasants. Quite numerous among them were directors of sovkhozy, of M.T.S.s, and secretaries of raion party committees, for what clearly was either a defence of kolkhozy from impossible exactions or a fight to defend the economic viability of their own outfits.[54]

It is of particular significance that many officials of the political departments of the M.T.S., this crack unit of administrators sent at the beginning of 1933 to install obedience and order in the country-side, engaged themselves in such activities. They criticised unrealistic plans, often defended kolkhoz managements from accusations of embezzlement, and refused to endorse criminal prosecutions against them.[55] One modern writer frankly takes their side: these people, he states, well knew that the crop data were exaggerated and therefore that delivery quotas based on such data were unjustified.[56]

In conclusion, however scarce the data, it becomes clear that what the hard-liners from Komzag called 'organised sabotage of the *zagotovki*', as we have quoted above, was quite a serious affair; many local administrations, including the political departments, were reaching conclusions about the state of agriculture and the lines to follow which differed substantially from the prevailing tendency in Moscow. The irritated reaction of the Politburo proves this point. The political departments were now found guilty of 'having become identified (*sroslis'*) with local people' and thus outlived their usefulness for Moscow. At the end of 1934 the departments were dissolved.[57]

Notwithstanding pressures from below and the debate and hesitations in the centre, some of the legislation pertaining to *zagotovki* and policies in the countryside shows a persistent tendency to go on with the type of *vykolachivanie* policy which Kirov would have liked to mitigate. Against one concession to peasants – the arrears of deliveries for 1933 were cancelled and repayments of seed loans spread over three years[58] – several new measures were announced, surpassing in their anti-peasant fierceness many of the previous enactments. First, the kolkhozniki who grew some grain on their plots saw their norms of delivery raised to the level hitherto applied only to private peasants – 10 per cent more than kolkhozy were paying in zones not served by M.T.S.s.[59] This meant that a treatment reserved only to an openly discriminated category was now extended to all kolkhozniki. The same tendency is apparent in yet another decision, according to which obligatory deliveries of meat, milk and eggs by private peasants and kolkhozniki alike would not depend on their economic situation: they should supply these products even if they had no livestock of their own.[60] At a time when the numbers of cattle were declining and millions of peasant families had no stock, it seemed particularly sinister to impose on them deliveries of animal foodstuffs. Or was it intended as an incentive to spur peasants to acquire stock? If it was meant to provide such an incentive, the Government soon reached the conclusion that it had better help peasants to acquire private cows. Poverty was a sufficient incentive for a peasant family to want a cow, but they had no means to get it. 'Cowlessness' was a disaster, and Molotov promised solemnly that in just two years the problem would be solved[61] – though it eventually took more than two years to endow all kolkhozniki with this vital support.

The link between *zagotovki* and the collectivisation drive, the pressures, that is, applied to peasants to join kolkhozy with *zagotovki* quotas as a whip, can be illustrated by events which took place in the second half of 1934, pertaining to the remaining 5 million peasant families which had managed to stay outside the collectives. It was still a considerable mass – some 20 per cent of all peasant households – but their share in the country's agricultural production was already very small. This was not, as officially claimed, a result of the 'superiority of the kolkhozy'. It was rather the oppressive delivery quotas, special taxation and other vexatious measures that made their lives unbearable, and served both as a boost to join kolkhozy and to ensure such 'superiority' of kolkhozy.

In 1931 the delivery quotas of these smallholders were made bigger than those paid by kolkhozy. They were assessed according to sowing plans which were imposed on them, and dues were exacted from them often without regard as to whether they had actually sown that much, or indeed whether they had sown anything at all. Their sowings incidentally could be – and often were – just taken away from them, their horses subject to mobilisations for the benefit of kolkhozy, and cases were reported of whole families mobilised to work for kolkhozy, though such treatment was on some occasions condemned by the leadership as having been a 'deviation from the party line'.[62]

Somehow, during 1933 – and despite continuing harassment – the mass of the unenrolled peasants were given a sort of respite; local officials, who were hard pressed to show results in collections, preferred to concentrate on kolkhozy, as it was an easier job to get considerable amounts from them rather than to chase after the numerous evasive smallholders. Some of those officials obviously thought that in any case there was not much left that could be taken from the small fry. Therefore, though delivery quotas were demanded from them, there was less repression applied to them during this period, and especially not much pressure to join kolkhozy.

The officials were right in this sense. There was enough trouble in running the kolkhozy as they stood, and many kolkhoz members and managers did not see much interest in accepting new people, who in any case would dispose of their horse or cow before joining, if they still had any left. It may even be that some local authorities explicitly forbade the acceptance of such people.

But some time during the summer of 1934 the Central Committee found this situation wrong and stepped in forcefully. The existence of 5 million 'speculators' was found undesirable. The July plenum therefore launched a new campaign to complete collectivisation by enrolling the remaining millions of families. There was no more talk this time of dekulakisations or violent repression in order to achieve their aim. As Stalin advised a gathering of secretaries in July 1934, the method should consist of 'strengthening the taxation press'; what he meant by this can be gathered from the measures taken by the Government to make this 'press' work. In October an extraordinary levy in cash was decreed on the private peasants – and the decree did not even bother to explain why this had to be done.[63] Another decree, enacted soon after the plenum, was in fact even harsher: the delivery quotas for the smallholders, which stood at 10 per cent above the quotas for kolkhozy (not in M.T.S.s), were now raised to 50 per cent. All the allowances which had previously existed for sowing above the plans were abolished, and a special new law was added to allow for confiscation of all but a few specified personal belongings for failure by smallholders to meet the quotas.[64]

Such monetary and grain taxation went beyond the solvency of the smallholders. The Government was going 'for the kill'. Only two ways were left (for those who could not go to the cities): either to join the kolkhoz or to become salaried labourers in sovkhozy, if these were around. By signing up with a sovkhoz the peasant would become exempt from *zagotovki*. The role of the *zagotovki* as a whip for driving peasants to kolkhozy is thereby once more illustrated.

Before closing this section, it would be illuminating to listen to a frank explanation by a leader of why this renewal of the collectivisation drive took place. It was offered, once more, by Kirov, in one of his speeches. Kolkhozy, he explained, were often very weak producers and their standards of living lagged behind the non-enrolled peasants. The kolkhozniki – and the others – saw no advantage in the kolkhoz; they were worse off in the kolkhoz than the private peasants who could still find some escape-valves (some sales on the black markets, for example) which were not open to the kolkhoznik. Therefore, Kirov concluded, the coexistence of the kolkhozy with private smallholders had become an anomaly which had to be ended.[65]

Not much additional comment seems necessary. Here was a frank and bitter admission that kolkhozy could not stand competition and comparison even with the pauperised smallholders of those days.

IV. ZAGOTOVKI UP, OUTPUT DOWN: 1928-41

We should now have a look at the output figures of Soviet agriculture during the Five-Year Plans, between roughly 1928 and 1941, to be better able to assess some of the results of procurement policies (and of collectivisation for that matter). It was officially admitted prior to 1958 that during the First Five-Year Plan agricultural production suffered, but this was presented as an unavoidable cost involved in the complex undertaking of creating a radically new organisation of agriculture. The slump could not but be transitory and, it was claimed, after 1932 things were cheerfully improving.

But a statistical handbook published in 1959 showed that reality was very different and the situation in the pre-war countryside much gloomier than even the figures computed by Naum Jasny were implying. In the same 1959 a Soviet expert gave the first detailed account of the crop-assessing practices after 1932.[66] This is quite a complex story, describing different methods of doing the job, including notions like 'the optimum barn-yield' which was practised first, some intermediate way coming next, and finally, from 1939 on, the strictly speaking 'biological crop' or 'standing crop' (*na kornyu*). In any case, the results of these assessments were not published, and the crop statistics in physical units became during the Second Five-Year Plan a state secret. Only the figure for the bountiful 1937 crop was made known.[67]

A special administration which we have already referred to – the Central Commission for Assessing Yields and Crops (Ts.G.K.) – was entrusted with the job and, characteristically, was not interested in discovering the amounts of grain which were actually reaching the peasants' barns. It preferred to compute one or another of the variants of 'biological yields', meaning the estimate of the 'standing crops' before the harvest, without discounting realistically figures for losses which took place before the grain reached the barn. But the norms of delivery were based on such hypothetical assessments and the peasants found themselves taxed, to a great degree, on non-existing income, because the inflated assessment base had been higher than the actual yield by some 30 per cent. This was one of the basic reasons for the 'reductionist tendencies' referred to above among some local administrators, who tried to defend the peasants from this peculiar governmental form of cheating.

As in the case of taxing the products of non-existent cows, over-taxing through the device of 'biological crops' might have had behind it some strategy aimed at making the peasants improve the quality of their work and reducing the losses in grain occurring during and after the harvest. Such losses were staggering, and the leaders became acutely aware of it in the middle of 1934. Kirov in particular seemed deeply disappointed by this state of affairs. He quoted estimates showing 40 per cent of the crops in important agricultural areas being lost because of poor husbandry, and he could not but brood regretfully over the big improvement in the situation which could be achieved if only such losses could be reduced.[68] This topic was certainly among those being debated at the top leadership level, as some would tend to explain the losses as resulting from Government policies, but the hard-liners, notably Stalin and Molotov, would prefer to explain things in terms of 'kulak propaganda' or 'petit-bourgeois mentality', and to see the losses as grain actually wasted by the peasant. It was up to the peasants – so this position seemed to imply – to stop this nonsense; the method of teaching them the right way, advocated by these leaders, was to be implacable on *zagotovki* targets.

Mentality obviously counted for something, but this should include the mentality of leaders too. The *zagotovki* as 'incentive' did not seem to work. The figures emerging after Stalin's death show a picture of declining agricultural output not only during 1928-32 but also up to 1937. Some improvements in subsequent pre-war years could not make good the damage and significantly improve on the figures in the pre-collectivisation or pre-revolutionary years. The following tables will illustrate our point. As we do not dispose of definitive and authoritative data on the whole period, our data are compiled from different Soviet sources without checking or recalculating them; the figures are therefore not entirely consistent, especially the percentages which refer to crops differently estimated by the sources, and they have to be seen as an illustration rather than as any definitive computation. Annual figures for subsequent years in Table 1 were not available to me, except for 1937, with its fabulous crop of 97·4 million tons and 31·8 million tons of collections; we shall therefore use the

Table 1

Grain Crops and Government Grain Procurements
1928-40

Year	Crop (all grain) (million tons)	Procurements (million tons)	Share of procurements in total crop (%)	Share of procurements in crops of kolkhozy (%)
1928	73·3	10·7	14·7	—
1929	71·7	16·8	22·4	55·7
1930	77·1	22·1	26·5	27·5
1931	69·4	22·8	32·9	37·8
1932	69·8	19·0	26·9	27·5
1933	68·4	23·6	34·1	35·5
1934	67·6	26·9	38·1	35·3
1935	62·4	28·3	37·8	39·1
1936	—	—	—	—
1937	87·0	31·9	—	—
1938	67·0	—	—	—
1939	67·3	32·1*	—	—
1940	95·6†	36·6†	38·0	—

* The average per year for the whole period of 1938-40.
† This figure probably includes the grain from the territories incorporated after 17 September 1939. Therefore to be comparable to the previous figures it should be diminished, but the point is not clear to me.

Sources:
Yu. A. Moshkov, *Zernovaya problema v gody pervoi pyatiletki* (Moscow, 1966) p. 225, and his contribution to *Istoria sovetskogo krestyanstva i kolkhoznogo stroitelstva v SSSR* (Moscow, 1963) p. 270; I. E. Zelenin, in *Istoria SSSR*, no. 5 (1964) p. 18; M. A. Vyltsan, *Ukreplenie materialno-tekhnicheskoi bazy v gody vtoroi pyatiletki* (Moscow, 1959); I. A. Gladkov (ed.), *Sotsialisticheskoe narodnoe khozyaistvo SSSR, 1933-1940* (Moscow, 1963).

Table 2

Production of Grain and Procurements in Tsarist Russia
and during the Five-Year Plans in the U.S.S.R.
(annual averages, in million tons)

Years	Crop	Yield (quintals per hectare)	Procurements
1909-13	72·5	6·9	
1928-32	73·6	7·5	18·1
1933-7	72·9	7·1	27·5
1938-40	77·9	7·7	32·1

Sources:
Narodnoe khozyaistvo SSSR v 1958 godu, p. 352. For the pre-five-year-plan period, according to one source the yearly crop for 1924-8 was 69·3 million tons which is not small. Another author quotes for 1925-9 a yearly crop of 73 million, with a yield per hectare of 7·9 quintals. See M. A. Vyltsan, *Sovetskaya derevnia*, op cit. p. 41 and V. P. Danilov, *Sozdanie materialno-tekhnicheskikh predposylok kollektivizatsii selskogo khozyaistva v SSSR* (Moscow, 1957) pp. 94-5.

Table 3

Index of animal produce, 1928-40
(1913 = 100)

Year	Animal produce
1928	137
1929	129
1930	100
1931	93
1932	75
1933	65
1934	72
1935	86
1936	96
1937	109
1938	120
1939	108
1940	114

Source:
Narodnoe khozyaistvo SSSR v 1958 godu, p. 350.

available official annual averages to complete the picture (see Table 2).

If subjected to closer scrutiny, some of these figures too would be doubted, for example the yields in Tsarist Russia. In any case, for the general picture to be clearer, some additional figures would be useful,[69] especially for animal produce.

These figures are sufficiently eloquent, although they are still embellishing the situation somewhat. Value estimates are in this case less reliable than data in physical units, which are given in Table 4 for some selected, but important, items of animal produce.

Table 4

*Production of foodstuffs (of Animal Origin)
for 1913, 1928 and 1940*

Year	Meat and lard (live weight, million tons)	Including procurements (million tons)	Milk (million tons)	Eggs ('000 million pieces)	Wool ('000 tons)
1913	5·0	1·8	29·4	11·9	192
1928	4·9	1·6	31·1	10·8	182
1940	4·7	1·7	33·6	12·2	161
in kolkhozy alone*	0·9	0·2	5·6	0·5	78

* This means production of the collective farms but not including the output of the family plots of the kolkhoz members.
Source:
I. A. Gladkov (ed.), *Sotsialisticheskoe Narodnoe Khozyaistvo SSSR, 1933-1940* (Moscow, 1963) p. 360.

It is worth repeating that stock breeding did begin to recover slowly from 1935 onwards,[70] but this could not yet improve the situation much prior to 1940. The 1913 level was not reached by then either in numbers of heads or in production of foodstuffs from animals. Characteristically, the role of kolkhozy in this sensitive field remained insignificant. The bulk of animal foodstuffs was produced by the kolkhozniki on their private plots and from their privately owned stock.

Thus, the general picture of agricultural production, both grain and animal husbandry, showed first an absolute decline, with a slight improvement during the three pre-war years but without any serious breakthrough: output of animal foodstuffs was lower than before the revolution, and the grain output was not substantially higher than in the N.E.P. or before the revolution; it was gathered from a much larger sown area and had to support a bigger population. The one branch which did produce substantially more were the technical crops.[71]

But as grain crops fell or stagnated, one column in Tables 1 and 2 displays a pronounced upward trend: the *zagotovki*. Whatever the state of the branch, whether its output kept falling or improved somewhat, the size and share of *zagotovki* kept growing. In some years, as we can see, the share of *zagotovki* in the gross output almost reached the 40 per cent mark – an extremely heavy toll to be taken from the small crops and low yields of those years. It will be noticed that all the improvement of 1938-40 was swallowed by the increase of *zagotovki*. The device of 'biological crop' estimates helped to achieve such a result, as this high percentage of the *zagotovki* share in the grain outputs became evident only after the crop statistics were appropriately deflated. *Vykolachivanie* was indeed doing what Kirov felt it would: strangling agriculture as a branch (and peasants as a class – which is another matter to be considered). For the bulk of the Russian peasant population, grain was not just a product such as most industrial outputs are. It played here a unique manifold role: besides being the output of the farm, it also constituted its means of production (seeds), its raw material (forage), its circulating capital in part, as well as the subsistence means and wage fund of the producers. Grain was thus – and still often is – a complex life-stuff for the branch and not just food for the cities or means of getting foreign currency. The Government seemed not to be interested in this sort of consideration. N.E.P. peasants, who, as we know, produced not less on the whole than the kolkhozy some three *pyatiletkas* later, did not market more than 22 per cent of their grain output. They needed, in very rough figures, some 12 per cent for seeds, 25-30 per cent for their livestock, up to 30 per cent for feeding themselves, and the rest for reserves. By taking 30-40 per cent from poor, sometime falling, crops, the whole production cycle was heavily damaged. The still extremely feeble kolkhozy were given an unmanageable task. They were given no chance to prosper. This will become even more evident when another major aspect of the *zagotovki* policy is examined – the prices paid to producers.

On the whole, this pricing problem is simple: prices paid to producers for their deliveries remained at practically the same level between 1928 and 1953.[72] But not so the cost of living and of producing. Some rises were given in 1935, but this did not alter the overall picture much. These prices were inadequate and, as a Soviet writer put it, soon became no more than 'symbolic'.[73] It is not easy to explore this problem fully. Price indices were not published, probably not even computed, in the 1930s and the costs of production in kolkhozy were never studied at all during those years. But cost estimates did exist for sovkhozy, and prices paid to them for grain were probably the same as those paid to kolkhozy. Some of these data can give us an inkling of the problem.

According to a competent Soviet author using archival sources, the cost of producing a quintal of grain in sovkhozy in 1933-8 was 27 roubles on average (with a maximum of 33·9 roubles in 1934 and a minimum of 17·7 roubles in the abundant year 1937). But the producer's prices were of the following order (for 1935, after a small increment): rye 6 to 6·2 roubles a quintal; wheat, 9·1 to 10·4 roubles; oats, 4·9 to 5·5 roubles. Not surprisingly, the sovkhozy were showing huge cumulative deficits, especially when it is considered that up to 80 per cent of grain was taken away from them without regard to their internal needs. The state subsidies to which they were entitled as state enterprises were not sufficient to cover such deficits.[74]

For kolkhozy, we can quote one Soviet estimate for a later year, 1953, which sums up the economic policies in the countryside during twenty-five years. With producer prices remaining on the same level during the whole period and the value of the rouble having dwindled tenfold, the story is told. In 1953 the prices paid to producers (for nine basic grains and animal products) covered producer's costs no more than to the extent of two-fifths. Grain prices covered only 19 per cent of their cost, and no more than one-fourth of the cost of animal products was met.[75]

Such a picture of devastating exploitation would at least have the merit of simplicity. But producer's prices evolved into a more complicated pattern than just the simple price for the delivery (*postavki*), and it is worth sketching out some of this pattern because of its economic implications. Two additional price categories have to be mentioned: the purchases (*zakupki*) and the 'decentralised procurements', each with a set of prices of its own.

Zakupki were introduced in 1933. The peasants were told that after their deliveries to the state and to the M.T.S., they would be asked to sell to the Government, additionally, a certain amount of grain for a higher price than normal *zagotovki*, and with the additional incentive of the scarce industrial goods to be supplied to sellers. The relevant decree promised that the kolkhozy would be entirely free to decide whether they chose to sell.

This was said in January 1934; but the promise was broken in another decree, signed by Molotov and Stalin on 31 August of the same year, which made the whole 'selling', in fact, a compulsory affair.[76] The decree prescribed that the distribution of grain to kolkhozniki for the *trudodni* they earned would not begin before more grain was offered in the form of *zakupki*. Consequently, the 'purchases' tended to be organised as the regular *zagotovki*: quotas, distributed and handed down to every village, pressure exerted on peasants to comply, and all the rest of it.

This was another instance of breaking promises. With such *zakupki*, on top of payments to the M.T.S., the solemn intention of the 1933 reorganisation, to give the countryside some sense of stability and predictability with regard to procurements, had vanished. As the share of such 'purchases' and M.T.S. payments kept growing in the subsequent years, the fixed and predictable part of it – the state tax (*postavki*) – became a small share of the whole. Once more, the total of deliveries in all their forms became an unpredictable shifting quantity, bringing back to the kolkhozy much of the insecurity of the

First Five-Year Plan, which had made the planning and managing of their farms a more than tricky endeavour.

The peasants well knew that the *zakupki* would not be what the state promised. They listened to speeches of Politburo members castigating kolkhozy for refusing to 'sell', they heard and read enough of the familiar tunes about 'kulak choirboys' and understood very well that *zakupki* would become just another additional tax. 'A new tax' was in fact their own term for these *zakupki*.[77]

'Decentralised *zagotovki*' became an additional channel for acquiring extra animal products and vegetables for the cities. They were introduced in 1932 and allowed factories, city co-operatives and other institutions to go shopping in the countryside for animal products, potatoes and vegetables, after the basic deliveries to the state had been made. A special network was created of 'convention bureaux' at all administrative levels to fix prices for this trade and to regulate it. Not more than three agencies were to have licences to operate in any administrative region (raion) to avoid competition, though this was to be no more than a pious wish. Such agents would purchase the products from kolkhozy or preferably sign long-term contracts with them, for sales which were to be paid at high 'conventional' prices and additionally rewarded by help offered to kolkhozy by these agencies in acquiring production means and other industrial goods.

Space does not allow us to deal in detail with this interesting 'decentralised *zagotovki*'. They soon became permeated, as everything else, with elements of compulsion – kolkhozy were too vulnerable to pressures from local authorities, deprived of rights and defenceless as they were – but such pressures were much less prominent than in the case of *zakupki*. The central Government did not meddle with it too much and the whole operation soon became a predominantly chaotic market affair. Swarms of agents from cities descended upon raiony which had something to offer; they bribed officials to get the trading licences – a whole 'black market' for such licences developed in 'good' raiony – and engaged in quite lucrative deals with kolkhozy, based on barter and spin-offs to local officials.

This activity did add something to the diet of industrial workers and officials, but not less, probably, to channels of speculation on black markets. The cost of these agencies and of their bargains was huge. In 1934 a total of 859 million roubles worth, of potatoes and vegetables mainly, was purchased, but the cost of the agencies included in this total oscillated between 29 and 55·8 per cent. The anticipated norm of operational costs should have been only 14 per cent.[78]

We can now sum up the phenomenon of multiple prices which developed, contrary to initial intentions or anticipations, in the wake of the *zagotovki* policy. As we know, a certain rather 'symbolic' price was offered for the basic *postavki*, the part of overall *zagotovki* which was officially presented as a compulsory state tax. For the second category, the *naturplaty*, nothing was paid to peasants. These were considered as payments in kind to the M.T.S. for its work; it looked like a kind of sharecropping system with not much say for the share-cropper in fixing the rates, as was the case in most such systems.

The next category – *zakupki* – were paid 20-25 per cent more than the basic *postavki* rates; this was the case in 1933-4, with some rises during the following years which did not take this price, in any case, substantially any further from the basic rate. Some premia could be paid for *zakupki*, and industrial goods were made available to com-plying kolkhozy, though goods never materialised in promised quantities, as they were either not available at all, or not supplied to the countryside, or embezzled – facts which the press abundantly illustrated.[79]

The next price category emerged in the kolkhoz markets where kolkhozy and kolkhozniki could trade their surpluses after having received permission to do so. Here the prices might have been as much at 13·2 times higher than those in private commerce in 1928 (for five basic agricultural products), and it was by selling a small share of their production on kolkhoz markets that peasants made about 60 per cent of their whole monetary income.[80]

The prices for grain reaching the illegal 'black markets' were even higher than on the kolkhoz markets, as speculators took very con-siderable risks to operate their trade; but they existed and seemed irremovable, though the scope of this trade cannot be gauged.

For animal foodstuffs a four-tier price system evolved: the official *zagotovki* price; the 'conventional price' for decentralised *zagotovki*, some three to four times higher than the official price; the kolkhoz market price; and the black market.

Thus some compensation would accrue to the producers, heavily underpaid for the bulk of their output, through the practice of higher prices on *zakupki*, kolkhoz market prices and some black market sales; but these could not make up the losses made on the bulk of the output. These compensations did not change the general picture of a branch of the national economy allowed to cover only a fraction of its costs.

The underpayment and the multiple-tier pricing had a profound effect on the kolkhozy. Not enough study has been done to analyse the impact of such pricing, but one phenomenon can be pointed to, following one rather angry statement by a modern Soviet writer. According to him, the fact that a kolkhoz was paid different prices for different lots of the same product played havoc with the kolkhoz economy. The poor and inefficient kolkhozy – these were, no doubt, the majority – did not have much to offer over and above the quantities levied as compulsory state quotas. Such kolkhozy were particularly hard hit and their poverty was thereby perpetuated. Some of the better or luckier kolkhozy who did happen to have grain above the compulsory quotas could be rewarded by getting additional income for *zakupki*, and premia for extra grain over the *zakupki* minimum, then more income from sales on kolkhoz markets and eventually even more on black markets. They could in this way make quite a lot of money and even become rich. The existing price system, complained the author, wrecked the poor and enriched the rich, and this situation was 'worse than the capitalist anarchy'.[81]

V. SOME CONSEQUENCES

The facts and figures as they emerge from this scrutiny point to a two-fold conclusion: the Soviet state was successful in organising a large-scale squeeze of agricultural output from the peasantry, but failed as a manager and organiser of successful large-scale agricultural production. It was, in fact, the very successful facet of the operation which was accountable for the failure of some other vital facets. To base the economic activity of a whole branch, and of a social class, on 'taking' without rewarding would be inconceivable without the application of mass coercion on a permanent basis. But tools and energies needed for such a compulsory process were different from and contradictory to tools and energies which were necessary for promoting kolkhozy as successful producers and a viable socio-economic structure.

Incidentally, the extraordinary display of mass coercion, without which this type of *zagotovki* would not work, contributed heavily to the hardening of Stalin's Russia into a bureaucratic police state. Violence applied to millions of peasants year after year was a training ground for institutions and methods which could later be applied to other groups. With the treatment of peasants in the First Five-Year Plan as background, the gloomiest years of the subsequent purges of cadres, however bloody, look like a re-edition on a smaller scale.

All the sources agree that the state made the *zagotovki* quite explicitly its central activity in the countryside. The leadership made no secret of it, and kept hammering into the heads of peasants and officials that the *zagotovki* were the principal, most important campaign in the life of the whole state, not just of the countryside. It is enough to leaf through *Pravda* between September and November of, say, 1934, to discover that during these months even industry is somehow in the shadow. Kirov in the same year put it bluntly: the *zagotovki* 'are the concentrated expression of the totality of our policy in the countryside, the kolkhoz, the sovkhoz and the smallholders'. Another leader, Vareikis, saw in this activity the main way of educating the peasants; Chernov would add that *zagotovki* were helping the kolkhozniki in overcoming the limitations of their petit-bourgeois psychology. The delivery, another text explained euphorically, is the supreme test of the socialist essence of the kolkhozy.[82] Even religious overtones were used to instil into the peasant a sense of the sanctity of the delivery: *zagotovki* became the 'supreme commandment' for the kolkhoz.

For the peasants, all this meant that the grain was no longer his but the state's. And the same attitude applied to the whole kolkhoz. The peasants learnt this lesson after a display of terror and an 'education' which heavily concentrated, among other methods, on administering starvation as a way of teaching.

The peasants yielded to superior force, but never really accepted the rule that the state's interests were more important than their own. As long as they could, the peasants behaved according to different rules, such as 'no bread, no work', or 'a pound of labour for a pound of bread'. And one big lesson which they learnt especially was best expressed as follows: don't trust the state, they don't care for peasants.

In the prevailing conditions, there could be no such thing as the shedding by peasants of their 'petit-bourgeois psychology'. Quite the opposite was true. As the peasants learnt that the state did not consider their interests as important, the obvious lesson for them, borne out by a mass of facts, was to take care, as far as possible, of their own interests. The emergence of a collectivist psychology was hardly possible here – unless as a defensive group or class posture. Squeezing peasants to the core bred apathy among them and forced the state to look for ways to overcome this apathy by instilling some stimuli and incentives into them, so they would become interested in doing something for their kolkhozy. The irony was that all such incentives were catering for the very petit-bourgeois mentality and self-interest which the state was allegedly out to eradicate. Such measures as re-establishing the right to keep a private cow, to have a private plot, to trade on kolkhoz markets, special prices and premia, were medicines for curing ailments which the *zagotovki* were hard at work to inflict.

Applied simultaneously, such treatments were self-defeating. They contributed to the creation of a peculiar hybrid system with deeply seated, inbuilt disincentives and fetters. As the authorities were poised for the squeeze and the peasants for the defence of their livelihood, production could not become the main worry either of the one side or the other. The state wanted the quick organisation of threshing with 90 per cent of its proceedings going straight to its elevators; and if at the same time much of the yield remained unharvested, or not properly put in stacks and liable to get wet and rotten, it did not interest the officials very much. It would be up to the factor who was the last to be paid to carry the brunt. There is no lack of material for documenting such a state of affairs.

The peasants knew it. They therefore responded by doing the minimum on collective fields as their way of perceiving realities. Facing such a mass expresison of what became popular wisdom, the state was forced to take direct responsibility over a growing range of agricultural activities for which the N.E.P. peasants used to care themselves: ploughing, sowing, weeding, harvesting became a state activity, to be planned and regulated by quotas and indicators. It led to a new interference in every aspect of kolkhoz life, in minute detail. When to begin to sow, where and what to sow, how to work and how to remunerate, how to take care of horses – all was handed down from above, and different officials sent in to ensure the execution of the detailed plans.

The situation verged on the ridiculous. It was the normal peasant stuff and needed their zeal to be done properly. But as long as the *zagotovki* were the state's central worry, it led to warfare with the peasants instead of winning them over. As the peasants responded, in fact, by a protracted *grève de zèle*, the estrangement on both sides exhibited a tendency towards self-perpetuation. The state, deeply distrusting the peasants, took over ever more responsibilities for the agricultural cycles with which it was unable to cope; the peasants learnt new ways of evasion and looked to their private plots and cows.

The system which grew out of such interaction was an agriculture in which peasants saw their main means of production taken away from them, the threshing taken over, estimates of crops made over their heads, planning of their sowings dictated from above. Furthermore, no autonomy of any consequence was allowed to the kolkhozy and no important sphere of their work left without interference. The formally proclaimed democratic organisation of kolkhozy had no meaning, as their management was imposed on kolkhozy, and any chairman who engaged in defending his outfit would be demoted and replaced by another nominee. The state wanted the internal administrations to be watch-dogs of the *zagotovki*, not representatives of the producers. This accounted for a constant turnover among kolkhozy chairmen who all too often had no chance to accumulate enough experience in running a complicated enterprise.

For the kolkhoz to become an efficient producer it needed conditions in which to acquire a personality of its own, a sense of pride and belonging. It needed dedicated leaders to preside over the kolkhozy and to help these leaders to acquire enough experience and authority in the eyes of fellow kolkhozniki. But Government policies were hard at work against the emergence of this type of solidarity in kolkhozy. Through constant interference and petty tyrannies by its local officials, through the unpredictability of its exactions and the whole essence of its agricultural policies, the state kept, in fact, disorganising the kolkhozy. Without a minimum of rights, independence and *esprit de corps*, the kolkhoz was condemned to stagnation.

Peasants, of course, could not escape their own condition. They had to feed themselves, but the small plot in which they invested a disproportionate amount of their labour and energies was too small to supply the family with bread and enough forage. It was a physical impossibility to live without participating in the kolkhoz works, not to consider the legal constraints to participate. Once in the kolkhoz field, the minimum of *trudodni* were imposed, norms and some labour discipline were demanded, supervision and pressures by management and party officials, and on occasions security organs too, helped to keep things going. There was no other way than to accommodate to the conditions, to earn *trudodni* and to sell something in the kolkhoz markets in order to make ends meet. It was the cruder incentive of elementary needs which made the system tick, rather than stimuli of a higher order. Because income on the kolkhoz field was only an unpredictable residual after many other claimants had been satisfied, much dedicated labour was wasted on the tiny plot because it actually gave some secure food minimum, and much sluggishness and indifference was deployed in the modern, large-scale sector equipped with machinery, but a low-yielding and insecure remunerator. In this way the peasants continued to perpetuate themselves as a separate peasant class, but they were not allowed to be either efficient smallholders or dedicated co-operators.

Neither was the peasant a citizen, even in the Soviet sense. Compared with the N.E.P. period, the social status of the peasants deteriorated. Under the N.E.P. the peasants, however poor, had some reason for self-esteem. The majority of them felt they were independent producers and saw themselves as *khozyaeva* in their own right, a class which had recently emancipated itself from the degrading conditions of serfdom.

But during the next period they were transformed into a mass deprived of rights, surrounded by discriminatory practices and limitations and submitted to an entirely new regime. The passport system and restrictions inside kolkhozy deprived them of much of their freedom of movement. They were subjected to compulsory state *corvées*, like road building and timber cutting, which did not apply to city dwellers. They had no representation of their own, no right to organise themselves for the defence of their interests. Peasants paid special higher prices for the means of production and for some consumer goods. They were submitted to a labour system which reminded them all too often of the conditions from which the revolution seemed to have redeemed them for ever. Peasants in Stalin's times were indeed legally bound to their place of work, submitted to a special legal regimen, and – through the kolkhoz – to a form of collective responsibility with regard to state duties. They were transformed, not unlike as in pre-emancipation times, into an estate placed at the very bottom of the social ladder.

Some twenty years after Stalin's death many changes have occurred and numerous discriminatory traits of the special regime have gone. Peasants in the Soviet Union today are paid for their labour and allowed to make profits; they have salaries and pensions, and produce much more and better than twenty years ago. But these are very recent developments. Soviet agriculture has not yet managed to effect a real technological revolution similar to the one which took place some time ago in other developed countries. Agriculture is still rather primitive and a great problem; and there is no doubt that the consequences of the first quarter of a century of kolkhoz history still weigh heavily and are far from having been definitively overcome.

NOTES

1. This is O. Lange's term; see his 'The Role of Planning in Socialist Economics', reproduced in M. Bornstein (ed.), *Comparative Economic Systems* (Homewood, Ill.: Irwin, 1965) p. 200.

2. The Soviet term is, in fact, *vzyat' khleb* ('taking bread'), and party leaders would say, triumphantly, that this year 'we took' such and such a quantity of grain. The term expressed the reality of the procedure.

3. The procurement campaigns would begin almost simultaneously with the harvest and last well into the spring of the next calendar year. But the entire action was included in the 'economic year', say 1928-9 (beginning on 1 Oct 1928 and ending on 30 Sep 1929). Thus, 'the 1928-9 procurement campaign' means procurement of grain from the harvest which grew in the (calendar) year 1928. From 1 Jan 1931 the 'economic year' was abolished, and planning and other economic activities were subsequently to be conducted in the framework of calendar years. Hence the procurement campaign of, say, 1933 means the campagn based on the harvest grown in 1933. It would, in the past-N.E.P. years, be virtually finished by the end of the same year.

4. The figures are in A. A. Barsov, in *Istoriya SSSR*, no. 6 (1968) p. 71.

5. Whether peasants did actually engage in any deliberate sabotage at that time is more than doubtful. Many top leaders believed then that the 'crisis' had nothing definitive to it and could have been averted or mitigated by appropriate policies. This opinion was held not only by the leaders of the 'Right' (Bukharin, Rykov, Tomsky) but also by such supporters of Stalin as Mikoyan. According to archival sources, he believed in 1928 that the difficulties of the 'grain crisis' resulted to a considerable degree from policy errors, and such errors could have been avoided. Quoted in E. I. Turchaninova, *Podgotovka i provedenie sploshnoi kollektivizatsii selskogo khozyaistva v Stavropolskom Krae* (Dushanbe, 1963) pp. 106-7.

6. The events of the 'grain crisis' are described in E. H. Carr and R. W. Davies, *Foundations of a Planned Economy, 1926-1929*, i (London: Macmillan, 1969) chaps 2 and 3; and in my own *Russian Peasants and Soviet Power* (London: Allen & Unwin, 1968) chap. 9.

7. S. Kossior, the Ukrainian Party Secretary, admitted in *Pravda*, 26 Apr 1930, that 'the worst side of the grain *zagotovki* – the method of pressure – was applied automatically to collectivisation' – exactly as the critics were saying earlier. But what Kossior stated here with regret very soon became common practice, including on the part of Kossior himself.

8. Organising the campaign, launching and supervising it, became the task of the party secretaries at the administrative levels. The technical apparatus for actually doing the job of collecting was provided by the agricultural co-operative organisation Khlebotsentr and its local branches, but the grain had to be turned over to the state agency Soyuzkhleb, created in 1928 under the auspices of the Commissariat for Foreign and Internal Trade (from 1931, under the Commissariat of Supplies which became separated from the Commissariat for Foreign Trade); Soyuzkhleb would also collect grain from sovkhozy directly through its own local branches, and the same was true for the milling tax (*garnets*). The central planner of the campaign was Mikoyan, the head of the Commissariat, acting in co-ordination with other bodies, especially with the Commissariat for Agriculture (headed by Yakovlev). A body called the 'Special Council for Zagotovki of Grain' was created inside Narkomtorg, including representatives of all the other commissariats and agencies concerned. The appropriate decrees can be found in *Sobranie Zakonov i Rasporyazhenii Raboche-Krestyanskogo Pravitelstva*; a good detailed description of the functioning of the whole system is in M. A. Chernov (ed.), *Spravochnik po khlebnomu delu* (Moscow, 1932).

9. The norms are in *Kollektivizatsiya selskogo khozyaistva. Vashneishie postanovleniya* (Moscow, 1957) pp. 534-44. On depriving peasants of reserves, see Yu. A. Moshkov, *Zernovaya problema v gody sploshnoi kollektivizatsii* (Moscow, 1966) pp. 72-3. This is an excellent book which we shall be using very often.

10. On the faulty distribution of quotas, see the article by Vinogradsky, in *Ekonomicheskaya Gazeta*, 16 June 1930. This type of target planning was applied to other agricultural activities too, not only to *zagotovki*.

11. Cf. ibid. The author urges the drawing-up of such balances and basing the imposition on them, in order to avoid undermining the production capabilities of the countryside. Soon such demands would come under attack as 'anti-state', and sometimes the very drawing-up of balances would be forbidden.

12. See ibid., and Moshkov, *Zernovaya problema*, p. 163. The reader will find data on the 'inter-village' grain circulation in R. W. Davies, 'A Note on Grain Statistics', *Soviet Studies*, XXI 3 (Jan 1971), commenting on Jerzy Karcz's article, in *Soviet Studies*, XVIII 4 (Apr 1967). Both articles will introduce the reader to the problems of 'Commercial grain'.

13. Another step is worth mentioning here which further contributed to weakening the resources of the countryside: from 1928, the milling tax (*garnets*) was to be paid exclusively to the Government. In order to make it work, all private mills were nationalised. This tax added some 2 million tons of grain to the Government's income. See Chernov (ed.), *Spravochnik po khlebnomu delu*, p. 25.

14. Cf. A. Mikoyan, in *Bolshevik*, no. 1 (1931) pp. 12-14, 16.

15. Chernov (ed.), *Spravochnik po khlebnomu delu*, pp. 27-8.

16. For details, see ibid. There were private peasants who had to sign, and some who did not have to, but the latter had to engage in so-called 'self-impositions' which were, in fact, prescribed by the authorities. To avoid unnecessary complexities, we do not enter into such details in this article. In any case, the Government made opposition to delivering grain liable to prosecution under para. 61 of the Criminal Code, with penalties ranging from a fine up to five times the value of the arrears (in market prices), to two years' imprisonment, with or without deportation. According to explanations of the Supreme Court, penal clauses had to be avoided with regard to non-kulaks, who were to be punished by fines and deprivation of different services and allowances – but not so any more if they persisted; in such cases the full sting of this law was to be applied. See *Code pénal de l'R.S.F.S.R.* (Paris, 1935) pp. 53, 288-9; and *Sbornik raz'yasnenii verkhovnogo suda, RSFSR* (Moscow, 1932) pp. 293-4.

17. Moshkov, *Zernovaya problema*, p. 152.

18. N. I. Nemakov, *Kompartiya-organizator massovogo kolkhoznogo dvizheniya* (Moscow, 1966) p. 258.

19. The sources on ways of evading *zagotovki* are numerous, especially in the journal of Komzag (Committee for Procurements), *Na Fronte Selskokhozyaistvennykh Zagotovok*; see, e.g., no. 14 (1933) pp. 3-6, dealing, among other phenomena, with the 'hairdressers'.

20. Moshkov, *Zernovaya problema*, pp. 155-6 and *passim*; also *Sovetskaya Yustitsiya*, no. 11 (1931) p. 18, for sample figures on court cases.

21. Cf. M. Lewin, 'Who Was the Soviet Kulak', *Soviet Studies*, XVIII 2 (Oct 1966).

22. Further material on repression can be found in M. A. Chernov, in *Bolshevik*, no. 21 (1931) p. 49, and in an article by Ganzha, in V. P. Danilov (ed.), *Ocherki po istorii kollektivizatsii selskogo khozyaistva v soyuznykh respublikakh* (Moscow, 1963) pp. 199-200.

23. Chernov, in *Bolshevik*, no. 21 (1931) pp. 50, 52.

24. *Na Agrarnom Fronte*, no. 1 (1932) pp. 23, 27; *Sotsialisticheskoe Zemledelie*, 14 Nov 1931; ibid., no. 1-2, 28 Jan 1932, p. 14.

25. For the political difficulties, see Danilov (ed.), *Ocherki po istorii kollektivizatsii*, *passim*; Moshkov, *Zernovaya problema*, p. 194; I. E. Zelenin, *Istoricheskie Zapiski*, no. 76 (1965) p. 44.

26. *Kompartiya Ukrainy v rezolyutsiakh i resheniakh s'ezdov i konferentsii, 1918-1957* (Kiev, 1958) p. 569.

27. Ibid., pp. 569-70.

28. Moshkov, *Zernovaya problema*, p. 202.

29. For the appeals of the Ukrainian C.C. on its session on 9 July 1932, see *Kompartiya Ukrainy v rezolyutsiakh*, p. 576.

30. For details, see V. N. Kleiner, in *Planovoe Khozyaistvo*, no. 4 (1933) pp. 17, 19, 27. The 1931 Circular of the Commissariat of Justice is in *Code pénal*, p. 227.

31. Kleiner, in *Planovoe Khozyaistvo*, no. 4 (1933) p. 29. Kleiner was deputy chairman of Komzag. The chairman himself, Chernov, stated the same in *Na Fronte Sel.-khoz. zag.*, no. 11 (1933) pp. 1-2. He blamed the leniency of the previous period, which had made the repressions indispensable later.

32. Moshkov, *Zernovaya problema*, p. 211.

33. Ibid., p. 214.

34. Stalin, in *Bolshevik*, no. 1-2 (1933) p. 19.

35. For events in the Northern Caucasus, see speech by N. S. Khrushchev, in *Pravda*, 10 Mar 1963, quoting the exchange of letters between Sholokhov and Stalin; Moshkov, *Zernovaya problema*, p. 217; Zelenin, in *Istoricheskie Zapiski*, no. 76 (1965) pp. 43-4.

36. On the famine, see Dana G. Dalrymple, in *Soviet Studies*, no. 3 (1964); Zelenin, in *Istoricheskie Zapiski*, no. 76 (1965) p. 47; Roy Medvedev, *Let History Judge* (London: Macmillan, 1972) pp. 94-6, quotes several sources; W. H. Chamberlain, in his *Russian Iron Age*, published in 1935, gave a detailed account based on personal observation.

37. Moshkov, *Zernovaya problema*, p. 186.

38. For figures on exports of grain, see *Istoriya SSSR*, no. 5 (1964); on imports of grain in the spring of 1932, see ibid., no. 4 (1962) p. 104, which added that even the modest food rations of city dwellers had to be curtailed, and in some regions supplementary *zagotovki* of grain had to be conducted.

39. For the main decrees concerning the creation of Komzag, see *Sobranie Zakonov*, no. 10 (1932) para. 53, and ibid., no. 11 (1933) para. 58.

40. The political departments (*politotdely*) were established by the decision of the January 1933 plenum of the Central Committee. See *KPSS v rezolyutsiakh i resheniakh s'ezdov*, ii (7th ed., 1957) 187-98. For a good book on the M.T.S.s and a chapter on *politotdely*, see Robert F. Miller, *One Hundred Thousand Tractors* (Cambridge, Mass.: Harvard U.P., 1970).

41. The basic decree is in *Sobranie Zakonov*, no. 4 (1933) para. 25; detailed instructions on how to prepare and operate the campaign in all its stages are in ibid., no. 16 (1933) para. 95 and the instruction which follows this paragraph.

42. A. Ya. Yakovlev, *Voprosy organizatsii sotsialisticheskogo selskogo khozyaistva* (Moscow, 1933) p. 119.

43. Decree of 25 June 1933, in *Sobranie Zakonov*, no. 39, para. 234.

44. By 1937, payment-in-kind to the M.T.S.s supplied almost 50 per cent of the state's income in grain (as against 15·7 per cent in 1933). The share of the tax-in-kind, i.e. the basic *zagotovki* lot (*khlebopostavki*), fell to about 35 per cent. The rest was collected in the form of so-called 'purchases' (*zakupki*) which we describe later. It goes without saying that for both the Government and the peasants all these categories were just *zagotovki*, and the official statistics subsumed all the categories (often including also the income from the milling tax) under the rubric of *khlebozagotovki*.

45. For this hint, see *Planovoe Khozyaistvo*, no. 4 (1933) p. 25.

46. The Central Commission for Assessing Yields and Crops (Ts.G.K.) was constituted in December 1932 under V. V. Osinsky, and attached to Sovnarkom.

The instructions for its composition and organisation are in *Sobranie Zakonov*, no. 3 (1933) para. 46; no. 44, para. 279; no. 17, para. 97a. There were more decrees and quite a hectic activity around these Commissions, with Stalin and Molotov signing the most important enactments. But *Istoriya SSSR*, no. 5 (1964) p. 13, derided the whole thing as a waste of time and contended that the objective of the Ts.G.K. was to inflate artificially the 'commercial surpluses' of the kolkhozy, by producing exaggerated crop assessments.

47. M. A. Chernov, in *Na Fronte Sel.-khoz. Zag.*, no. 11 (1933) p. 4; *Selskoe Khozyaistvo RSFSR*, no. 22, 1 Aug 1931, pp. 10-11.

48. *Planovoe Khozyaistvo*, no. 4 (1933) p. 25.

49. The latest account about Kirov, his role and his assassination is in Medvedev, *Let History Judge*, chap. 5. For earlier sources which Medvedev probably did not know, see B. Nicolaevsky, *Power and the Soviet Elite* (London: Pall Mall Press, 1966).

50. S. M. Kirov, in *Pravda*, 19 July 1934.

51. Leading article in *Na Fronte Sel.-khoz. Zag.*, no. 19 (1934).

52. Ibid., no. 27-28 (1934) pp. 2-3, for example. Such sources are numerous. We should remember that this review is an organ of Komzag, which was attached to Molotov's office and therefore obviously voiced his opinions.

53. Zelenin, in *Istoricheskie Zapiski*, no. 76 (1965) pp. 77-8.

54. *Na Fronte Sel.-khoz. Zag.*, no. 17-18 (1934), has much correspondence from districts reporting on this kind of repression of officials.

55. Zelenin, in *Istoricheskie Zapiski*, no. 76 (1965) pp. 76-7; see also *Na Fronte Sel.-khoz. Zag.*, no. 17-18 (1934).

56. Zelenin, in *Istoricheskie Zapiski*, no. 76 (1965) p. 57.

57. The political departments in the M.T.S.s were dissolved in November 1934 (see *KPSS v rezolyutsiakh*, pp. 260-5), but they continued to function in sovkhozy until 1940.

58. Decree signed by Molotov and Stalin, *Pravda*, 28 Feb 1934.

59. Decree of 3 Apr 1934, in *Sobranie Zakonov*, no. 18 (1934) para. 139. This, as were many others that we quote, was signed by Molotov and Stalin, which meant that this was a Government and Party enactment – a common practice in those years. At that time fewer than half of the kolkhozy (but more than half of the sown area) were served by the M.T.S.s. The kolkhozy which could escape signing up with the M.T.S.s were relieved because the M.T.S. did its job badly and cost a lot of grain. To reward kolkhozy which were serviced by the stations, the delivery norms for such kolkhozy were quite substantially lower than for the others.

60. This decree is in *Sobranie Zakonov*, no. 46 (1934) para. 362.

61. Molotov, in *Pravda*, 8 July 1934.

62. Lyubchenko, in *Bolshevik*, no. 11 (1934) pp. 21-2.

63. A decree on the levy is in *Sobranie Zakonov*, no. 49 (1934) para. 380. Stalin is quoted from archives in *Istoriya SSSR*, no. 5 (1964) p. 24.

64. *Sobranie Zakonov*, no. 48, para. 370, and no. 49, para. 380.

65. S. M. Kirov, in *Stat'i i Rechi* (1934) pp. 130-2.

66. *Narodnoe khozyaistvo SSSR v 1958 godu* (Moscow, 1959) pp. 350, 352; M. A. Vyltsan, *Ukreplenie materialno-tekhnicheskoi basy kolkhoznogo stroya* (Moscow, 1959).

67. Vyltsan, ibid., p. 125.

68. Kirov, in *Stat'i i Rechi* (1934) pp. 106-7. His probable source is the estimate of the Commission of Yields and Crops, presented by Bryukhanov in

Pravda, 20 July 1934. Samples taken in different grain-producing regions invariably showed a discrepancy of 30-40 per cent between the estimates of the yields *na kornyu* ('standing crop') and the crops actually harvested.

69. The figures for the three years 1925-7 show an average of 73·3 million tons of grain per year. For the five pre-collectivisation years, 1925-9, the estimates vary between 73 and 74 million tons per year, substantially the same as during the subsequent quinquennia, but with higher yields per hectare, as sown area was considerably expanded during the First Five-Year Plan. Cf. V. P. Danilov (ed.), *Sozdanie kolkhoznogo stroya materialno-tekhnicheskikh predposylok Kollektivizatsii selskogo Khozyaistva v SSSR* (Moscow, 1957) pp. 94-5.

70. The catastrophic drop in numbers of cattle stopped in 1934 (for cows, in 1935) and henceforward a slow improvement in numbers of heads began, but towards the beginning of 1941 the figures were still far below the 1916 level.

71. *Narodnoe khozyaistvo SSSR v 1958 godu*, p. 355, shows increasing crops of the main technical plants, but substantially dwindling yields; as to the population, it remained stationary in the countryside between 1913 and 1940, but grew in the cities from 28,420,000 to 63,112,000.

72. For data on prices and the value of the rouble, see A. A. Barsov, in *Istoriya SSSR*, no. 6 (1968) p. 72; Lazar Volin, *A Century of Russian Agriculture* (Cambridge, Mass.: Harvard University Press, 1970) p. 251. Producers' prices were even lowered in 1931, but later rose by some 28 per cent for grain and 20 per cent for animal foodstuffs; but rises of this scope did not change very much.

73. *Istoriya SSSR*, no. 5 (1964) p. 19.

74. I. E. Zelenin, *Zernovye sovkhozy SSSR, 1933-1941* (Moscow, 1966) pp. 181-7 and *passim*.

75. V. G. Lopatkin, *Tovarnye otnosheniya i zakon stoimosti pri sotsializme* (Moscow, 1963) pp. 366, 243; Volin, *A Century of Russian Agriculture*, quoting a study by Holtzman, estimated that procurement prices rose by about 25 per cent but prices of consumer goods in shops rose seven times, and on kolkhoz markets seventeen times.

76. Cf. Zelenin, in *Istoricheskie Zapiski*, no. 76 (1965) p. 58.

77. Cf. Kirov, in *Stat'i i Rechi* (1934) p. 155; *Na Fronte Sel.-khoz. Zag.*, no. 19 (1934) p. 31.

78. Numerous data can be found in *Na Fronte Sel.-khoz. Zag.* during 1933 and 1934, notably no. 3 (1934) p. 18.

79. On prices paid for *Zakupki*, see Vyltsan, *Ukreplenie*, p. 132; also data in *Na Fronte Sel.-khoz. Zag.*, no. 19 (1934).

80. Barsov, in *Istoriya SSSR*, no. 6 (1968) p. 19.

81. See Lopatkin, *Tovarnye otnosheniya*, pp. 46, 236; for angry criticisms by other authors of the destructive effects of the *zagotovki* policies on the rural economy for a whole generation, see, e.g., G. S. Lisichkin, in *Novyi Mir*, no. 9 (1965) p. 221; Moshkov, *Zernovaya problema*, p. 220 and *passim*; Nemakov, *Kompartiya-organizator*, p. 261.

82. For this type of statement, see Kirov, in *Pravda*, 19 July 1934; Chernov, in *Na Fronte Sel.-khoz. Zag.*, no. 11 (1933) p. 1; Kalinin, in *Stat'i i Rechi* (1935) p. 81; S. Leikin, in *Na Agrarnom Fronte*, no. 2-3 (1935) p. 61; Vareikis, in *XVII-aya konferentsiya VKP(B)* (1932) p. 190.

14 Some Historical Reflections on Planning and the Market

MAURICE DOBB

IN speaking of the period of the N.E.P. in the Soviet 1920s, Mr E. H. Carr has said that 'the economy remained fundamentally a market economy' and that 'the connection between the State sector and individual agriculture through the market dominated all other economic relations';[1] with the implication (presumably) that it was upon the relation between industry and agriculture, as this existed at the time, that the character of the system as a 'market economy' depended. This was certainly the prevailing Soviet opinion at that period; and it was perhaps as an echo of this that Stalin shortly before his death, and referring to the kolkhoz agriculture of this later period, attributed the continuing survival of 'commodity production', or market relations, to the existence of two (different) forms of what he called socialist property in industry and agriculture.[2] Later in the same volume of his monumental history Mr Carr describes, with unsurpassed richness of detail, the two central controversies that were to develop as the decade approached its close: the rather abstract and not very fecund debate between 'teleologists' and 'geneticists', and the assault by the champions of centralised planning, wedded to a high tempo of development, against concepts like 'equilibrium' and 'balance' and 'proportionality' – concepts that were associated with market relations with their implications for policy and for planning methods and objectives. (This was, of course, incidental to the mounting attack on the 'right-wing tendency' and on Bukharin in particular, with his advocacy of 'gradualist' transition within the framework of N.E.P., a cautious tempo of collectivisation and avoidance of any rupture in the *smychka* with the mass of the peasantry.) The tenor of discussion at the time as well as the outcome of developments in the 1930s certainly suggested that market relations and planning stood in a simple inverse relationship as polar antitheses: the former could be predominant only at a primitive and undeveloped stage of planning, and in the degree to which socialisation was extended and planning developed, market relations must wither away. So widely was this kind of view adopted at the time that few, if any, could have imagined that in the 1960s, after several decades of planned development, the question of again enhancing market influences and finding a revived role for *khozrashchot* would have appeared so prominently on the agenda alike in the U.S.S.R. and in most other countries of Eastern Europe. The fact that it has done so inevitably casts some doubt on the sufficiency of the former view that we have mentioned, with its simple antithesis. Perhaps some may even feel inclined to question whether the interpretation of N.E.P. as consisting *solely* of a 'deal' with an individualist peasantry can be allowed to stand.

Certainly, the logic of events in the 1930s was in the direction of increasing centralisation; and both the degree of it and the forms that this took were evoked at least as much by the nature of the actual problems that arose in the course of this decade as they were by the demands of theory. At the same time, the nature of the situation in this period and its associated problems cannot be separated from the policy objectives being pursued at that time. These consisted of an exceptionally high rate of investment and of development; moreover, the development was of a kind to involve bold structural shifts in the economy and also strains and tensions of a special, as well as specially severe, kind. Many of the problems of this period resembled those of a modern 'war economy';[3] and this became increasingly true as the decade advanced, and to the construction of heavy industry, of a fuel and power base and of a transport network were added also rearmament and the building of war industries, all of which in combination dominated the economic scene. In such circumstances, with these policy objectives, it was almost inevitable that an increasingly tight control should be exercised from the centre over the detailed specification of constructional schemes and of the investment expenditures involved in them; as it was also that, in face of increasingly severe supply shortages, initially of constructional materials, subsequently of an increasingly wide range of metals and of fuels and energy resources (despite early progress in electrification), centralised rationing of scarce supplies should be adopted via the system of 'funded commodities' and their detailed allocation – a system which started with a few hundred items and expanded until in the 1950s it covered something approaching 10,000 items.[4] Even the current expenditures of *khozrashchot* units (not to say their investment expenditures) were tightly controlled through the system of credit control developed in the early 1930s, which Professor Davies has described in some detail;[5] and the 'own funds' of enterprises were reduced to the bare minimum (to 'average' or 'normal' requirements) in order to render this control of expenditures effective. Not only were plan targets for industries and individual enterprises laid down in overall terms, whether in physical units or in gross value, but as time went on these were increasingly broken down into stipulations about the detailed 'assortment' of output, with the addition of various 'limits' and 'indices' covering the wages bill and employment, increase of productivity and the like, so that the obligatory plan for a productive unit could have as many as three or four hundred different 'indices'. Such a system can be attributed again, in large part at least, to the need to combat the tendency of enterprises to hoard materials and skilled labour in a situation of general scarcity, accentuated if not occasioned by overtight plan targets associated with a high tempo of growth. In the absence of the latter, it is at least arguable that such detailed and stringent controls would have been unnecessary, and more of the latitude previously accorded to individual productive units ('trusts' as they were then mostly called) in the preceding period could have been preserved.

In order to acquire a proper perspective on such questions, the judgement of one recent commentator on Soviet planning could well be noted and underlined:

> Whereas economists of the Lausanne school have always conceived of the economic mechanism as something for which one can formulate general rules independent of the real historical situation, there are certain things which are on the historical agenda and certain things which are not.... The advocacy of full *khozraschet* in 1928 was about as relevant to Soviet economic policy as the advocacy of the market by Hayek in 1939 was relevant to British economic policy at that time.[6]

To emphasise in this way the relativity of the issues raised in the earlier debate to contemporary policies and problems implies that one should also view the new debates about economic reform in the 1960s in the light of the new and changed circumstances of this more developed situation of three decades later. Yet ideas and attitudes generated in that earlier discussion, with its rather *simpliste* counterposing of planning versus market, have exerted a continuing influence in recent years. Certainly notions and assumptions generated in the late 1920s continue to influence the thinking of relative 'conservatives' like Strumilin (who was prominent in those earlier discussions as well as in plan-making), and may go some way to explain the extreme caution towards reform proposals displayed in some administrative and planning circles – a caution that has sometimes amounted, it seems, to an unco-operative dragging of feet even after proposals for decentralisation and greater flexibility have been officially sanctioned. It is not impossible, of course, that the changes of the 1960s will turn out to have been no more than comparatively minor modifications of a hypertrophy of centralisation of decision which had developed in conditions of war economy and its immediate aftermath, and that in its essential framework and *modus operandi* the system that the 1930s developed will turn out to have survived. In this case, talk of a new stage of 'market socialism', appropriate to a second and more mature phase of socialist development, will prove to have been no more than a deviating minority view. On the other hand, Hungary, which has carried the economic reforms of recent years furthest in the socialist camp (apart from Yugoslavia), has advisedly used the term 'new economic mechanism' to describe its new policy-turn towards a more decentralised structure of economic administration. (This term refers to the termination of supply allocations, a decentralisation of a substantial proportion of gross investment, and even the unfreezing of some prices.) Even in the Soviet Union the reintroduction of 'wholesale trade between enterprises' is officially spoken of as the *ultimate* outcome of the 1965 reform;[7] and Professor A. Birman has spoken of the changes of the mid-1960s 'as the third all-round economic reform in the history of our country; in scale and importance it is equal to the first two: the New Economic Policy of 1921 and the reorganisation of management in 1930-2'. This he underlined by adding: 'If some of us fail to realise the full scope and diversity of the present reform, that is because we are contemporaries and participants in it.'[8]

The genetic versus teleology issue was, of course, essentially that of the respective roles of the subjective versus objective factors which has always played a large part in Marxian controversy at all levels (e.g. of 'class consciousness' as opposed to material conditions, of theoretical concepts and historical situations, of 'leadership' versus 'spontaneity'). In a controversy among Marxists one would scarcely expect the extreme teleologists' position (that 'purposive action' and human will could overcome any obstacle) to be acceptable – save as a tactical overemphasis tolerated for a season in order to overcome an opposite and conservative emphasis on limiting factors latent in the existing situation that was regarded as sapping the will to innovate and to change. In any other circumstances and time one could have expected the heirs of Marx and Lenin to have rejected as 'utopianism' and 'infantile voluntarism' the idea that purposive revolutionary initiative and action can flout 'economic laws' and suffice to storm heaven. Indeed, Stalin's later pronouncements about economic laws, and their continuing (if hazily defined) role, could be said to have been aimed at redressing the balance of the earlier debate and silencing the more extreme advocates of the 'teleological' position (after their tactical role was finished) as it was also, clearly, aimed against those who held that market influences were totally excluded once a planned economy, on the basis of a socialised industry and agriculture, had been established.

There seems to be little reason to doubt that the kind of intensive development achieved in the 1930s, with its structural changes and high tempo of growth, would have been impossible (in Russia's existing circumstances, at least) without a very high degree of centralised decision-making and control – control that went far beyond mere 'steering' of the actions of lower commands and that involved detailed tutelage of actual plan implementation. Even so, top-level policy did not always get its way, as some of the examples cited by David Granick indicate (such as the attempt of top planning bodies to achieve process specialisation in engineering for the sake of its technical economies, which seems to have been frustrated by the urge of managements towards vertical integration as a safeguard against supply shortages).[9] At any rate, it seems fairly clear that throughout this period considerably more *de facto* independence remained with managements of larger enterprises, at least, than would appear on paper. When such independence had the effect of frustrating, rather than aiding, planning intentions – whether in range of product assortment, or by inflating costs or employment and wage-bill totals – the reaction of Gosplan and/or the Ministries was, not unnaturally, to extend the range of plan directives and to make these more precise or more detailed. Possibly some incentive (e.g. a bonus) would be attached to fulfilment of the newly stipulated task or target that experience had shown was liable to be neglected in favour of others; with a resulting multiplication of so-called 'success indicators', some of which inevitably conflicted with others, and as a collection were almost bound to carry unequal weight.[10] This was essentially pragmatic improvisation to meet particular situations. The net result was greatly to inflate the intricacy of plans and the tasks of planners, as well as to place more reliance upon commands and directives being actually fulfilled, without evasion and distortion, than could realistically be expected. As Professor R. W. Davies has pointed out:

if planning from the centre is taken too far on paper, the possibility of shaping the economy can be destroyed. This is not simply because over-centralisation can stifle innovation, and thus limit economic growth. If central powers are extensive, the inevitable weaknesses in the paper plan can up to a point be corrected by the emergence of unofficial markets ... under-the-counter and illegal methods.... But if the authority of the central planners is taken too far, so that these devices are put to an end, it may stifle itself.[11]

Something very like this situation had apparently been reached by the beginning of the 1950s; and some re-examination of the whole question of centralisation of decision versus a more decentralised system was evidently required.

The initial attempts to deal with this situation after 1953[12] amounted to no more than an administrative redistribution of responsibilities among the top layer of planning and ministerial bodies. In the process the number of targets and indices settled by Gosplan at an all-Union level (and/or confirmed by the Council of Ministers) was considerably reduced, and those within the competence of republican Gosplans or Ministries were extended. This phase of *soi-disant* 'decentralisation', indeed, was criticised later, when discussion of the whole problem had become bolder, as 'solving complicated economic problems by administrative measures ... a most fallacious approach'.[13] One result, however, was to reduce the number of targets included in the central plan for major industrial products. So far as the lower units were concerned – the production units and operational management – little was changed: even if rather less detail was written into their plans, the ministerial *glavki* could (and apparently did) make up for this by issuing their own supplementary directives; and the main weight of the system continued to rest on obligatory directives handed down to industrial managements, who were left little discretion or scope for initiative. Substantially the same remained true of Khrushchev's apparently more drastic changes of 1957, with their emphasis upon geographical decentralisation to regional bodies and liquidation of the top-heavy structure of all-Union industrial Ministries.

What seems to have contributed quite powerfully to the recognition of the need for something more crucial by way of change than administrative reshuffles at higher levels was a fuller realisation of the distorting effect of the various methods of expressing plan targets, and hence of measuring productive achievement: e.g. in weight of output, in length or area or number of items, or alternatively (where the product was heterogeneous) in gross value (since this was easy to calculate as quantity multiplied by selling price). Examples of the distorting effects of such methods are now too familiar to need repeating. Some of the most adverse effects can be removed, of course, by simply changing the basis of measurement, without any more drastic alteration in the system: as, for example, the shift from *gross* value (with its encouragement of 'material-intensive' types of product)[14] to *net* value, which was adopted first of all in the clothing industry in 1959 and then extended more widely. But *some* degree of bias attaches to almost any physical index, to the extent that it gives importance to a particular dimension to the neglect of others; and accordingly in some degree attaches to the very system of controlling production by detailed plan directives and orders, since these inevitably emphasise results in terms of quantity (and by some particular, rather arbitrary, dimension as measure of quantity) irrespective of whether achievement of such a quantity target is at the expense of quality or of enhanced cost. Attention was accordingly turned towards finding a 'synthetic' index of performance (as Liberman called it) that would surmount the bias of the purely quantity-of-output kind; and once interest was concentrated upon a 'synthetic' index – an index that would take account of input cost as well as output, as also of the *kind* of output – it became clear that this had to be of a balance-sheet, or *khozrashchot*, type. Once such a shift was made, of course, the door was open to the granting of much greater latitude and discretion to the enterprise concerning the detail of its output and input policy. Such lower-level decisions, once they cease to be taken simply in response to orders and directives from above, must be taken according to some species of market criteria; and what the upshot will be will of course depend on prices (whence the importance of the Soviet price discussion of the 1950s, and the coupling of measures of reform of the economic mechanism with measures of price reform). It also followed that, as a means of influencing these lower-level decisions, planning bodies and Ministries must increasingly resort to 'economic instruments' (as they have been termed) rather than 'administrative' ones. With renewed interest in *khozrashchot*, it was not unnatural that increased attention should be paid to the way in which things worked in the 1920s when *khozrashchot* as a principle of operation came into vogue.

Viewing the matter in historical terms, one can say that what gave a new perspective to discussion in the 1950s and 1960s was a change in the basic situation and in the demands this laid upon policy in two main respects. Firstly, the intensive stage of industrial construction, characterising the pre-war decade, was bound to be followed by at least some easing-off in the earlier 'priority of development for heavy industry', if not an actual shift of priority towards the production of consumption goods. Such a shift certainly did occur in the later 1960s in the Soviet Union (and again for the first quinquennium of the 1970s). Whether large or small, the consequence of such a shift was to give more prominence to production for the retail market and hence greater weight in economic policy to market influences and to market demand. Secondly, the onset (or at least approach) of labour scarcity, with the absorption into industrial employment of the previous rural labour reserve, precluded the older type of 'extensive growth' by means of expanding employment, and increasingly obliged economic growth, if this were to continue, to take the form of progressively raising productivity by means of continuous technical innovation. It is here that there have been some signs of a lag during the past decade. Technical innovation is by no means the achievement of the scientific research laboratory alone; its adoption in practice demands a high degree of initiative and adaptability at the level of production and on the part of managements of industrial plants. It seems fairly clear that managerial personnel schooled and policed to carry out obediently decisions and directives of superiors are likely to be unsuited to such an innovatory role (and of this Soviet experience to date seems to afford some evidence at least).

There are those whose comment on any such discussion of decentralisation would be to cite the computer as a technical advance capable of solving all the problems of centralised planning and of obviating the need for decentralisation; at any rate for decentralisation to an extent that would involve reintroducing market relations and links (e.g. between industrial enterprises). This is a viewpoint to be met with both in Western and in Eastern Europe:[15] it is found, as one might expect, among more conservative defenders of the old system surviving from the 1930s, but it is also voiced among more moderate spokesmen for planning who are not themselves without criticism of *over*-centralisation. An example of the latter is the late Oskar Lange in what must have been almost his last written statement, 'The Computer and the Market',[16] which concluded with this emphatic declaration:

> Mathematical programming assisted by electronic computers becomes the fundamental instrument of long-term economic planning, as well as of solving dynamic economic problems of a more limited scope. Here, the electronic computer does not replace the market. It fulfils a function which the market never was able to perform.

It is not to be denied that the computer can very greatly assist and simplify the work of centrally planned decision. On the theoretical level it certainly provides an answer, as Lange himself observes,[17] to the Hayek–Robbins objection (of the 1930s) that comprehensive planning would involve the solution of thousands of simultaneous equations. Yet it remains extremely doubtful whether the computer can provide the answer to the whole problem, or even the major part of the problem, of centralisation in an advanced and complex industrial society – an answer in the sense of permitting any degree of centralised decision about micro-economic adjustment and obviating the need for decentralising the latter. Those who seek to silence all discussion of a possible *via media*[18] between plan and market by extolling the magical quality of the computer as a planning instrument deserve to be treated with more suspicion than respect.

There are a number of reasons why the computer cannot provide the *whole* answer to the complex problem of economic mechanism. Firstly, there is the practical consideration that computers as at present devised cannot handle the full range of industrial product varieties, e.g. in an input–output matrix, without a quite high degree of aggregation into product groups; and they seem unlikely to suffice to do so in the foreseeable future. The number of items, for example, in the Soviet official nomenclature list of 1960 amounted to 15,000, and this was far from being exhaustive. No input–output table yet devised for analysis of Soviet plans has included more than a few hundred product groups at most (that constructed by the Central Statistical Office for 1958 contained 157 product items).[19] With anything like this degree of aggregation for purposes of computerised central decision about output and allocation, the scope for decentralised micro-decision within each product group remains very considerable (or, alternatively, for well-known reasons, the balance method is subject to a significant degree of approximation, and hence of 'play' and inaccuracy, in the adjusting and allocating process).

Secondly, what a computer yields is dependent upon the information that is fed into it; and it is far from certain that planners and administrators will be in possession of enough unbiased detailed information for the purpose of reliable and precise decision about a mass of detail. Thus there is an information limit on the number and type of decisions that can be taken centrally. Take, for example, the crucial 'technical coefficients', defining the inputs required to produce a given quantity and kind of output. These differ from one plant to another according to their technical equipment and their specialisation, and are subject to change over time. Only those closely acquainted with the production process and the plants in question are capable of knowing what these are at first hand. For transmission to higher administrative levels, these data will almost inevitably have to be averaged to an extent dependent on the degree of aggregation; and the weighting appropriate to this averaging will depend on what the relative outputs of different items as well as plants are intended to be. Suppose that the plan of relative outputs is changed in the course of plan preparation and plan adjustment – as in some degree must inevitably happen. It is almost inconceivable that the planners will themselves possess enough detailed information to recalculate the average weighting of the coefficients themselves; and it would be an impossibly cumbrous and time-wasting procedure for them to refer the matter back to the plant level every time the draft plan was changed in the preparatory iterative procedure. Hence the coefficients used are almost bound to be no more than *approximately*, and not precisely, accurate. Accordingly, the internal consistency of the plan as it emerges is likely to be no more than approximate. At the macro-level and for macro-relations this degree of approximation, or margin of error, may be tolerable, in the sense of being too small proportion-ately to seem to matter. But at the micro-level (e.g. in the production of individual products and particular styles, sizes, grades of a product item) it may be crucial, and the lack of consistency (e.g. between inputs and required output) may be damaging to a major degree. Experience has shown this to be the Achilles' heel of the supply-allocation system and a not negligible weakness of the 'balance method' used to achieve internal plan consistency or coherence.

To this must be added the consideration that information fed from lower units to higher in the course of plan preparation almost inevitably contains a bias.[20] It would be surprising, indeed, if such bias were absent, since those supplying the information well know that what they supply will affect what is later imposed as an obligatory task upon them. If they were supplying it for a purely academic exercise the position might be otherwise. But the management and responsible personnel of lower units would scarcely be human if they did not seek to give themselves some elbow-room by overstating supply require-ments and understating productive potentiality or reserves, in the hope of encouraging plan targets to be on the lenient rather than the severe side, and avoiding interruptions of production owing to supply shortages. The planners, suspecting such bias, may, of course, seek to offset it by tightening up the technical coefficients with which they have been supplied and scaling up output targets. But the degree to which they can safely do this is bound to remain largely guesswork; and experi-ence has abundantly shown that to err on the side of optimism and over-tight planning only serves cumulatively to enlarge the basic problem (i.e. the information bias); and it very soon defeats its own purpose by causing dislocations of production through supply short-ages and non-deliveries of components. (The economist Kalecki, when he was attached to the Polish planning commission, used to say that he dreaded a good harvest since it encouraged over-optimism in drawing up plans for the coming period, with the risk of damaging consequences.)[21]

Even if central planning decisions are well and realistically based, there remains the problem of transmitting them as directives or instructions to the operative units (plants and enterprises), and the effect of the form in which this is done upon their practical implementation. We have already said something of the manner in which targets expressed in a physical dimension can have seriously distorting effects on the product that is actually turned out and on the manner of its production – distorting effects which, though they may be fewer, are not necessarily absent when targets are expressed in terms of value. If the attempt is made to counter such negative influence by multiplying the number of additional indices (e.g. cost-reduction ones, or employment limits or premia for fulfilling a stipulated 'assortment'), this not only complicates the planners' task considerably, but probably results in conflict between the various success indicators, which almost inevitably have different weights, some being ignored and others given prominence, probably in a quite random and incalculable fashion. What is not always appreciated in discussion of these matters is that transmission of instructions in such forms is an almost unavoidable consequence of centralised decision about the *detail* of production; and that even if a plan is perfect in its design and intention, much may go wrong with its actual implementation. This would be true even if the function of plant managers could be reduced to that of mechanically obedient sergeant-majors, 'theirs not to reason why'; it is very much more so to the extent that those in charge at the production level need to contribute something positive in the way of adaptation and initiative.

The alternative is to leave operational control over detail to management at lower levels (even, as in Hungary, year-to-year decision on their own output programmes within the framework of a centrally determined longer-term plan); and for this purpose to rely on some 'synthetic index' of performance – the *khozrashchot* principle of the 1920s. If enterprises (and/or 'associations') are to frame their actions according to balance-sheet criteria, then prices become crucial – relative prices of different inputs as substitutes and of different products. This immediately brings price policy, and the question of price controls (or, at least, of price limits and ceiling prices), into the centre of the stage, since an economically 'incorrect' price structure could have as damaging effects upon output 'assortment' and on choice of inputs as any set of centrally imposed target indicators (linked with *ad hoc* bonuses for fulfilment) can have. It would look as though an all-but-necessary corollary of such latitude for enterprises to make their own production decisions would be to restore at least some degree of latitude to enterprises to procure their supplies by direct contractual relations with other enterprises, thus giving them scope for 'shopping around' for what they need and laying down their own terms as regards quality, design, cost, as well as delivery dates and quantities. Thus there would be restored *some* form of market between socialist enterprises (in place of the allocation system), in addition to a retail market for consumers' goods.

Decentralisation of decision over a mass of micro-detail of this kind, such as previously congested the agenda of central planning bodies, would enable the latter to concentrate their attention, and their refined techniques, upon the macro-economic relations and magnitudes of the system, defining and establishing the structural framework within which the (limited) autonomy of enterprises would operate. Here it may not be easy at first sight to see where the line between macro and micro could or should be drawn. To draw the boundary too much at the expense of the sphere of the former would give market influences too great leeway at the expense of planned control; to draw it too much in the opposite direction might mean perpetuating many of the negative features of over-centralisation on which we have touched. Ultimately, of course, decision upon the location of such a boundary line must rest on results of experience and experiment. But a rather obvious, if by no means precise, line of division presents itself in the shape of the economist's distinction between investment decisions and decisions about current output. If the former were centrally planned and controlled, at least in the main, and defined so as to include all *new* plant construction and all major reconstructions or extensions (e.g. above a certain size) of existing plants, basic productive capacity and its distribution between industries and industrial branches would be established as a matter of planning policy; while decentralised decision-making (and market influences upon it) would be confined to current output policy *within the limits* of existing technical equipment and productive capacity of plants and enterprises.[22] This would, indeed, constitute the major difference from those 'decentralised models' of the pre-war *Wirtschaftsrechnung* debate in the West, associated with the names of Dickinson and Lange. It might then seem to be a secondary question whether or not the discretion of industrial managements was additionally limited by the setting (in the plan) of general quantity targets for enterprises either year by year or over a series of years.

In conclusion, there are two additional considerations that seem worth mentioning in this context, even at the expense of repetition of what has been said elsewhere. Firstly, the question of workers' participation in industrial management, or at least in policy-making, is evidently a highly controversial one, at any rate as regards the degree of it and its appropriate form. In the form of elected works councils, with rights of participating in policy-making decisions, it has been implemented only in the case of Yugoslavia, and for an experimental period in Poland after 1956 and in Czechoslovakia during the 'Prague Spring' of 1968. Yet if there is to be any such extension of what was at one time called 'industrial democracy', this can have little content in practice unless an appreciable amount of autonomy in economic decision-making rests at the level of the industrial enterprise. Such participation can be little more than formal if it is to be no more than operational, in the sense of finding ways and means of putting into effect decisions already arrived at by superior bodies. Political considerations of this type, accordingly, can reinforce very strongly the purely economic reasons for decentralisation that we have considered here; and unless such democratic participation by workers in industry is ruled out as a practical component of a socialist system, the type of question that we have been discussing cannot be decided on economic considerations alone. Even if it were quite feasible to take all decisions centrally, and to co-ordinate them satisfactorily according to some optimising principle, democratic considerations might well point the way to rejecting so bureaucratic a solution.

Secondly, it has to be borne in mind when considering changes of economic mechanism that there may be a degree of interdependence between various elements or factors in the situation such that, if some of these are changed without others to complement them, the new and reformed situation may be no improvement upon what it replaces, and may even be inferior thereto. There may be, in fact, a minimum of associated and complementary changes that are needed to make the more decentralised mechanism function coherently. If this be the case, too hesitant and piecemeal a reform – excessive attachment to Fabianesque 'gradualism' – may prove to be self-defeating (as in some respects it looks as though the rather limited and cautious Soviet economic reform of the second half of the 1960s may turn out to have been). The most obvious example of this would be if autonomy of enterprises were considerably extended on the basis of the old pre-reform price system. But there may be less obvious linkages than this of which serious account ought to be taken. We have mentioned the tendency of over-tight planning in the past to produce a chronic state of short supply, which not only occasions interruptions in the flow of production, but also places the supplying unit in the strong position of adopting a 'take it or leave it' attitude to purchasers (whether other enterprises or the final consumer) with regard to type or quality of product. It also causes a tendency to hoard excessive stocks of scarce supplies, so far as this is possible – hoarding which cumulatively accentuates the shortage situation elsewhere. Such a situation of 'sellers' market' has become a fairly common feature of Soviet industry, the remedy for which is not easy to prescribe, at any rate consistently with some major objectives of planning policy. But it may well be that to find a way of ending this situation (even of transforming it, for a time at least, into its opposite) is a prior condition for enabling any more decentralised mechanism to work efficiently and to show satis-factory results.

NOTES

1. E. H. Carr and R. W. Davies, *Foundation of a Planned Economy, 1926-9*, ɪ (London, 1969) pt 2, p. 787.

2. *Economic Problems of Socialism in the U.S.S.R.* (Moscow, 1952) p. 32. A few pages earlier (p. 23) Stalin had, indeed, mentioned the sale of consumer goods for individual consumption as an example of 'commodity circulation' (and a 'sphere of operation of the law of value'); but this was accorded no more than passing mention and in the sequel was apparently forgotten.

3. Professor A. Nove has quoted a passage from B. Higgins's *Economic Development* (New York, 1959) stressing the similarity in nature of the problems of planning a war economy and planning development in an underdeveloped country: 'The process required the breaking of a succession of critical bottle-necks. . . . In short, "total war", like planning development of poor and stagnant economies, involves marked and discontinuous structural changes and resource allocation without reference to the market.' Quoted in A. Nove, *The Soviet Economy* (London, 1961) p. 290; cf. ibid., pp. 145-7.

4. Cf. V. S. Nemchinov, *Ekonomiko-Matematicheskie metodi i modeli* (Moscow, 1962) p. 69, mentions a figure of 10,500 as commodity balances handled by the 'organs of material-technical supply and sale'.

5. R. W. Davies, *The Development of the Soviet Budgetary System* (Cambridge, 1958) pp. 229 ff.

6. Michael Ellman, *Soviet Planning Today*, Occasional Paper No. 25 of the Department of Applied Economics (Cambridge, 1971) p. 185.

7. Presumably after the leading cases of short-supply products have been remedied by appropriate output increases to match demand.

8. In *Literaturnaya Gazeta*, 11 Feb 1970. This may perhaps be deemed an exaggeration of the changes as these actually emerged; but it serves to illustrate, none the less, what many even fairly moderate advocates of economic reform had in mind in those years.

9. D. Granick, *Soviet Metal Fabricating* (Madison, Wis., 1967) pp. 143 ff.

10. Citing Polish experience, Dr J. G. Zielinski has said that even as late as 1960 the number of 'success indicators' in use, and applying to industrial enterprises, amounted to as many as fifty. *On the Theory of Socialist Planning* (Ibadan and Oxford, 1968) p. 164. More generally, for 'success indicators' and

their problems, cf. Nove, *The Soviet Economy*, pp. 155 ff.

11. Davies, *The Development of the Soviet Budgetary System*, p. 328.

12. Among the first official public criticisms of over-centralisation seems to have been a resolution of the Central Committee of the Party and the Council of Ministers of 14 Oct 1954, which spoke of 'exaggerated centralisation'.

13. Statement in *Pravda*, 1 Nov 1964, quoted in the present writer's *Soviet Economic Development since 1917*, rev. ed. (London, 1965) p. 377.

14. i.e. of products with a relatively high proportion of materials bought from outside the enterprise as compared with the value added in the enterprise itself. Particular examples were tools made only with expensive metals and clothes made of expensive rather than cheap materials.

15. Although in the latter *not* so far as I am aware among the mathematical economists of TSEMI (Central Mathematical Economic Institute of the Academy).

16. In C. H. Feinstein (ed.), *Socialism, Capitalism and Economic Growth: Essays Presented to Maurice Dobb* (Cambridge, 1967) pp. 158-61.

17. Ibid., p. 158: 'Let us put the simultaneous equations on an electronic computer and we shall obtain the solution in less than a second. The market process with its cumbersome *tâtonnements* appears old-fashioned. Indeed, it may be considered as a computing device of the pre-electronic age.'

18. Perhaps one should speak of 'synthesis' – and in the sense of *aufhebung*.

19. Putting it in this way, it is true, rather overstates the technical limitations, since, given suitable conditions, there is the possibility of so-called 'decomposition' of the total problem into sections. Even so, however, there remain fairly strict technical limits, (*a*) as to the degree of accuracy of such methods, (*b*) the number of successive 'iterations' possible within the time-scale in question.

20. Ota Šik has even spoken, as regards investment allocation from the centre, of 'investment demands backed by distorted information and reports to central bodies'. *Plan and Market under Socialism* (Prague, 1967) p. 90.

21. Edward Lipiński, in *Polish Perspectives*, xiv 9 (Sep 1971) p. 32.

22. Cf. the present writer's *Welfare Economics and the Economics of Socialism* (Cambridge, 1969) pp. 140-3. Cf. also Ota Šik: 'Central economic plans should be expressly *macro-economic* plans giving direction only to the basic structure and most general proportions of branches of production, the fundamental regional allocation of production forces, the basic processes of distributing the national income, the basic proportion between domestic production and foreign trade, etc. At the same time the central body must provide overall policies ... in regard to finances, prices, wages, foreign trade, but leaving to local management the details' (*Plan and Market under Socialism*, p. 144).

PART FOUR
Related Studies

15 Lenin's *Imperialism* in Retrospect

MARY HOLDSWORTH

THIS essay attempts to examine Lenin's *Imperialism* and his attitude
to national problems in the light of modern studies in the politics of
development, in particular the conceptual approaches worked out by
groups of American and some British scholars concerned with the
study of modernisation and development. The reasons which have
suggested this study are diverse. One is that the new conceptual
approaches widen the range of inquiry beyond the by now very well-
studied area of how and why Soviet nationality policies have petered
out in a static and uniform system, and stimulate one to ask why this
particular legacy of Lenin nevertheless remains a relevant political
factor today. It is in this range of political studies that Leninism is
most often discussed. Another reason is that the modern functional
approach moves away from polarities, both of the established
communist/non-communist type, and of the traditional/modern type
of thinking, and works in terms of a continuum, with overlapping
stages, or of a 'mix' which varies in the relative importance of its
components but which nevertheless remains a 'mix'. This methodology
and these attitudes seem particularly relevant in approaching the
legacy of Lenin.

Coming closer to the subject in hand, an assessment of Lenin's
legacy to development studies may serve as a fresh angle on the study
of imperialism in its historical perspective.[1] Without limiting itself to
the study of political domination by a metropolitan country of areas
beyond its confines, it nevertheless uses the experiences of nation-
building within both traditional continental and in colonial empires.
It is superfluous to point out that Lenin based his analysis on a
specific and in fact fairly short-term period in the history of
imperialism, but it is important to assess what the views he came to
from that intensive study had on his own subsequent thinking and on

that of his followers. This kind of inquiry might also link what Lenin described as 'semi-colonies' and the contemporary concept of neo-colonialism, or at any rate suggest questions on the content and validity of the latter concept.

I have drawn the concepts on development in the main from Professor Apter's studies.[2] Professor Apter presents a variety of models relevant to a modernising situation. From this variety comes the necessity of constant government choice, which every modernising government has to face. This includes decisions as to what social group can be relied on or called into existence for support, or alternatively destroyed as a potential opponent. He discusses what ideas and attitudes activate the different groups, how the opinions are formed, how altered. Since the majority of modernising states which Professor Apter has studied in detail and over a long period fall into the group of 'colonial' and 'semi-colonial' (with the exception of Japan), it is not surprising that the legacy of Lenin remains alive. But it is not Leninism as a solid body of doctrine, or indeed as crude unassimilated propaganda by Cominform agencies or lecturers at the Lumumba University in Moscow, which survives. The conceptual approach uncovers the needs and aspirations of individual governments, the ideas they look for in their need to bridge the gap between expectation and reality and to cope with the discontinuities which arise between static social structures and the new 'social system that can constantly innovate without falling apart ... and a social framework that can provide the skill and knowledge necessary for living in a techno-logically advanced world'.[3] And it is in this group of ideas, which embraces a very wide political spectrum, that it is possible to pick out key topics which appear in various combinations and with changing degrees of intensity over the spectrum as a whole.

The first of these is what Professor J. L. Talmon has called the 'political messianism model', but which indeed goes back throughout the history of political thought, and rests on the belief (or, in cruder form, the assumption) that there exists a single and exclusive truth in politics. In the context of contemporary modernising African states, Professor Apter has called the adherents of this model the modern Jacobins. They practise what is basically a mobilisation system of development, weighing up to a greater or less degree hindrances or severe incompatibilities within their particular society to this model of modernisation.

Another group of ideas and problems clusters round a broad head-ing of traditionalism. This includes adherence to a religion, an ethnic and linguistic identity and strong attachment to it, a strong folk tradition as regards means of livelihood, usually agricultural but not exclusively so. These have faced the majority of modernising states as immediate political problems. The problems have obviously been intensified in new states which are not ethnically homogeneous or homogeneous in their religious beliefs. At the opposite end to tradi- tionalism, but without the revealed certainty of political messianism, comes the search for an ideology that can win support and legitimise reform and the activities of the reforming agency. In this situation an ideology that can claim a scientific basis has a certain appeal. For the late comers on to the 'wide stage of history' (Lenin) or the 'rendez-vous de l'histoire' (Senghor), a philosophy of history which seeks to map out a scientifically based orderly development of human societies has an immediate and understandable appeal and can be a powerful factor in legitimising a government's action in difficult and diffuse transitional stages. In a similar way, an appeal to 'scientific socialism' can meet a genuine political need.

But the 'scientific' is only one of the attributes of socialism which is relevant to the politics of development. Another attribute is when socialism appears as the counterpart to colonialism – both the colonialism familiar to all the newly established states and, in a more problematic way, the vaguely defined 'neo-colonialism' which remains a preoccupation of many developing countries in trying out their inter- national roles. The empirical fact that socialism had to share with nationalism the struggle against colonialism and that in most cases the latter was the senior partner does not eliminate the former from the area of preoccupation but merely brings a further group of prob- lems and interim solutions. Similarly, the pragmatic need for economic aid or the rearrangement of external economic relations does not eliminate the fear of neo-colonialism; it raises problems of inter- national identity, of acceptable speed of change, and of finding resources.

It is around these interrelated groups of key topics that I should like to trace whether and in what way Lenin's ideas are still relevant, in what way they have been internalised by modern leaders and in what situations and in what sense they have been rejected or modified. It is more useful to speak of 'Leninism' rather than disentangling the adaptations or distortions of Marx. This whole discussion is concerned with the formative influences on today's leaders and influential groups engaged in the politics of a specific type of situation. Lenin has long seemed the most important mediator of Marx to the contemporary world in his role as successful revolutionary – one of the 'doers who are writers, and shapers who are thinkers'[4] – and this in itself is of considerable significance.

Leninism as the model *par excellence* for the elite party working out political truth and schooling itself for transforming it into political action has no serious contender. Those modernising states which have adopted this type of structure have adopted to a greater or lesser extent the political philosophy that produces it. Though the content of what the elite party claims to bring about has seldom been a mere replica of the Bolshevik programme, the structure, internal discipline, selective recruitment, and above all the position of the party leader, have strong overtones of the party Lenin created. The importance the leader attaches to the party as a political force in government, its relation to other consultative or administrative structures, is also Leninist. Composition and even size of the party have varied in different situations, notably those where nationalism was the major emotive force. But homogeneity and strong anti-factionalist measures, selection and retention on criteria of personal loyalty and effective performance rather than on those of inherited status or high position in an ethnic group, as well as a large degree of mobility in the party's service – all these were in the first instance Leninist characteristics. The programme content will be discussed later in conjunction with interpretations of socialism.

The cluster of problems loosely described as traditionalism confronts all leaders and indeed all groups in modernising states. It is interesting to trace in this context echoes of Lenin's own controversies over nationalities policy with his peers both in the formative years of the Bolshevik Party and in its first years in power. The fact that Lenin both as a creator of a political programme and as ruler of a multinational state had to contend with the problems of communalism is of immense significance. Without this extra dimension to the October Revolution's modernising problems, the Bolshevik experiences would have been much less relevant to the problem of the majority of African and Asian political leaders. In experimenting with problems of this type, Japanese experience, for instance, would make much less impact. If one looks at policy statements first (as opposed to their application), those which reverberated in people's minds, and which in a transmuted way continue to reverberate still, are Lenin's stated adherence to the risk of self-determination up to and including the right to secession, and his denunciation of Russification and support of minority languages. The fact that from the start Lenin grasped the potential tug-of-war between socialism and nationalism and repeatedly stated that the claims of nationalism or secession must give way to the claims of the socialist revolution detracted very little from the creation of Lenin's anti-imperialist image. That he very much under-estimated the strength of both ethnic solidarities and linguistic attach-ments when he supposed that secession and the flourishing of minority languages would in due time provide the solid and contented base for integration into one socialist whole has merely meant that the new leaders gradually find how sophisticated the political skills have to be to contain, let alone solve, these intractable problems. It is realised that one must extend Lenin's time scale but not move away from his original premise that, somehow or other, the two can be reconciled in a non-imperial, non-capitalist way.

It is interesting to look back at Rosa Luxemburg's vehement criticism of Lenin on this issue – a criticism which she adds to her famous condemnation of his negation of mass participation and his staking all on an elitist party. She argues against the need for national self-determination as a stepping-stone to socialism even in the multi-ethnic and multi-lingual empires with which both she and Lenin were familiar. She held that the socialist revolution would in itself right these wrongs and solve these problems, and that self-determination, linguistic states and the rest would injure the socialist cause, and postpone socialist solutions. Yet in the event he was right and she was wrong, and if the right to secession had not been written into each successive Communist Party programme and into all the early pro-gramme documents and constitutions, the legacy of Lenin in the minds of a wide spectrum of leaders and politically active groups in the modernising states today would have been to that extent diminished.

There is obviously a great deal more to be said on the integration of traditionalism, nationalism and socialism, since containment, let alone acceptable solutions, has proved to be the most difficult assign-ment of the new successor states. That containment in the Soviet Union itself was in the end achieved by severely centralising means, backed by armed force and police purges, has contributed to the repudiation of the Soviet Union as an ideal model. But the effort to preserve the image of successful integration on Leninist lines continues to be made by the Soviet leadership; for instance, the 1967 conference on 'Socialism and the Liberated Countries' was held in Baku.

One must admit, however, that in this range of problems the con-ceptual analysis seems somehow inadequate. It seems likely that these particular intransigences of human group behaviour will eventually become accommodated. As Professor Apter describes, in the continuum towards modernity one moves from 'the more "primordial" sentiments based on race, language, tribe, or other factors, which although not

relevant to the development process, may be relevant to the maintenance of solidarity or identity. What I call "nationalism" is the ideology
that embodies these primordial sentiments. It is well to bear this special
meaning in mind as we discuss the relationship between nationalism
and socialism.'[5] But at the close of 1971 this tidy though relevant
analysis hides a craggy and abrasive hinterland of bloody conflict.

Coming now to Lenin's study of imperialism and trying to connect
up some of its analytical approaches and conclusions to modern
development policies, the point of key significance is the definition of
imperialism as the last and highest stage of capitalism and the consequent linking-up of the overthrow of one with the overthrow of
the other. Post-imperialist systems of economic development must
thus be socialist, however variously defined; they cannot be carried
out by capitalist monopolies which by definition are located in the
metropolitan capitalist countries. Such monopolies would, as hitherto,
create their surplus value from colonial labour and transfer it back
to the metropolitan country, where among other things it would be
used to corrupt the lower bourgeoisie and favoured proletariat away
from its historic mission of speeding on the socialist revolution. This
in its simplest form was the core of a complex of suspicions, caution
and ambivalent attitudes in regard both to patterns of internal
economic economic development and in some measure to external
political alignment, which characterised particularly the earlier years
of political independence. But there were further, perhaps less obvious,
ramifications. One concerned the schools of development economics
in some of the modernising countries. Lenin, as indeed his contemporary Marxist political economists, stressed that profits on capital
always flowed back to the capital's source. The consequent doctrine
of the primacy of investment in heavy industry if a country were ever
to be truly independent was prominent in the thinking of important
successor governments for a considerable period, and eventually
converged with various policies of prestige spending, which latter,
however, one would hesitate to lay at Lenin's door. But certainly,
attitudes engendered by Lenin's *Imperialism* led to much heart-
searching on the source of capital accumulation, and to some mistaken
choices of development priorities.

The 'Notebooks' in preparation for *Imperialism* illustrate vividly
Lenin's preoccupation with the contemporary phase. There is little
concern for the history of imperialism, or for studies in culture contact.
There is little research in source material. The notebooks are a compendium of notes and extracts from books and journals published
almost wholly in a span of some twenty years, and of abstracts of

current statistical material, illustrating and elaborating the Hilferding thesis on the wide-flung workings of finance capital. But looking back at the notebooks over fifty years later, the following points strike the reader. First, Lenin was reading and quoting scholars and publicists writing within the living heritage of Marx and Engels and within the varied group of German and Austrian writers of the immediate post-Marxist circle. (Krupskaya's phrase on 'Lenin conversing with Marx' is a suggestive metaphor for describing this immersion in the key issues of the day and for working at them from a certain standpoint.) This is not to say that Lenin did not use the work of a number of British historians of the period writing on the Empire, but to underline why he aligned himself with Hobson rather than with the traditional British gradualist view of the evolution of Empire, and the applicability of the Westminster model. But perhaps a more subtle relevance lies in methodology. First, the massive use of statistical data – the empirical approach, the effort to quantify, to present evidence from socio-economic analysis by methods taken from the physical sciences. Among the journals he read and used are *Zeitschrift für die gesamte Staatswissenschaft, Die Neue Zeit, Schriften des Vereins für Sozialpolitik,* in which the early generation of continental sociologists also wrote. A good deal of this was turgid, polemical, over-laid with all kinds of controversies and enmities now totally irrelevant, but in spite of all this it was the prolegomena to a whole school of modern social investigation. And it is this aspect which remains relevant in the 'politics of development'. At one level it links up with the belief in the efficiency of the 'scientific' approach as a guideline to change, and at another with the view that one of the main objects in studying society is to know how best to change it.

The 'semi-colonies' and the various 'dependent' though politically sovereign states which figure prominently in Lenin's own work and in much of the writing of his contemporaries obviously raise issues which are not solved by political independence in the post-imperial era. Problems of investment in developing countries, of aid programmes, of the relative merits of different priorities and techniques have today a vast and highly professional literature of their own. Lenin's contention that political emancipation cannot of itself be the end of the story is subsumed in much of these discussions. But on the whole he himself has little to say on dependent economies as it were from within – which is surprising in view of his analysis of the socio-economic structure of late nineteenth-century Russia. Rosa Luxemburg's chapters on the impact of developed capitalism on subsistence economies have remained more relevant in drawing attention to the disruption and imbalance brought about by the crude shocks of haphazard economic exploitation, and may be among the influences prompting the search for more integrative and controlled policies of economic and social development.[6]

Two further points seem relevant to this retrospective glance at Leninist influences in development. One is to discover how and in what respects the impact of Leninism has changed over the years. The other is to record a tentative new approach to development studies by recent Soviet writers. One of the lessons of modern political studies is that a popular image, or 'cognitive map' to use H. Hyman's more sophisticated phrase, should not be ignored as a political force.[7] The particular 'cognitive map' in this context is the view that only socialism can provide the long-term solution to the aspirations of all peoples formerly downtrodden by imperialist rulers or held in the grip of unequal economic relationships. In the half-century which saw the emergence of more new nations than any previous period, several contradictory yet simultaneous processes can be identified. One is the partial disenchantment with the Soviet model. And one could add to the obvious and by now frequently documented reasons for this the extreme paucity of contemporary Soviet sociological studies on, say, the impact of modern industrial development on traditional societies, assimilation or otherwise of new settlement groups, impact of secondary education on Moslem families, etc. (A few very good studies exist, but they are few and far between in comparison with the wealth of experience that has accumulated by now, and with the mass of such studies in most other parts of the world.) Another development is the proliferation of interpretations of socialism, the search and experimentation with patterns to suit individual situations and to absorb or adapt existing national strengths. This is in the Marxist tradition. But though Engels's phrase on not exporting any one brand of socialism is recorded by Lenin in his *Notebooks on Imperialism*,[8] the Leninist image has been ambivalent in this respect. The ambivalence was inherent in his own statements and actions. It was also prominent in the attitudes and writings of a whole middle generation of Soviet experts and journalists writing on Africa. Lenin's stress on the necessity of class conflict is another feature which has been partially superseded (though it had a very strong impact for a considerable period, perhaps more in Asian countries than in African). Looking back at Bukharin's and Preobrazhensky's *The A.B.C. of Communism*,[9] which, as its title suggests, was a popular statement of the Bolshevik programme, one is struck by the obtrusiveness of the class component in relation to the nationalist one in the section on 'Communism and

Nationality'. Again, one cannot claim a dramatic change. Obviously Lenin's strong and repeated warnings about the shortcomings of the national bourgeoisie had considerable impact, but equally obviously in the event it proved extremely difficult to obtain any kind of independence without the existence of a national bourgeoisie. It is not particularly fruitful to draw up a balance sheet of the legacy of Lenin in the politics of development as defined today. Differing attitudes and differing emphases exist simultaneously in people's minds and emerge in different situations. It is thus quite possible for a dis-enchantment with the actual Soviet model to coexist with a sustained belief that the ways to desirable goals are nevertheless in the general Leninist direction.

A few comments on the recent work of Soviet and East European students of development may help to round off this study. Two main impressions emerge from a perusal of books and articles on African problems published since about the middle-1960s.[10] The first is an almost trenchant realism, and the second a familiarity with modern con-ceptual approaches and a growing freedom in the use of modern social science vocabulary. The sense of reality appears, for instance, in the acknowledgement that the Soviet model is not necessarily the one for the non-capitalist road to socialism, some writers going as far as to say that it emphatically is *not* the model and explaining why. Attempts to rationalise antagonism to the Soviet Union among recently created African or Asian regimes no longer take refuge in a stereotype of 'imperialist machinations'. Concepts of class and their relevance or otherwise to the society in question are analysed anew and include an appraisal of situations where the state appears to be above the class struggle. A variant of the classical class stereotype relevant to many modern African states is acknowledged, namely that the young working class represents the priviliged class vis-à-vis the peasants and hence that it is rather disinclined to be the revolution-bearer. Acknow-ledgement of repeated setbacks, instabilities, and of the fact that interim models have to be worked out, gives a freshness long absent from much Soviet writing on the Third World. Among examples of the use of modern approaches one could cite an analysis of a develop-ing government which shows it as a fully autonomous economic and political mechanism, unsupported by even remotely adequate social structures, and hence having an insupportable burden hoisted on to it. Similarly, in leadership studies one author observes that the destinies and tasks of revolution are identified with the personality of the leader, which produces an inherently unstable situation. An interest-ing socio-psychological analysis works out why an army cannot really carry through a revolution without endangering the purpose of the revolution itself, and also lists the juxtaposition of circumstance and socio-political relationships which favours an army *coup*.

These new insights and the much wider range and pertinence of inquiry are due, among other things, to greatly increased first-hand knowledge of development problems in areas well outside the U.S.S.R. itself. Interchange of ideas at conferences must have some impact, even if many of them are of the 'in-group' type, such as the Cairo 1967 seminar on 'Africa: National and Social Revolution'. Also, modern American and British publications in the social sciences are increasingly reviewed in Soviet journals. The post-Stalin climate of opinion has enabled inquiries into certain areas of the social sciences to become less rigid. Soviet studies on the developing world have moved from a foundation of excellent studies of ecology and material culture in the pre-revolutionary and early post-revolutionary years and have gone through a long period of rigid inquiry, circumscribed by immovable positions in which the politics of development had to be taken as given and the economics of development held the stage. The move in recent years to inquiry into the politics and sociology of development brings Soviet studies in this field gradually nearer to the prevailing modern approach.

What of Leninism in this changing phase? As one would expect, in recent literature, a good many of the articles and symposia discussed above are headed 'Leninism and the Struggle against Bourgeois Ideology', or 'Some Problems of National Liberation in the Light of Leninism', or 'The Leninist Concept of Non-capitalist Development'. Probably the only interim assessment one can make, pending deeper and more comprehensive studies of Lenin's legacy in the political thought of the 1970s, is to repeat that one no longer looks for a self-perpetuating body of doctrine, but instead for lines of inquiry, attitudes, preconceptions, and a reinterpretation of dogma. In the case of Soviet social scientists one must also take into account that they have had their whole training in a fairly closed and circumscribed atmosphere.

NOTES

1. G. Lichtheim, *Imperialism* (New York: Praeger, 1971) gives a modern historical analysis, and covers the main interrelated problems.
2. D. Apter, *Some Conceptual Approaches to the Study of Modernisation* (Englew and Cliffs, N.J.: Prentice-Hall, 1968). G. A. Almond and J. S. Coleman, *The Politics of the Developing Areas* (Princeton U.P., 1960) was one of the pioneer books in this field.

3. Apter, *Conceptual Approaches*, p. 197.

4. Ibid., p. 198.

5. Ibid., p. 243.

6. R. Luxemburg, *The Accumulation of Capital*, Introduction by Joan Robinson (London: Kegan Paul, 1951).

7. Herbert Hyman, *Political Socialisation* (Glencoe, Ill.: Free Press, 1959), quoted by Almond, op. cit.

8. V. I. Lenin, *Collected Works*, xxxix (London: Lawrence and Wishart, 1968) 672, quoting Engels's letter of 12 Sep 1882.

9. Petrograd, 1920. Now available in a Penguin edition, 1968, with an excellent introduction by Mr E. H. Carr.

10. Excellent critical summaries of this work, with ample quotations, are published by Mr D. Morrison in *Mizan*, Central Asian Research Centre, London N.1 (Aug 1971; Oct 1970; July-Aug 1969; Jan-Feb, July-Aug, Sep-Oct 1968; Mar-Apr, Nov-Dec 1967; Nov-Dec 1966).

16 Graetz and Dubnow: Two Jewish Historians in an Alien World

LIONEL KOCHAN

WHEN Mendelssohn and a group of followers undertook to enlighten Eastern European Jewry, they attributed to the knowledge of Jewish history an important share in the process of enlightenment. They endeavoured to commission Solomon Maimon either to prepare a Hebrew version of Basnage's *Histoire des Juifs depuis Jésus-Christ jusqu'à présent* (1706-11) or to compose an entirely new work of Jewish history. Neither scheme had any success. Maimon comments that history, natural theology, morals, 'being easily intelligible, would not instil any regard for science into the more learned Jews, who are accustomed to respect only those studies which involve a strain upon the highest intellectual powers'. Then there was the certain conflict between these subjects and 'religious prejudices'. 'Besides,' Maimon concludes, 'there is no proper history of the Jewish nation: for they have scarcely ever stood in any political relation to other civilised nations and, with the exception of the Old Testament and Josephus and a few fragments on the persecution of the Jews in the middle ages, nothing is to be found on the subject.'[1]

Maimon was of course no historian and he lived in a non-historical age. Even so, this episode does illustrate the widespread conviction that even if the Jews did have a history – an arguable proposition *per se* – then virtually nothing was known of it, or interest taken in it. Numerous later writers have maintained the same proposition – though they have accounted for the phenomenon in varying ways.[2] A recent Jewish religious philosopher, Franz Rosenzweig, in presenting the Jews as the 'eternal people' has, for this very reason, argued that they are thereby removed from 'all the temporality and historicity of life'.[3] This restates a traditional affirmation in the existentialist terminology of the twentieth century.

But Mendelssohn's initiative does show that, at the end of the eighteenth and beginning of the nineteenth century, the attitude to historical study was already beginning to take a more positive form.[4] The movement towards concern with the Jewish past gained further impetus from the *Wissenschaft des Judentums* – so much so, that it is impossible to conceive either Graetz or Dubnow save in the light of that movement. Even so, though the study of Jewish history did establish itself at the beginning of the nineteenth century as an autonomous discipline (in, e.g., the work of I. M. Jost), nothing in the nature of a historical school or a modern historiographical tradition could yet develop. The difficulties confronting Graetz and Dubnow cannot be underestimated – most notably, perhaps, that difficulty arising from the relationship between the Jewish historian of the Jewish people and his non-Jewish intellectual environment. Graetz (1817-91) and Dubnow (1860-1941) were both contemporary with the great rise of European historiography, especially in Germany. How did they react to this pressure? Moreover, the pressure emanated from a world that had consistently denied the very existence of Jewish history, since the collapse of the Second Temple. The work of Basnage at the beginning of the eighteenth century stands out as the sole attempt by a non-Jewish historian to treat of events in the Jewish world subsequent to 70 C.E. The very subject-matter of Jewish history had to be made authentic amid Gentile indifference and hostility, and Jewish lack of interest. To what precise influences were Graetz and Dubnow subject? What did they select and what reject from their environment? How do the two Jewish historians compare in this respect?

This cluster of problems will be our major concern. But before talking of differences, a word first as to similarities. Both, from youth onwards, saw themselves as historians. Both saw in the history of the Jews a phenomenon of surpassing and distinctive value and importance. Outstanding in its intensity, moreover, is the self-identification of the two Jewish historians with the fortunes of their people. The story goes that when Zunz was told of Graetz's intentions, he asked: 'Another history of the Jews?' Graetz riposted: 'Another history, but this time a *Jewish* history.'[5] The same passionate identification is characteristic also of Dubnow's work. The two historians feel with their people, suffer in its tragedies and rejoice in its triumphs. By the same token, neither confines his sympathy or denunciation to the past but readily participates in contemporary battles – Graetz in his polemic with Treitschke, Dubnow in his *Letters on Old and New Judaism* (1897-1907). 'What profit does anyone find today in denouncing the sins of Charlemagne or of Napoleon?' asks Carr, the agnostic.[6] He is echoed by Knowles, the Catholic, whom Carr quotes in his support.[7] But to refrain from passing judgement was unthinkable to the two Jewish historians. The reason is perfectly obvious: if you cannot condemn Napoleon's 'infamous decree' (1808), then must you not likewise overlook even the actions of, say, the Crusaders, the Inquisitors, Khmelnitzki, Petlura, etc.? On what grounds, further, can you then condemn Hitler in the present? Not for nothing did Dubnow give the title 'In Haman's Times' to an open letter in a Yiddish journal that he published in 1939.[8]

Of course, though Graetz and Dubnow were at one in this emotional identification with the whole experience of their people, great differences emerge as soon as attention is turned to the sources of their outlook, and their treatment of the same subject-matter. Attempts have been made to demonstrate some sort of parallelism or affinity between Graetz and Ranke.[9] But no convincing evidence has been adduced. Indeed, it has been more persuasively argued that 'it is impossible to recognise in Graetz's work any true contact with the great upsurge of the historical sciences in contemporary Germany'.[10] Be that as it may, there is certainly stronger reason to argue that Graetz's approach to the understanding of the totality of Jewish history owed much to Hegel. Graetz had been introduced to Hegel's thought in the early 1840s as a student of Professor Braniss, at the University of Breslau.[11] Of course, Hegel's principal historical contention that the Idea is progressively embodied in different peoples or worlds was utterly untenable for any such devout Jew as was Graetz. Here the views of S. R. Hirsch and Z. Frankel were far more powerful. Graetz must resoundingly reject Hegel's view that Judaism belonged to a transitional phase of the 'Oriental World'.[12] Graetz himself speaks of Hegel's 'crass prejudice' vis-à-vis Judaism.[13]

But this still leaves room for a Hegelianism modified so as to accommodate the centrality of Judaism. To this early period of Graetz's career belongs his programmatic essay, *Die Konstruktion der jüdischen Geschichte* (1846). This reconciles the understanding of Judaism as law (Mendelssohn) with the understanding of Judaism as spirit (Steinheim, Formstecher).[14] But in so doing, the essay, within the limits imposed by Graetz's prior commitment to Judaism, is suffused with Hegelian ideas, in particular the idea that the history of a thing makes manifest its character. To the opening question 'What is Judaism?' Graetz replies that it is precisely the history of Judaism that will bring together the many divergent views and interpretations, each on its own necessarily one-sided and incomplete. 'The totality of Judaism is only recognisable in its history; in history its whole essence, the sum of its powers, must be made explicit.'[15]

Thenceforward, Graetz argues that 'Jewish history in all its phases, even in the apparent vagaries of the haphazard, makes manifest a uniform idea.... If one surveys Jewish history, its active as well as its passive side, in accordance with broad categories, if one holds fast to the natural nodal-point, then one has the very factors which have brought it into life, then one has the buds which the idea of Judaism has, as it were, borne in its lap.'[16]

The idea of Judaism, according to Graetz, undergoes a threefold development. The first two are played out on the *Heimatsboden*, in pre-exilic and post-exilic times. The former is marked by a politico-social character and its exponents are 'political burghers' (*politische Bürger*), warriors, kings 'with but slight religious *élan*'; the latter epoch is marked by its religious character, and its bearers are men of piety, sages, teachers, pupils, sectarians 'who have but a weak social interest'. The prophets, especially the later ones, form the transition between the two periods, at the time of the Babylonian exile. 'If, in the first period, the political factor (*das Staatliche*) stood forth with exclusive one-sidedness, then in the second the religious factor took up a one-sided position, to the extent that it negated all political independence; Judaism ceased to be a basic state law and became religion in the accepted sense of the word.' But neither of these exclusivities 'can wholly represent' the character of Judaism – neither the purely political nor the purely religious.[17]

It is only the third and culminating period of the Diaspora that, despite 'its apparent disintegration and incoherence' (*Zerrissenheit und Zusammenhangslosigkeit*), will reconcile the contrasting claims of politics and religion. Whereas the latter bears the traces of 'unreflecting immediacy', religiosity in the third period, that of the Diaspora, 'sinks itself in the inwardness of reflection'. This is the work of scholars, thinkers, philosophers of religion, systematicians – even sceptics and apostates, Graetz adds, 'for scepticism is a necessary ingredient in the purificatory process of knowing'.[18] The objective of this process is 'not to remain standing in the realm of the abstract or theoretical ... but to produce consciously and in the present a practice in accordance with theory, a religio-social reality'.[19] At the end of the *Konstruktion* Graetz argues, not only that these three *Momente* must have been present in the original idea of Judaism, 'as the tree in the seed', but also that 'it seems to be the task of the Jewish idea of God, to organise a religious state-constitution conscious of its activity, its aims and its connection with the world as a whole'.[20]

Graetz remained true to this Judeo-centric view of history and the world to the end of his life. In 1888, more than forty years after the *Konstruktion*, he was still writing: '... Judaism is the science alike of humanity, of monotheism, and of religious nationalism. It has still its function to play, its mission to fulfil, in bringing these ideals to reality.'[21] However, long before this, it had already become apparent that in important respects the quasi-Hegelian Graetz of the *Konstruktion* was writing his *Geschichte der Juden* in a different spirit. There is already in the *Konstruktion* a certain ambiguity, in that the concept of the evolving idea of Judaism seems to coexist with a static Judaism as spirit, contrasted with paganism as nature.[22] Graetz's practice as a historian is to some extent at variance with his earlier theoretical stance. His main concern continues to be the intellectual and spiritual history of Judaism. By comparison, to the economic and social history of the Jews very little attention is given. It is therefore beside the point to castigate Graetz for disregarding precisely those aspects of Jewish history that he considered unimportant to his main theme.[23]

The relevant question, it seems, if we are to consider those influences with which Graetz was associated, is to move from the theory of the *Konstruktion* to the reality of historical treatment. This confirms a point made in the early days of Graetz interpretation by David Kaufmann, who rejects the attribution to Graetz of any 'prejudged Hegelianising' (*voreingenommene Hegelei*).[24] What Graetz does in fact present as Jewish history is very largely a history of thought and martyrology. Moreover, the idea of Providence is dominant, e.g.:

> the Diaspora was a blessing in the development of the world's history, for Israel could, by means of its wanderings, fulfil its mission to bring light to the nations. It scattered some sparks at Alexandria, Antioch and Rome, and thus gave rise to Christianity. It scattered some seeds in Mecca and Medina, and thus gave rise to Islam. From a few traces of light left by it was derived the scholastic philosophy in the second half of the Middle Ages, and the Protestantism of the Continent in the sixteenth century....[25]

Apart from Providence as expressed in the centrality of Judaism, Graetz as a historian operates with two other essentially religious categories. These are quite simply body and soul, sometimes equated at the beginning of Jewish history with the political and the religio-moral.[26]

In the Introduction to volume IV of the *Geschichte* this is clearly expounded. This, the first volume to be published (in 1853) treats of the collapse of the Jewish state to the completion of the Babylonian Talmud, *c.* 500. It inaugurates the study of the whole Diaspora which, in Graetz's view, is to be seen under a double aspect: 'on the one hand enslaved Judah with wanderer's staff in hand; his countenance turned heavenwards surrounded by dungeon walls, instruments of torture and the glow of branding-irons; on the other, the same figure with a questing look on the transfigured features, in a study filled with a vast library in all the languages of man ... the image of a slave with a thinker's pride'. The history of suffering is the external history of the Jews; their inner history is the history of thought. 'To seek and to wander, to think and to endure, to learn and to suffer take up the long stretch of this epoch.' With this as his *point de départ*, Graetz then subdivides the Diaspora period into markedly and unmistakably religio-spiritual chronological categories: first, from the foundation of the Sanhedrin and school in Yavneh to the collapse of the Gaonate and the Babylonian schools (70-1040); the foundation of the rabbinical schools in Spain to the split between *Denkgläubigkeit* and *Stock-gläubigkeit* (1040-1250) the struggle for free inquiry to the beginning of the new period under Mendelssohn (1230-1780).[27] The period subsequent to Mendelssohn is that of 'growing self-consciousness' – the subtitle to volume XI.

This schema of Graetz is not altogether reconcilable with his *Konstruktion*. The skeleton of the latter's programmatic analysis is formed of three distinct periods in Jewish history of which the third denotes the union of its two predecessors to form 'eine religiöse Wirklichkeit', and thus they bring to a triumphant climax the germ-cells borne within Judaism since its very beginnings. The actual history, on the other hand, operates with the categories of suffering and thought. If, therefore, the intention is to view Graetz in the light of his relationship to contemporary historiographical influences, then it appears evident that he remained unaffected.

Far more rewarding is it to remove Graetz entirely from this framework and to consider him as a representative – perhaps the *last* representative – of a traditional type of Jewish historiography. The latter as asserted earlier, is by no means well developed, for a variety of reasons. But what does exist can be grouped into precisely those categories which form the framework of Graetz's own work, i.e. martyrology and the unfolding of a religious, philosophic and spiritual tradition. Clearly, this does not of itself exclude the use of history as a means to emphasise this or that aspect of the tradition, to use history for special pleading, to denigrate certain religious claims, to exalt others. These categories are likewise separable from the identification and analysis of changes within the genre itself.[28]

But the two basic themes cut across these changes. Take, for example, the *Letter* of R. Sherira Gaon (tenth century), Abraham ibn Daud's *Sefer Ha'kabbalah* (twelfth century), Abraham Zacut's *Sefer Yuhasin* (fifteenth to sixteenth century), David Gans's *Tsemah David* (end of sixteenth century), etc. These exemplify those works that are devoted to the exposition of a chain of thought, scholarship, religious tradition. Very little overt reference is made to other aspects of Jewish life.

Their counterpart in respect of history as martyrology and chronicle is to be found in the histories of the Crusades, or Joseph Ha'Cohen's *Emek Ha'bacha* (sixteenth century), or Nathan of Hanover's *Yeven Metzula* (seventeenth century).[29]

It is to this tradition that Graetz belongs; or rather, his work combines the twin themes of Jewish suffering and Jewish learning, treated with much of the scholarly aparatus and technique of the nineteenth century. In other words, as far as the selection and treatment of his material is concerned, Graetz's relationship to contemporary schools of historiography is emphatically negative. Graetz brings to a triumphant climax and fusion the dominant preoccupations of his forerunners. The student and teacher at Breslau University and the contemporary of the great age of German and European historiography bent the achievements of his age to the fuller exposition of a native Jewish tradition.

With Dubnow we are in a recognisably different world. No road led from Germany to Russia. Western European ideas, especially those with a secular emphasis, held greater sway in the Russian Pale than in the provinces of Posen or Silesia – at least as far as concerns the writing of Jewish history. It seems that Dubnow's outlook represents a blend between local Russian elements and a certain type of Jewish-nationalist outlook. It is not difficult to see one reason why this should be so. In Germany the battle for Jewish emancipation had been won and the 'national' rights of German Jewry was a question posed by nobody of influence; in Russia, on the other hand, not only was the battle still being fought, but the question of 'national' Jewish rights was raised within a context of small nations engaged in a similar struggle. Thus, in a general way, Dubnow's nationalist emphasis on the Jews as makers of history, and not merely as a people that subjectively experienced a history imposed on them by others, has an obvious affiliation with the assertion of the rights of small nations in the second half of the nineteenth century. He writes as follows, for example, in the fourth of his *Letters on Old and New Judaism* (1897-1907):

Despite the present reaction, the course of history is directed, not toward the subjection of national groups, but toward their liberation. In the same way that the principle of a ruling Church gave way after a bitter struggle, so too the principle of a ruling nationality is bound to be discarded. If the ninteenth century was able to secure the legal recognition by the community of the principle of freedom of the individual, the twentieth century is faced with the task of establishing the freedom or the autonomy of the national individual. The struggle by nationalities for this ideal will not cease until it is crowned with victory. Israel is not alone in this struggle.[30]

In the Russian historiographical context this has been described as the 'federal idea', its aims being to correct the idea of 'Muscovite egocentricity'.[31]

Independently of this adventitious political situation, however, Dubnow's views can also be related to a particular period in the history of the Jewish Enlightenment, the *Haskala*, and the Russian intelligentsia. A determining influence on Dubnow's outlook came from his reading of English and French thinkers, as distinct from the German thinkers who had earlier been dominant in the *Haskala*. At the same time Dubnow can also be seen in the context of the Russian social thought that developed in the nineteenth century. In this perspective we can perhaps see in Dubnow a curious blend of Westerner and Judeophile. This particular treatment of Jewish history is fully in keeping with Belinsky's exhortation to pass 'from the blue heavens into the kitchen'. Again, it can well be supposed that Dubnow would readily echo Belinsky's declaration: 'for me, to think, feel, understand and suffer are one and the same thing'. Dubnow as the heir of the *Haskala* does not only welcome the secularisation of Jewish life (though with a difference, as we shall attempt to show), but also incorporates in his work much of the outlook and values of the Russian intelligentsia of the nineteenth century. He is no Bazarov or Pisarev in their denial of spirituality, but the cast of his mind is undeniably secular, rationalist and utilitarian in the spirit of the men of the 1860s and 1870s. In adolescence, when Dubnow rejected the traditionalist Jewish values of his early background and upbringing, the materialism and positivism of Belinsky, say, or of Chernyshevsky and Dobrolyubov, or the populism of Mikhailovsky, became important factors in the formation of his outlook.[32] Dubnow would well have concurred with Mikhailovsky in the latter's choice of intellectual heroes: '... for myself I would like only one thing: a little plot of land and as many books as possible ... and read all those Spencers, Darwins and Huxleys

in the original'.[33] Moreover, Russian was in a sense Dubnow's mother
tongue. He wrote all his major works in Russian (save his *History of
Hassidism*, which is in Hebrew), spoke Russian at home with his
family, wrote his autobiography in Russian, generally used Russian
for his public declarations and, in fact, spent most of his life up to
1918 in such Russian cultural centres as Odessa and St Petersburg.
He lived physically remote from the Yiddish-speaking centres of the
Pale (though without for one moment decrying the value of Hebrew
and Yiddish as national languages).[34]

The work of John Stuart Mill, an influence common both to the
Russian social thinkers and to Dubnow, yet had a special meaning
for the latter. Mill's philosophic liberalism and individualism gave
Dubnow powerful personal and intellectual support at a time when
he stood in opposition to his environment:

> The problem that he [i.e. Mill] encountered in the matter of the
> freedom of the individual, the liberation of the soul of the individual
> from the dominance of the public or the tyranny of public opinion
> was close to my heart because of my own bitter experience. Was I
> not myself a victim of this tyranny which gave my parents freedom
> to give me an education accepted in its time ... and were not my
> wanderings and restlessness to a large extent caused by the fact
> that with my ideas of freedom I could not live among the religious
> zealots of my native town? And now appeared the great thinker,
> one of the greatest of his generation, and proved irrefutably that
> it is not enough to fight for the political freedom of the collective
> against the tyranny of the ruling minority but that there is also a
> need to wage war for the freedom of the individual against the
> tyranny of the majority, against prevailing traditions and accepted
> views.[35]

For many years pictures of Mill and Shelley stood on Dubnow's
table.

Of equal importance in the formation of Dubnow's outlook was
his encounter with Comte, whose theory of the three stages of thought
Dubnow describes as 'a revelation'. To put sociology, as did Comte,
at the summit of the sciences, seemed to Dubnow 'the highest truth'.
Further suspicion of metaphysics came to Dubnow from his reading of
Feuerbach and Büchner. Herbert Spencer's theories of evolution
reinforced the influence of Comte.[36]

Dubnow's understanding of the Jewish nation and Jewish
nationalism best illustrates the variety of influences to which he was
subject. This understanding is itself reached through a process of

evolution in Jewish historical thought derived from Comte's law of the three stages of thought. Thus, in Dubnow's application of this concept, we have first the *theological* understanding of the Bible. This is followed by the *spiritual* understanding (e.g. of a Zunz or a Graetz) which denied to the Jews, through their lack of territory and state, an active share in the determination of their own history but condemned them to be the passive object of the history of other peoples; the periodisation of their works is correspondingly attuned to the history of literature and culture; third, what Dubnow terms 'the purely scientific conception of Jewish history, the *sociological*', is reached in modern times. This takes its stand on the view that 'the Jewish people at all times and in all countries has always and everywhere been a subject, a creator of its history, not only in the intellectual but also in the sphere of social life. Both in the period of the state and the period without a state Judaism stands forth with the deeply impressed character of a nation, not merely as a religious community among other nations.'[37] The Jewish religion, on this view, is a creation of the nation and God is created in the image of the people. 'This was a historical God, who directed the historical destinies of the people but was also at the same time their product.'[38] Dubnow deplored the absorption of the national into the religious so that a Spinoza, for example, was forced out of Judaism on religious grounds, whereas, had the criterion been national, no such loss would have been necessary.[39]

A secular conception of Jewish nationality, established in this way, was by no means unique to Dubnow, but it was he perhaps who made it the foundation of his system. On the one hand, in the first of his *Letters on Old and New Judaism*, Dubnow rejected the view that any one nation can embody and transmit the same unaltered idea throughout its history. He quotes Lavrov with approval: 'but can it really for a moment be imagined that the prophets of the time of the first fall of Jerusalem, the medieval cabalists, talmudists and translators of Averroes, and the contemporaries of Heine, Rothschild, Meyerbeer, Marx and Lassalle have all embodied one and the same idea in history?'[40]

On the other hand, Dubnow's doctrine of Jewish nationalism does require an ineradicable subjective sense of national consciousness: '... a nation may be defined as a historical-cultural group which is conscious of itself as a nation even though it may have lost all or some of the external characteristics of nationality (state, territory, language), provided it possesses the determination to continue developing its own personality in the future. Objective criteria of nationality are giving way to subjective factors.' The references here are to Fichte (though with reservations), Renan, Fouillée, and Rudolf Springer (Karl Renner).[41]

Of these exponents of the nationalism of the nineteenth century it is Fouillée, author of the *Esquisse psychologique des peuples européens* (1903), who provided Dubnow with the framework that encompassed the evolution of Jewish history. Dubnow used the *Esquisse* to expound a threefold development which in its final phase validated the uniqueness of Jewish nationalism. In the light of Fouillée's theory, Dubnow saw the evolution of a national type 'from the material to the spiritual and from external simplicity to inner complexity'. Initially, the nation takes shape as a mere product of nature, a racial or tribal group, formed by a common origin, territory and climate which, in their turn, determine the physical and mental characteristics of the tribe. In time, as a result of economic co-operation and other forms of human association, a further degree of organisation is reached, i.e. a civic union or state. The tribe's territory, hitherto merely part of the natural environment, becomes an active political factor uniting one or more tribes into a nation, with an organised political authority to determine laws, defend frontiers, assert the rights of the nation, etc. At this point what Dubnow terms the 'territorial-political type of nationality' emerges. It is marked by the growth of spiritual creativity, by the elevation of religion to 'a comprehensive world-view', by a deepening of the moral sense, etc. The testing time of the maturity of such a territorial-political nation is reached, however, when it is not only deprived of its political independence but also loses its territory: 'if ... such a nation still maintains itself for many years, creates an independent existence, reveals a stubborn determination to carry on its autonomous development – such a people has reached the highest stage of cultural-historical individuality ...' History has chosen for this unique status the people of Israel: 'the spiritual elements outweighed decisively the material and political elements'.[42] Jews are thus the most historical of all peoples because Jews, and Jews alone, have lived through all stages of human history thus far.

The presentation of Jews as the spiritual nation *par excellence* is the very substance of Dubnow's understanding of Jewish history in general. It is at the root, for example, of his rejection of Zionism (though this was attenuated in practice). Whereas Zionism was 'principally based on the experiences of the nineteenth century', Dubnow claimed that his theory of 'spiritual nationalism' was derived from 'the whole course of Jewish history'.[43] He saw Jewish history as a succession of autonomous centres – in Babylon, Spain, France and Germany, Poland – and at the turn of the century he hoped and expected that the Russian-Jewish immigrants to the United States would re-create beyond the Atlantic an American version of an institution, the origins of which stretched back to Babylon. The Diaspora was not, as the Zionists claimed, an anomaly, but, as Dubnow argued in the article on the Diaspora that he contributed to the *Encyclopaedia of the Social Sciences*, the scene of 'substitutes for state forms', i.e. autonomous communities controlling not only religious life but also social relations, and with their own educational and charitable institutions and enjoying in some cases powers of taxation and judicial administration. This is what Dubnow meant when he wrote to his English translator, Israel Friedländer, in December 1913: 'I occupied myself with the history of the people, not with the history of literature, and history is essentially the development or decline of the national self in relation to the environment.'[44]

Dubnow largely made subjective criteria the criteria of nationality. Not the least of these was a common history: 'by our common memory of a great stirring past and heroic deeds on the battle-fields of the spirit; by the exalted mission allotted to us ... by such moral ties we Jews, whether consciously or unconsciously, are bound fast to one another'.[45] But Dubnow does not rely solely on subjective criteria to guarantee the continual existence of the Jewish people, and he makes a distinction between state and nationhood, familiar to the numerous advocates of the rights of small peoples in the multi-national empires of the world before 1914.

Although Dubnow wrote shortly before the appearance of Springer's *Der Kampf der österreichischen Nationen um den Staat* (1902), his favourable reference to this work not only illustrates his receptivity to the ideas current in the non-Jewish world but also his notion of Jewish autonomy. Springer quotes for example a resolution of the Austrian social-democrats of 1899 urging the re-formation of the Dual Monarchy into a federal state of nationalities with a system of national elective chambers enjoying legislative power within their respective domains.[46]

From one point of view the difference between Graetz and Dubnow can in part be seen in terms of their reactions to the socio-political status of their respective Jewish environments. But it is intellectually more rewarding to see the difference, as does Steinberg, in terms of a contrast between the external and internal histories of Jews and Judaism. Steinberg writes, for example, that Graetz was 'so deeply bound up (*versponnen*) in the inner history of Judaism' that he disregarded the external history of the Jews.[47] The contrast has also been seen as that between an 'ideological conception' of Jewish history and a 'sociological'.[48] Certainly, one theme in Jewish historiography dominating the fifty-odd years between the publication of Graetz's last volume (1876) and Dubnow's first (1925) is indeed an attempt to overcome Graetz's neglect of daily life and the material life of the individual.[49] Dubnow saw the distinction between Graetz and himself as the result of Graetz's lack of 'a clearly elaborated and fully matured national ideology that he could have set against the firm and rounded system of assimilation. Indeed, Graetz was far from claiming the state's recognition of the national rights of the Jewish people, a demand to which only the nationally-minded spokesmen of later generations were emboldened, and, moreover, beyond the frontiers of Germany.'[50]

This in its turn is involved in Dubnow's relationship to non-Jewish thought, to which he was far more receptive than Graetz. Ahad Ha'Am in fact – no less an admirer than Dubnow himself of Mill and Spencer[51] – accused Dubnow, through his advocacy of Yiddish, of attempting to create 'new literary and cultural values which will be a sort of imitation, a reflection of a reflection, of foreign cultures, as do the Lithuanians and the Ruthenes, etc., then I can see no reason and no need in such a lowly national existence'.[52] But is this fair? The commitment to a secularised historiography undoubtedly had dangers, for which the exaltation of Jews as a nation unique by virtue of its spirituality was inadequate compensation. On the other hand, it is important to note that whatever Dubnow did or did not take from the non-Jewish world he transmuted into a personal version of the uniqueness of Jews. When, in an early essay, he described Jewish history as 'the only history stripped of every active political element',[53] and saw its uniqueness in its spirituality, he was, despite his secular commitment, rewording the theory of the chosen people. By way of Mill, Comte, Spencer, Fouillée, etc., Dubnow rejoins Graetz in a traditional affirmation.

NOTES

1. S. Maimon, *Autobiography*, Engl. trans. (London, 1954) pp. 154-5.

2. D. Kaufmann, *Gesammelte Schriften*, ed. M. Brann, I (Frankfurt am Main, 1908) 247; S. Rawidowicz, in Elbogen, Meisl and Wischnitzer (eds), *Festschrift zu Dubnows 70. Geburtstag* (Berlin, 1930) p. 58; J. Meisl, *Heinrich Graetz. Eine Würdigung des Historikers und Juden* (Berlin, 1917) p. 27; M. Güdemann, 'Heinrich Graetz', *Monatsschrift für die Geschichte und Wissenschaft des Judentums*, Jg. 61, Heft 9/12 (Dec 1917) p. 348; L. Zunz, *Literaturgeschichte der Synagogalen Poesie* (Berlin, 1865) p. 1; A. A. Neumann, 'Shevet Yehuda and Sixteenth Century Historiography', in *Landmarks and Goals* (Philadelphia, 1953) p. 82; S. Bernfeld, 'Dorshei Reshumot', *Ha'Shiloah*,

II 3 (1897) 193; S. W. Baron, *A Social and Religious History of the Jews* (Columbia U.P., 1952) I 26; E. Tcherikower, 'Jewish Martyrology and Jewish Historiography', *Yivo Annual of Jewish Social Science*, I (New York, 1946).

3. F. Rosenzweig, *Der Stern der Erlösung* (Heidelberg, 1954); first published 1921 and now available in an English translation, *The Star of Redemption* (London, 1971) pt III, pp. 55 ff.

4. See, e.g., I. Barzilay, *Shlomo Yehuda Rapaport* (Massada, Israel, 1969) p. 49.

5. P. Bloch, *Heinrich Graetz: A Memoir* (London, 1898) p. 60; see also M. Brann, *M.G.W.J.* (Dec 1917) pp. 339-540, and Bernfeld, in *Ha'Shiloah*, II 3, pp. 396-7.

6. E. H. Carr, *What is History?* (London, 1961) p. 72.

7. Ibid., p. 71.

8. S. Dubnow, *Nationalism and History*, ed. K. Pinson, Engl. trans. (Philadelphia and New York: Meridian Books, 1961) pp. 354-9.

9. H. Liebeschütz, 'Jewish Thought and Its German Background', in *Year Book of the Leo Baeck Institute*, I (London, 1956) 217 ff.; idem., *Das Judentum in deutschen Geschichtsbild von Hegel bis Max Weber* (Tübingen, 1967) pp. 152 ff.; S. W. Baron, *History and Jewish Historians* (Philadelphia, 1964) pp. 269-75.

10. Y. Baer, *L'Berur ha'matzav shel ha'limudim ha'historiim etzlenu* (Jerusalem: Sefer Magnes, 1938) p. 35.

11. Bloch, *Heinrich Graetz*, p. 21.

12. N. Rotenstreich, 'Hegel's Image of Judaism', *Jewish Social Studies*, XV 1 (Jan 1953) 33-52; see also introductory article by S. Ettinger to *Graetz darkhe ha'historiya ha'yehudit* (Jerusalem, 1969) pp. 14-15.

13. H. Graetz, *Die Konstruktion der jüdischen Geschichte* (repr. Berlin, 1936) pp. 93-4.

14. N. Rotenstreich, 'Nisyono shel Graetz b'filosofiya shel ha'historiya', *Zion*, VIII 1 (1943) 51-9.

15. *Die Konstruktion*, p. 8.

16. Ibid., p. 9.

17. Ibid., pp. 19-20, 31, 56.

18. Ibid., pp. 50-1.

19. Ibid., p. 52.

20. Ibid., p. 96.

21. H. Graetz, 'The Significance of Judaism for Present and Future', *Jewish Quarterly Review*, I (Oct 1888) 13.

22. Ibid., p. 11. This relationship has been attributed to the influence of Steinheim; cf. H. Cohen, *Jüdische Schriften*, III (Berlin, 1924) 204.

23. The judicious remarks of E. J. Cohn in this respect ('Heinrich Graetz', in G. Kisch (ed.), *Das Breslauer Seminar*, Tübingen, 1963, p. 195) compare favourably with the intemperate attack of G. Herlitz, 'Three Jewish Historians', *Leo Baeck Year Book*, IX (London, 1964) 78 ff.

24. Kaufmann, *Gesammelte Schriften*, I 277.

25. H. Graetz, *Historic Parallels in Jewish History* (London, 1887) p. 12. See also S. Ettinger, 'Mifalo Ha'historiografi shel Graetz', in *Historionim ve'askolot historiyot* (Jerusalem, 1962) p. 85.

26. e.g. Introduction to *Geschichte der Juden*, I (Leipzig, 1874) xxxiiii.

27. Ibid., IV 1-5, Introduction; cf. also Introduction to vol. V.

28. For a study of this in reference to the historiography of the medieval

period, see H. H. Ben-Sasson, 'L'Magamot ha'kronografiya ha'yehudit shel y'mei ha'benayim ubayoteha', in *Historionim*, pp. 29-49.

29. For fuller accounts of these and other works, see Bernfeld, in *Ha'Shiloah*, II 3, Neumann, in *Landmarks and Goals*, and Tcherikover, in *Yivo Annual of Jewish Social Science*, I.

30. Ed. and introduced by K. S. Pinson under the title *Nationalism and History* (New York: Meridian Books, 1961) p. 141. See also A. Tartakover, 'L'Bikoret shitato ha'sotziologit shel Dubnov', in S. Rawidowicz (ed.), *Sefer Shimon Dubnov* (London, 1954) p. 79.

31. Cf. Anatole Mazour, *Modern Russian Historiography*, 2nd ed. (Princeton, 1958) pp. 146 ff.

32. J. Meisl, 'Chaye Shimon Dubnov', in Rawidowicz, *Sefer Shimon Dubnov*, pp. 27-8.

33. Quoted in J. H. Billington, *Mikhailovsky and Russian Populism* (Oxford, 1958) p. 83.

34. Cf. Sh. Auerbach, *Shimon Dubnovs Shtellung tzu Yiddish un Hebräisch*, in A. Steinberg (ed.), *Simon Dubnow: The Man and His Work* (Paris: World Jewish Congress, 1963) pp. 162-4.

35. Quoted in R. Mahler, 'Ha'kitot ve'hazramim ha'tarbutiim b'divrei yemei Yisrael l'shitat Dubnov', in Rawidowicz, *Sefer Shimon Dubnov*, p. 117; see also S. Dubnow, *Mein Leben*, ed. Hurwicz (Berlin, 1937) p. 50, and S. Dubnowa-Erlikh, *Zhizn i Tvorchestvo S. M. Dubnova* (New York, 1950) pp. 37, 49, 219.

36. Dubnow, *Mein Leben*, pp. 50-1; Mahler, in *Sefer Shimon Dubnov*, pp. 116-17.

37. S. Dubnow, *Weltgeschichte*, I (Berlin, 1925) xiv-xv.

38. Ibid., I 64.

39. Ibid., VII 475.

40. Pinson (ed.), *Nationalism and History*, p. 94; P. Lavrov, *Istoricheskie Pisma* (St Petersburg, 1906) p. 204.

41. Pinson (ed.), *Nationalism and History*, pp. 86-7.

42. Ibid., pp. 76 ff.

43. Dubnow, *Weltgeschichte*, X 346.

44. M. Davis, 'Jewry East and West: The Correspondence of I. Friedländer and S. Dubnow', *Yivo Annual of Jewish Social Science*, IX (New York, 1954) 26-9.

45. S. Dubnow, *Jewish History*, Engl. trans. (London, 1903) pp. 22-3.

46. R. Springer, *Der Kampf der österreichischen Nationen um den Staat* (Leipzig and Vienna, 1902) p. 247; Pinson (ed.), *Nationalism and History*, p. 87.

47. A. Steinberg, 'Die weltanschaulichen Voraussetzungen der jüdischen Geschichtschreibung', in Meisl, Elbogen and Wischnitzer (eds), *Festschrift zu Dubnows 70. Geburtstag*, p. 40, n. 1.

48. Elbogen, 'Von Graetz bis Dubnow', ibid., p. 7.

49. Ibid., p. 17.

50. Dubnow, *Weltgeschichte*, X 31.

51. *Igroth Ahad Ha'Am*, vol. V: 1913-1917 (Jerusalem and Berlin, 1924) p. 247.

52. Ibid., vol. IV: 1908-1912, p. 100.

53. Dubnow, *Jewish History*, p. 16.

Bibliography of the Works of E. H. Carr

BERYL J. WILLIAMS

THIS bibliography does not claim to be complete, or exhaustive. The most important publications, however, have been included.

All translations in foreign languages, and American editions, have been omitted.

Over a period of many years E. H. Carr was a distinguished contributor to *The Times*, and during the war years wrote many of its editorials, on foreign and other affairs. For the *Times Literary Supplement* he wrote extensively; some of the articles were re-published in his *Studies in Revolution*, and in *1917: Before and After*, and reviewed a large number of books. The majority, which were not included in the above-mentioned books, have been deliberately excluded from this bibliography – or, more accurately, check-list.

BOOKS AND PAMPHLETS

Dostoevsky, 1821-81: A New Biography (London: Allen & Unwin, 1931).

The Romantic Exiles: A Nineteenth Century Portrait Gallery (London: Gollancz, 1933; Harmondsworth: Penguin Books, 1949, repr. 1968).

Karl Marx: A Study in Fanaticism (London: Dent, 1934).

Michael Bakunin (London: Macmillan, 1937).

International Relations since the Peace Treaties (London: Macmillan, 1937; new and enlarged ed. 1940). Reprinted as *International Relations between the Two World Wars* (1947).

Great Britain as a Mediterranean Power, Cust Foundation Lecture (Nottingham, 1937).

Britain: A Study of Foreign Policy from the Versailles Treaty to the Outbreak of War (London: Longmans, 1939). One of a series called 'Ambassadors at Large: Studies in the Foreign Policies of the Leading Powers', of which he was a General Editor.

Propaganda in International Politics, Oxford Pamphlets on World Affairs, No. 16 (Oxford: Clarendon Press, 1939).

The Twenty Years Crisis, 1919-38: An Introduction to the Study of International Relations (London: Macmillan, 1939; rev. ed. 1946).

The Future of Nations: Independence or Interdependence?, The Democratic Order, No. 14 (London: Kegan Paul, 1941).

The Future of International Government (with S. de Madariaga), Peace Aims Pamphlet, No. 4 (London: National Peace Council, 1941).

Conditions of Peace (London: Macmillan, 1942).

Nationalism and After (London: Macmillan, 1945).

The Soviet Impact on the Western World (London: Macmillan, 1946). Chap. 1 is a reprint of *Democracy in International Affairs*, Cust Foundation Lecture (Nottingham, 1945).

The Moral Foundations for World Order, in 'Foundations for World Order' (Denver: Social Science Foundation, Univ. of Denver, 1948).

Studies in Revolution (London: Macmillan, 1950; London: Cass, 1962). Articles and reviews which originally appeared in the *Times Literary Supplement*.

The New Society (London: Macmillan, 1951).

German-Soviet Relations between the Two World Wars, Albert Shaw Lectures on Diplomatic History, 1951 (London: Oxford U.P., 1952).

A History of Soviet Russia:
  The Bolshevik Revolution, 1917-23, vols. I-III (London: Macmillan, 1950-3; Harmondsworth: Penguin Books, 1966).
  The Interregnum, 1923-4 (Macmillan, 1954; Penguin Books, 1969).
  Socialism in One Country, 1924-6, vols. I-III (Macmillan, 1958-64); vols. I-II (Penguin Books, 1970).
  Foundations of a Planned Economy, vols. I-II (Macmillan, 1969-71). Vol. I in collaboration with R. W. Davies.

What is History?, The George Macaulay Trevelyan Lectures delivered in the Univ. of Cambridge (London: Macmillan, 1961; Harmonsworth: Penguin Books, 1964).

1917: Before and After (London: Macmillan, 1969). Previously published essays marked in this bibliography with an asterisk (*).

INTRODUCTIONS TO BOOKS

to *Nationalism* (Royal Institute of International Affairs, London, 1939).

to M. Litvinov, *Notes for a Journal* (London: Andre Deutsch, 1955). Proved to be a forgery.

* to N. G. Chernyshevsky, *What is to be Done?* (New York: Vintage Books, 1961).

* to N. Bukharin and E. Preobrazhensky, *The A.B.C. of Communism* (Harmondsworth: Penguin Books, 1969).

ARTICLES IN LEARNED JOURNALS

'Turgenev and Dostoevsky', *Slavonic Review*, VIII (1929-30).

'Was Dostoevsky an Epileptic?', *Slavonic Review*, IX (1930-1).

'Bakunin's Escape from Siberia', *Slavonic Review*, XV (1936-7).
'What Makes the Worker Work?', *Welsh Review*, IV 1 (Mar 1945). Reprinted as chap. 3 of *The New Society*.
'Two Currents in World Labor', *Foreign Affairs*, XXV (1946-7).
'Radek's "Political Salon" in Berlin, 1919', *Soviet Studies*, III (1951).
'Some Notes on Soviet Bashkiria', *Soviet Studies*, VIII (1956-7).
'The Origins and Status of the Chekha', *Soviet Studies*, X (1958-9).
'Pilnyak and the Death of Frunze', *Soviet Studies*, X (1958-9).
'The Russian Revolution and the Peasant' (The Raleigh Lecture, 1963), *Proceedings of the British Academy*, XLIX (1963).
* 'Some Random Reflections on Soviet Industrialisation', in C. H. Feinstein (ed.), *Socialism, Capitalism and Economic Growth: Essays presented to Maurice Dobb* (Oxford U.P., 1967).
* 'Revolution from Above: Some Notes on the Decision to Collectivise Soviet Agriculture', in K. H. Wolff and Barrington Moore, Jr (eds), *The Critical Spirit: Essays in Honour of Herbert Marcuse* (Boston: Beacon Press, 1967).
* 'Isaac Deutscher: An Obituary', *Cambridge Review*, 14 Oct 1967.
* 'A Historical Turning Point: Marx, Lenin, Stalin', in R. Pipes (ed.), *Revolutionary Russia* (Cambridge, Mass.: Harvard U.P., 1968).

REVIEWS IN LEARNED JOURNALS

in *Soviet Studies*

'From Munich to Moscow', I (1949) 2 parts, reviews the following:
  Nazi–Soviet Relations, 1939-41 (Dept. of State, Washington).
  Documents and Materials relating to the Eve of the Second World War, 2 vols. (Ministry of Foreign Affairs of the U.S.S.R.).
  Documents on British Foreign Policy, 1919-39, 3rd series, vol. I.
  L. B. Namier, *Diplomatic Prelude*.
  Max Beloff, *The Foreign Policy of Soviet Russia*, vol. II: 1926-41.
R. Fischer, *Stalin and German Communism*: I (1949). Also reviewed in the *T.L.S.* (see *Studies in Revolution*, pp. 181-99).
N. Rubenstein, *Soviet Russia and the Capitalist States, 1921-2*: I (1949).
R. Pipes, *The formation of the Soviet Union*: VIII (1956-7).
M. Djilas, *Conversations with Stalin*: XIV (1962-3).
I. Maisky, *Journey into the Past*: XV (1963-4).

in *Slavonic Review*

Vospominaniya A. M. Dostoevskogo: IX (1930-1).
B. Lazitch, *Lénine et la IIIème Internationale*: XXX (1951-2).

in *History*

G. Mayer, *Friedrich Engels*: XIX (1934-5).
J. M. Billington, *Mikhailovsky and Russian Populism*: XLIV (1959).
R. Pipes (ed.), *Karamzin's Memoir on Ancient and Modern Russia*: XLV (1960).
N. Riasanovsky, *Nicholas I and Official Nationality in Russia*: XLVI (1961).

370 *Essays in Honour of E. H. Carr*

S. Monas, *The Third Section: Politics and Society in Russia under Nicholas I*: XLVII (1962).

M. Malia, *Alexander Herzen and the Birth of Russian Socialism*: XLVII (1962).

A. P. Mendel, *Dilemmas of Progress in Tsarist Russia: Legal Marxism and Legal Populism*: XLVII (1962).

J. L. H. Keep, *The Rise of Social Democracy in Russia*, L (1965).

G. C. Thaden, *Conservative Nationalism in Nineteenth Century Russia*: L (1965).

E. Lampert, *Sons against Fathers: Studies in Russian Radicalism and Revolution*: L (1965).

S. Lukashevich, *Ivan Aksakov*: LI (1966).

L. Kochan, *Russia in Revolution, 1890-1918*: LI (1967).

H. Kapur, *Soviet Russia and Asia, 1917-27*: LII (1967).

S. Schwarz, *The Russian Revolution of 1905*: LIV (1969).

ARTICLES IN *The Listener*

'The Mediterranean', XX, 2 Nov-29 Dec 1938:
1. 'Italy's Ambitions' (discussion with G. Martelli), 3 Nov 1938.
2. 'Spain's Key position' (discussion with E. Monroe), 17 Nov 1938.
3. 'Nations Bordering on the Adriatic' (discussion with R. W. Seton-Watson), 24 Nov 1938.
4. 'Turkey and the Black Sea Straits' (discussion with A. J. Toynbee), 1 Dec 1938.
5. 'The Near East' (as interlocutor to Sir Ronald Storrs), 8 Dec 1938.
6. 'Strategy in the Mediterrainean' (with Admiral Sir Herbert Richmond), 15 Dec 1938.
7. 'Trade Interests in the Mediterranean' (with C. J. S. Sprigge), 22 Dec 1938.
'The Political Scene in the Mediterranean' (supplement), 29 Dec 1938.

'Taking Stock' (discussion with Colin Brooks), XXIV, 10 Oct 1940.

'British Foreign Policy', XXXVI (1946):
1. 'The Case for a Planned Foreign Policy', 10 Oct 1946.
2. 'Striking a Balance', 17 Oct 1946.
3. 'Planning our International Trade', 24 Oct 1946.
4. 'Foreign Policy Begins at Home', 31 Oct 1946.

'The Pattern of Soviet Foreign Policy', XXXIX, 1 Jan 1948.
'Problems of Writing Modern Russian History', XL, 7 Oct 1948.
'World Revolution and Soviet Foreign Policy', XLI, 3 Feb 1949.
'The Real Meaning of the Soviet Elections', XLIII, 20 Apr 1950.
'The New Society', XLV, 10 May-14 June 1951.
'Memories of the League of Nations', XLVII, 1 May 1952.
'The Puzzle of Anglo-German Relations', XLVIII, 3 July 1952.
'The Bolshevik Revolution in Perspective', LIII, 21-28 Apr 1955.
* 'The Structure of Soviet Society', LIV, 4 Aug 1955.
'What is History?', LXV, 20 Apr-25 May 1961, and letter, 1 June.

'The Russian Revolution and the Peasant' (shortened version of Raleigh lecture), LXIX, 30 May 1963.
* The Significance of the Russian Revolution', LXXVIII, 9 Nov 1967.

Notes on the Contributors

C. ABRAMSKY, B.A.(Jerusalem), M.A.(Oxon). Goldsmid Professor of Hebrew and Jewish Studies, University of London, and Senior Associate Fellow, St Anthony's College, Oxford. Formerly Reader in Jewish History, University College, London. Joint author with H. J. Collins of *Karl Marx and the English Labour Movement*; author of *Kamenev on Machiavelli*, *The Biro-Bidjan Project*, and many articles on Marx, modern Jewish history and modern Jewish art.

SIR ISAIAH BERLIN, O.M. President, Wolfson College, Oxford, formerly Chichele Professor of Social Philosophy, University of Oxford. Author of *Karl Marx*, *The Hedgehog and the Fox*, *The Age of Enlightenment* (ed.), *Four Essays on Liberty*, *Moses Hess*, and many articles.

ELEONORE BREUNING, B.A.(Oxon.), D.Phil.(Oxon.). Lecturer in Russian History, University College of Swansea. Assistant editor, *Documents on German Foreign Policy*.

G. A. COHEN, B.A.(McGill), B.Phil.(Oxon.). Lecturer in Philosophy, University College London. Author of articles on Marx and on philosophical topics in British and American journals. He is currently writing a book about historical materialism.

R. W. DAVIES, B.A., Ph.D. Director of the Centre for Russian and East European Studies and Professor of Soviet Economic Studies, University of Birmingham. Author of *The Development of the Soviet Budgetary System*, *Science and the Soviet Economy*, *Science Policy in the U.S.S.R.* (co-author) and *Foundations of a Planned Economy, 1926-1929*, I (co-author), and many articles. He is currently writing an economic history of the U.S.S.R. in the 1930s.

MAURICE DOBB, F.B.A., D.Litt.(Hon.). Emeritus Reader in Economics in the University of Cambridge and Fellow of Trinity College, Cambridge. Author of, *inter alia*, *Soviet Economic Development since 1917*, *Papers on Capitalism*, *Development and Planning*, *Welfare Economics and the Economics of Socialism*.

JOHN ERICKSON. Professor of Politics, University of Edinburgh; Lees-Knowles Lecturer, University of Cambridge (1971-2). Author of *The Soviet High Command, 1918-1941*, *The Military-Technical Revolution: Its Impact on Strategy and Foreign Policy* (ed.), *Soviet Military Power*, and many articles.

MARY HOLDSWORTH, M.A. Principal, St Mary's College, University of Durham. Articles and bibliographies on minorities in the Soviet Union and Soviet contacts with Africa. Contributions to L. Schapiro and P. Reddaway, *Lenin* (1967) and to E. Luard (ed.), *The Cold War* (1964).

MICHAEL KASER, M.A. Reader in Economics, University of Oxford; Professorial Fellow of St Antony's College, Oxford. Formerly with Foreign Office and U.N. Economic Commission for Europe, Geneva. Author of *Comecon: Integration Problems of the Planned Economics*, and *Soviet Economics*, joint author with J. F. Zielinski of *Planning in Eastern Europe*, and many articles.

LIONEL KOCHAN, M.A., Ph.D. Bearstead Reader in Jewish History, University of Warwick. Author of *Russia and the Weimar Republic, Acton on History, The Struggle for Germany, 1914-1945, Russia in Revolution, 1890-1918, The Jews in Russia since 1917* (ed.).

ARTHUR LEHNING, Member of the International Institute of Social History, Amsterdam. Author of *The International Association, Archives Bakounine* (ed.), *From Buonarroti to Bakunin: Studies in International Socialism, Michael Bakunin: Selected Writings*, contribution to the preliminary history of the First International (Leiden, 1938).

MOSHE LEWIN, Docteur en Histoire (Sorbonne). Reader in Soviet History and Politics, Centre for Russian and East European Studies, University of Birmingham. Author of *The Russian Peasant*, and *Lenin's Last Struggle*.

ROGER MORGAN, M.A., Ph.D. (Cantab.). Deputy Director of Studies, Royal Institute of International Affairs; formerly lecturer at the University of Sussex. Author of *The German Social Democrats and the First International, Modern Germany, Britain and West Germany* (co-editor), *West European Politics since 1945, The Study of International Affairs* (co-author and editor), *High Politics, Low Politics: Toward a Foreign Policy for Western Europe, The United States and West Germany, 1945-73*.

ALEC NOVE. Professor of Economics and Director of the Institute of Soviet and East European Studies, University of Glasgow. Formerly Reader in Russian Social and Economic Studies, University of London. Served in the Civil Service at the Board of Trade and the British Embassy, Moscow. Author of *The Soviet Economy, Was Stalin Really Necessary?, An Economic History of the U.S.S.R.*, and many articles.

MONICA PARTRIDGE, B.A., Ph.D. Professor of Russian and Head of Department of Slavonic Studies, University of Nottingham. Author of *Aleksandr Gertsen: ego angliiskie svyazi, The Young Herzen, Alexander Herzen and the English Press*, and many other papers on Herzen.

D. C. WATT, M.A. Professor of International History, University of London (L.S.E.). Author of *Britain Looks to Germany, Personalities and Policies, A History of the World in the Twentieth Century*, editor of *Documents on*

German Foreign Policy, 1918-1945, has written many articles on international affairs.

BERYL J. WILLIAMS, B.A. Lecturer in History, University of Sussex. Author of contribution in the forthcoming volume of the *New Cambridge History of British Foreign Policy*.

Index

Index

Action Francaise, 4
Adenauer, K., 173, 177
Adler, Max, 20
Afghanistan, 102, 110, 111, 113, 114, 115, 119n
Agrarian Marxists, Conference, 262, 265, 267, 277
Agricultural Guarantee & Guidance Fund, 178
Ahad Ha'am (Ginzberg, A.), 364, 366
Aland Islands, 117
Albania, 160
Aledogsky, A., 227n
Alexandria, 356
Algeciras Conference, 110, 122n
Alexander (The Great), 35(n4)
Alexander I, 234
Alexander II, 36, 38
Alexinsky, G., 121n
All Russian Supreme Staff, 207, 208, 213, 214, 221
Alston, L., 236, 242, 247, 250n, 251n, 254n
Almond, G. A. and Coleman, J. S., 350
Al'tfater, V., 227n
America, United States of, 115, 136, 144, 166, 168, 173, 176, 177, 234, 239, 241, 243, 244, 245, 249, 261-2
Amur, R., vii, 111, 112, 114
Anabaptists, 32
Anan'ich, B. V., 119n
Anderson, C. A., 254n
Antioch, 356
Anglo-Irish Treaty, 1921, 173
Anglo-Japanese Alliance, 105, 111, 122n
Anglo-Russian Agreement, 1907, 104, 115, 116, 117, 120n, 122n, 124n
Annettenhöh, 126
Anti-Comintern Pact, 153
Anti-Semitism, 21
Anweiler, O., 252n
Apter, D., 342, 345
Aralov, S. I., 226n
Assmann, K., 170n
Astakhov, G., 162, 163, 164
Aster, S., 166n
Athens, 33

Attolico, B., 167n
Auerbach, S. H., 366
Australia, 243, 244
Austria, 72, 117, 143, 363
Averroes (Ibn Rushd), 361
Azerbaijan, 113, 116

Babeuf, F. N., 18, 59, 78
Baer, Y., 365
Baghdad Railway, 113, 117
Baku, 149n, 345
Bakunin, M., viii, 4, 20, 21, 26, 37, 43, 47, 51-2, 53, 55, 57-81
Balkans, the, 101, 116, 118, 120n
Baltic, the, 106, 111, 117, 118, 153, 204, 218
Baltic Republics, 239, 240, 241
Baluyev, P. S., 209, 219, 222
Bandar Abbas, 103
Baranov, V. K., 212
Barbès, A., 49, 60
Baron, S. W., 365
Barrere, C., 124n
Barres, M., 4, 16, 21, 29
Barsov, A. A., 319, 323
Barzilay, I., 365
Basle, 52, 74
Basle Congress, 74
Basnase, J. C., 352-3
Batkis, G. A., 251n
Batum, 112, 149n
Batyushkov, V. R., 277-8
Baudelaire, C. P., 7
Bavaria, 191
Beck, J., 159
Becker, J. P., 80
Beesly, E. S., 35
Beethoven, L. van, 19
Belgium, 25, 61, 138, 243, 249
Belinsky, V. G., 359
Bell, The, 36, 37, 38, 41-2, 44, 46
Bell, C., 180n
Beloff, M., 165n, 169n, 170n
Belorussia, 258, 265
Ben-Sasson, H. H., 366
Benckendorff, A., 102, 106, 111, 114, 117, 118, 123n

377